INDIA AND SOUTHEAST ASIA

INDIA AND SOUTHEAST ASIA

Cultural, Economic and Strategic Linkages

Editors
Prof. Satish Chandra,
Prof. Baladas Ghoshal

GYAN

India and Southeast Asia

₹ 750

ISBN: 978-81-212-1130-7

Published in 2011 in India by
Gyan Publishing House
23, Main Ansari Road, Darya Ganj,
New Delhi-110002
Phones: 23282060, 23261060
Fax: 011-23285914
E-mail: books@gyanbooks.com
Website: www.gyanbook.com

Leser Type Setting by: 21st data infosys, Delhi

Printed at: Chawla Offset Press, Delhi

Contents

PART–V
ARC OF PEACE AND PROSPERITY

Preface

Dr. Karan Singh

The relations between India and South East Asia have been very close. These relations can be studied under various headings: political relations, trade and commerce and cultural relations. Our relations are very close because of the impact of India on South East Asia, as well as the feedback to India. But colonial domination for several centuries really sundered these relations, and the colonies were exploited. It is only in the second half of the 20th century that colonialism finally retreated and collapsed. I think I am right in saying that India's freedom in 1947 really breached the citadels of colonialism because after that in many countries their freedom struggle came to fruition. But soon after that, we were hit by the Cold War. The Cold War, lasted from 1945 to 1990. So, first we had to view everything through the colonial prism, then we came to view things from cold war prism. It is only in 1990, after the collapse of the Cold War that we were in a position to get our act together and to see what we can do in Southeast Asia.

The 20th century has been a most extraordinary century. It has seen the rise and fall of all sorts of ideologies — of Tsarism, of Marxism - Leninism, of Maoism. All of these ruled in the 20th century and fell in the 20th century. And all of them have left their mark upon India and upon South East Asia. But before I come to South East Asia, let us say a word about South Asia. We are here caught in a ring of fire — Afghanistan is on fire, Pakistan is on fire, Nepal is on fire, Bangladesh is on fire, Sri Lanka is on fire. So South East Asia *ki baari to baad main aayegi* (the turn of Southeast Asia will come later), our immediate concern is the fire all around us. Every single SAARC country, with the exception of Maldives and Bhutan, is in a state of turmoil. It is a most extraordinary situation. And I think political scientists and thinkers will have to apply their minds to this, to what is happening. Why is it that despite promising starts, none of the experiments seem to be going anywhere? Although we are committed to democracy, I think our primary foreign policy concern at this point of time has to be South Asia. Because it is South Asia where our interests are jeopardized directly and vitally. The attack on the Sri Lankan cricketers was one of the more ugly manifestations of the growth of fundamentalism and fanaticism in this entire region. This is something, which can be called a new ideology, because, as I have mentioned, other ideologies have disappeared. I would not call this ideology Islamic fundamentalism; I would call it Islamist fundamentalism meaning thereby using Islam for certain political purposes. This is a new rising ideology of the 21st century. And in the same way, that we had to confront and finally defeated those other ideologies of the 20th century, I think the main task for us in the next few years will be to meet, deal with and finally defeat this new ideology, which, like communalism, is not confined to any one country. It is spread all over the world. Like Communism at one stage as also Marxism - Leninism, it is a worldwide philosophy.

South East Asia is comparatively more stable than South Asia, although you have problems in Thailand, in Myanmar and so on. But our relations with ASEAN need to be strengthened. In the vast triangle of China, Indonesia and India, between them is half the population of the world. All the States in the area should, if it is possible, try and maintain it as a region of peace and progress. This will mean various treaties, various geo-political and strategic arrangements with all the countries of the region. We must not let South East Asia get caught in the flames that are engulfing South Asia. So I think we need a coordinated strategy between India and the countries of South East Asia. And I would say that a seminar like this can help a great deal in that respect.

As far as culture is concerned, it is astounding how for example Angkor Vat was built a thousand years ago, when Rajendra Chola built the Brihadeshwara temple in Thanjavur. Surayavarman was the King, who built Angkor Vat, the largest place of worship in the world. It is a wonder, it is a marvel. I do not know the Seven Wonders of the World, but I think Angkor Vat could figure in the list of any wonders. And the extraordinary detail: it was first Hindu, and then it was Buddhist. The freezes Vaishnava then Buddhist are quite breathtaking. In Java the great temple of Borobudur, which of course is an *apbhramsha* (corruption) of Bhadra Vihara. Bhadra Vihara means great vihara. There was also Prambanan, (Param Brahman) temple. These are all standing there. I must congratulate the Government of Indonesia for protecting these monuments all these years and not allowing them to fall prey like the Taliban, who in an act of unspeakable outrage shattered the great Buddha in Bamiyan. There are many temples in Bali also.

The point is that the three great religions that have influenced South East Asia and India are Hinduism, Buddhism and Islam. Unless we get a working relationship between these religions we are never going to have peace, because it is not so much a clash of civilizations as it is now a clash of religious fundamentalisms. We have to be very careful, particularly the intellectual community as to how this triangle works out. For example, what form do the various worshippers adopt? I think that the basic concept that we have to work upon is the Rigvedic hymn, *Ekam Sat Vipraha Bahudha Vadanti* (The truth is one. The deluded ones may call it by many names). Until people begin to realise that there are multiple paths to the divine, there will never be peace in this world. Because if there is a Divinity, the Divinity has decided that there will be many paths. There is no one path to the Divine, there are many paths to the Divine. This is essential.

The Indian influence: Hindu - Buddhist influence in Vietnam, Laos, Cambodia, Thailand, Indonesia has been extraordinary. And, of course, Islam has played a major role. Of the several caps that I wear, one is President for Indian Council for Cultural Relations. We are beginning to look east. We have also so far followed the usual colonial hang over of looking west. And let me inform you that this year hopefully, we will open cultural centres in Beijing, in Tokyo, in Kuala Lumpur, in Bangkok and in Dhaka. And we already have centres in Jakarta, in Bali and in Sri Lanka. So what we try to do is to promote Indian culture. But also base it upon the whole concept of multi-culturalism, of pluralism, of inclusivism, Huntington's thesis, although we might decry it and deplore it, was a brilliant piece of political analysis. If you want to rebut it, the only way would be to develop the confluence of civilisations rather than the clash of civilisations. The Huntington thesis was a self-fulfilling prophecy. Ever since he wrote that book, everybody has been talking about the clash of civilizations. In reality, there is a clash of fundamentalisms. So what we have to do is, instead of decrying it as people do, we have to come out of it. Where is the Asian scholar who has written a counter to Huntington's book? To counter it, it has to be well researched, and equally well argued.

I think what we really need to do is to grapple with some of the more fundamental questions that are arising in the post colonial and post-cold war world. The Cold War totally distorted perceptions in the entire world. In the first decade of the 21st century, the great problems that await us as follows. First of all, climate change and global warming. This is probably the most serious problem. The glaciers are melting at a most alarming rate, you can see them falling to pieces. And if that continues, several countries are going to disappear from the face of the globe. And there will be millions of ecological refugees.

The second, continuing problem is the abolition of poverty. That you still have millions and millions people living below the poverty line, is not acceptable. And in some countries, more people are going under the poverty line then going over it.

The third problem is the spread of religious fundamentalism. There are fundamentalisms of all kinds. Here in India we not only had the East West axis of fundamentalism, we have the North-South Naxalite axis of fundamentalism, which is equally lethal. That is not a religious based fundamentalism — It is an anarchist based fundamentalism.

So, the threat of fundamentalism, the threat of global warming, and the necessity of poverty alleviation, these, I would say, are the three major tasks before all of us in this century.

Introduction

Prof. Satish Chandra
Prof. Baladas Ghoshal

Before the advent of thé Western imperial powers in the sixteenth century there were fairly close links between Southeast Asian countries, and its neighbours. There was extensive trade, both inter-regional and that with India, Sri Lanka and China. The strong cultural and religious links were reflected in the mutual interchange of scholars and literature. Thus Ramayana in a modified form became the culture of Indonesia and it has a strong presence in Thailand, Cambodia, Laos, etc. In religious matters there was interchange not only of Hindu and Buddhist scholars but later of Islam. Islamic divines from Gujarat and Bengal played a significant role in Islamising Malaya and Indonesia, and in carrying forward the syncritic traditions of Sufism. Buddhist traditions in modified forms, remained strong in Thailand, Laos, Myanmar, and to some extent in Vietnam.

These links were shattered with the advent of colonialism. Monopolies were set up by the different Powers so that inter-regional trade dried up and communication and other links were confined to the trade between the metropolitan power and its colony. In cultural and educational matters the local cultures were overlain by the culture of the colonizing country and, with the gradual exclusion of indigenous traders from international trade, society became more land-locked and rigid, both in structure and outlook.

Today all the countries of the region are resurgent, economically and culturally. While a lot of attention is being devoted to economic development and trade, not sufficient attention has been paid to culture and education. There is much that the countries of the region including India can learn from each other. What for example underpins the relatively moderate Islam of Malaysia and Indonesia? To what extent was it influenced by the moderate Islamic culture and Sufism which had developed in India? Does India's success at managing a multi-lingual, multi-ethnic society has any significance for other countries facing similar problem? How do indigenous cultures impact on social, economic and strategic formations today?

These and many other issues facing India, Malaysia, Indonesia, Singapore, were discussed early in 2008 at a seminar at New Delhi organized by the Society for Indian Ocean Studies. The seminar was co-sponsored by the Nehru Memorial Museum and Library, and the Institute of Southeast Asian Studies, Singapore, with financial support from Ministry of External Affairs, Ministry of Culture, Indian Council of Historical Research and Indian Council for Cultural Relations. The inaugural address was delivered by Dr. Karan Singh, M.P., Chairman, Indian Council for Cultural Relations (ICCR).

The papers presented at the seminar and those commissioned subsequently have been brought together in this volume. The volume has been divided into five sections – History and Culture, Trade and Colonialism, Multiculturalism, Economic Development, and Arc of Peace and Prosperity. The attempt is to present a holistic picture which could provide a useful basis for further detailed studies.

Southeast Asia is considered to be the key to the domestication of rice and of some major species such as certain yams, aroids (specially taros) and banana. Some include even sugarcane in this. Southeast Asians were among the first to domesticate the chicken and the pig. It also witnessed the earliest sea crossings of the world into the Pacific and up to Australia and Madagascar. Thus, they were keen farmers, experienced sailors and ship builders having an inexhaustible supply of timber and bamboo.

Geographically Southeast Asia has generally been divided into two broad segments – the mainland comprising modern Vietnam, Burma (Myanmar), Thailand, Cambodia, Laos, and northern Malaysia, and the maritime area comprising Indonesia, South and East Malaysia, Brunei and the Philippines.

The three main centers of political, economic and cultural activity on the mainland which arose in the 3rd century A.D. were the Vietnamese of North Vietnam with their capital Hoa-Lu (near modern Hanoi) and economic centres near the Red River, the Khmer state of Funan which dominated Cambodia and the northern area around Ankor, and third, the Burmese-Mon rule with its capital at Pagan upland. Of these, North Vietnam had always to contend with China which absorbed its energies for long, allowing only some forays into the South Mekong area.

Analysing the structure and functioning of the Khmer state which arose around the third century and continued to dominate the region till the 9th century it is pointed out that the Ankor rulers set up standards of state control and culture which influenced the wider region. Indian influence came mainly from traders. Images of Siva and Vishnu and later the Buddha as also depiction of Ramayana and popular legends can be seen at the temples at Ankor which were built by each ruler from 6th to 9th century. In its agrarian expansion, and in the expansion of international trade, the temples – both those built by the central rulers and those by local elites, played an important role.

The most powerful kingdom in maritime Southeast Asia was the Srivijaya state with its capital at Palembang in South Sumatra. Srivijaya had a powerful navy, which enabled it to dominate the Spice Islands in the east, Sumatra, and ports along the Malacca Strait. These ports had become more profitable with the shift of trans-Asiatic trade to China from the 4th century onward, from the

Kra Isthmus to the Malacca Strait. The Srivijaya Empire which declined in the 11th century was replaced by the Majapahit Empire based on Java. The Majapahit Empire was double the size of Srivijaya, and the centre of international spice-trade. It was the Majapahit domination of the Malacca Strait and its control of the growing trade to China which led to the series of Chola expedition to the area in the 14th century.

The countries of Southeast Asia had an economy which depended largely on wet-rice cultivation, supplemented by cloves and black pepper in some areas, mining of metals, but above all, growing international trade concentrated on port towns, Relationship with the isolated village communities and port towns was tenuous, leading to a decentralized polity.

Turning to culture, Kapila Vatsyayan argues forcefully that while in the countries of Southeast Asia, identities are fluid and cannot be absolutely fixed, various analysis show that there is a very special Asian sense and sensibility. Thus, there is the dynamics of interpenetration and co-existence rather than confrontation, specially in the pre-colonial period. This is evident in the sphere of culture, especially monuments such as Borobudur, Prambanan, Ankorvat, etc. She argues that there was communication and confluence in the realm of art and architecture, and that indigenous traditions amalgated with others, and continued to have the capacity and potentiality of holding many cultural identities together.

Carrying the theme further, in her article on "Textiles as a Means of Cultural Exchange" Hema Devare traces the cultural saga of Indian textiles in Southeast Asia from the 1st century A.D. Thus, the *Devaraja* concepts of the Khmer and Thai were translated into figures from Hindu mythology which were reproduced. Gold played an important role in the royal fabrics, Ceremonial fabrics – painted or dyed – known as kling clothes were especially popular with Thai royalty. Indian textiles also became an important part of the temple décor. Textiles acquired a ritual significance which was far more important than their utilitarian need. Silk patolas from Gujarat came to be associated with protective elements Malay warriors were given patola sashes when they went to battlefields.

Mrs. Devare Southeast Asians were not passive recipients. They were specific in their tastes, and adapted Indian designs to local clothes. Even today, textiles of Southeast Asia, resonate Indian iconography and imagery. Yet they are not Indian.

Analysing the nature of the interaction between India and Southeast Asia, Himanshu Ray says that the basic disjunction took place in the 18th century with the introduction of the steamships. The traditional coastal groups could not cope with these mechanized vessels, and were reduced to being fishermen. The evolution of modern ports and expansion of Western colonies in the nineteenth century completed the process.

Himanshu Ray discusses the historiography of how Indian influence in the region has been seen during the 20th century. During the last sixty years, archeologists have tried to unearth "indigenous cultural matrix, how countries of the region had reached cultural complexity by the early centuries of the common era with selective assimilation of Indian culture.

Discussing the various channels of communication which influenced countries of the region, the author emphasizes the role of epics and fables mainly in Sanskrit which were repeated in early Malay and Indonesian societies. She discusses the various legends about Indian connection in state building. Role of trade networks, and temples is also analysed.

The attempt in this paper has been to highlight the location and archaeology of religious structures, thereby placing religious architecture on its wider social base. According to her, a comprehensive appraisal of coastal centres and maritime communities, the intertwined strands of religious architecture, economic activity and political intervention need to be examined and understood.

From Indonesia Taufik Abdullah traces the rise of Islam in Malaysia and Indonesia. He shows that following the decline of the Srivijaya Empire in the 11th century, a number of small independent states arose in Sumatra and in Malacca which had been a centre of international trade with China, the Persian Gulf and India. It was in Malacca where a small prince converted under the influence of traders. But Malacca remained a pluralistic society, tolerating differences of custom, religion or place of origin. The major communities were the Gujaratis, Tamils, the Javanese and the Chinese who had their own *shah-bandars*. There were also a few thousand Bengalis, Persians and Arabs. The Malays also were engaged in international trade because Sultan Mehmud of Malacca ordered an expedition to go to India to purchase cloth.

In the introduction of Islam in Indonesia, Malacca, Aceh and Pasai in North Sumatra played important roles. According to, Taufik Abdullah "the Islamization of Pasai began when an Arab man of religion who must have come from Gujarat, landed on a small fishing village in North Sumatra at the end of the 13th century. He converted the village chief and made him king of the small territory."

While noting the close relationship of Aceh--Darussalam with Hejaz, Yemen and Egypt, the author underlines its close trading relationship with Gujarat and Malabar. A powerful sufi movement was started from Aceh by Hamzah Fansuri who emerged as one of the towering figures in the history of Islamic thought and literature in the archpilego. Hamzah Fansuri's foundations were at Ayuthia in Siam where many Indian and Persian as well as Arab and Turkish men of religion were living. As a result of the rise of these centers, following the downfall of the Hinduized kingdom of Majapahit with its capital near present Surabaya of East Java, the 16th and 17th centuries became the period of political and military conflict and the propagation of Islam in the region.

Farish Noor from Singapore emphasizes that the process of cultural interchange did not end with the Islamization of maritime Southeast Asia that began in earnest from the 13th century. He argues that "Indian Muslims played the key role as transmitters of knowledge and religious praxis." Tracing the ancient links between India , Sri Lanka and countries of Southeast Asia, Farish Noor says that the South Asians were neither colonialists, nor conquerors. The arrival and settlements of Hindu and Buddhist traders, scholars and missionaries further entrenched the process of Indianisation, and eventually gave to Southeast Asia its normative political, economic and religious culture, traces of which could be found even today. But he warns, it would be wrong to conclude that there was a process of passive absorption of all that was Indian. "This would negate or undermine the role of local genius and the agency of the rulers and peoples of the archipelago themselves, who were never passive recipients of these new ideas, beliefs, values and customs from abroad."

Briefly tracing the history of India and the Hindu interaction with Southeast Asia, the author points that the spread of Islam in India mirrored the spread of Islam in Southeast Asia. Just as their predecessors had done before them, the rulers of Southeast Asia turned to India both for inspiration and help when it comes to governing and managing their communities. Thus by the 13th - 14th centuries, prominent Indian Muslim merchant adventurers had established themselves in many of the newly Islamized Malay – Indonesian kingdoms. Some of them were even able to establish their own kingdoms.

Farish Noor argues that there were two factors which account for the ease with which Islam penetrated and eventually consolidated its hold on Southeast Asia. The first was the familiarity with Indian Muslims who were seen as inheritors of the mantle of *idealization* that was pioneered by their Hindu-Buddhist counterparts much earlier. Second was the medium that was used by Muslim traders and missionaries - the discourse and praxis of popular folk Sufism. This helped to develop a localized and syncretic idiom which could be easily understood and followed. Warning against the rise of ethno-nationalism and exclusivism, the author emphasizes the need of history writing that assesses the continuity of development and cultures during the long period of religious and cultural conversions.

In the section on trade and colonialism, using Chinese sources, H.P. Ray argues that in the early phase, between 2nd century B.C. and 5th century A.D, trade with countries of Southeast Asia and China was characterized by the predominance of Yue (Viet Namese) and Indian traders who controlled the shipping. They were joined later by the Persians and Kunlun traders. Primary focus of trade uptil the 11th century, according to him, was the Chinese market and he discusses the composition of the commodities, traded, with *karpasa* (cotton) playing an important role.

The author argues that unlike the Arabs or the Indians, the Chinese were not a maritime nation, but they became one after the Southern Song dynasty shifted their capital to the coastal city of Hangzhou. At first, their efforts were to fight the pirates infesting the area. By the early Ming period (late 14th to early 15th century A.D), China had become a naval power which enabled the Chinese to maintain control over trade in the high seas in the Pacific Ocean adjoining China, and counter the pirates. The height of this activity was attained by the seven voyages of the Chinese Admiral, Cheng He between 1405 and 1432. These voyages have been much discussed. According to, in these voyages the Chinese demonstrated an acute sense of realpolitics in manipulating south and Southeast Asian politics. They put their loyal allies in power in places of strategic and commercial importance like Palembang (Samudra) and Singhal (Ceylon). The author does not discuss whether these voyages had any lasting effect, especially after the ban of foreign trade by the Chinese emperor after 1432. However, using Chinese sources, Ray throws light on the commodities especially various types of textiles exchanged between India, China and maritime Southeast Asia.

Lakshmi Subramanyan's paper is an attempt to look at the dynamics and processes of identity formation among trading communities whose social profile was predicated upon cultural and commercial practices within the Indian Ocean. The Indian Ocean functioned as a trans-national zone of interaction with connections extending far across discrete civilisational units from which migrant merchant communities were drawn and thrown together to negotiate cross cultural and commercial interflows and overlaps.

Looking at a unitary notion of a diaspora especially in the pre- colonial period, it is argued that the majority of Indians were temporary residents and also that the community of migrants was differentiated in terms of class and occupation. There was in fact, no long-term separation from a real or originary homeland and that the invocation of the nation was only one and often provisional strategy in the formation of identities.

The author examines in detail the role of the Chulias whose presence in the trading world of the Indian Ocean especially in the Bay of Bengal segment during the seventeenth century which constituted the golden period of Indian overseas trade was a marked feature. Despite opposition of the English and the Dutch, the Chulias were able to maintain their trade with the Malays. This was not only on account of their commercial skill, and their close connection with the Arabs, but their willingness to marry local women, adopt local customs, and be both Malay at one end and Indian at the other. Although the Chulias were Muslims, the term Kling continued to be used for them. But, the author says, "Religion in this case was not only a spiritual space but a civil and political case as well. They were welcomed in the new port cities and states where they made local alliances and functioned in important capacities."

The Chettis, starting as salt merchants in the 18th century, gradually rose to be important merchants and money-lenders. The author says "In contrast to the Chulias, the community seemed distinctly more insular in spite of their very close integration into local economic exchanges".

Using the Dutch archival sources and the published records Jayasheela Stephen examines the nature and pattern of the trade in textiles conducted from the Coromandel Coast by the Tamil and Telugu merchants and the Dutch East India Company with various ports of Indonesian Archipelago during the Seventeenth Century. Scholars have so far mentioned that the Dutch purchased various types of the textiles without actually naming the variety of cloth. Further, various ports such as Pulicat, Devanarnpattinam and Nagapattinam from where the Dutch exported cloth had not been properly highlighted. The role of the Tamil and Telugu traders who signed the textile contracts has been largely ignored. The available literature on Coromandel trade mentions in general terms the textile exports without pin pointing the various markets in the three islands of Indonesia such as Java, Sumatra and the Spice Islands (Moluccas, Makassar). The volume of Dutch textile trade and the value in florins had swelled up from 1617 to 1678 and the purchase and selling prices also increased. Owing to the demand, the Dutch began to purchase cloth from various places in Coromandel and exported them to Aceh, Jambi and Palembang, the three main Sumatra markets. Textiles for the Java markets in Jakarta and Makassar also picked up.

The author lays special emphasis on the role of Chettis and Marakkayars (part of the Chulia merchants). These sections had been continually carrying textiles in their ships to Banten and Aceh. The author shows that cloth was bartered for spices, and also sold in exchange for Minangkabau gold. Gold, silver and copper which came to Jakarta from China and Japan was, in turn, sent to the *Dutch* factors in South India where it was minted. The author traces in detail the movement of trade by Chettis and Marakkayars, and how gold and bullion moved from China and Japan, highlighting the three-way trade, with Indonesia being an important conduit.

Comparing the colonial experience of India and Indonesia, Aditya Mukherjee challenges the revionist view of portraying colonialism in a positive light particularly in the context of India, Indonesia, and Korea, etc., which have developed rapidly during in recent years. Analysing colonialism he argued that structurally, it disarticulates the colonial economy in a manner that makes transition to capitalism more difficult. "Colonialism and capitalism are not even parallel paths which can never meet. They are actually divergent paths". The paper forcefully argues this proposition. Thus, it is shown that colonialism under develops by appropriating surplus at all stages, viz. the merchantilist phase, second the free trade modernizing phase which saw the establishment of railways, communication systems, and third the financial phase.

According to the author, the mode of surplus appropriation is a function of a complex set of factors such as the specific need of the metropolitan country and the capacity of the colony at different stages of world capitalism over time. In the pre-industrial revolution era, *labour* was the key factor of production in world capitalism, one witnessed either labour being transported away as slaves or indentured labour, or the produce of labour working in the colony being taken away for free. When, aided by the above transfers the process of industrialization begins in the metropolitan countries and *capital* becomes the key factor of production in late 18th and early 19th century, one witnesses major transfer of capital from the colony, leading to drain or tribute or unrequited transfer of produce of the colonial people, from the colonial empires to the metropolitan countries. This period also saw the capturing or monopolization of the colonial markets for the capitalist production of manufactures of the metropolitan countries. And, similarly, now when knowledge is becoming the key factor of production in the so called post industrial society what is being transferred is not labour or capital but primarily knowledge.

While comparing the mercantile phase of colonialism in India and Indonesia the author notes that though the Dutch East India Company which controlled Indonesia gets dissolved in 1798, nearly *half a century before* the English East India Company which controlled India is dissolved in 1858, yet in Indonesia this first stage type of colonialism involving direct appropriation of surplus where colonial monopoly trade essentially constituted the tribute, continued for nearly fifty years after it stops in India.

It has been calculated that Indian tribute, i.e., capital transfers from India in the late 19th century helped Britain balance its balance of payment deficit with the rest of the world to the tune of about 40 per cent when the British deficit was in part due to the huge investments it was making in the colonies at that time. The tribute from Indonesia called *Batig-slot* which had fallen drastically in the early 19th century rose dramatically with the introduction of the Culture System. The massive Indonesian tribute to Netherland which had ceased in the early 19th century rose to an annual average of 18 million guilders between 1831 to 1877. Another estimate put it at $ 8 million of tribute per year in that period. With the introduction of the 'Ethical Policy' in 1900 the tribute was said to have risen to $ 150 million per year by World War II.

The tribute which took away anything between 5 to 10 percent of the GDP of the colonial countries prevented the process of primary accumulation which was a necessary condition for the transition to industrial capitalism for any economy. Nine percent of the GDP of the British territories in India were drained out through tribute in 1801 when Britain was investing only seven per cent of its GDP as the first country undergoing industrialization.

Aditya Mukherjee concludes by reiterating that in the case of both India and Indonesia the growth that we witness in recent years is not a function of what was left behind by their respective colonial experiences but of breaks from their colonial legacy. At independence both countries had similar problems to face. Whether it was Nehru or Sukarno, the first task was to unstructure colonialism so that conditions could be created whereby these countries could participate in the globalization process not merely as victims but as partners, who with the help of the independent national state could wrench major economic benefits for it.

In the section on Multi-culturalism, all the three writers – show concern at the gradual rise of Islamic conservatism in many countries of Southeast Asia. Tracing the gradual spread of Islam in Indonesia from the 13th century onwards largely on account of foreign merchants and sufi saints, Dilip Chandra says this process led to the rise of syncretism, and the acceptance of many tradition and rituals. However, the 19th century, emergence of the reformist Wahabi movement in Arabia, and the struggle against Dutch ruler strengthened Islam as a political force. When the Dutch finally left Indonesia in 1949, Islam was one of the most potent and vibrant force in Indonesian socio-political life, having played a crucial role during the freedom struggle. However, during the Suharto regime, and especially after 1985, Islam took a back seat, with the new leaders laying emphasis on making Islam a strong social force.

Argues that in the final analysis, in Indonesia Islam has maintained its unique syncretistic character in spite of strong influence on it from the Middle Eastern countries and the political developments there.

Baladas Ghoshal explores the world of Islam in Southeast Asia and finds rise of creeping intolerance in the region's plural societies. Ghoshal traces the recent changes to pressures of globalization, political compulsions and opportunism, and ideas and money flowing from the Arab world. This new form of identity is premised on an understanding and a belief that to be a true Muslim one has to be different from 'others' in every aspect of life and that there cannot be a meeting ground between Islam and other religions. A strong sense of grievance and victim mentality has also reinforced Islam's role as a medium for asserting identity. The external manifestation is the wearing of Middle Eastern clothes by men and *hijab* or veil by women. In Indonesia Sanskrit names are being replaced by Arabic ones. Strict observance of fundamentalist Islam is also a means of asserting identification with reform and protesting upper-class corruption which is wide-spread in Indonesia and elsewhere. Arabization has long term implications both for the future state structure in Islamic countries in Southeast Asia, but also for regional security.

Ghoshal points out that under the influence of Arab ideas and finance, even in countries like the Philippines, Thailand, Cambodia and Myanmar, Islam which is only a minority religion there and had an indigenous flavour in terms of customs and practices, has now assured a much more conservative character. Growing violence and appeal of radical Islamic ideology among the Muslims in these countries makes news.

The countries of Southeast Asia are not only multicultural, but their leaders also take pride in managing such societies with great success. In reality, however, there have been wide gaps in the profession of policy and practice, as the process of assimilation is far from complete or peaceful. Using Malaysia as an illustration, Utham Kumar Jamadhagni examines three cases that call into question the policy of multiculturalism in this region. Freedom of religion one of the basic guarantees in a multi-ethnic society has been undermined in the case of Lina Joy a Muslim-converted to Christianity.

The next case is the "bhumiputera" concept and its associated issues. Finally, the HINDRAF movement and how a multicultural state is being threatened by Islamism and other divisive tendencies. According to Utham Kumar, the present government has moved away from defining Malaysia as a multicultural country by declaring it an Islamic state. The erstwhile Prime Minister Abdullah Ahmed Badawi had promoted a theory of government based on the Islamic principles known as *Islami hadhari* (civilisational Islam). But it has to counter the undercurrent of Islamic fundamentalism at home. Public schools are becoming more Islamized. More women are wearing the headscarves. The influence of the *ulema* or religious teachers is growing. The Muslim moral police also known as JAWI detain hand-holding couples and threaten "deviant" Muslims to be sent to rehabilitation centers.

Utham concludes by saying that the rise of Islamic fundamentalism in the Southeast Asian neighbourhood together with the process of Islamization could destabilize the much-touted multiethnic social fabric.

In the section on Trade and Development, paper begins with the fundamental question about ASEAN: after four decades: where does it stand on the path of regionalism? Is it a cohesive, well integrated grouping of countries of Southeast Asia or a mere conglomerate of countries loosely bound together by the considerations of expediency and convenience? Has the organization over the years made serious efforts to overcome the principal constraint of sovereignty? According to Sudhir Devare, ASEAN has steadfastly supported the principles of sovereignty and non-interference in internal affairs, which has been brought to bear from time to time when there were bilateral disputes or serious violations of human security within an ASEAN country. The examples are: the dispute between Thailand and Cambodia on an ancient Buddhist temple located near their boundary bringing the two countries to a military conflict; Indonesia and Malaysia had come close to an armed clash in the Ambalat Sea off Sulawesi over the question of rights for oil and natural gas four years ago. But there are several bilateral issues among ASEAN members which remain unresolved that have the potential of disrupting peace and security in the region. The Chinese claim sovereignty over all the South Sea Islands, although they follow a policy of friendly and co-operative relations. However, the Chinese government protested when the Philippines passed a law about its ownership of Kalayam Islands, a part of Spratlys. There is no effective mechanism within ASEAN (though the General Council has the powers, in principle) which can deal with such inter-state issues.

ASEAN's principle of non-interference in other's internal affairs has come under criticism from outside powers and lately even from within. The Myanmar situation has become a test-case on this score which is often cited as ASEAN's inability to influence or shape the course of events in defence of democracy and human rights.

Some scholars in Indonesia which is the largest country in the region, are of the opinion that in order to address the issues of security, peace and economic development in the Asia-Pacific, there should be a 'Concert of Powers' which should include eight large powers namely, the U.S, China, Japan, India, South Korea, Russia, Australia and Indonesia with ASEAN as an associate member. Devare points out 'ASEAN's relevance is often being questioned by scholars and academics from ASEAN. They ask the question: can ASEAN handle the challenges created by the rise of China and India? Devare also raises the question of strategic and maritime security of the region, and also points out that the neglect of the area by Bush led to a vacuum which was sought to be filled by China. But Obama is likely to take a closer interest in the region.

Devare argues that political cohesion in ASEAN is still an on -going process. Currently, ASEAN states are faced with serious consequences of the global economic downturn. In the circumstances, the march towards a credible regionalism in ASEAN will be anything but gradual and far from being spectacular. However, he contends that the policy framework that ASEAN have put in place is in the right direction. That includes their several cooperative arrangements with major powers of the region and outside world. With their own Charter having been adopted ASEAN have now a roadmap before them.

For India, ASEAN has become an important hub in promoting trade and investment in the wider Asia-Pacific region. India can also leverage the brand-name of Singapore or Thai or Malaysian companies in doing business in China, Japan or the U.S. There are more than 2000 Indian companies based in Singapore doing business all over the world from there. Besides, Indian companies also learn best business practices followed in ASEAN, some of which are top class in the world. Thus there is a natural fit, complementarity between India and ASEAN which both recognize and seem to value today.

Amita Batra examines the India-ASEAN economic relationship in the context of Asian economic integration. Based on trade and investment trends the economic potential of regional economic integration In Asia is highlighted. Alternative approaches to the alignment of regional economies towards the formation of a regional trade bloc/regional economic integration are evaluated, as also the challenges that need to be tackled in this context. She brings forth the central role that has to be played by the ASEAN in bringing to shape and life a new regional economic architecture in Asia. She underscores the critical importance of the global financial crisis in providing the region with a renewed opportunity for economic integration. In the above context, Batra undertakes a review of the economic consequences of the emerging new regional architecture in Asia comprising both India and China and provides insights on whether the emerging relationship between these two economies can be characterized as either competitive or co-operative. In her view, the two are not competitive. The contribution of the two economies to world growth is significantly different which she analyses in detail.

Reiterating the dictum that Free Trade Agreements (FTAs) hamper rather than facilitate free trade for those left out. Scrutinizes the cost benefit of FTAs between India, Thailand, Singapore and ASEAN. In the 2004 FTA between India and Thailand, he argues, much of the gains have accrued to Thailand on account of items such as colour picture tubes, auto parts and electronic goods. Production of these items are more expensive in India. The CECA with Singapore was a win-win situation for both. Bilateral trade and investments have surged, with Singapore providing a base for Indian companies for investing in ASEAN and East Asia. However, commercial services have languished in the absence of an agreement on professional services.

Regarding the recently concluded FTA between India and ASEAN, Chandra Mohan points out that the India-ASEAN FTA is likely to be the country's most important and ambitious trade agreement. ASEAN's GDP of $1.5 trillion is not very different from that of India's GDP of $1.2 trillion. An FTA is bound to open up a substantial market for our goods. India, too, can benefit from services trade with ASEAN. An FTA, thus, will spur the globalizing drive of India Inc eastwards as it forms partnerships, alliances and joint ventures to leverage the bustling business potentiality of this region during the 21st century. However, despite its evident importance, India's stance in its negotiations with ASEAN has been defensive in nature. Indian industry, for its part, nurtures a deep-seated ambivalence over the benefits of such bilaterals, including the one with ASEAN due to the persisting domestic handicap of inverted duty structures. This contributes to a skewed pattern of trade tilted against India. There is also concern over the prospect of diversion of foreign direct investments (FDI) from countries like Japan, whose companies can use their bases in countries like Thailand as a staging ground for their assault on India's domestic market in automobiles and consumer electronics. Nevertheless, closer economic engagement with ASEAN cannot proceed without a greater degree of self-confidence on the part of stakeholders like India Inc.

Discussing comparative management systems in India and Southeast Asia, Vinayshil Gautam showed that in respect of financial decisions pertaining to new investments, the bottom of approach was found to be more popular in the US and Japan, the top down approach found greater receptivity among the top management in Indian firms. For financing of investment, designing of capital structure, the Indian corporate sector has shown a marked preference for debt, including international loans which he calls "an instrument of neo-slavery".

Emphasizing the role of Indian telecom industry, which is amongst the fastest growing industry in the country as well in the world, Vinayshil Gautam concludes that by promoting a common identity of ASEAN, expanding its network to make the effort towards ASEAN + 6 would help increase its clout in the global arena.

In the concluding session, Rajiv Sikri looks at the prospect of an 'arc of peace and prosperity' encompassing the region from South Asia up to the Pacific, covering all the East Asian and the South East Asian countries, plus

Australia and New Zealand, which are on the periphery of this 'arc'. Both Prime Minister Manmohan Singh and former Prime Minister Atal Behari Vajpayee have publicly spoken about the enormous potential of this region where there should be free movement of people, goods, capital and ideas across this vast space. Even as there are developments in Asia that brighten the prospects of this 'arc of peace and prosperity' becoming a reality, one should not ignore some real problems that are likely to be encountered in this path. One fundamental problem, of course, is that while many countries do share India's vision there are differences among Asian countries on how to realize this vision. These differences came out most graphically in the setting up of the East Asia Summit (EAS); India had a difficult time to become a founder member. However, a long-term vision combined with successful Indian diplomacy ensured that India was a participant in the inaugural EAS summit. Against this is the competing vision of the ASEAN+3, which brings together ASEAN, Japan, China and South Korea, being pushed primarily by China, which thinks that through this mechanism it would be able to dominate the region. It is precisely because of such fears that countries like Japan, Vietnam, Indonesia and Singapore have been keen to involve India so that there is some kind of balancing factor to Chinese hegemony over East and Southeast Asia. Now as the process of building a community in East Asia gets under way, the ongoing struggle that can be expected to intensify is about the nature of this 'arc of peace and prosperity.' Would it be centered on the EAS, or the ASEAN+3?

Sikri points our that one cannot envision an 'arc of peace and prosperity' without factoring in what the United States will do and what kind of pressures it will bring upon the countries to make sure that it is included. US membership of the EAS will undoubtedly change the balance and the dynamics of the EAS. Russia too has been very keen on joining the EAS, but has not succeeded so far. Another, bigger, question is: what would happen to Taiwan and North Korea? One cannot have any 'arc of peace and prosperity' that ignores these two sore thumbs sticking out in East Asia. If India integrates with East Asian and South East Asian countries, how does India handle its South Asian neighbours? Are they going to be left behind? What happens to Bangladesh? From the Indian perspective, it is obviously to India's advantage that it is a member of this grouping.

Then there is the ill-conceived and short-lived 'Quad' that brought together India, Japan, the United States and Australia a couple of years ago. However, as a result of vehement opposition from China, and also because of a change of governments in both Japan and Australia, the Quad has been given a quiet burial. Australian Prime Minister Kevin Rudd has been pushing the idea of an Asia-Pacific Community, comprising the United States, Japan, China, India, Indonesia, and unspecified 'other states in the region'. It is possible that this is a Chinese attempt to prevent the emergence of the India-Japan-US- Australia 'Quad'. What they are doing is essentially to try to spike the idea of the 'Quad' by expanding it to include China, as well as Indonesia, which because of its geographical location and size, is a very important country for China's trade and energy SLOCs. Another problem with the Rudd proposal is that it divides ASEAN and all the ASEAN countries (other than Indonesia) that have been left out of the proposed grouping will oppose this proposal tooth and nail.

Sikri urges India to develop a psychological and a real counter to ongoing Chinese activities in the Indian Ocean. India needs re active in this regard. This can be done bilaterally, through exercises, training or other cooperative activities with individual countries. It can also be through confidence-building regional mechanisms like the Indian Ocean Naval Symposium (IONS), the MILAN exercises, the ASEAN Regional Forum (ARF), and Track II mechanisms like CSCAP and the Shangri-La dialogue. Japan is obviously going to be a key player and India has rightly been giving considerable attention and focus to engaging Japan. The problem, however, is that Japan has a somewhat inconsistent view of India that appears to be considerably dictated by the state of its relations with China. In addition to engaging Japan, we also need to continue to engage South Korea.

Sikri talks about two other 'arcs' in which India will have to take a natural interest. One is the 'arc of energy' extending from the Persian Gulf through the Caspian Sea and going on to Siberia and the Far East. The final arc, perhaps the most difficult one, is the 'arc of instability. 'From Pakistan, right up to the Mediterranean is a very unstable region and one of the most turbulent and problematic areas of the world. The whole region – Pakistan, Afghanistan, Iran, Iraq, Lebanon, Syria, Israel, and Palestine – is a virtual tinderbox. Now the fire is spreading towards India.

Finally, feels that India has to take a view whether it can, or indeed whether it should, piggyback on the US? Linked to this is another key question: how does India have a strategic relationship with the US when India's naval fleet as well as the development of India's naval equipment and systems is so heavily dependent on Russia? At a time when U.S. and Russia are again entering a period of strategic competition, the Russians will hardly be inclined to give India their hi-tech products if India is entering into a strategic relationship with the United States.

Vice-Admiral Chauhan deals with the Indian Navy's approach toward maritime security in the Indian Ocean. He argues that India's thinking about maritime security is now firmly established within a new construct that incorporates military, political, economic, societal and environmental dimensions, and recognises the many linkages between them. The Indian Navy's thinking is increasingly influenced by the UNDP list of as many as seven additional components of 'Human Security' : *Economic Security, Food Security, Health Security, Environmental Security, Personal Security, Community Security*, and, *Political Security*. Today, there are several significant threats to human-security, including wars and international terrorism. Drugs and arms smuggling are very real threats that continue unabated. Demographic shifts — whether caused by migration or by other factors — continue to haunt security organisations. Environmental degradation and its security overtones is another. Energy, food and water shortages are all moving up the ladder of security-related threats that are becoming inseparable from military threats. These have led to the formulation of new concepts such as 'comprehensive security' and 'cooperative security'. Cooperative Naval constructs such as the IONS (Indian Ocean Naval Symposium) and the WPNS (Western Pacific Naval Symposium) are, in fact, founded upon these 'Non-Traditional' security-concepts, involving 'cooperative' rather than 'competitive' security and 'comprehensive' rather than narrow 'military' security. Hence, security issues within the maritime domain need to be referenced more towards common interests rather than threats. At a regional level, common interests are, the same 'Human Security' Issues. 'Constructive Engagement' between navies enables the gaining and sharing of operational, and, doctrinal expertise... as also transformational experiences... the examining and imbibing of 'best-practices'..... the generation of inter-operability, and, the enhancement of Maritime Domain Awareness through a variety of information-sharing mechanisms.

According to Chauhan the improvement of the security situation in the Strait of Malacca offers a striking example of the success that can be achieved through cooperative and collective security constructs. Concerted actions by the littoral states have caused incidents of piracy to dwindle very significantly, which Chauhan attributes to the praiseworthy actions of the littoral states of Indonesia, Malaysia, Singapore and Thailand. He, however, admits that even in the Straits of Malacca there is clearly much that remains to be done. The Strait remains very vulnerable to terrorist attack. At its narrowest point, the strait is less than 1.5 nm wide, and, a successful attempt to sink a ship in this bottleneck could have severely-adverse fallout on merchant traffic.

In order to maximise beneficial gains, all navies in the Indian Ocean region need to engage in both directions along the axis of perceived maritime-capability — not just with navies that are considered to be as advanced or more advanced than one's own — but equally, with navies for whom ***the collective*** engagement will ***build*** capacity and ***enhance*** capability. Argues that it is precisely this patient and step-by-step process of building capacity and enhancing capability, especially amongst the smaller littoral states of the region that will transform some of the security-related fragility of the Indian Ocean littoral into robustness born of self-confidence and self-sufficiency.

Chauhan envisages a move towards connectivity with the Shanghai Cooperation Organisation that might eventually lead to the pan-Asian security construct. The Indian Navy believes that the Indian Ocean Naval Symposium (IONS) and the Western Ocean Naval Symposium (WPNS) movements constitute the key to addressing the many challenges that face us in the within the Asia-Pacific maritime domain.

Tracing the historical factors which delayed India's interaction with Southeast Asia, argues that India's ASEAN economic relations carry a sub-regional developmental promise in the sense that their trade routes would contribute to India's northeastern (NER) region which is contiguous to Southeast Asia. In fact, the NER is conceived as India's gateway to the ASEAN region. Development by highways, railways, airways, shipping services and energy linkages would lead to significant development of this region.

Notes that the Asia-Pacific region is looming large economically and strategically, with the rise of China. To safeguard its interests, India has made multiple engagements with the countries of the region which he illustrates by a diagram. The Indian Navy too is a potent foreign policy force to establish closer relations with Asian countries by visits, naval exercises, etc.

By subscribing to various regional trade groups, India has established her economic presence in Southeast Asia, though the latter is yet to be convinced about India's ability to deepen mutual economic partnership. Strategically, India has carved out a bigger role for itself in the Asian geo-political landscape. Through membership in fora of regional bodies, combined with sustained display of her naval power, India has staked her political claim to be a legitimate actor in the Asian power structure. Major powers like the US, Japan, China and the medium ASEAN powers acknowledge India as a significant regional power. Thus, on balance, India's strategic presence outweighs her economic activism in Southeast Asia. Though it is a historical anachronism to search for close parallels between early Indian role in Southeast Asia and her present role therein, there is no doubt that India has gained back much of the lost ground in the region.

Asad-ul Iqbal Latif gives a view from Singapore about China's and India's interactions with Southeast Asia. Although historically Southeast Asian countries were tribute paying entities of the Middle Kingdom, and some writers have advocated a likely enunciation of a similar policy, the Chinese leaders have shown little inclination towards such an approach, though this configuration could arise in the future. India too has rejected the neo-Curozian view of trying to establish an arc of domination from Aden to Singapore. Latif finds that India's rediscovery of Southeast Asia, in the form of its Look East Policy in the 1990 has transformed its relations with the Association of Southeast Asian Nations (ASEAN). In tandem, India's appearance as a swing state in relations between the United States and China has made New Delhi an important part of the strategic calculus in Southeast Asia. However, like China, India needs to eschew any return to a past when colonialism absorbed the Indian Ocean into alien orbits of influence. The pre-colonial 'mandala' system would be a better model. Even as India's hard power grows, its exercise of soft power-drawing on its strength in intellectual pluralism, political liberalism and secularism – would underpin its interests in the region as a benign yet credible power. Indeed, the history of India's pre-colonial relations with Southeast Asia cries out for a reformulation of that cultural role. The region is far more receptive to India's soft power than Central Asia or West Asia is likely to be.

Suggests two concrete ways in which India could give its Look East Policy greater cultural depth. First, the idea of setting up Tagore Institutes around the world. This would fulfill the need for Indian culture to have a permanent, instantly recognizable and iconic presence abroad. Tagore Institutes would do this and bring India into the league of countries whose cultural diplomacy fuels their formidable soft power. Examples are, Britain with the British Council, France with the Alliance Française, Germany with the Goethe-Institut, and now China with the Confucius Institute. Secondly, New Delhi should move expeditiously with the proposal to set up a revived Nalanda University on the site of what was one of the world's first residential universities. The Nalanda Project, which is chaired by Amartya Sen and to which Singapore is aimed at advancing the concept of an Asian community and rediscovering old relationships. To quote: "Ultimately, culture is the story of the mind outliving the depredations wrought by nature and man. The exercise of soft power in India's relations with Southeast Asia would have a firm foundation in that ancient promise of culture."

In the last chapter, Tridip Chakraborti focuses on ASEAN's record in dealing with the outstanding issues like the problem of forest fires and trans-boundary environmental pollution; the scourge of terrorism after 11 September, 2001; South China Sea imbroglio; Cambodian crisis in 1979; the financial crisis of 1997; minimizing the gap between rich and poor ASEAN members; island disputes among the member countries, natural disasters, swelling of infectious diseases etc. He describes the initiatives ASEAN members have taken in their endeavour to resolve them, based solely on dialogue, consultation, cooperation, engagement and mutual interaction, without breaking away from the principle of non-intervention. In fact, the majority members have felt that, since the principle of non-intervention has been inherent in the very nature of the organization, having contributed to ASEAN's success in the past, it would continue to do so in future, and discarding it would not make ASEAN any stronger. For the sake of regional cohesion, the members have tried to strike a balance between what is desirable and what is possible, the idyllic and the realistic, desired ends and available means and international involvement and national sovereignty. Its consensus model has always served this Association and its members splendidly. To the ASEAN members, their very own 'ASEAN Way' is not at all a typical conflict-resolution mechanism, but has rather evolved as a conflict-avoidance instrument, relying on the software arms of regional understanding rather than the hardware elements of formalized, rule-based instrumentalities. During its long years of experience, ASEAN has never been visualized as a mechanism for conflict-settlement and conflict-resolution. It has rather been able to establish itself successfully in conflict-mitigation.

The signing of the ASEAN Charter in November 2007, which seeks to establish ASEAN as a legal entity and formally move the region towards an

EU-style economic community by 2015, has greatly increased ASEAN's institutional capacity and ability for autonomous action, including the realm of counter-terrorism. Thus, after more than four decades, ASEAN has not only survived, but has developed into an important force internationally, being upheld as an exemplar of regional unity, worthy of emulation. Through its policy of trial and triumph, based on the mindset of regional cohesion, ASEAN has come to play a very constructive and prominent role in developing a sense of regional identity in Southeast Asia and has been successful in reducing tensions for the maintenance of peace and stability in the region, as opposed to any other third world regional organization such as SAARC, which is inadvertently plagued by narrow selfish interests and political differences among the member countries.

PART–I. HISTORY AND CULTURE

CHAPTER 1

History and Society in Southeast Asia before 1500 – An Outline

Prof. Satish Chandra

Despite differences in languages, the countries of Southeast Asia had social structures, which had much in common, and they interacted with each other socially, economically and culturally. Historically, Southeast Asia was never an isolated or self-contained unit because of its cross-road situation on the map of Asia. It had, therefore, been a meeting ground of commerce, culture and civilizations, situated both in the Indian Ocean and the Pacific.

Settled agriculture and the rise of primitive states in the region can be traced back only to the 3rd century B.C. The peoples of the area made significant contribution in ship-building, long distance voyaging on the sea, domestication of rice and harvesting of crops such as sugar-cane, yam, sago, banana and cocoa-nut. They also assimilated and developed sophisticated metal technology which included bronze, brass, tin and iron, and of course, gold.

Like early India, which had no tradition of history writing but for a few exceptions, the Southeast Asian countries, excluding Vietnam, too, lacked an historical tradition. Most of their written history is a recent creation, much of the task being the outcome of labours of western scholars. May of these scholars have, however, consciously or unconsciously, often applied western values and social concepts in their writings on Southeast Asia. A comparative study of Southeast Asian countries' social organization, political structure, economy and culture with those countries, such as India, Sri Lanka with which they had close economic and cultural ties would, therefore, be rewarding.

Southeast Asia has generally been divided into two broad segments – the mainland comprising modern Vietnam, Burma, Thailand, Cambodia, Laos, and northern Malaysia, and the maritime area comprising Indonesia, South and East Malaysia, Brunei and the Philippines. The three main centers of political, economic and cultural activity on the mainland were the Vietnamese of North Vietnam with their capital Hoa-Lu (near modern Hanoi) and economic centres near the Red River; the Khmer state of the southern Mekong region which spread to Cambodia and to the northern area around Ankor, and third, the Burmese-Mon rule with Pagan upland, later extending to the Irrawady valley dominated by the Mons. Of these, North Vietnam had to contend for long with China which absorbed its energies, allowing only some forays into the Central and South Mekong areas. Culturally also Vietnam remained much nearer to China than the rest of Southeast Asia.

The Khmer state arose around the third century and continued till the 15th century. It had various capitals near the coastline at first, but in the 6th century it expanded inland and occupied the Torb Sap or Great Lake, a natural reservoir for annual monsoon floods of the Mekong. The shift of the Khmer polity to Ankor region which was situated on the northern of the Great Lake is linked with the name of Jayaverman-II. The Chinese record keepers used the word Funan, top of the mountain only to the period before the shift to Ankor. But the word Funan is often associated with the Khmer kingdom for its entire existence.

Ankor was next to rich rice land areas, and provided the means to successive rulers, such as Bhavavarman, Mahendravarman, Jayavarman - I & II to expand over modern Cambodia. It was Yasovarman who began to reside at the actual site of Ankor. He was a great builder, and built sanctuaries at Ankor and almost one hundred temples or monasteries throughout the realm. These temples contained images of Siva, Vishnu and the Buddha and had accommodation for the monks who lived there. The temples contained legends from the *Ramayana* and *Mahabharata*. Although each king built a temple at Ankor to mark his memory, the great temple Ankor Vat, was built by Suryavarman-II in the middle of the 12th century.

The Brahmanical priests strengthened the position of the king in various ways. Thus, in 802 C.E, Brahman priests performed a ceremony that proclaimed Jayaraman-II as the supreme ruler, and all subordinate rulers as his vassals. The Ankor rulers set up standards of state control and culture which influenced the wider region. Indian influence came mainly from traders at the coast, as also from traders traveling to China who disembarked at the Kra Isthmus and carried their goods across the Khmer kingdom to the sea. The Brahmanical concept of a Universal God superior to all local deities helped the ruler to become supreme in other ways too — he claimed to be representative or chief servitor of supreme God Siva or Vishnu. Legend of a marriage of a local princess of the ruling house with a brahman also strengthened the prestige of the successors. The brahmans in the temples provided a literate bureaucracy. However, these factors, which played an important part in the rise of a large, powerful state in the region have to be seen in a wider socio-economic context, viz. the expansion of wet-rice cultivation in place of the earlier slash and burn system of isolated communal groups. Strong monarchies rather than local chieftains were in a better position to build water works needed for wet-rice cultivation. We are told that brahmans improved rice cultivation by introducing the technique of rice re-transplantation. But more evidence is needed to support this.

According to a modern historian, "The Khmers were consummate hydraulic engineers: they cut canals, dredged and straightened rivers, built dikes into the floodplain to deflect and hold back flood waters, dug moats around their temples and some residential areas, and built countless reservoirs to tap the high water-table found in the region.... Several prominent Khmer kings also engaged in large scale public work projects to build enormous *baray* (great lakes) so large that they are visible from space by satellite."[1]

In the agrarian expansion, and growth of international trade, the temples – both those built by the central rulers and those by local elites, played an important role. They acted as centers of investment (banks) from the offerings and lands, the investment being redistributed to individuals or cultivators, or used for international trade. Second, temples were repositories of technical information and knowledge and supported scholars, astrologers, musicians, dancers, etc. Third, they were agencies which helped in the task of strengthening agrarian infrastructure by building water-works for which money and labour were needed. The temples could provide both more easily than the local elites because any task undertaken by the temple was considered holy. The monasteries could also act as royal outposts.

It will be seen that the temples in the Khmer kingdom served functions similar to temples in South India.

The Khmer empire reached its maximum extent under Jayavarman VII (1182-1218 CE). Imperial expansion also meant construction of monuments: great stone temples, and rest houses, hospitals, raised roadways and bridges, and *barays* (lakes). But the end of Jayavarman's rule, marked the beginning of two centuries of Khmer decline. Among other things, it is linked to ecological changes, and the silting up of some *barays*. Ultimately, Thais overwhelmed Ankor in the fifteenth century.

Pagan, upland at the Irrawady river, was able to dominate the entire Irrawady valley. As a modern historian, Keith A. Taylor, says, "Pagan was the ideal site to concentrate the rice-surplus of the two regions. Mimbu downriver and Kyaukse upriver which had emerged as important rice-producing areas through the development of extensive irrigation systems." Lower Burma, Arakan and Tenassirn were important centers of international trade and culture, but "the history of Pagan reveals that in that time and place, the inland agrarian polity was better able to concentrate people and wealth than were coastal entrepots".

The rise of Pagan began in the early 11th century. It had to contend with the Shan people from the North, and the Mons from the south who considered themselves culturally superior. The Mongols penetrated Pagan from Yunan in the 13th century, but were defeated by the Shans of North Burma. The Burmese moved to Ava down the river, but Arakan and the Mons became separate kingdoms leading to the fragmentation of Burma.

What political and cultural legacy Pagan left has been a matter of controversy. The ethnic division between the Burmese, the northern Shan and other tribes, and the Arakanese were never resolved. However, Buddhist monasteries played an important role in the Irrawady valley. Moral authority granted by the Buddhist monks to rulers was considered important, although no clear concept of a supreme ruler sanctified by the monks emerged. Large lands were donated for the support of monasteries by rulers and nobles which sometimes led to conflict with the state.The Sarvastivadin and Theravad Buddhists of upper and lower Burma had close links with Sri Lanka, many of the monks being sent there for improving their knowledge of the sacred lore. Lower Burma also had close trade links with Sri Lanka, although Arakan, which had gradually become Muslim, had close economic links with Bengal.

Both the Burmese and the Khmer kingdom contested for the domination of small coastal kingdoms. Of these the largest was Champa with its capital at 'Panduranga, Kanthãva', etc. Ayuthya was another kingdom which was an island state. Both of these kingdoms were strongly influenced in their cultural and religious forms by Indian traders. Ayuthya had a strong navy which it used to raid and plunder coastal cities. Following the disintegration of the Khmer kingdom in the 14th century, Dai Viet (Vietnam) remained the most powerful kingdom. It pressed down the Mekong valley against Champa. Ayuthya located on the Chao Pharaya river off the Gulf of Thailand expanded inland, and clashed both with Vietnam and Burma. Ultimately, in 1767, Burma invaded and destroyed Ayuthya. A new kingdom, Siam or Thailand, dominated by the Tais arose in its place, but could never equal Ayuthya in trade or naval power.

As compared to the mainland countries, the maritime countries of Southeast Asia were much more influenced by the sea and by trade since they sat astride the trade lines from India, China and the Middle East-area from which at first Persian, and later Arab merchants came, along with a few Jews. Trade between these countries, and the Mediterranean world, and the maritime states of Southeast Asia prospered. Countries from Southeast Asia also had many goods to contribute to this trade, apart from gold and tin. These included forest produce such as camphor, sandal wood, ivory, etc. Later, the fine spices and ungents became main items of trade. The spices were obtained by local traders from the spice islands of Moluccas (or Maluku) in exchange for rice, metals, etc. The spices were then exchanged for textiles from India, and silk and porcelain from China. The Javanese economy was monetized by the tenth century. The metallic coinage system included both gold and silver currency.

The two biggest empires which arose in the maritime states were the Srivijaya empire (7th to 11th century), based on South Sumatra, and the Majapahit empire (late 13th to 16th century) based on Java. From its capital Palembang, situated upriver on river Musi on the south west coast of Sumatra which was navigable to the sea and could protect ships from the fury of the monsoon, Srivijaya was able to control ports from the north-eastern ports of

Java and many North Malay ports. Thus, they could control both the Malaka and the Sunda straits for trade between India, the Middle East and China, and able to procure spices from the Malukus. Srivijaya was able to control and incorporate the ports and their rice-producing hinterland not so much by force as by sharing with them foreign goods brought by the traders, and by protecting their sea-shores from pirates. The hinterland of the Musi river which was under the direct control of Srivijaya provided both rice and sailors.

Srivijaya faced the hostility of the Sailendra rulers of Central Java or Mataram. But there were marriage alliance between the two, and in the middle of the 9th century, when the Sailendra ruler was defeated, he went to Palembang, and was incorporated in the royal household. The dynasty began to be called the Sailendra dynasty. The Sailendra rulers of Srivijaya had close links with both India and China. The links to India and China is testified to by the visit of the Chinese pilgrim I-tsiṇ to Srivijaya in 672. He stayed for six months to study Sanskrit. On return from India, he stayed again for four years, and then went back to China. In 850-60 C.E. there was a grant to a Buddhist monastery at Nalanda where the donor is called *kulaputra* of Maharaja Samaragriva, who was himself son of a king of Yava-bhumi (Java)" "ornament of the Sailendra dynastry".

Control of the seaports linking the growing trade to China seems to be the basis of the series of naval raids by the Chola rulers. The Chola navy sacked and burnt Palembang in 1025. They also invaded North Malay in 1085-86. While this does show the strength of the Indian navy at that time, no attempt was made to establish control over any of the ports, or create a monopoly of any goods. Thus, the tradition of open sea-trade continued.

The gradual weakening of Srivijaya over North Malay and the Malay Straits was due not to the Chola intervention, but the assertion of local independence by ports of the region, sometime with the help of the Chinese who found it advantageous to deal with local rulers. Internal factors, and the rise of Majapahit in Java also played a role.

It is generally not realised that the Majapahit empire, based on Java, not only carried on the traditions of Srivijaya, but was more extensive, powerful and wealthy. As a modern writer says, 'Majapahit was the last and the greatest of the empire in the pre-1500 Southeast Asia island realm. Its kings came to possess a degree of central control in East Java that went beyond previous precedent, and they furthermore created a state centre that established varying degrees of hegemony over central Java, and an overseas realm almost three times the size of what had been Srivijaya's......"[2]

Thus, it included North Malay, all of Sumatra, Bali, and a vague control over the spice Islands or Maluku where it had a port. It also controlled Brunei and a part of the Philippines.

Although Majapahit rose to prominence in the late 13th century, its political and cultural antecedents were much older. Thus, Central Java was home to a Hindu, and East Java of a Buddhist kingdom much before the rise of Srivijaya. East Java is known for the magnificent temple at Borobodur. The rulers of Central Java consecrated in 856 C.E. a magnificent temple at Prambanan on the Deng plateau, dedicated to the trinity of Siva, Vishnu and Brahma.

Central Java or Mataram was ruled over at first by the Sailendras who took the title of Maharaja. Central Java was a rice bowl, and closely allied to Srivijaya. But it was not so much interested in trade as East Java which was the centre of spice trade from the Molukas for which all international traders came. Marco Polo came here, and praised their wealth. Despite mutual wars and internal dissensions, the Majapahit rulers combined both the rice producing lands of Central Java, and the rich ports and hinterland of East Java. They extended cultivation by building dams on the Brantas river, and built roads across the area. Further, they carried out a synthesis of Buddhist, Saiva, and Tantra rites with Malay rituals. This was demonstrated in the Chaitra festival held at Babat, near the capital, Majapahit. Babat was a market town to which all traders, domestic and foreign, including those from India, and artisans gathered. The festival, held in March or April, consisted of a series of ceremonies which not only exemplified social and cultural life but enhanced the position of the Majapahit ruler. In the ceremonies brahmans and Buddhist monks prayed for the prosperity of the royal house, and holy water was offered to the king. In a stately procession princess in golden attire, nobles, scholars and judges of the realm (brahmans), moved to the beat of ceremonial drums and the blowing of conch-shells and trumpets. This was followed by a week's public amusements in which the court participated. The ceremony was then shifted for a week to the capital.

By all accounts, the 14th century marked the high tide of the inter-Asian trade. Growing foreign demand for spice was accompanied by increased production of rice from the hinterland, and artisanal production.

From this brief survey, a few conclusions may be drawn. First, beginning with small states, both mainland and maritime areas were able to develop large empires which not only maintained law and order but expanded agriculture — mainly rice cultivation, and promoted and participated in overseas trade.

Second, they were open to and assimilated civilizational and cultural values and forms, both that came from outside, and those developed by countries of the region. They successfully established a symbyotic relationship between the various cultural elements, and evolved a pluralistic order, avoiding inter-sectoral strife. Religion was closely integrated with social traditions and political forms.

Third, although political conflict over territory, prestige and trade continued sporadically, society was not organized on military lines. Thus, standing armies were small, there was hardly a military or bureaucratic hierarchy. Land revenue and taxes were collected with the help of local elites (granted hereditary *sima* rights in Java), traders and temples. Thus, the polity was more decentralized than centralized.

Fourth, the sea played a much more important role in the social and political structures, and the mental make up (mentalities) of the peoples of the region. Sea-daring and adventure was part of their psychology which also led to considerable piracy but was put down sternly by naval states, such as Srivijaya and Majapahit.

Fifth, there was a tradition of rulers, the elites and temples taking part in domestic and over-seas trade. Thus, the traders were a powerful community, respected and promoted by the ruling classes. It was this balance between the rural elites and traders which was upset when the colonial rulers monopolized foreign trade, and forced the traders to look inland for profits.

Sixth, despite the importance of over-seas trade in the economy of the countries of the region, little effort was made to create trade monopolies, or close their ports to foreign traders. Thus, the tradition of open sea-trade continued.

Lastly, some countries of the region had powerful navies and a strong tradition of boat-building. But their navy or traders do not seem to have played an active part in the Bay of Bengal region or South China Sea. Although Chinese merchant ships came to Malabar, and even to Gujarat, no such tradition of traders from Southeast Asian countries coming to India is available.

This, as well as similar social and cultural structures between India and countries of Southeast Asia need a deeper study.

REFERENCES

1. Miriam T. Stark in *Southeast Asia: from pre-history to history*, ed. Ian Glover and Peter Bellwood, Routledge Curzov, 2004. p.108.
2. Kenneth R Hall, *The Cambridge History of Southeast Asia*, O.U.P., 1992, Vol. 1, p. 215.

CHAPTER 2

Asian Sense and Sensibility, Monuments and the Oral Tradition

Dr. Kapila Vatsyayan

For different parts of the geographical entity called Asia or Southeast Asia, all our identities are largely fluid and cannot be absolutely fixed. Each constituent of the area called South-east Asia and South Asia becomes a part of the kaleidoscope where different configurations take place in time and space. Through all these configurations a distinct Asian sensibility is clearly distinguishable. This belies the theoretical position taken by some scholars that there is no such thing as Asian civilization. Erudite and devoted Asian and Indian scholars have addressed themselves to this issue, which permeates the specific disciplines of history, maritime trade, economics as also archaeology and art.

I would like to restrict myself only to underline the diversity of approaches.

If one looks at some of the scholarly writing it would appear that there have been three approaches. The first is purely *chronological.* The critical writing in the *cultural* sphere has predominantly adopted religious affiliations as indicators. Thus the culture of this region has been understood and assessed as Hinduism, Buddhism, Islam or Christianity. Some of this writing speaks of syncretism. Whether this is a phenomenon of syncretism or something else has to be accepted or re-visited. The third approach endeavours to trace the nature of trade and economics, goods and services, and touches upon the impact of trade on culture and politics.

It will be obvious that no one approach can present the fascinating dynamics of a complex communication system which is evident in the pre-colonial, colonial and post-colonial period, as also the causes and effects of maritime trade, etc. In much of these spheres, what becomes evident is that there is a very special *Asian identity and sensibility*. Would it be too much to state that largely there is the dynamics of interpenetration and co-existence, rather than confrontation, specially in the pre-colonial period. Fluidity rather than fixity is the nature of this dynamics. Identities do not undergo a total change. Instead, there is overlap. This phenomenon of multi-identities can be identified in societal formations and religious affiliations and is most explicitly evident in the sphere of culture, especially in the monuments in South-east Asia. Each monument appears to provide testimony to the fact that none can be categorized either in terms of linear chronology or in terms of a single affiliation, Hinduism, Buddhism or Islam, or from the point of trade, commerce and political power.

Let us take as an example the most well-known monument, which has been declared as a world heritage site. How do we interpret Borobudur? Is this a stupa replicating those in India? Even far more, does it have important antecedents in respect of concept, form and significance? One scholar, i.e., the French scholar Paul Mus, has convincingly argued that at a conceptual level Borobudur is a concretization of the schematic design of the Vedic yajna. He further argues that the formal design is in conformity with *mandalas*, both Hindu and Buddhist.

Thus, when one begins to examine the nature of a monument like Borobudur, it is no longer a question of restricting that interpretation to its being only a Buddhist monument or a typical stupa. Equally important is the historiography of the identification as also conservation of this monument. Once we begin to look at this, then it becomes necessary to address the historiography of such monuments in pre-colonial, colonial and now post-colonial period. It is not necessary for me here even to refer to the impressive body of not only archaeological but also interpretative critical work on Borobudur. Despite this volume of very impressive body of critical literature, there is scope to examine how the monument could be a multi-meaning structure both at the time of conception as also construction. I say so because I have a personal recollection of the history of the efforts that were made for the restoration of this monument and as someone peripherally involved in the UNESCO project. It was obvious to me through repeated visits that the monument would continue to compel us to ask many more questions beyond the work of the distinguished Dutch and other European scholars.

Now, if we turn our attention from the monument of Borobudur to Prambanan, we are faced with a similar situation in terms of the complexities of identification, classification and straight-jacketed affiliation to particular religious cults. This is not the occasion to raise some deeper questions in regard to the monuments in Prambanan, but only to bring home in our context the fact that can Prambanan be looked at as a purely funerary temple? Or identified with Vaishnavite or Shivaite cults?

The history of restoration of this group of monuments is also known and well documented. However, each restoration brings up a new set of problems. I do not have to refer to the seminal work of Stutterheim and of the Indonesian archaeologists, specially Satyawati Sulaiman.

This argument could be extended to the great complex of monuments temples in Cambodia. Even Angkor Wat belies straight-jacketed classification in terms of replication of Indian models, or for that matter, if it has ever been a Hindu or Buddhist monument. I need say no more here because the latest archaeological work on Angkor complex has made it evident that no single religious category fits the monument.

To repeat in half lines:

Angkor Wat – is it India repeated? Is it paradigmical model of Kailash – yes or no? Is it only a representation of Chola power – partially yes and partially no? Further, are the myths which have been carved on those walls only a representation of pauranic Indian? The Amrit Manthan of the third gallery is concurrently a visual representation of a pan-Asian myth, a political statement and a distinct art style. Thus, in the case of each of these major monuments mentioned above, and many, many others, these complexities face the researcher if he or she is to follow only a single approach.

The same phenomenon can be seen in Vietnam and Thailand. In the case of Vietnam, a neat definition between Indian and Chinese influence does not serve the purpose of interpreting meaning or form. The distinctively Vietnamese character even within a multiplicity of styles only shows that there was communication and confluence in the realm of art and architecture, and not confrontation. The indigenous traditions amalgamated with others and continued to have the capacity and potentiality of holding many cultural identities together.

While the archaeological evidence is a clear statement, there is a vast amount of work which needs to be done on the inscriptions, on the manuscript material and in the co-relation of the archaeological, epigraphic and literary evidence. Understandably, despite the popularity of these monuments and archaeological sites, today deeper research work is still a necessity.

At this point I think we have to face candidly some disturbing facts. It will be agreed that the number of scholars in India – and I can speak only about India – who have the ability to read original inscriptions as also manuscripts is rare. The number of traditional scholars who were competent to do this is fast shrinking. Alas, the university system at the graduate or post-graduate level does not make it mandatory for scholars to learn an ancient language or a script or be in command of primary material. Thus, there is dependence on secondary material and translations. While the earlier generation of Indian scholars was in command of some of these languages, I doubt if one can make an impressive list of those who can do so now.

One has also to face the fact that learning and competency in languages belonging to either a country or associated with a monument is a necessary pre-requisite. In some of the departments in countries abroad they insist that the scholar first holds a command over the corpus of literary material, whether as inscriptions or manuscripts. There is no such insistence in the present university system in India. There are no doubt some traditional scholars in this country outside the university system who could be identified as specialized human resource, but they are seldom called upon because the university system does not recognize them.

Thus the questions we have to ask ourselves are whether there is a need for a future generation to investigate these aspects of cultural dynamics in this region, or could we rest on our oars by only tracing linear history and either speaking about a greater India or 'wave upon waves' from India or typical indigenous trends or in terms of the Hindu, Buddhist and Islamic heritage? The argument could be extended to other spheres, particularly the sphere of performing arts, but this I shall not touch upon here.

Finally, may I submit that there should be a serious effort to train a future generation of scholars who would be competent in deciphering inscriptions, looking at original primary material and also to be competent in multiple languages. In the absence of this, we shall continue to be conditioned by our own limitations of either accepting or rejecting earlier theoretical positions.

I go further in terms of the knowledge, beyond the knowledge, into the other point that was raised. Often we say that there is a well-chiselled system of oral communication. Now, if the oral communication is so effective, how does a whole civilization depend upon the efficacy of the spoken or the heard word? And where in the worldview does it give primacy to the word heard rather than the word written in a certain way? This raises extremely important questions at the levels of both ontology as also epistemology. In the Indian context, the Vedas, which are supposed to be the foundation of many knowledge systems, by volition spoke about the Shruti as the primary and the Smriti as the secondary. If that permeated into what we call the systems of transmission of knowledge through oral communication, then we cannot go into the anthropological paradigm of having a hierarchy of civilizational ratings from the 'primitive' to the 'civilized', from the non-literate to the literate. That is the theoretical puzzle that I wish to place before you.

You are well aware of the history of the prioritization of the written over the oral in the early 20th century discourse. This categorization had deep implications for the understanding of those traditions, which had shown unprecedented continuity and today called 'the developing world'. It is time that we in Asia should go beyond the pre-colonial, colonial and post-colonial and also global discourse, but instead try to identify this very special methodology of communication, which is pervasive in all of Southeast Asia and South Asia. The oral traditions cannot be categorized as some minor folk traditions but have to be looked at differently. Perhaps this volume and its follow up will suggest a new methodology of work most suited and appropriate for the evidence rather than accepting the theoretical position first and then try to fit the evidence into that theoretical position. As academics I think we realize this. But the pressure of accepting earlier hypotheses is great and the work becomes comparatively easier. However, if we are conscious of a very distinctive Asian sensibility and identity, conscious of the nature of fluidity and over-layering, then obviously the present paradigmical models do not fit the reality of the Asian phenomenon.

CHAPTER 3

Textiles as Means of Cultural Exchange: India and Southeast Asia

Hema Devare

Introduction

A cultural synthesis of the original and local is an ever present theme in the story of India's relations with Southeast Asia. Beginning from the pre-Christian era Indians have had close cultural interaction with this region. India's relationship with Southeast Asia was varied and colourful as the hues and designs of textiles, because the flow of ideas, thoughts and customs was not from one source in India but came from various regions and their transmission too, was not confined to one culture but to several of them.

Indians entered Southeast Asia for commerce and business. They crossed the eastern seas with a great spirit of adventure and enterprise. The economic contact was mainly started by people from south India with bead trade. Archaeological evidence to that effect has been found in Malaysia, Indonesia and the Philippines.[1] By 200 B.C the long distance axis stretching from the Mediterranean to China was established. It was connected by land and sea routes including the famous Silk Route. The Asian mainland and archipelago were fully integrated into this axis via India and China. Several Jataka stories before the Christian era refer to voyages between India and Suvarnabhoomi (general name for the lands and islands in the Far East)[2] Kautilya's *Arthashastra* (323 to 300 B.C) mentions India's trade with lower Burma in *tailparnika* (sandal-like paste).[3] There were a number of migrations from India to Indochina before and after the Christian era. There is a reference to Indian settlements in Takkola (present-day Malaysia) and Yavadwipa (present-day Indonesia) in Palinidesha (247 B.C)[4]

In addition to the merchants, princes also traveled across the sea to seek fortune.[5] Along-with them went brahmans, many of whom married local princesses, like Kuandinya, who married Soma, the daughter of the Naga king of Funan, and the brahman, Durgaswamy, who married the princess of the royal family of Kamboja. Prevalent religions, Hinduism and Buddhism also went to Southeast Asia which flourished there and left an indelible imprint in the form of monuments, sculptures, inscriptions, language, literature, customs and arts.

India played a principal role in the textile history of Southeast Asia which also provides a window to the history of Southeast Asian societies. The woven fabric has been very important everywhere as it expresses the tradition and culture of a society. Cultivation of cotton traces its roots to India. The amalgam of Indian and Southeast Asian cultures can be seen in textiles, where familiar motifs and patterns are discernible giving a sense of déjà vu. Those trade textiles which had once upon a time been vehicles of culture can still be seen in the temple sculptures and wall- paintings of Southeast Asia where they have been documented. Indian textiles formed a base on which cultural relationship with Southeast Asia was built. How did this happen? To find out we have to reconstruct the entire cultural saga and travel back in time when textiles were beginning to enter Southeast Asia.

The Arrival of Indian Textiles in Southeast Asia

In the beginning of the 1st century AD, India was having a flourishing trade in luxury articles with the Roman world which was enhanced by Indian textiles. India was so advanced in the art of spinning and weaving of cotton and silks, their brilliant colours and rich repertoire of designs that Roman women had fallen for Indian muslins, and the state had to empty its treasuries to pay for them. *Periplus of the Aerythreai Sea* (written in 196 AD) speaks of fine cotton stuffs in Urayur (present-day Tanjore). It also describes Paithan (centre known for silk weaving) as an important trade centre.[6] *Manimekhalai*, an early Tamil classic speaks of artistic patterns of cloth and expert weavers.[7] Porunararuppadai, an early Tamil poem mentions cotton cloth, thin like the slough of a snake with floral designs and refers to silk with its threads gathered in small knots.[8]

By the 2nd century this trade had reached beyond India to Southeast Asia and China. *Brihat Jataka* also mentions trade in cloth.[9] There are references in early Buddhist sources to local merchants who booked the share of incoming cargo from India by paying money in advance.[10] Ships carrying cargoes between India and China stopped at ports along the coast of Southeast Asia to barter and exchange. Trade between the Malay peninsula and Sumatra in the east and Malabar in the west was in the hands of Tamil merchants. Their main objective was to acquire forest and sea products and mineral wealth of the region for sale in China which they did through the medium of textiles. Indians used to carry cloth to Southeast Asia on the way to China while Southeast Asians re-exported it along with other commodities.[11]

In the 4th century, Chinese pilgrim Fa Xien mentions Indian merchants who were conducting trade with his country. He calls the fabric of India 'Po-tie' which is connected with Pota or Patti in Dravidian language.[12]

The history of the Chinese Sung dynasty refers to the arrival of a mission from Ho La Tan (a locality situated in Sumatra). Among other things that the envoys brought with them included Indian textiles. This is the first reference to the export of Indian textiles from India to Southeast Asia.[13]

The maritime trade was dominated by Arabs, Chinese and Indians among whom Gujarat, the Coromandel coast, and Bengal specialized in the export of quality textiles. Tang dynasty records show that in the 7th century heavy trade in luxury cloth was triggered by growing demand for robes of honour, ritual banners, palace hangings and other fabrics. [14]

Historical records show that Indian textiles were the most important element in the ancient Asian trade which flourished for over fifteen centuries. It is interesting to see that fragments of textiles depicted in stone point to ancient links between India and Southeast Asia. For example, the four thousand year old motif of overlapping circles, (enclosing a flower appeared on a ceramic excavated from Mohenjodaro) was also seen on the balustraded windows of Bayon of the Angkor period. The same pattern was found on the cloth discovered at Fustat (Egypt, 9th-13th centuries). Indian textiles and Indonesian spices were the main characters of the Asian trade. Painted and printed textiles from Gujarat and Coromandel coast were closely knit with spice trade. They consisted of plain woven cottons, decorated either by mordent dyeing or mordent dyeing in combination with resist dyeing. The Southeast Asians bartered their spices primarily in exchange for these textiles. So popular were the Indian textiles that the traders in the Spice Islands of the Moluccas (the world's first source of cloves) were, according to John Gilow ('in *Indonesian Textiles*') were reluctant to take gold and silver for their spices, but were eager to trade for painted, brocaded or ikkated cotton and silk cloths brought in abundance from the Indian coast. They were known as 'Sarsa' (painted cotton textiles), 'Chitta' (spotted cloth) or 'Sembagi' (printed textiles in Malay world). Literary texts and fictional epics also refer to them. Maritime trade also figures in the Jain literature in India of the 10th-11th centuries. They refer to items such as elephants, ivory and silk.[15] Merchant guilds like Manigramam and Aiyyahole developed economic networks in Southeast Asia between the 9th to 14th century. They traded in textiles, dyes and foodstuffs.[16] Patterned cloth of Indian origin had high circulation in Southeast Asia. Changes in textile pattern illustrated on Javanese statuary in the 10th-11th centuries reflect growing popularity of Indian export cloths at that time.

Although Chinese silks were coming to Southeast Asia, Indian silks became a luxury commodity for centuries. Silk is known as sutra (derived from Sanskrit) throughout Southeast Asia. In the 13h century, Zhou Dougan, a member of the Chinese diplomatic mission resident at the Cambodian capital mentions that in the king's palace much use was made of double-woven silk spangled with gold gifted by foreign merchants. This could have been patolas of Gujarat.[17] Patwala is also mentioned in the Javanese inscriptions in the 15th century. Tsiuan-tcheon, the Chinese inspector of commerce says that in the middle ages the principal textile exporters to Egypt as well as the Far East were the Indians. During this period hundreds of thousands of metres of Indian cloth, predominantly cottons but also silk was shipped to Southeast Asia.

Indian textiles which came to Southeast Asia not only served as apparel for the royalty and masses, but more importantly, they carried in their stresses cultural elements inherent in them. Apart from being functional, Indian textiles had ritualistic uses. They reflected the complexity of the Indian society.

Cultural Flow

The current of Indian culture had entered Southeast Asia in the natural course of events without any political or military power. There were no major conquests. Inter-marriages also helped the spread of cultural influence and courtly life. Indian ideas, use of Sanskrit language, concept of a city state (nagara) and spiritual practices and the theory of deification of kings (devaraja) strengthened the process of Indianization.

By the 6th century Indianized kingdoms had already taken roots in Southeast Asia including Funan in Cambodia, Champa in Vietnam, Srivijaya in Sumatra and Kedah in Malay peninsula.

The Indian way of life combined with local elements was first adopted by the royal courts and elite of Southeast Asia. Over a period, Hindu-Buddhist elements were absorbed into Southeast Asian cultures. Since then Buddhism provided a lasting influence on the mainland southeast Asia. Even today Theravada Buddhism remains the major religion of Burma, Thailand, Laos, Cambodia and Vietnam. Malay Indonesian societies were greatly influenced by Indian values. The Sailendra rulers of Java (750 to 850 A.D.) had maintained close contacts with the Pala rulers of Bengal.

The royalty also adopted Indian textiles and the dress code the evidence of which can be seen from sculptural art and ancient paintings as well as the temple architecture in the Indianized Southeast Asia. The earliest example of this comes from the Mi Son temple in central Vietnam in the kingdom of Champa, one of the earliest Indianized states where dancing Shiva wears a garment (a short dhoti with a long tail with several pleats hanging from a belt made of fabric) used by Indian kings of the same period. The Apsara of the Pedestal of Tra-Kieu dated to the 10th century wears a richly decorated cloth which is skin tied and fits closely to the legs. It corresponds to the costumes of sculptures representing dancers and female deities from south India in the same period, known as Chandataka in Sanskrit.[18]

The Angkor period is defined as 7th to mid-15th centuries. The Khmer costumes of the Angkor period have a remarkable influence of Indian costumes.[19] The jacket and bodice styles of the Khmer kings and soldiers are similar to the style of Kushan and Gupta images of Indian kings.

According to the Indian scholar, Shri Motichand, Indian costumes may have initiated new styles of clothing in Southeast Asia. For example, *chwang kabun* of the Angkor period might have been derived from 'dhoti', *selendang* of the Malay world, and *sabai* of the Thai people may have been derived from a garment –like sari, the end of which is worn over the shoulder. The rulers of the early Indianized kingdoms wore long skirts draped or folded in front, held with belts, decorative sashes and clasps. They wore jewelry everywhere including ear and head ornaments. According to Ananda Coomarswamy, the people of Srivijaya wore clothes similar to the Indian dhoti. Like the Khmer and Thai women, Javanese women of Majapahit kingdom wore a cloth around the upper part of their body. The Bhrukti image of Chandi Jogo in Java has the left breast completely and the right partially covered by the Pala style uttariya. The bodice used in the Sringasari period in east Java was a replica of what contemporary women of India were wearing.

Hindu-Buddhist sculptures from the 9th to 11th centuries provide evidence of similarities with Indian patterns. The early 10th century image of Manjushree from Semarang in central Java is wearing cloth decorated with parallel of four petalled flowers similar to the Khmer patterns and similar to contemporary depiction of deities in eastern illustrated manuscripts suggesting Bengal muslin. Javanese Ganesha sculpture (1239 AD) is wearing cloth with interlocking circles identified with Gujarat from early centuries of the millennium. Both idols are wearing imported Indian cloths.[20]

In the 12th century, the Khmer kings Suryavarmàn I and II had encouraged links with the Chola dynasty of India leading to closer cultural ties. In the Khmer period, the royal regalia included fans and parasols. Reliefs show that patterned cloth was used to make the blinds for windows, screens, curtains and parasols-all essential indicators of the royalty.[21] The Thai kings followed Khmer conventions. Although the Thai society was Theravada Buddhist, the Thai Royalty followed the ritual paraphernalia of brahmanical fashion. Ceramic sculptures and statues of devas from the Dwaravati period (6th to 9th century) (for example, the sculpture at the Chula Praton Pagoda in Muang district or the sculptures in Kubua, Rachaburi province) show that people wore long ankle-length cloths but did not wear blouse or shirt. Women wore *sabai* (like Indian pallu) and lots of necklaces.[22] Similarly, in Sukhotai period (12th-13th centuries), women wore sarongs in dhoti style called *pha chong kraben*. Their breasts were bare; men wore dhoti style trousers pleated or tied at the waist. This style remained popular in Ayutthaya period as well. (1350- 1717 AD) Since that time, *pha chong kraben* and *pha nung* (lungi) became the established costume styles for both men and women.

Generally throughout Indianized Southeast Asia textiles remained simple, rectangular and largely untailored.

The Khmer and Thai followed the Devaraja concepts. This was translated into textile designs. Celestial deities and figures from the Hindu mythology were the designs favoured in the court décor. Thepanom (yakshas, gandharvas, kinnaras normally seen on the temple entrances of India) and apsaras, were especially popular.

Association of Gold in Royal Fabrics

In the Indianized Southeast Asia gold played the most important role in royal clothing. *Rigveda* also mentions *hiranya drapi* (cloth of gold).[23] Association of fine textiles with royalty was an ancient concept in India. Gods are described in scriptures as wearing woven garments. In *Mahabharata*, Yudhishthira was presented a shawl with golden embroidery. *Mahabharata* also describes cotton as one of the fabrics used by brahmanas. In Ramayana, Janaka gave to his four daughters a range of fabrics which included cottons and silks.[24] According to *shastras*, silk was accorded 'pure' status; silk with gold thread was considered auspicious for Hindus. Megasthenes, a Greek envoy staying at Pataliputra, the Maurya capital wrote in his journal (Ta-*Indica*) about the richness he saw, especially in the clothes of the court. He writes, 'Indians are garbed in the finest flowered muslin clothes and the rich ruling class in magnificently embroidered gold thread.' [25]

The immortal nectar as gold occurs in several contexts in old Sanskrit texts. In Southeast Asia, too, the gold's glitter was the symbol of royal presence and such decorated cloths became suitable for royal and ceremonial use. The Chinese records supply details about the use of gold for clothing accessories in early Southeast Asia. In the 4th century the King of Champa (Linyi) wore a hat decorated with gold flowers .

In the poem entitled '*Nagar Kartama*' written in 1365 by Prapancha describes the court life of Majapahit king. It says that at sun rise, on a major festival the prince of Majapahit put on golden clothing and is carried on a sedan chair.[26]

In Cambodia the bride continued to be dressed in costume with silver and gold thread. According to Hindu beliefs tracing to Angkorian times the metal was a purifying agent and was supposed to protect the bride.

In Hindu- Buddhist courts, one of the decorative techniques was to embellish naturally dyed ikkat fabrics with supplementary gold weaving. In Thailand, Sumatra and Bali the gold leaf was used to highlight certain patterns already dyed on the cloth. The popular local gold brocade patterns were applied to Indian trade cloths to accentuate the block painted design[27]

Valuable silk and gold fabrics became a symbol of power of the royal houses of Southeast Asia. The courts of Thailand, Cambodia, Malay peninsula and coastal Indonesia were renowned for their sumptuous gold brocades. Silk weft cloths were embroidered with gold thread for royal use. In some cases the gold was applied on the surface. This technique was common in Indonesia and Malaysia known as '*prada*' and '*telepuk*'. The most time consuming elaborate textiles were the gold and silk brocades known as '*songkets*' which were meant for royalty.

Ceremonial Textiles and Culture

Coromandel fabrics (painted and dyed cloths) known as 'kling' cloths were especially popular with Thai royalty. (Klings were Tamil-speaking people from the Coromandel coast region which under the Cholas extended up to Kalinga. Later kling cloths were associated with Masulipattanam and Pulikat.) For court use they were embellished with gold work. (*Pha Kiang Thong*)

Ma Huan in 1433 describes the Malay royal dress as having a long garment of a fine patterned blue cloth fashioned like a robe and a fine white foreign cloth to wind round his head. This patterned cloth could be from Coromandel and the white cloth Bengal muslin.[28]

One of the most distinguished Javanese dresses which used this cloth was 'dodot', an oversized wrap worn in combination with patola or batik sarong or trousers. It was a ceremonial garment specially designed for Priyai or nobility.[29]

Patolas of Gujarat with their complex designs and subtle striking shimmering colours fascinated Southeast Asian royalty. With its high value and elegance they became valuable possessions. Known as '*cinde*' in the Southeast Asian world, patola was the most sought-after cloth by the Indonesian royalty. Javanese Sultans used patola on everything royal the furnishings, clothes and puppets. Thai royalty coveted them. The right to wear patola was claimed as a prerogative of nobility throughout Southeast Asia. The highest quality were those with elephant and an octagonal star known as *jalamprang*. In the royal courts of Southeast Asia, double ikated patolas of Gujarat and painted and printed cottons were essential elements of royal ceremony. The use of canopy of Indian 'chintz' (European term for Coromandel painted and printed fabrics) was a universal practice.

Indians textiles served widely for display for ceremonial and spiritually important occasions. Most textiles depicting legendary scenes were intended as hangings at temples, monasteries and palaces. They drew their themes from mythology. *Jataka* legends describing the lives of Buddha were used to create Burmese kalagas. (elaborate hanging) The latter also appeared as court hangings. A pagoda, symbolizing mountain, the abode of Shiva was a popular image that appeared on many silk hangings like 'pidan' of Cambodia. Ramayana battle scenes against plain white background popular in Bali could be traced to South Indian temple hangings. In India, narrative textiles were used as a backdrop for dramatic performances of scenes from religious epics. Javanese didactic cloth paintings and Balinese *klungklung* (court paintings) could be related to Kalamkari tradition. The cloth hangings from Gujarat depicting hunting scenes were meant for ceremonial use in eastern Indonesia as described by Zhao Rukua in the 13th century.[30]

On the mainland, Indian textiles became an important part of the temple décor. In the monasteries they were used to separate the sacred world from the temporal. In homes, they were used as a backdrop at religious ceremonies performed by monks. Buddha's figure invariably rested against imported textile. Painted motifs on the ceiling at the Thekyamuni temple at Pagan in Burma was the standard design in printed cotton cloths. Textiles are represented in the Shiva chamber of Chandi Loro Jonggrang (Prambanan) temple at Yogyakarta.

The spiritual symbols of Indian iconography also took roots in Southeast Asian textiles. Southeast Asians readily accepted them because of their own belief in the upper world of birds and lower world of reptiles.[31] For example, the Naga, the ruler of water kingdom appears in many guises on Southeast Asian cloths. Garuda, the mythical bird of Hindu legends, the mount of Vishnu and a central figure in Ramayana appears on royal textiles. Garuda and Naga, the prominent symbols of royalty in Southeast Asia appear on the Javanese batik and silk weft cloths of Khmer. Mount Meru, the abode of Hindu gods appears on Javanese batik in the form of a stylized motif of Alasan. The Hindu concept of Panchdevata and trimurti (Brahma, Vishnu and Mahesh) merge with the ancient notions about the organization of the universe and its opposing colours of red and black.[32] Throughout Indianized Southeast Asia, the circle, the star and lozenge became identified with lotus, the charka (Vishnu's weapon) and Mandala motif.

The courts of Javanese sultans kept alive classical forms of theatre with Hindu legends which required display of rich costumes.

In maritime Southeast Asia, *Mahabharata* became the most popular Indian epic providing the basis for most *wayang kulit* (leather puppet) shows performed with village rituals. On the mainland it was Ramayana that had the most lasting impact on artistic representation. Prince Rama's search for Sita, abducted by the evil, Ravana is the basis of most themes in dance performances as well as in the shadow theatre. The rich costumes worn by the characters reflect the Indian influence.

Even today in classical dance performances in Cambodia such as the Apsara dance, costumes are created from gold and silver thread work. In mask dance, the dancers wear hip wrappers over pants with ornamental edges showing below. The velvet satin short jackets with sequins for men are the reminders of Angkor bas reliefs. These dance performances provide the glimpses of the cultural past and the ancient civilization since they keep alive the customs and the costumes of that period.

The colours of the week are observed in royal ceremonies of Cambodia even today. This custom dates back to Hindu origins as well. The queen before the coronation of the king wears cwang kabun (dhoti) of colours specified for each day. It is a mark of respect for the deity of the day.[33]

In Bali, black and white checked cloth called poleng is draped around temple deities, guardian figures as well as temple dancers. They symbolize the duality of life, good and evil, a concept traced to Hindu origins.

Hierarchy Through Textiles

Indian textiles in their inherent characteristic of being ceremonial and royal brought some subtle changes in the social structures of Southeast Asian societies. They began to play an important role in the court hierarchy. A more rigid distinction developed between the rulers and the ruled. The foreign or local origin of the cloth, the texture, the design, the manner in which it was worn were all ways of distinguishing the rulers from the ruled. In Kalidasa's works (500 AD) it was possible to know the status of a person by the dress he wore.

In Thailand, only the king and the queen wore gold brocaded satins. Some ministers elevated to nobility were allowed to wear restricted designs. Their wives and royal servants were dressed in graded fabrics.[34] In the Angkorian society, social distinctions could be demonstrated by wearing particular designs. As pointed by Zhou Dougan in 1296, wearing of fabrics patterned with recurring groups of flowers was permitted only to the elite and princes. Ordinary officers were allowed to wear only two groups of flowers. In Indonesia, the manner of wearing head-cloths and the length of the skirt cloths over breeches was decided for court officials. No ceremony was complete without parasols of silk and velvet as was the case in India with chakravartin and maharajadhiraja. The sacred canopy, the royal umbrella, weapons, became visual symbols of royal regalia.

This distinction between the aristocracy and the masses through the dress code was evident in the Malay-Indonesian world till the 13th-14th century. Although religious affiliation changed after the adoption of Islam which was mainly introduced by Gujarat and Tamil traders, court practices continued in the same manner. It is interesting to note that like Hinduism and Buddhism, Islam also came to Southeast Asia from India. Textiles remained an important part of ceremonial ritual and the legacy of customs carried on.

Cultural Legacy

In southeast Asia textiles have a ritual significance which is far more important than their utilitarian need. They are integral to all life cycle ceremonies and they are revered.

Although Indian textiles arrived as items of trade in Southeast Asia, because of their exotic appearance and complexity of designs and also due to their association with royalty, they were absorbed in the hierarchies of Southeast Asian society and art. These trade textiles became a part of sacred heritage. They were not only absorbed in textile usage, but their ritual value surpassed that of local cloths. Indian cloths having come in the distant past became an important element in all rites of passage including birth, marriage and funerals. They also found an important place in mythology and customary practices. Indian textiles continued to take on meaning and function unique to the cultures of Southeast Asia. They were put to uses which were very specific and indigenous and were ascribed protective powers.

The painted and mordant-dyed cotton fabrics ('*saudagiri*' on the Southeast Asian mainland and 'semabgi' in the archipelago and later on well-known as 'chintz' all over the world). were used as gifts helpful to establish social relationships. The 9th century Javanese inscriptions establish textiles as very important ceremonial gifts of the period especially sponsored by the royal elite.[35] The gifts and ritual offerings in the Javanese inscriptions of that time abound with cloths identified by their colours. In Thailand, textiles formed a part of state gifts to visiting ambassadors and envoys. The flowered Indian cloths do figure in such lists. Thai monks and nuns wore saffron or white robes but on special occasions they received painted cloths of highest quality from the nobility.[36] In the Malay court protocol, after the king gave a set of clothing for the honoured guests they often gave Indian textiles as a return gift. In Malay weddings they were displayed on silver trays and were known as 'kain telepuk'.

These textiles were widely accepted as a form of storing wealth in Southeast Asian societies, a convertible form of wealth which could be used in the settlement of business or social debts. Ritual exchanges occurred at all levels–from the individual to the state with the aim of securing allegiances and loyalties. In Thailand, the distribution of imported cloths had been used since the Ayutthaya period as a method of expressing favour, privilege and rank.

In Sulawesi, Indonesia, these fabrics are called *Ma'a*. They were described as having come from a mythical sea in mythical times and hence became sacred treasures. They were associated with marriages and funerals. In Toraja, central Sulawesi, people build a huge staircase of bamboo ladder to which hundreds of rolls of Indian textiles are attached. It towers above the proceedings. It is a symbolic invitation to ancestors. Even in the predominantly Muslim society of Indonesia, the Coromandel textiles retained their magical status. Painted cloths with flowers and a tree were prized as canopies. It was a symbol which linked the people of deified ancestors with the world of humans stretching to watery lower realms.

Silk patola from Gujarat, in particular, came to be associated with protective elements. Malay warriors were given patola sashes when they went to battlefields.[37] Soldiers at Thai court wore Indian-made painted jackets featuring ferocious monsters to ward off enemies on all sides. Patolas with their elephant motif were magnified and put on walls for decoration as well as protection. In Bali, scraps of patola were used to cure a sick child. Grinsing of Bali (the only other place apart from Patan in Gujarat where double ikat is woven) came up as a local therapeutic cloth which wards off the disease.

Over centuries, the give and take continued in the realm of textiles. Southeast Asians were not passive recipients. They were specific in their tastes; very often they dictated the demands and Indian artisans created the requisite textiles for them. For example, the Thai textiles made in India looked strikingly Thai. Tome Pires, a Portuguese official had observed that in the beginning of the 16th century Coromandel cloths were decorated in the fashion of Siam.[38] The four petalled rosette, a motif common in Thai art since Dwaravati times (8th century) is the most popular motif on Indian textiles for the Thai market.

Southeast Asians adapted Indian designs to local cloths. The diamond and eight pointed star of Patola has penetrated the local designs of Lao skirts, Malay songkets, Indonesian batiks and ikats, khmer weft silks and Mindanao textiles of the Philippines. Pelangis in Jambi, Indonesia made of silk are fashioned on the same lines of Bandhani from India and are used during weddings. The naga and Garuda bird's wings are evident on Palembang songkets. The South Sumatran region where Buddhism first took roots is even today rich in Mandala designs. The latter are coverings for food and gifts for ceremonies.

So much interaction took place between the two textile cultures that like the progeny of intermarriages Southeast Asian textiles acquired a face that was local yet Indian. This was a cultural heritage shared equally by India and Southeast Asia which evolved over the time into a fine layer for the fabric of Southeast Asian society.

Even today, textiles of Southeast Asia resonate Indian iconography and imagery. Yet they are not Indian. Rabindranath Tagore when he visited Indonesia in 1927 said "I see India everywhere but do not recognize it."

May be that is the essence of the cultural assimilation which is reflected in the textiles of South East Asia.

REFERENCES

1. H.B. Sarkar, '*Cultural Relations between India and Southeast Asian Countries*', ICCR and Motilal Banarasidass, 1985, p. 248.
2. R.C. Majumdar, *Hindu Colonies in the Far East*, Calcutta, 1944, p. 9.
3. H.B Sarkar, as in 1 above, p. 249.
4. *Ibid*, p. 249.
5. Himanshu Prabha Ray, Article 'Far-flung fabrics-Indian textiles in ancient maritime trade' from '*Textiles in Indian Ocean Societies*' edited by Ruth Barnes, p. 25.
6. Yashodhara Agarwal, 'Silk Brocades', p. 90.
7. Neelkanta Sastri, '*The Colas*', Published by the University of Madras, 1975 (First edition 1937), p. 88.
8. *Ibid*, p. 88.
9. Om Prakash, '*European Commerce and Enterprise in pre-Colonial India*', Cambridge Uni. Press 1998, p. 207.
10. As in above 5, p. 25.
11. Har Prasad Ray, '*Trade Routes between India and China, c 140 B.C. to AD 1500.*' Published by Kamal Mitra, for Progressive Publishers, Calcutta, p. 161.
12. *Ibid*, p. 162.
13. H.B. Sarkar, as in 1 above, p. 252.
14. Ruth Barnes, 'Textile in Indian Ocean societies', p. 117.
15. H.P. Ray as in 5 above, p. 23.
16. *Ibid*, p. 23.
17. John Guy, '*Woven Cargoes, Indian Textiles in the East*,' Thames and Hudson. 1998 p. 58.

18. '*Through the Thread of Time*' Edited by Jane Puranananda, The James H.W. Thompson Foundation Symposium Papers, Published by River Books, Thailand, 2004, p. 138.
19. *Ibid*, p. 123.
20. John Guy, *Woven Cargoes*, p. 62.
21. Gillian Green, article 'Textiles at the Khmer court, Angkor'.
22. Matibelle Gittinger, *Textiles and the Tai Experience in Southeast Asia. The Textile Museum*, Washington D.C. 1992, p. 18.
23. Ajit Mukerjee, edited '*Banaras Brocades*' p. 11.
24. Yashodhara Agarwal, '*Silk Brocades*', p. 14.
25. *Textile Arts*, p. 310.
26. *John Milsik*, p. 35.
27. Robyn Maxwell, '*Textiles of Southeast Asia: Tradition, Trade and Transformation*,' Revised Edition, Published by Periplus Editions (HK) Ltd. 2003, p. 183.
28. John Guy, *Woven Cargoes*, p. 69.
29. *Ibid*, p. 99.
30. *Ibid*, p. 111.
31. Robyn Maxwell, as in 27 above, p. 198.
32. *Ibid*, p. 203.
33. Gillian Green, '*Traditional Textiles of Cambodia: Cultural Threads and Material Heritage*' Published by River Books Co. Ltd. 2003, p. 191.
34. Susan Conway, *Thai Textiles*, Published by British Museum Press, London, 1992, p. 98.
35. Gillian Green, as in 33 above, p. 117.
36. John Guy, *Woven Cargoes*, p. 146.
37. Robyn Maxwell, as in 27 above, p. 215.
38. John Guy, *Woven Cargoes*, p. 131.

CHAPTER 4

Society and Culture in Southeast Asia and India's Contacts [before 1500 AD]

Prof. Himanshu Prabha Ray

> "From around the middle of the eighteenth century a long process began, which led over the next hundred years to a very dramatic change in the history of the ocean and its peoples. Over this comparatively short stretch of time people from outside the ocean took over most of the lands around the ocean, while the ocean itself became dominated by one naval power. Government policy and technological advances combined to undercut millennia-old indigenous maritime activities, with naval force always available as a back-up."[1]

This quotation from Michael Pearson's book succinctly sums up the disjunction in maritime activity in the Indian Ocean in the eighteenth century. Perhaps the single most significant point of disjunction was the introduction of steamship navigation in the nineteenth century. Historical evidence indicates that as a result, the indigenous system underwent radical changes. Seafaring activity shifted from being 'fair weather' to 'all weather'. Instead of the traditional communities, liner companies now dominated maritime trade. The skilled man-power required for manning these mechanised vessels could no longer be provided by the littoral sailing communities, and this led to the marginalisation of coastal groups to traditional fishing activities.

The disjunction between the indigenous sailing pattern and European intervention is nowhere more marked than in the evolution of ports and harbours along the Indian coast from the nineteenth century onwards. An apt example of this is the development of the Calcutta port from medieval villages in the colonial period and the transformation in the entire landscape of the Hooghly. Prior to these changes, elaborate structures and harbour installations were non-existent in the region, nor were they necessary. In the pre-colonial context, Bernier's quotation is worth repeating: "Nowhere else in India do the rivers terminate in such estuaries, nowhere does the tide penetrate so far up the streams, enabling a close contact between maritime navigation and an inland water transport, which has always been the most active in the world."[2]

The nineteenth century also marked the acquisition of new colonies by European powers, which opened up different routes and intensive connections across the ocean and a case in point is the linkage of South Asia with Australia. This paper addresses changes in the pre-existing linkages between South and Southeast Asia across the Bay of Bengal as a result of colonial intervention and the extent to which these colonial histories have influenced recent writings. The basic premise that this paper questions is: can the history of the ancient period be understood without discussing the generation of knowledge about the past over the last three hundred years? Can new forms of knowledge introduced in the colonial period and based on elaborate documentation, such as archaeology and art history, be termed scientific? To what extent were supposed 'nationalist writings', such as those of R. K. Mookerji or Nilakantha Sastri, which took recourse in traditional accounts and Sanskrit texts attempts at harking back to a glorious Indian past?[3] How does one factor in the generation of an academic discourse about the subcontinent's past into the writing of maritime history of the ancient period?

How then does one reconcile the contrasting views that emerged in the early 20th century: one, focussed on Hindu imperialism and the colonisation of parts of Southeast Asia; the other, emphasised universal history and India's cultural capital? In 1912, Radha Kumud Mookerji had published his doctoral thesis completed at Calcutta University under the title *Indian Shipping: A History of the Sea-borne Trade and Maritime Activity of the Indians from the Earliest Times*. The frontispiece of the book showed a relief from Borobudur with a sailing ship under the caption 'Indian Adventurers sailing out to colonize Java'.[4] Chapter VI, titled 'The Period of Hindu Imperialism in Northern India', dealt with the maritime activity of the Bengalis based on a collection of poems of more than fifty authors describing sea voyages titled *Padma Purana* or *Manasamangala*.

> In the same manner that Shakespeare's Antonio had "an argosy bound for Tripoli, another for the Indies, a third for Mexico, and a fourth for England" is our Indian S'rimanta represented to possess merchantmen trading to the Coromandel coast, to Ceylon, to Malacca, Java and China.[5]

A little later, Rabindranath Tagore embarked on a sea voyage on 15 July 1927 on the French ship *Amboise* to Java and other countries of Southeast Asia.[6] It was an intellectual pilgrimage and Tagore's only motive, Bose argues, was "to collect source materials there for the history of India and to establish a permanent arrangement for research in this field."[7] Bose stresses Tagore's attempts at highlighting the theme of cultural exchange between the two regions and the creativity of the Javanese and other peoples of Southeast Asia in negotiating with Indian cultural forms and products. Tagore was also aware of regional differences in historical developments within India and the fact that relations of the Srivijaya kingdom (6th to 14th centuries AD) were largely with the Palas of eastern India.[8] How does one categorise the writings of Tagore?

The 'Indianisation' model has continued to affect archaeologists working in South and Southeast Asia over the last five decades, though it is seldom that the genealogy of the process itself has been scrutinised. It is indeed unfortunate that in the post-Independence discourse on ancient Indian History, the work done by the Greater India Society should have been shelved under the rubric of 'Nationalist' historiography and little attention paid to shipbuilding and maritime communities in historical writing. Notwithstanding the Nationalist tag, a pioneering work on shipping in the Indian subcontinent that is yet to be replaced is Mookerji's study of 1912. Perhaps the first contribution of Mookerji's study was to provide a comprehensive compilation of textual references to seafaring, including the use of the Sanskrit work, *Yuktikalpataru*, a treatise on ship-building attributed to king Bhoja and dated to the 11th century. Another theme dealt with by Mookerji was the prominent place of Bengal in ancient maritime trade. He based his discussion on the sixteenth century collection of poems in Bengali known as *Padma Purana* or *Manasamangala* and composed by more than fifty authors in celebration of the glories of the goddess Candi. Many of these contained descriptions of sea voyages and are an addition to an earlier text on the same theme, the graphic account of the sea voyage of Chand Saudagar by the thirteenth century poet Narayandeva. The depictions of watercraft on the terracotta temples of Bengal escaped Mookerji's notice, though writers such as Dasgupta[9] and Deloche[10] later documented these. In spite of these beginnings, studies on ship-building activity and on the archaeology of religious architecture continue to be neglected.

In contrast, archaeological work over the last six decades in Southeast Asia is often seen as establishing that the region had achieved social complexity by the early centuries and that Indian influence was selectively assimilated into the pre-existing cultural base. The focus continues on identifying the 'indigenous cultural matrix' and its unilinear progression towards urbanisation and statehood. The achievements of the past in terms of "the age of the state, the longevity of settlement sites, and the inventiveness of early bronze or ceramic technologies have been of vital importance to contemporary national communities, an importance that is translated into issues for today's scholars."[11] This paper is divided into two sections: in the first, I present an overview of available writings on Society and Culture in Southeast Asia; and in the second I broaden the canvas to highlight the maritime network across the Bay of Bengal.

The Historiography

It is generally accepted that maritime contacts between South and South East Asia date to the middle of the first millennium BC, but there is no clarity on the nature of these contacts or their influence.[12] A majority of the inscriptions found in Southeast Asia are in Sanskrit, though there is evidence of vernacular epigraphs as early as the 7th century AD. Similarly the generally stated position of scholars working in Southeast Asia is that Indians never colonised Southeast Asia, but the impressive Indic temples constructed after the 7th century could hardly have come into existence without *considerable* India knowledge and bodily presence.[13] "Local rulers chose to adopt Indic gods and language to their own advantage rather than having Hinduism imposed upon them from outside".[14] How valid is this assumption of elite absorption of Indic values? It would perhaps be useful to remind ourselves of the channels of communication through which cultural flows took place in antiquity.

In Indonesia, for example, there is evidence to suggest that a large corpus of what may be termed narrative literature in Sanskrit was known, as indicated by writings in Old Javanese. as well as sculptures and reliefs on shrines and temple walls. These included the *Purānas*, the *Pañcatantra* or a collection of allegorical fables, the *Jātakamālā* or the Buddhist Garland of stories, and the rich source of the *itihâsa* / *mahākāvya* tradition provided by the epics the *Rāmāyana* and *Mahābhārata*. Blending local myth and folklore of Indonesia, this body of narrative developed into a fascinating mosaic of stories, which despite its varied origins bore a markedly Indonesian character. The Old Javanese *Rāmāyana* is in the poetic *kakawin* form using Sanskrit metres, and the Uttarakanda is in prose *parwa* form as are the books of the *Mahābhārata* preserved in Java. The Tantri stories of the *Pañcatantra* were written in the form of the *kidung*, a later poetic invention using local metres. These writings are often attributed to royal initiative, but it is evident that channels of communication also included oral transmission by priests and pilgrims, traders, wandering story tellers and entertainers, which provided a parallel stream that was incorporated into the Javanese tradition and widely disseminated through the performing arts.[15]

In the context of Malay literature, it was earlier believed that Malay tales about the heroes of the Sanskrit Epic the *Mahābhārata* were paraphrases of *kakawin* poems in Old Javanese. However it is now evident that the Malay versions show noticeable similarity to the plays (*lakon*) of the Javanese shadow play *wayang purwa* of which the repertoire was based on Javanese remakes of the *Mahābhārata*. Besides, a majority of Malay narratives based on the Sanskrit Epic have no analogies with *kakawin* and are obviously the result of the work of *dalang* directors and puppeteers of the *wayang* theatre.[16]

Thus it is crucial to factor in channels of cultural communication and the nature of interaction in any discussion on cultural interchanges across the Indian Ocean. This continues to be a neglected aspect, as scholarly interest has instead focused on the origins of early kingdoms or states in Southeast Asia and state formation has been a significant theme in the study of Southeast Asia over the last five decades. The secondary literature on the emergence of the early state as reviewed by Christie is substantial and need not be repeated here.[17] It is evident that perceptions of the state differ radically. Wolters for example, sees Funan, referred to in Chinese sources, as a tribal society, "which from time to time produced certain chiefs who were able to mobilize sufficient military power, family networks of relatives and their allies, and marriage alliances to other chiefs' groups to impose their hegemony over neighbouring chiefs. Such overlordship was of temporary duration and was made possible by the formation of a coalition of those who supported the adventurer seeking hegemony".[18]

In contrast Hall accepts the polity of Funan as a real state with a bureaucracy, an army, an infrastructure to produce and control agricultural production and to move trade goods.[19] According to Jacques, Funan is a Chinese term for mountain and has been described in the Chinese accounts as a single realm under a single leader.[20] In contrast the Sanskrit term refers to the polity as *parvatabhupalas* or the rulers of the mountain, indicating thereby a plurality of political control. It is nevertheless significant that there is, to date, no evidence of a local currency issued within Funan, though a number of silver coins originating in Thailand or Burma were among the finds from Oc-Eo.[21]

In the context of the Khmers, several legends regarding their origins are known and many of these are repeated in inscriptions both in Southeast Asia and India. For example, an inscription from Mison in Champa refers to the founding of a line of kings as a result of the union of the brahmana Kaundinya and Nagi Soma, the daughter of the Naga king and this legend is repeated in 3rd –4th century Chinese sources as well as in Pallava epigraphs. A 10th century inscription from Cambodia, on the other hand, ascribes the origin of the royal family to the marriage of the hermit Kambu Svayambhuva with the celestial nymph Mera given to him by the god Siva.[22] It is these Chinese accounts and genealogies mentioned in inscriptions that have often formed the basis of the study of early kingdoms in Southeast Asia, but in recent years there have been increasing inputs from anthropological models. For example, Michael Vickery has been a strong proponent of the notion that kings in lowland Cambodia emerged from local elites in the 7th-8th centuries and that an analysis of the titles adopted by the kings indicates a conical clan.[23]

The Devarāja cult or the cult of the divine god king has often been termed as one of the prominent features of ancient Khmer society, especially from the ninth to eleventh centuries AD, as first proposed by George Coedés. In the Cambodian cult of Devarāja, Coedès argued that Saivism came to be more conspicuous than in India and that it was the king who was the great god of ancient Cambodia to whom all the temples and religious monuments were dedicated. Kulke re-examined the issue and concluded that the "Devarāja was a calantî pratimā or mobile image in the form of a bronze sculpture representing Siva in one of his divine embodiments. This sculpture was worshipped in successive capitals, either in the palace or within the palace grounds in a special building, which, in the style of the royal palaces of Angkor was built for the god who is the king of perishable but valuable material."[24]

As compared to studies on political developments in Cambodia, there has been somewhat inadequate attention paid to economic activities that formed the basis of the kingdom of Angkor. Archaeologists and historians have accepted the crucial role of agriculture and water in the emergence of early civilisations, but it is only in recent years that the focus has shifted from individual crops to agricultural systems. Nevertheless the significance of rice cultivation in supporting large populations is evident, the issue that is more complex relates to the role of the kings in building and controlling large irrigation structures. Recent research establishes that domestication of rice took place around 6500 BC in the Yangzi valley in China. In Cambodia the evidence for early rice-cultivation comes from the site of Samrong Sen in central Cambodia and dates to 2200 BC. There is mention of rice field workers in the inscriptions from Angkor, but no details are available and while the bas-reliefs of the Angkor monuments depict warfare and fishing, agricultural activities are singularly un-represented.[25]

B.P. Groslier and Jacques Dumarçay argued that in the 9th century there was a change in the system of production ushered in by Indravarman who got the Indratataka or the baray of Lolei excavated. In addition Indian settlers brought with them knowledge of reclaiming land from the marshes and from this time onwards the erection and maintenance of waterworks was considered the religious duty of kings.[26] Adhir Chakravarti writing in 1978 questions this suggestion and argues that the construction of the barays was confined to the Angkor region, while the country at large was left to its own traditional devices.[27] Archaeologists using remote-sensing techniques have identified ancient field-systems in parts of the Angkor region and it is estimated that more than 50 million bunded fields were cultivated between 9th and 15th centuries using a combination of floating rice and flood recession techniques. These methods continue to be in use today in the region and indicate the continuity of traditional practices, rather than reliance on irrigation. Hence Khmer-built dams may have functioned as flood retardation devices rather than for irrigation and the ponded water was primarily intended for temples.[28]

Trade is another theme that has often been credited with introducing social change in Southeast Asia and here it is generally argued that carriers of this maritime trade were members of Southeast Asian trading communities. In his pioneering study of Indonesian trade and exchange based largely on Chinese textual accounts Wolters argued for the entrepreneurship of early coastal polities in western Southeast Asia, which thrived on commerce with India in the first five centuries AD and only later with direct exchange with China.[29] This trading network had earlier beginnings and we know that late prehistoric settlements of the 2nd and early 1st millennia BC in mainland Southeast Asia regularly occur in small stream valleys, which feed the major river systems. These perhaps quite isolated villages were linked by far-reaching exchange networks, which saw marine shell ornaments being taken over 1,000 kilometre from the coast and copper and tin ingots and artefacts entering communities far removed from the ore sources. Although our knowledge of intra-regional trading networks is uneven, archaeology provides evidence enough to demonstrate that they were already dynamic and expanding before they became interlinked. These networks were greatly stimulated by their integration into Indian trade to the west.[30]

As early as the 3rd century AD there is archaeological evidence for the presence of small coastal polities centred on urban centres in Southeast Asia enclosed by palisades or walls with rulers living in palaces. In the 3rd century many of these coastal polities were integrated into the social space of Funan as indicated by Chinese sources. These communities knew writing, practised agriculture and patronised craftsmen, but with the exception of seals and sealings no Buddhist or Brahmanical structures have been brought to light.[31] It is only in the 3rd and 4th centuries that Indian inspired political and religious strategies began to be adopted and by the 5th century these coastal polities in peninsular Malaysia became full-fledged city-states. These city-states provided the first impulse for the diffusion of Indian artistic forms, both Vaisnava and Buddhist and perhaps the best known in Oc-Eo, which thrived on maritime trade, but was abandoned around 7th century AD.[32] In 670 the state of Srivijaya came into existence by consolidating smaller polities scattered along the Straits of Melaka and in the 9th and 10th centuries its power and prestige was acknowledged over an extensive area in the Indian Ocean, though it lost its commercial importance in the 11th to 13th centuries and was replaced by the city-state of Melaka in the 15th century.[33]

In the context of the civilisation of Angkor it is often argued that the capital was the religious and ritual centre of the kingdom and the emphasis has been on the king who was imbued with divinity. There have been several studies on political thought and administrative theory among the Khmer[34] and the structure of the Khmer kingdom and its characterisation as a feudal state. Several scholars have suggested that the brahmanas introduced political treatises in Cambodia and that these have largely influenced the Khmers. Chakravarti refers to the recruitment of officials after taking tests (*sarvopadhāśuddha*) and suggests that the administrative system may be regarded as analogous to that in China.[35] Others have argued for a change in the mode of production and the emergence of a hydraulic society as discussed above. In this formulation the emphasis has been on agrarian expansion and slave labour rather than on trade. Chakravarti, on the other hand, suggests that the identification of the city-states shows that they lay along the route from lower Burma via Thailand to Cambodia.[36]

In contrast to this somewhat artificial dichotomy between agriculture and trade or between the sacred religious centres and secular village administration, Claude Jacques highlights the essential fact that all the inscriptions be they in Sanskrit or in the vernacular were placed in temples or sacred areas and either concerned directly with the gods or with the administration of god's properties.[37] Thus the crucial element in the Southeast Asian landscape was the religious shrine and it is important to understand its role in society. Scholars have written about fiscal immunities granted to religious bodies from the 10th century onwards and recorded in inscriptions,[38] as well as to the network of temples as evident from *miśrabhoga*, the requirement that local temples forward a portion of their income to a central temple.[39]

Unfortunately there have been very few studies that have attempted to locate religious structures in a social context and to analyse their interaction both spatially with other temples and shrines and vertically with a range of communities. The religious affiliations of Khmers rulers is often seen as oscillating between allegiance to Hinduism and Mahayana Buddhism, with Theravada Buddhism appearing somewhat later in the 13th century. A study of religious architecture however indicates that a Buddhist shrine did not differ markedly from a Hindu temple and a good example is that of Bat Chum inaugurated in 953 AD where the Buddhist settlement followed the same architectural pattern as that of others dedicated to Siva or Visnu. Though inscriptions refer to Buddhist monasteries and to 10th century hermitage or âúrama dedicated by Yasovarman, none of these have been identified in the archaeological record.[40]

An analysis of the inscriptions of Jayavarman VII indicates that both Ta Phrom and Preah Khan were enormous complexes. While the former was home to eighteen priests, 2740 officials and another 2202 supporters including 615 female dancers, the records from the latter mention royal temples supporting 306,372 people divided into 13,500 grâmas, the reference being to 'servants of the gods' rather than to slaves.

> "Feeding and clothing this multitude involved the provision of rice, honey, molasses, oil, fruit, sesame, millet, beans, butter, milk, salt and vegetables, all the quantities being scrupulously listed for appropriation from the royal foundations and warehouses. Clothing was also required, and even the number of mosquito nets is set down. Assigned to supply the temple were 66.265 men and women, a figure rising to 79.365 if you include Burmese and Chams. The inscription then provides an inventory of the foundation's assets: gold and silver vessels; 35 diamonds; 40.620 pearls; 4540 precious stones such as beryl; copper goblets; tin; lead; 512 silk beds; 876 veils from China; cushions; and 523 sunshades. There were musical instruments 'to charm the spirit' and with nightfall or for rituals, there were 165.744 wax torches. There was also a highly organised healthcare system. The foundation was responsible for the administration of 102 hospitals strategically placed across the kingdom, some of which have been identified on the basis of their own inscriptions."[41]

The history of Buddhism in Cambodia and Vietnam is still inadequately researched. Nevertheless by the 7th century there are references to visiting teachers from India including Punyodhana from central India who promulgated Vajrayana Buddhism in Champa.[42] From the 7th to the early 10th century there is evidence for the spread of Mahayana Buddhism in Champa with links with the religious traditions of Thailand and Java. In the 9th century, Jaya Indravarman II founded a vihara and dedicated the grand temple of Dong-duong, 25 kilometres south-west of Mi Son to the Bodhisattva Lokesvara Svabhayada and gifted land, slaves, silver, gold, etc. The temple complex was larger than any other religious foundation in Champa and had relief carvings on the wall depicting narratives from the life of the Buddha.[43]

An inscription dated AD 902 from An Thai in Quang Nam records the consecration of Lokanātha in the vihara of Pramudita lokesvara and the beneficiary was the monk Nagapuspa, a friend of king Bhadravarman. The next king Indravarman confirmed the endowments and exempted the monastery from tax. Another important inscription from the same period comes from Nhan Bieu in the southern part of Quang Tri and is on four faces of a stele. It records the consecration of a Siva temple and a Buddhist monastery dedicated to Avalokitesvara in honour of their ancestress Princess Lyan Vrddhakula.[44] This inscription is a good example of the Siva Buddha association found in Champa and with close parallels to the prevailing situation in Java.

Thus the extensive network of the temple is evident. At the beginning of the eleventh century, lineage temples probably constituted a fairly large group of sanctuaries and it is suggested that members of the lineage managed the property attached to these temples. Jacques also cautions against placing too much emphasis on the large stone temples that survive without taking into account the smaller village temples and shrines that must surely have existed and formed an extensive network of religious shrines in Khmer country. Similarly the history of Angkor cannot be studied in isolation and without reference to that of the sea-facing Chams. It is this regional and maritime network that the next section attempts to highlight.

The Maritime Network

By the ninth century the major states on the islands of Java and Bali, especially the central Javanese state of Mataram had developed complex economic infrastructures and had integrated diversifying agricultural systems into a web of regional and long-distance trade networks. Sanskrit language inscriptions from Buddhist sites refer to religious teachers travelling to the region from Gujarat, Sri Lanka and Gaur in Bengal. Mataram also produced maritime Southeast Asia's first standardised indigenous coinage based on gold and billon (silver-copper alloy) divided into weight-value units integrating local and Indian systems. By the tenth century coins based on the same system of weights and values were beginning to be minted across the maritime region from Sumatra to Bali and to the Phillipine island of Luzon.[45]

From the ninth to the mid-fourteenth centuries two of the merchant guilds that dominated economic transactions in south India were the Manigramam and the Ayyavole. Associated with these two merchant guilds were associations of craftsmen such as weavers, basket-makers, potters, leather-workers and so on. As late as the 17th century, the Ayyavole seemed to be concentrated in the cotton producing areas of Andhra Pradesh. Though these two guilds originated independently of each other, from the mid-thirteenth century onward, the Ayyavole association became so powerful that the Manigramam functioned in a subordinate capacity to it. Not only did these merchant associations develop powerful economic networks, but also employed private armies.[46] The range of their operations extended well beyond the boundaries of the Indian subcontinent into Southeast Asia.

Several clusters of Tamil inscriptions have been found on the eastern fringes of the Indian Ocean from Burma to Sumatra. Of the seven mid ninth to late thirteenth century Tamil or part-Tamil language inscriptions so far found in Southeast Asia, one has been found near Pagan in Burma, two just south of the Isthmus of Kra in the Malay peninsula and four in north and west Java. Perhaps the easternmost record is the bilingual Tamil and Chinese language inscription found associated with the remains of one of the two Siva temples at Quanzhou. These inscriptions connect merchants associations operating out of south India with the founding or the endowing of temples or other structures for the use of resident Indian merchant community. In the 1060s and 1070s Chinese records report that the Imperial Court received missions from the Chola kingdom as well as from the ruler of Srivijaya, but by the last decades of the eleventh century the Chinese court had begun to encourage Chinese traders to venture out to the sea.

Perhaps the most relevant example for this paper is the Buddhist monastery at Nagapattinam, which was a major landmark on the Tamil coast from the sevnth to the nineteenth centuries AD. A Buddhist temple was erected at Nagapattinam specifically for Chinese Buddhists at the instance of a Chinese ruler during the reign of the Pallava king Narasimhavarman II (c. AD 695-722) and the Chinese monk Wu-hing visited the site on his way to Sri Lanka. One of the later Srivijayan king, Maravijayottunga varman, is known to have provided for its construction and the Chola king Rajaraja I granted revenues of a large village Anaimangalam for its upkeep in AD 1006.

In the tenth century, local versions of these merchant guilds termed the *manigrama* appeared in the north coast ports of both Java and Bali, especially at Julah on the Balinese coast. There are seven Javanese inscriptions dating from 902 to 1053 AD that refer to merchant associations called banigrama and to the various tax concessions granted to them. While some foreign merchants may have been included in these groups, these appear largely as indigenous organisations associated with the local economic networks as tax-farmers.[47]

Inscriptions dating from 840 to 1305 AD from Java are especially significant for this discussion as these list foreigners involved in trade and tax farming on the island.

> "All of these inscriptions that survive in their original form are, in fact, *sima* charters connected with communities located away from the coast. The settlements that received these charters, like the settlements that supported kabanyāgān merchant enclaves, formed important links between the domestic marketing network and the ports downstream. This group of charters stands apart – by virtue of the detail that they provide – from the larger number of inscriptions that merely contain vague references in tax collecting lists to *juru kling* (head of the Indian/foreign community) – and later occasionally the juru barata and juru cina (heads of the Indian Ocean? And Chinese communities?)."[48]

The term 'kling' was widely adopted in Indonesia as a blanket-term covering all South Asians and in some cases all foreigners. The earliest inscription to contain such a list dates to 883 AD and is from Yogyakarta in central Java. The list includes foreign members of the tax farmer group from Champa, lower Burma and Cambodia or Kmira, as well as Kling, Pandikira, Aryya and Singhala from South Asia. These groups continue to find mention in four 11th century inscriptions issued by the rulers of Mataram in central Java, though an additional appears, that of the Drawida, soon to be replaced by the Colika and Karnataka. After the middle of the 11th century there was a hiatus in inscriptions containing lists of foreign tax farmers and these reappear in 13th – 14th centuries when an important addition is that of China, though Kmir (Khmer) and Champa retain their position.[49] The Javanese text Nāgarakertāgama completed in AD 1365 mentions merchants from Jambudvipa (India), especially from Karnataka and Bengal, from China and various parts of Southeast Asia.

One of the enigmatic issues of Khmer history is that there is no evidence of monetised transactions from 802 AD to the latter part of the 13th century when inscriptions refer to taxes being collected in kind and exchanges based on barter. In the 13th century there are references to Chinese cash, hemp cloth, gold and silver. A similar situation prevailed in Champa where there is no evidence of local coinage, though 9th-10th century inscriptions occasionally refer to *pana* possibly signifying a gold or silver coin. It is only during the 12th-13th centuries that gold and scented wood served as a measure of value.[50]

There are occasional references to merchants or *vanik* in 10th – 11th century inscriptions from Angkor and to merchant quarters, but the question relates to the presence of monetised exchange.[51] In 8th century inscriptions from Cambodia land value was often expressed in terms of silver or cloth, but this changed subsequently and it is only in the 10th and 11th century that inscriptions record the actual price paid for land. In place of the simple payment of silver and cloth, these inscriptions append long lists of objects given up in exchange for land, such as cattle, paddy, spittoons, copper, elephants and slaves, though their valuational component is not clearly defined.[52] Another interesting practice was to gift goods to a religious complex before using them for the purchase of land.

This ties in with references in Chinese sources. Zhou Daguan, a member of a Chinese diplomatic mission to the court of the Khmer king Indravarman III was resident at the Cambodian capital in 1296-7 and provides us details of life and customs at the Khmer court. He refers to three types of transactions. For small transactions, the Khmers used rice, grain and Chinese coins, for somewhat larger ones they used hemp cloth, while for large transactions they used gold and silver. It is significant that silver is found in north Indochina and although some gold-bearing sand are known to exist in Cambodia, gold must have been imported from elsewhere in Southeast Asia, such as Sumatra, the Malay peninsula, the Philippines and Borneo.

Zhou Daguan's comments on textiles are particularly relevant.

"Among the fabrics worn by the sovereign are some, very rich and sheer, which are valued at three or four ounces of gold. Although certain fabrics are woven in Cambodia, many are imported from Siam [Thailand] or Champa [Central Vietnam], preference being given to the Indian weaving for its skill and delicacy".[53]

The Chinese observer continues that cloth for royal use included Indian textiles, which were valued in gold and that foreign merchants brought double-woven silks spangled with gold, which may perhaps be a reference to trade in what later came to be termed patola. In addition we also know that there was a growing influence from the Chinese trading community, which in addition to silks, brought porcelain and furniture. This description is further corroborated by floral designs represented on costumes in reliefs on the monuments of Angkor, which duplicate those found on Indian statuary. Many of these patterns continued to be repeated on Indian textiles made for the Thai and Cambodian markets in the 18th and 19th centuries.[54]

Thus though it is evident that the Khmers actively participated in the regional and long-distance world of the Indian Ocean, several gaps remain in our understanding of the organisation of this trade. For example, while Chinese, Indian and Javanese participation in these trading networks has been highlighted, the role of the Khmers is only now being recognised. Secondly, in the absence of coins, working out the value of the list of commodities mentioned in the purchase of land remains a challenge. The emphasis in earlier studies has been on divine kingship, control of water and the magnificent art and architecture of the monuments at Angkor and it is in recent decades that resources such as remote-sensing and aerial photography are being tapped to provide inputs regarding settlements and location of habitation sites.

Finally I would like to reiterate that the histories of religious sites include not only their date of origin, name of patron and architectural plan but more significantly the survival of these monuments through time and their discovery, since colonial intervention changed the terms of reference of the debate on religion and especially religious architecture. No doubt, there are several gaps in our understanding of the social history of temples. In the 18th-19th centuries with the discovery of the temple, the stakeholders in the temple also underwent transformation given the newly emerging religious and cultural identities in the 19th and 20th centuries. New disciplines such as archaeology and art history were created. While the conclusions reached as a result of these new methodologies are repeated in the study of the past, there have been few analyses of the methods involved or the social and cultural context of the archaeologists involved.

Conclusion

In the final analysis, the history of maritime communities is evident from the donations that they made to religious establishments. Thus trade and trading activity cannot be studied in isolation from the diverse religious landscape that developed in early South Asia. The continued focus on the state, the identification of place names mentioned in textual accounts and enumeration of commodities involved in maritime commercial transactions are somewhat inadequate to comprehend the complexity of maritime travel in the ancient period.

The attempt in this paper has been to highlight the location and archaeology of religious structures, thereby placing religious architecture in its wider social base. For a comprehensive appraisal of coastal centres and maritime communities, the intertwined strands of religious architecture, economic activity and political intervention need to be examined and understood.

The religious landscape influenced the trading system in several ways from moulding cultural preferences and choices to active participation. Religious shrines were both consumers of a variety of commodities used in ritual, as well as important locales for trading activity as indicated by shops and markets within or in the vicinity of temple premises from the ninth-tenth century onwards. At the same time there are several instances of a differential tax on commodities required for religious purposes. More importantly, of course several commodities such as textiles were imbued with multiple meanings and were both items of common consumption as well as products for elite and religious requirements. Finally, the building of new temples stimulated economic growth thereby transforming both the geographic and social landscapes of the region.

At this stage, certain conclusions may be drawn. First, information on seafaring communities from historical and archaeological sources indicates that their make-up cut across ethnic boundaries. Hence attempts at categorising them within present national boundaries may be in keeping with current aspirations, but will find little support historically. Second, while trade provided an important motive for sea-travel, it was by no means the only reason for travel by sea and needs to be studied within a wider perspective of seafaring activity and maritime networks. Third, the role of religions, such as those of Buddhism, Hinduism or Islam in motivating and supporting seafaring activity needs to be recognised and accepted. Finally, for an appreciation of cultural interchanges across the Bay of Bengal, it is crucial to highlight the diverse channels of communication, which also included oral transmission by priests and pilgrims, traders, wandering story tellers and entertainers. It is only then that a holistic understanding of cultural interaction across the maritime world will emerge.

REFERENCES

1. Michael Pearson, *The Indian Ocean*, Routledge, London-New York, 2003, p. 190.
2. J. Deloche, *Transport and Communications in India*, Oxford University Press, New Delhi, 1994: 117.
3. "The issue of territoriality acquired a new edge as Indian art history spilled over its national boundaries to tell the story of the spread of Indian art and religion across China, Japan and Southeast Asia." Guha-Thakurta proposes this served as "a major sop to national pride" and reinforced the idea of India as the source of Asian art, Tapati Guha-Thakurta, *Monuments, Objects, Histories*, New Delhi: Permanent Black, 2004: 187.
4. Radha Kumud Mookerji, *Indian Shipping: A History of the Sea-borne Trade and Maritime Activity of the Indians from the Earliest Times*, London: Longmans Green and Company, 1912.
5. Mookerji 1912: 158.
6. Sugata Bose, *A Hundred Horizons*, New Delhi: Permanent Black, 2006: 245.
7. Bose, 2006: 245.
8. Bose 2006: 259.
9. T. Dasgupta, Shipbuilding and Commerce in Ancient Bengal, *Journal of the Department of Letters*, University of Calcutta, 1923, 10: 111-28.
10. J. Deloche, Boats and Ships in Bengal Terracotta Art, *Bulletin de l'Ecole Francaise d'extreme-Orient*, 1991, 78: 1-23.
11. Craig J. Reynolds, *Seditious Histories: Contesting Thai and Southeast Asian Pasts*, Seattle and London: University of Washington Press, 2006: 5.
12. H.P. Ray, *The Winds of Change: Buddhism and the Maritime Links of Early South Asia*, New Delhi: Oxford University Press, chapter 4. Kishor K. Basa, Indian Writings on Early History and Archaeology of Southeast Asia: A Historiographical Analysis, *Journal of the Royal Asiatic Society*, volume 8, part 3, November 1998: 395-410. Bérénice Bellina, Beads, Social Change and Interaction between India and South-east Asia, *Antiquity*, 77, no. 296, June 2003: 285-297.
13. Ian Glover, Peter Bellwood, eds., *Southeast Asia. From Prehistory*

to History. London and New York: Routledge Curzon, 2004: 37.
14. Charles Higham, *The Civilization of Angkor*, London: Weidenfeld & Nicholson, 2001: 9.
15. Malini Saran, A System Of Knowledge Transmission: The Narrative In Indonesia In The Early Hindu Buddhist Period, Himanshu Prabha Ray edited, *Sacred Landscapes in Asia: Shared Traditions, Multiple Histories*, IIC – Manohar, New Delhi, 2007.
16. Vladimir I. Braginsky, *The Heritage of Traditional Malay Literature*, KITLV Press, Leiden, 2004: 114.
17. J. W. Christie, State Formation in Early Maritime Southeast Asia: A Consideration of the Theories and the Data, *Bijdragen tot de Taal-, Land- en Volkenkunde*, 151,2, 1995: 235-88.
18. Wolters, O.W., 1979, Khmer Hinduism in the Seventh Century, Smith, R.B. and Watson, W., eds., *Early South East Asia*, New York: Oxford University Press.
19. K.R. Hall, *Maritime Trade and State Development in Early Southeast Asia*, Honolulu: University of Hawaii Press, 1985.
20. C. Jacques, Smith, R.B. and Watson, W., eds., *Early South East Asia*, New York: Oxford University Press, 1979: 371-9.
21. Robert S. Wicks, *Money, Markets, and Trade in Early Southeast Asia*, Cornell University Studies on Southeast Asia, 1992: 186.
22. D.G.E. Hall, *A History of South East Asia*, London: Macmillan Education, 1981 (reprint): 26-7; 105.
23. Michael Vickery, Some Remarks on Early State Formation in Cambodia, David G. Marr and A. C. Milner edited, *Southeast Asia in the Ninth to Fourteenth Centuries*, Singapore: Institute of Southeast Asian Studies, 1986: 95-115.
24. H. Kulke, *Kings and Cults: State Formation and Legitimation in India and Southeast Asia*, New Delhi: Manohar Publishers, 1993: 361.
25. Higham, 2001: 15.
26. B. P. Groslier, *Angkor et le Cambodge an XVI siécle*, Annales du Musée Guimet, LXIII, 1958: 109-112. Jacques Dumarçay, *The Site of Angkor*, Oxford: Oxford University Press, 1998.
27. A. K. Chakravarti, *The Sdok Kak Thom Inscription*, Calcutta: Government Sanskrit College Research Series, 1978: 19-20.
28. R. Acker, New Geographical tests of the hydraulic thesis at Angkor, *South East Asia Research* 6, 1, 1998: 5-47. W. J. Van Liere, Traditional Water Management in the Lower Mekong Basin, *World Archaeology*, 11, 3, 2002: 265-80.
29. O.W. Wolters, *Early Indonesian Commerce: A Study of the Origins of Sri Vijaya*, Ithaca: Cornell University Press, 1967.
30. H.P. Ray, *The Archaeology of Seafaring in Ancient South Asia*, Cambridge: Cambridge University Press, 2004.
31. Pierre-Yves Manguin, The Archaeology of Early Maritime Polities of Southeast Asia, Ian Glover and Peter Bellwood edited *Southeast*

Asia: From Prehistory to History, London and New York: Routledge Curzon, 2004: 294-5
32. Manguin, 2004: 296.
33. Manguin, 2004: 306.
34. Jean Imbert, Histoire des Institutions Khmères, Phnom Penh, 1961; S. Sahai, *Les Institutions Politiques et l'Organanisation Administrative du Cambodge Ancien (VI-XIII siècles)*, Paris: EFEO, 1970.
35. Adhir Chakravarti, Some Recent Trends in Old Khmer Studies, *Journal of Ancient Indian History*, XIII, parts 1-2, 1980-2
36. Chakravarti, 1980-2.
37. Claude Jacques, Sources on Economic Activities in Khmer and Cham Lands, David G. Marr and A. C. Milner edited, *Southeast Asia in the Ninth to Fourteenth Centuries*, Singapore: Institute of Southeast Asian Studies, 1986: 327-334.
38. S. Sahai, Fiscal Administration in Ancient Cambodia, *The Southeast Asian Review*, 1, 2, 1977: 123-38.
39. Robert S. Wicks, *Money, Markets, and Trade in Early Southeast Asia*, Cornell University Studies on Southeast Asia, 1992: 204.
40. Christophe Pottier, Yasovarman's Buddhist Asrama in Angkor, Pierre Pichard and Francois Lagirarde edited, *The Buddhist Monastery: A Cross-Cultural Survey*, Paris: EFEO, 2003: 199-208.
41. Higham, 2001: 126-7.
42. D. Snellgrove edited, *The Image of the Buddha*, Paris, 1978: 155.
43. Ian Mabbett, Buddhism in Champa, David G. Marr and A. C. Milner edited, *Southeast Asia in the Ninth to Fourteenth Centuries*, Singapore: Institute of Southeast Asian Studies, 1986: 299-300.
44. Mabbett, 1986: 302-3.
45. Jan Wisseman Christie, Asian Sea Trade between the Tenth and Thirteenth Centuries and its Impact on the States of Java and Bali, Himanshu Prabha Ray edited, Archaeology of Seafaring: The Indian Ocean in the Ancient Period, Delhi: ICHR Monograph 1, 1999: 222-3.
46. Meera Abraham, *Two Medieval Merchant Guilds of South India*, New Delhi: Manohar, 1988.
47. Christie, 1999: 242-5.
48. Christie, 1999: 246.
49. Jan Wisseman Christie, Javanese Markets and the Asian Sea Trade Boom of the Tenth to Thirteenth Centuries AD, *Journal of the Economic and Social History of the Orient*, 41, 3, 1998: 369.
50. Wicks, 1992: 183.
51. Wicks, 1992: 205, footnote 75.
52. Wicks, 1992: 217.
53. Chou Ta-kuan [Zhou Daguan], *Notes on the Customs of Cambodia (1296-97)*, Bangkok, 1967: 22-3.
54. John Guy, *Woven Cargoes: Indian Textiles in the East*, London: Thames and Hudson: 58-9.

CHAPTER 5

Indonesian Archipalago and the Indian Ocean

Prof. Taufik Abdullah

It was certainly not a co-incidence if by publishing his now classic article entitled "*Le royaume de Çrivijaya*" in 1918 G. Coedes had at the same time uncovered the riddles behind the many unexplainable bits and pieces of historical evidences. On the basis of the recently found four inscriptions written in the old Malay, Coedes convincingly proved that in the 7th century a kingdom that destined to become a great maritime empire, Srivijaya, had already been established in the Southern part of Sumatra. With this finding many of the hitherto unconnected evidences could finally make a clear historical picture on the dynamics of the Straits of Malacca and its relation to both the Indian Ocean and the South China Sea as well as with Java Sea. Without the knowledge on the historical existence of Srivijaya the origin of Malacca, the most important center of international trade in the 15th century, can never be properly explained.

According to the *Sejarah Melayu* (or The Malay Annals) the origin of Malacca can be traced to the time when Parameshwara, the prince of Palembang had to run away to Tumasik (present day Singapore) and later, when he realized the ruler from Javanese kingdom was still pursuing him, he crossed to Muar (on the Malay Peninsula) until finally he settled in Malacca. But what was the origin of Palembang that it was so late to enter into the record of history? Why the Javanese ruler was so eager to control Palembang? By proving that Palembang was the capital of the long forgotten Sriwijaya a host of many still unanswered questions could be solved. With the help of the knowledge of the existence of the Srivijaya Empire the historical significance of Chinese records on the existence of the kingdom of Kan-t'o-li or even the older P'an P'an by the 7th century can be properly understood. Then one could pose a possibility on the existence of the proto-Srivijaya empire in the region.

Indeed since the historical existence of Srivijaya had been "recovered" (as Bernard Lewis would have put it), a host of historical questions on the maritime dynamics of the Southeast Asian region can be more explainable. In one of his last articles Coedes offered a hypothesis that one time in the 8th century Srivijaya threatened the Khmer kingdom. It was the ruler of Srivijaya that was referred to as the *Maharaja* in a Khmer inscription. The place of Srivijaya as a center of Buddhist learning was reported by I- tsing, the 7th century Chinese monk, who chose to spend a few years in the capital city of *San-fo-tsi,* to deepen his knowledge on the teachings of the religion, before he continued his journey to Nalanda, the world center of Buddhism. The 9th century Arab sources also talk about the great maritime empire that had attracted many traders from all over the world to come. It was therefore understandable if that the world famous Buddhist temple, the 9th century Borobudur monument was built by the Syailandra dynasty that was at one time the master of Sumatra and Java. The Srivijaya Empire had undoubtedly played important role in the formation of a new cultural sphere in the Indonesian archipelago.

Under the rule of Srivijaya the Straits of Malacca became an important center of international trade. It attracted the traders and travelers from as far as the Persian Gulf in the West and China in the East. Because of its strategic position Srivijaya was not only able to expand its political and economic influences to the surrounding areas, it could also attract the interest of the other powers. From the beginning the rulers of Srivijaya had to be aware of the potentially destructive power of the Chinese empire. However how great was the thirst for power of the Chinese ruler he could usually be satisfied if the little powers were willing to acknowledge his position as the overlord with a simple token of royal tribute. The problem with the Chinese emperor might arise if he felt something wrong with the working of the tributary relationship. The other rulers, whose powers were on the rise, were apparently not so accommodative. They would prefer to settle the score with the use of power in the continuing delicate balance of power. That was the sad experience Srivijaya had to endure in time when its power began to decline.

In the early 11th century the king of Chola from India launched a massive attack on Srivijaya and captured the Maharaja of Srivijaya. It was perhaps due to the devastating impact of the attack that – as suggested by the Chinese records— the capital of Srivijaya had to move from Palembang to Jambi or Malayu. Not long after the devastating attack, the king of Singasari (East Java), Kertanagara, the devout follower of Tantrism, launched the so-called *Pamalayu* operation, with the intention of making Malayu, the new capital of Srivijaya, as his tributary state. Since then Srivijaya, the once great maritime empire, the master of the Straits of Malacca and the overlord of the so many maritime kingdoms and principalities in the region, gradually went down into historical oblivion.

However it was since the time of the Pamalayu operation the successive centers of power in Java – beginning from Singasari, Majapahit, and later in the 16th century the already islamized port cities of North Java and even the 17th great agrarian power with center in the interior of Central Java, the

Mataram empire – never forgot the important role of the Straits of Malacca. They would always try to dominate the strategic sea road. In 1369 the empire of Majapahit, with its capital in Trowulan, near the present day Surabaya, East Java, occupied Palembang, the abandoned former capital of Srivijaya that had for sometime become a basis of the Chinese pirates. The *Hikayat Raja-Raja Pasai* (The History of the Kings of Pasai), a traditional historiography, that nicely mixes history as the reconstruction of the past events with myths, the cultural answer to the unanswerable questions , and cultural testimony, tells a story of the attack of Majapahit on Samudra-Pasai, the first Islamic sultanate in Southeast Asia. In order to the continuation of his position the Sultan of Pasai offered his daughter as the wife of the king of Majapahit. However in spite of the defeat the reputation of Pasai as the center of Islamic learning remained. It was reported that one of the Nine Saints (*Wali Sanga)* of Java, the semi legendary Islamic proselytizers came from Pasai. The *Hikayat Patani* (The History of Patani), also a traditional historiography, tells the story that Patani was Islamized by an *ulama* who came from Pasai. He, as the text says, happened to be in Patani when the king of Patani was seriously ill, No local healer could help him until someone informed the royal officials about an *ulama* from Pasai who happened to be in town. The *ulama* said that he could only help the king if the king promised to convert into Islam. The king agreed but soon after he recovered he forgot his promise. He fell sick again and the *ulama* was summoned again to the palace and, as can be expected, the king was asked again to make the same promise. But the same event was repeated until the *ulama* threatened that it was his last visit to the palace. When finally the king did recover he did not any longer forget his promise. After converting into the Islamic religion, according to the traditional historiography, everything run as usual, except the king and the people abstained from eating pork and praying the *berhala,* the idols.

The continuing important role played by Pasai as the center of Islamic knowledge can also be found in one of the most famous history books in Malay tradition, the *Sejarah Melayu.* It tells a story that on one occasion the Sultan of Malacca had an important but very difficult question on the secret of God. But no one in Malacca could give a satisfactory answer to that question. He decided to send a delegation to Pasai, whose position as the center of trade and power had been taken over by Malacca, to search for the right answer. The Sultan of Pasai assembled the men of religion but again they failed to give a satisfactory answer. Finally the Sultan of Pasai whispered something to the head of the delegation. The right answer had been given. But it was apparently a secret answer that could not be easily given to the novice in mystical knowledge.

Malacca was "created, not developed into", as an historian puts it, a center of international trade. Established at the end of the 14th century in a relatively short time Malacca became an important trading and political as well as Islamic propagation center. Frequented by traders from many countries

Malacca emerged as a cosmopolitan and multi cultural trading center. There were four major communities settling in Malacca – the Gujaratis, the Tamils, the Javanese, and the Chinese. The early 16th century Portuguese traveler reported that in addition to the above communities there were also a few thousands Bengalis, Persians, and Arabs living in Malacca. The four major communities had their respective heads under the direct supervision of the *syahbandar,* the royal appointed port authority, who played a double role— the official of the kingdom as well as the representative of foreign traders. The *shahbandar* represented the royal court and the outside world. Since majority of the foreign traders were Muslims one could also say that he occasionally played the role of the mediator between the foreign Islamic communities and the royal court.

Although acknowledging the important role of the foreign merchants in Malacca. the *Sejarah Melayu* gives a very clear indication that the Malays themselves were very much active in the international trade. It says that Sultan Mahmud ordered an expedition to go to India to purchase cloth. A Portuguese traveler also reported that ships from Malacca sailed quite often to Ceylon. Tomé Pires went so far to state that Malacca could not live without Cambay, the Gujarati center of trade, nor Cambay, he continued could live without Malacca. To some extent the development of several northern Javanese ports, such as Demak— the new center of power after the demise of Majapahit— Japara, Ceribon, Gresik, Tuban and Surabaya, was very much dependent on their relationship with Malacca. In addition to being the major rice exporters these northern coastal ports also played important roles as the transit points for spices from the Maluku or the Spice Islands.

Ibn Majid, an Arab visitor to Malacca had really very low opinion on the religious behavior of the people. "They have no culture at all", he wrote. "The infidel marries Muslim women while the Muslim takes pagans as wife.... They (the Muslims) drink wine in the market and do not treat divorce as a religious act". He might be right in his impression but looking from another angle this statement only emphasized the fact that Malacca was really a pluralistic society that might not always insist on the religiously correct behavior to its settlers. Everybody belonged to same cultural bazaar despite the differences of custom, religion or places of origin. Malacca had apparently another face that could not always be properly seen by contemporary observer who only stayed for a short and busy period. The maritime kingdom not only had its own book on the family and maritime laws that were largely based on Islamic jurisprudence but also had made itself as a major center of Islamic propagation to the surrounding areas. Not less important was the fact that in the growingly competitive trade and political environment Malacca encouraged and developed some kinds of Islamic solidarity among the merchants. It was exactly the feeling of Islamic solidarity that helped to make the Indian Ocean by the 15th century "a sort of Muslim lake" or as another author once said "the sea of the Arab language".

In the beginning of the 16th century Malacca began to experience an internal crisis. In time when it had to face the challenges of its vassal states and the new element in the competitive world of trade, the Portuguese, the maritime kingdom began to experience an internal discord among its own elite. In order to solve the royal internal conflict Sultan Mahmud abdicated in favor of his son, Sultan Ahmad. But in about a year he retook the royal position. In time when the Portuguese were already planning to launch its massive attack on Malacca the Sultan introduced some kind of a religious policy that could easily disturb the social balance. He was reportedly to have said that "Malacca was to be made into Mecca". Whatever the reaction of the devout Muslims might be to this bold statement, the Islamic policy of the Sultan was sure—as the Portuguese sources indicate—to alienate a great number of the Chinese settlers. As the result the disgruntled Chinese merchant community willingly gave their supports to the Portuguese in their assault against Malacca. While he was leading the Malay troops in defending Malacca against the assault of the Portuguese Sultan Ahmad—again according to the Portuguese sources—was murdered at the order of his father. Shortly before the Portuguese occupied the city Sultan Mahmud and his royal entourage as well as the people who remained loyal to the court abandoned the city and moved southward. They finally settled in Johor and made the new settlement as the new capital.

Later in retelling and reflecting on the humiliating Malay defeat against the Portuguese, the *Sejarah Melayu.* the text that was written in the Johor palace (most likely by Tun Sri Lanang in 1612), offered some wisdom on the tragic event. The text looks at the political calamity as the sign of the punishment of God for the injustices that had been committed by the Sultan. It is exactly this kind of ethical judgment on political calamity that is also adhered to by the *Tajus salatin* (The Crown of all Kings), which was perhaps the oldest Islamic political theory in the Malay world, written in Aceh-Darussalam in the first decade of the 17th century. No act of treason, *durhaka,* should be conducted against the unjust but legitimate king, the *daulat,* because God would have His own way to punish the unjust ruler.

With the fall of Malacca an entirely new game began in the Indonesian archipelago. The spread of Islam was no longer simply a matter of the holy calling to enlarge the community of the believers; it had also become a way to compete with the Christian power. If in the beginning it was only a question of the accessibility of the ships from the archipelago to the Indian Ocean and the thriving internal maritime trade of the people in the region that really matter, with the coming the Europeans the trade competition, political ascendancy and religious calling could easily rolled into one and undivided source of conflict. The coming of the Europeans posed the unprecedented challenges to the region. They were not satisfied with the military victory that would end up with the recognition of the overlord position in the traditional vassal-and- overlord relationship they wanted to subdue and to occupy territories or royal capitals. They could occupy the upper hand in the competitive world trade they would insist on the right of the monopoly. And finally the Europeans, most notably the Portuguese and Spaniards, would also want to control the souls of the subjugated people, if necessary by the force of arms. The coming of the Europeans immediately changed the highly competitive world into the arena of cultural conflicts. The slow penetration of Islam under the auspices of the royal patronage to the surrounding territories had gradually become the past to reflect on.

The Islamization of Pasai began when an Arab man of religion, who must have come Gujarat, landed on a small fishing village in North Sumatra at the end of the 13th century. He converted the village chief and made him the king of the small territory at the end of the 13th century. When Marco Polo, the Italian man of adventure, visited the newly established kingdom he had the impression that the desire of the people to study Islam was quite high. By the beginning of the 14th century Pasai and its sister town, Samudra, had become a center of religious activities. Ibn Battutah , the North African traveler, who stayed for sometime in this oldest Islamic kingdom, (in 1345-1346) reported that the Sultan regularly surrounded himself with the religious experts who came from Islamic centers of learning across sea, discussing the many aspects of religious doctrine. The Sultan of Samudra-Pasai maintained good relationship with the Indian Islamic royal courts. He regularly sent missions to the nearby territories to spread the religion.

In many ways the Islamization of Pasai belonged to the same pattern to that of Malacca that took place one hundred years later. By converting the head of the small territory Islam helped to establish a kingdom and a royal tradition. In other words these kingdoms were relatively free from the burdens of the past. They could either to develop new cultural foundation and political tradition or maintained something from the past or even borrowed something else from foreign countries. They might continue the old tradition but changed the content of its symbolic meaning or simply introduced something new that could make them inseparable parts of the Islamic world. In many ways the newly emerging cultural paradigm can be called an integrative tradition that simply blurred the boundaries between the realm of politics and that of religion. A different type of political tradition would later emerge in Java, where the forces of Islam that had emerged on the port cities on the North coast of Java – as the local historical tradition never fails to emphasize— succeeded in abandoning their political allegiance to the decaying Majapahit, the once great Hindu empire that enjoyed its glorious time in the 14th century, Replacing the old political center the newly Islamic based centers of power were simply obliged by political necessity to deal with the questions of cultural continuity and political legitimacy. In the process not only the religious authority of Islamic *ulama* had to deal with the political power of the king, Islamic teaching had also to be properly translated into the already entrenched cultural tradition. It was in this situation some kinds of tradition of dialog gradually emerged. Some times the dialog could run smoothly but occasionally a cultural or even political confrontation between the representatives of royal tradition inherited from the past and that of the newly adhered religion could not always be avoided.

For a few years after the fall of its capital city the once united empire of Malacca fell into pieces. Several competing little kingdoms were formed in Sumatra, across the Straits of Malacca; some of them even sided with the Portuguese while some others made new alliances. Gradually, however, the old sense of unity returned, only now the overlord had made Johor as the new center of power. In the meantime the Portuguese never had a peaceful time in Malacca. Under its rule Malacca almost never had the chance to enjoy a peaceful time. It was consistently under the threats of the many, but sometime also competing, maritime powers in the archipelago. Jepara and Rembang, the small but energetic centers of maritime powers in the North coast of Java launched their rather massive attacks on the former Islamic center of trade. Aceh –Darussalam, the new emergent power, after the decline of Samudra-Pasai launched several unsuccessful attacks on Malacca. In the meantime the Portuguese not only tried to expand its sphere of political influence to the island across Malacca, Sumatra; it also sought alliance with the remaining Hindu kingdoms in the archipelago. In 1522 the Portuguese sealed an alliance with the kingdom of Pajajaran, the remaining Hindu kingdom of West Java, to halt the progress of the Islamic newly established kingdom, Ceribon and its sister kingdom, Banten. The stake in the conflict was the port of Sunda Kelapa. In 1527 the Portuguese sent its armada but for whatever reason the armada failed to reach Sunda Kelapa. As a way to commemorate the success of the forces of Ceribon to occupy coastal town the name of Sunda Kelapa was changed to Jayakarta, the victorious town, which was later better known as Jakarta.

One of the direct impacts of the fall of Malacca was the dispersion of the Muslim traders and the establishment of new political and trading centers. Aceh-Darussalam on the northern tip of Sumatra, the kingdom that had overcome and replaced Samudra-Pasai as the center of power in Aceh, emerged as both the strong contender to Malacca as well as the new center of Islamic propagation and thought. Aceh –Darussalam was also the only power that seriously tried to seal a system of alliances with the other Islamic centers of power. It was a response to appeals of Aceh-Darussalam that the Ottoman ruler, who claimed to be the *khalifah* of the Islamic world, militarily intervened on behalf of the oppressed Muslims in the Indian Ocean. The Ottoman Empire sent to Aceh artillerymen and gunsmith in 1564 and 1568.

About the same time the sultanate of Banten on the Java coast of the Straits of Sunda, established by Sunan Gunung Jati, the ruler of Ceribon, the double-kingdom of Goa-Tallo in South Sulawesi, and the sultanate of Ternate and its permanent competitor, the sultanate of Tidore, in the Spice Islands became as the most important trading centers in their surroundings. Later these kingdoms, like their predecessor, Malacca, also assumed the role of the centers of religious propagation. In due time these kingdoms also managed to expand their respective sphere of political controls and influences to their respective vicinities. It was in Goa-Tallo and in the Spice Islands Islam was really involved in—what a Dutch scholar says—"the race with Christianity". Ternate and Tidore, the two most powerful rulers of the Spice Islands were to be deeply involved in the Spanish and Portuguese conflicts.

The period from the early 16th century to the middle of 17th century can perhaps be said not only the time when international commercial activities could easily transform themselves into political and military conflicts but also the age when the proliferation of religious propagations took place. Not less important than that it was also the period when the *ulama* in this region began to get themselves actively involved in the Islamic discourses. The *ulama* not only addressed themselves to their own respective immediate social surroundings or even to the Malay speaking elite class but also to the cosmopolitan communities of the Islamic believers. Some of them wrote their treaties in Arabic though most of them preferred to use the highly "Arabized" Malay or other local languages. Almost without exception they were parts of the expanding networks of different branches of religious disciplines and Islamic schools of thought. The participating ulama played the roles of the intellectual brokers as well as the translators of Islamic teaching to the educated general populace. In the process the early pioneers of Islamic thinkers practically made the Malay language, the *lingua franca* of the commercial world of Southeast Asia, as an important language of religion.

This period can be safely said as the time when Malay Islamic religious literature began to flourish. As if out of the blue suddenly in the late 16th century Aceh-Darussalam, the sultanate that had managed to have a direct commercial contact with the Hejaz, Yemen and Egypt while maintaining its close trading relationship with Gujarat and Malabar, emerged as the center of religious discourses. The first important writer in Aceh-Darussalam and indeed in the Malay world as a whole was Hamzah Fansuri. As his name indicates he was born in Barus or Fansur, as the Arabs called it, a small town on the West coast of Sumatra, the world renowned center of the very high quality camphor, where according an inscription a small Tamil community had already established itself in the 11th century. A mystic, as his *syair* or poem indicates, who received his illuminating mystic foundation in Shahrnawi (Ayuthia), the capital city of the old Siam where many Indian and Persian as well as Arab and Tukish men of religions made their living. Hamzah Fansuri emerged as one of the towering figures in the history of Islamic thought and literature in the archipelago. Even until now, one can still enjoy and admire his mystical poems.

After the death of Hamzah Fansuri his position as the great thinker Islam was filled up by Syamsuddin as-Sumatrani (d. 1630) who occupied the position of royal Mufti of Aceh, under the great Sultan Iskandar Muda (1607-36). It was the time of the greatness of Aceh-Darussalam. The Sultan expanded the rule of the Sultanate to the western coast of Sumatra and Pahang, across the Straits of Malacca. However after the death of the Sultan the mystica. school of Hamzah Fansuri came under the theological assault of Nurruddin ar-Raniri, the great religious scholar, who came from Ranir, Gujarat. Before he came to the Malay world Ar-raniri had most likely studied the Malay language in Gujarat where a sizable Malay community had settled and a number of religious scholars had also frequented the Malay world. Ar-Raniri's uncle had at one time spent several years in Aceh. The trusted teacher of Sultan Iskandar Thani (1636-41) ar-Raniri stayed and taught in Aceh until a few years after the death of the Sultan. While he was living in Aceh he wrote a number of books, mostly written in Malay and a few in Arabic. The most famous was his book on Islamic law, *Siratal Mustaqin*, and the encyclopedic text *Bustanus salatin* (The Garden of all kings), which was supposed to be a response to *Tajus-salatin.* After the death of his patron he – as the Dutch records say—sneaked out of Aceh (1644) That was the time when a backlash against his rather harsh and intolerant persecution of the mystic orders took place. His position in the royal court—again according to the Dutch record—was replaced by an *ulama* from Minangkabau. A few years later another great mystic as well as a very prolific author, who also wrote the first *tafsir* or Quranic exegesis in Malay language, Abdur Rauf al-Singkili, or better known in Aceh tradition as Teungku Syah Kuala.

In short Aceh-Darusalam of the 16th century and 17th century was an Islamic sultanate that had brought the Malay world into the dynamic discourses of the Islamic world. As a consequence of the growing power of the district heads at the expense of the royal court and the emergence of the new political powers the sultanate Aceh-Darussalam gradually lost its leadership in religious learning and thought. However since that time the Islamic religious thinkers and authors could no longer pretend to ignore an important fact—the European power was there to be seen and their power were also there to be seriously taken into account.

After the coming and the dominance of the European colonial powers the Indian Ocean, the way to the centers of the Islamic world, could no longer offer a free and open sphere to be explored economically as well as intellectually. It took a major war and several national revolutions to re-open the ever culturally and intellectually challenging big ocean.

CHAPTER 6

The Arrival of Islam to Southeast Asia From India: The Second Wave of 'Indianisation' Revisited

Dr. Farish Noor

Men make history, and the leading members of the revolutionary generation realised that they were doing so, but they could never have known the history they were making .... What in retrospect has the look of a foreordained unfolding of God's will was in reality an improvisational affair made in the crucible of political crises.... If hindsight enhances our appreciation for the solidity and stability of (historical) legacy, it also blinds us to the stunning improbability of the achievement itself.[1]

History is about remembrance, and remembrance involves *re-membering* the broken pieces of what was once a united common memory held by many. This paper will address one aspect of our common history that has been broken apart thanks to the proclivity of post-colonial historians to re-write national histories that are circumscribed by the boundaries of modern post-colonial states: We will be focusing on one aspect of the common history of South and Southeast Asia, and that is the history of the coming of Islam from the former to the latter.

The bane of post-colonial national histories is that we take as the foundational premise the idea of the modern nation-state as the defining point of origin as well as the teleological end of history. We write our post-colonial histories with a skewered hindsight that has been narrowed by the confines of modern (and late) political boundaries. We adopt modern concepts such as racial and ethnic difference when describing the lives of the ancients for whom these words may not have had the same meanings, if at all. And these national histories still posit the notion that the destiny of our nations are determined by some linear trajectory that was pre-ordained in the past, even though it is embarrassingly evident that our ancestors who lived 2,000 years ago had no inkling whatsoever of the nation-states that were to come.

This narrow, nationalistic and ultimately reductionist manner of writing history is one of the causes of our poverty of memory today. From our first days at school we are taught that the history of the nation begins from the day of independence and that the central actor on the stage of history is the nation-state itself; reduced to its barest essentials as an entity endowed with will and purpose. The 'supremacy of the textbook' that is affirmed by its official provenance makes it even more difficult for students, scholars and laymen alike to read such official histories with a critical deconstructive eye.[2] A cursory overview of the state of official history-writing in the postcolonial states of South and Southeast Asia would be instructive in making our point here:

Beginning in South Asia we can start by looking at the state of official history discourse in India. For half a century now Indian historians (even those who wrote during the last stages of the British colonial era) posited the view that there has always been such a thing as India and an Indian identity. Historians like Majumdar (1952) and scholars like Radhakrishnan (1923) have written time and again about the 'Indian colonies' that once dotted the landscape of Southeast Asia, oblivious to the fact that these co-called Indian colonies were not necessarily peopled by communities who came all the way from the Indian subcontinent, but which may have just been Hindu-Buddhist societies whose members were local natives. Furthermore, the use of the term 'Indian colonies' again re-states the fundamental error that there was such a thing as 'India' then, and that consciousness of this concept was prevalent among South Asians, when we know for the fact that the very term 'India' only came into usage much later from the 17th century onwards thanks to the contact with Europeans.

The same bias can be found in the official history books of Pakistan and Bangladesh, which also take off from the starting point of present-day political realities. And yet in both instances, the notion of a Pakistani and Bangladeshi nation-state serves as the entry into a wider historical narrative that back-dates the presence of Pakistan and Bangladesh as the defining actors of their respective histories; partly with the intention of creating a linear teleology that posits the existence of these modern political entities as the end-points for a long historical process that dates back to the pre-modern era.

The official history of Sri Lanka likewise obscures its long historical links with the rest of the Indian subcontinent and there is precious little mention of the long historical links with Southeast Asia, particularly with Burma/ Myanmar, Thailand and Java. This is ironic considering the fact that Sri Lanka was the place where Buddhism thrived after its gradual marginalisation from India, and it was also from Sri Lanka that Buddhism was spread to places like Burma/Myanmar, Thailand, Cambodia, Laos and Java-Bali. Until today there can be found important historical sites of monks' residences in places like Anuradhapura where Buddhist monks from Java, Burma and Siam congregated, and from which monks were later despatched to Southeast Asia.

Turning across the Indian Ocean, we discover the same historical slippages and blind-spots in the official histories of Southeast Asian polities. While in predominantly Buddhist Thailand, Cambodia, Burma/Myanmar and Laos we still find references to the Sri Lankan roots of Buddhism, there has been little substantial work done to further explore the long process of transoceanic transfer of ideas, values, cultural norms, languages and plastic arts.

Meanwhile in maritime Southeast Asia we see an even greater denial of the shared past in the official histories of Malaysia, Indonesia and Singapore. In all these cases, India – and by extension the entire South Asian subcontinent – has been relegated to a marginal position as some faraway land where there was once some form of cultural and economic contact. Yet the official languages of Malaysia and Indonesia – *Bahasa Malaysia* and *Bahasa Indonesia* respectively – are both deeply marked by the common linguistic past that they share with Sanskrit, and until today one can frame entire Malay and Indonesian sentences where practically every word is Sanskrit in origin. In the domain of popular culture and the arts we likewise see the sharing of a common cultural heritage in the way in which so much of what makes up 'traditional' Malay and Indonesian culture – when understood in essentialist terms – is of South Asian origin. Malay and Indonesian cultural practices such as the *wayang kulit* (shadow puppet theatre) derives most of its mythology and narratives from the great Indian epics such as the *Ramayana* and *Mahabharatta*, both of which were later locally adapted to suit local needs and tastes.

And perhaps the most striking case of selective history writing has to be that of Singapore's, which dates its founding to the period and achievements of Stamford Raffles, the colonial official and governor of the British East India Company during the early stages of the 19th century. This selective appropriation of Raffles and the role of the East India Company effectively introduces a historical break in the continuity of Singapore's history, presenting it as a commercial *entrepot* that emerged *ex nihilo* outside the context of a wider, deeper and older historical milieu when the region was a cosmopolitan continuum binding South and Southeast Asia together. The net result being that most ordinary Singaporeans may not even know how and why their island state was named thus: *Singha Pura* being of course a Sanskrit name for what was once a Hindu-Buddhist polity that came into being during the era of the Majapahit empire.

How and why this erasure of the past came about is as much a question of history as it is a question about the politics of history and history-writing. We do not propose to embark on a long political critique of the political vicissitudes that have led up to the current impoverished state of knowledge about our past and shared histories here, but rather would like to take this opportunity to remind us of the common threads of temporality and historical continuity that once held together the two grand chambers of the common Greater Indian civilization, which saw the Indian Ocean as the corridor that connected us.

To lend weight to this claim, our focus here will be on the process of Islamisation of Maritime Southeast Asia that began in earnest from the 13th century, where Indian Muslims played the key role as transmitters of knowledge and religious praxis. But allow us to begin by offering a cursory sketch of the shape of the world then, before the coming of Islam and before modern ethno-nationalism divided the two halves of this expansive trans-oceanic culture and civilization.

Re-membering our Common Transoceanic Identity: A look at South and Southeast Asia during the Hindu-Buddhist Period

According to Sylvain Levi, 'India gave her mythology to her neighbours, who went to teach it to the whole world. She gave to three-quarters of Asia a God, a religion, a doctrine, an art. She carried her sacred language, her religion, her institutions to Indonesia, to the limits of the known world and from there they spread back to Madagascar and perhaps to the coast of Africa...'[3]

Let us start with this premise: Our ancestors lived in a time where the concept of nation-states, political boundaries, racial difference and citizenship were alien to them. We – the peoples of South and Southeast Asia today – are the descendants of communities and nations that were open to external influences to a far greater degree than we perhaps realise, and this is borne by the fact that the culture, religions and vocabularies that were used in the ancient past demonstrate an easiness with cosmopolitanism that would embarrass most of us today. In *re-membering* our past, we need to somehow imagine what it was like to live then, in an age free of narrow political identities and loyalties.

To remember our past, we need to recall the names and places, as well as geographical configurations, that have passed from memory: There was once a land called *Suvarnabbhumi,* whose western shores were turned towards the Indian Ocean, facing the eastern shores of the Indian subcontinent. Like two faces reflected by a common mirror between them, the developments on both sides of this great watery divide mirrored each other, bearing witness to the rise and fall of kingdoms and empires. It was towards this fabled land of gold, spices and aromatic woods that generations of Indian navigators steered their vessels, braving the monsoon winds and turbulent waters, hoping to make landfall in order to be able to return home with their hulls full of bounty.

By the first millennium India was already a cosmopolitan civilisation that was in contact with other great powers around it. The Indian kingdoms were engaged in trade with the outside world and Indian rulers were sending merchants and ambassadors to foreign lands at the time. Many of these trips abroad were aimed at gaining access to markets and to buy precious commodities and resources for domestic consumption back home. Coedes (1968) notes that India once imported gold from Siberia via the Bactrian route, but was forced to seek other sources of gold when these routes were cut thanks to the migrations in Central Asia. During the first century A.D., the Indians imported gold from the Roman Empire in the form of Roman coins. But with the development and expansion of Indian kingdoms (and the related expansion of their respective populations) the demand for materials and commodities naturally grew as well. The Indian Ocean was a natural conduit for trade with Southeast Asia and the Far East, and in time Indian sea-faring merchants and traders were sailing Eastwards in search of new markets and suppliers of commodities and resources. Many of these Indian merchants were Hindus or Buddhists, and Sylvain Levi (1929) has argued that most of the Indian Buddhist merchants were particularly devoted to Buddha Dipankara (The Calmer of the Seas). It is therefore not surprising to learn that many of the early *Jataka* tales found in Southeast Asia are related to maritime-related stories and adventures, as they were brought by seamen and sea-faring merchants and traders from India.[4]

The oldest statues of the Buddha that have been found in Southeast Asia remain as oblique indicators of the seafaring lives of the first mariners who came to the region from India by sea. Many of these statues – influenced by the Amaravati school that flourished in India up to the fourth century – feature the image of the Buddha standing upright with long flowing robes that fall from his shoulders to the ground. The gentle, sweeping flow of the folds of the Buddha's robe are no mere accident, for this image happens to be that of the Buddha Dipankara (The Calmer of the Seas), whose very name can be traced to the word *dvipa* (island) and who was worshiped as the protector of seamen.[5] The *Brihatkatha*, *Kathakosa* and other renditions of the Buddhist *Jatakas* refer to Bengali merchant-princes and fortune-hunters sailing eastwards from Tamralipta (Tamluk) in the Bengal region for *Suvarnadvipa* (Sumatra) and returning home with riches aplenty.

The region of Southeast Asia has been called by many names: 'Greater India', 'Farther India', the land below the wind. Sanskrit records refer to it as *Suvarnabbhumi – the land of gold* – and placed it firmly within the frontiers of the world as it was then known to the South Asians. However facts remain and endure despite the efforts of even the most determined among the revisionists, and geography remains as a mute testament to the realities of times long forgotten. The Indian Ocean was (and remains) the vast corridor that kept these two lands apart and together at the same time, and across this ocean what began as a sporadic series of trading expeditions eventually developed to be a continuous traffic of human bodies, goods and commodities as well as ideas and doctrines. As a result of this transcultural contact and exchange the social and cultural terrain of Southeast Asia was visibly altered thanks to the incorporation of Indian designs and motifs, traces of which remain till today in the plastic and utilitarian arts of Southeast Asia, from the ubiquitous Indon-Malay *keris* (dagger) to the design structure of boats and sailing vessels in the archipelago.[6]

The South Asians who came to the Southeast Asian archipelago were neither colonialists (in the Western sense) nor conquerors, and the arrival of the South Asians – as George Coedes[7] – has argued, could not be compared to Chinese colonisation that was happening at the same time or the arrival (and subsequent colonisation and conquest) of the Europeans who came centuries after.[8]

Debate still rages on till today about the exact routes that were used by Indian traders (and later Brahmin missionaries) as they made their way to Southeast Asia. Scholars and historians have attempted to track down the routes that were used by looking at the names of places and settlements as they were recorded in ancient texts, but most of these findings have proven to be inconclusive. As Coedes (1968) notes: 'the information we can draw from the Indian place names transplanted to Farther India is not very conclusive, for these names often appear for the first time in writings of a later date, and the choice of names like Champa, Dvaravati, Ayodhya and other famous cities of Puranic legend does not necessarily prove the Gangetic origin of those who transplanted them to foreign lands. Place names that are less well known offer better evidence. One can, for example, establish a relationship between Taruma, which the earliest Javanese inscriptions place on the western part of that island, and a locality of the same name located near Cape Comorin. Likewise the use of the name Ussa (Odra, i.e. Orissa) for Pegu and of Shikshetra (i.e. Puri) as an only name for Prome in Burma certainly indicates a relationship between these states and Orissa. The name *Kalinga* resembles that of Kling used by the Malays and the Cambodians to designate Indians. The appellation *Talaing*, applied to the Mons by the Burmese, seems to indicate that at a certain epoch Telingana, of the Madras region, was in particularly active relations with the Mon country. Following the same line of thinking we can recall the presence of ethnic names originating in the Dravidian line among the Karo Bataks of Sumatra: Chola, Pandhya, Pallava, Malayalam.' (p. 30) While it is still impossible to prove conclusively from which part of India that Indian influence was first brought to Southeast Asia, it is clear that by the third and fourth centuries there was a substantial volume of traffic between the Eastern coastal states of India and the Indon-Malay archipelago as well as mainland Southeast Asia.

What took place in Southeast Asia during the pre-Islamic and pre-colonial eras can only be understood in the context of an age where geo-political boundaries were fluid, porous and inter-penetrating; and local developments took place against a backdrop of transcultural exchange and translocal evolution. Our concern here is not to elaborate upon the (often contested and contentious) claims of numerous scholars who have tried to locate the precise date for the beginning of the 'Indianisation' process. By the 5th century Gupta influence and hegemony had extended to the Bengal region, and the Bay of Bengal became by extension the springboard from which Gupta power – and Indian cultural influence – would spread further abroad. Coedes drawing on material found in various archaeological studies, argues that the traces of Indian influence in Southeast Asia can be found even before the rise of the Aryan states and kingdoms in India. But these traces of Indian influence cannot be described as transcultural exchange in any real sense of the word: they rather point to parallel developments in both regions that were happening at the same time. It is still difficult, if not impossible, to pinpoint the exact date when the Indianisation process began. One of the earliest documents of any scholarly merit is the ancient Pali text, the *Nidessa*, which dates to the first centuries of the Christian era. According to him, the *Nidessa* contains several Sanskrit references to locations that Sylvain Levi has identified as belonging to Southeast Asia. Coedes' own prudent and cautious estimation is that 'Indian colonisation (of Southeast Asia) was intense in the second and third centuries A. D. and came to fruition in the fourth and fifth centuries.'[9] Most accounts tend to agree that the Indianisation process was already underway between the second and third centuries, and evidence of Indianised societies and polities in Southeast Asia can be found from the fourth to fifth – precisely the time when the Gupta dynasty of India had reached its peak and was spreading its cultural and political influence abroad from the Bay of Bengal. Chinese records testify to the existence of small Hindu-Buddhist polities on the Malay Peninsula around the second century, while Sanskrit inscriptions there do not go back any further than the fourth.[10] In the territories that make up present-day Malaysia, evidence of Hindu-Buddhist influence and Indianisation go back to the second and third centuries. Historical records and religious texts from both India and China refer to the presence of established Hindu-Buddhist kingdoms like Langkasuka-Kadaran, Tambralinga and Takkola.

The arrival and settlement of Hindu and Buddhist traders, scholars and missionaries in Southeast Asia contributed vastly to the development of the Hindu-Buddhist polities there, and also further entrenched the process of Indianisation that eventually gave much of Southeast Asia its normative political, economic and religious culture – traces of which can still be seen till today.

However it would be wrong to conclude that the Indianisation of the Indon-Malay archipelago was simply a process of passive absorption of all that was Indian, Hindu or Buddhist. This would negate or undermine the role of local genius and the agency of the rulers and peoples of the archipelago themselves, who were never passive recipients of these new ideas, beliefs, values and customs from abroad. Coedes' account of the Indianisation process between the second to fifth centuries points to a far more complex process (or processes) that operated on a number of different registers simultaneously. The Khmer ruler Yasovarman I (889-900) for instance, opened his court to a number of religious teachers and priests from the Vishnuite, Shivaite and Buddhist traditions, and his adoption of these beliefs was selective and deliberate.

Nor should we assume that the traffic of ideas, goods and bodies between India and Southeast Asia was always moving in one direction. The Indon-Malay world not only interacted with the Indian subcontinent, but there were also instances when ambitious Malay rulers would turn their attention westwards to India to fulfil their dreams of power and glory: The 12th century medieval chronicles of Sri Lanka, for instance, record the invasion of the island by a Malay ruler from Nakhon Si Thamarrat named Chandrabahanu. Not only did Chandrabahanu's army defeat the forces of the Singhalese rulers of Polonnaruwa, they also managed to claim the prized relic of the Buddha that was in the possession of the Polonnaruwa kingdom. Following their victory the Malays then established their own kingdom in the northern part of the island (close to the Jaffna region) and the dynasty only met its end in the early 13th century when the son of Chandrabahanu was killed by the Pandyan king of Southern India.[11]

The end result of this long process of transcultural exchange was the construction of new categories of identity and belonging, a reworking of social norms and values and the construction of a new epistemic order that actually contributed to the further evolution and development of Hinduism and Buddhism, as they filtered through the prisms of the local and vernacular. It was thanks to this process of Indianisation that South and Southeast Asia were brought closer together, to the point where a common linguistic, religious, architectural and aesthetic culture was shared by the communities that spanned the Indian Ocean. This long process of cultural transmigration and exchange in turn paved the way for the coming of Islam to Southeast Asia from South Asia, and it is for that reason that Islam's arrival on the shores of the Malay Peninsula, Sumatra and Java can aptly be described as the second moment or episode in the long drama of the Indianisation of the Malay archipelago.

The Second Wave of Indianisation: Islam's arrival and settlement in Southeast Asia via India

According to Brian Harrison, 'It was not to Persia or Arabia but to India that Southeast Asia had also looked for cultural inspiration combined with commercial prestige. The acceptance of Islam among the islands and the Malay Peninsula had, therefore, to await its acceptance by Indians who were predominantly engaged in overseas trade between South Asia and Southeast Asia.'[12]

Islam arrived on the shores of the Indon-Malay archipelago not clad in armour, but in the form of religious texts wrapped up amidst the prayer-mats and records of itinerant traders, humble Sufi mystics and scholars. And yet this *penetration pacifique* brought with it changes that were unprecedented on a popular level and were to remain in the centuries to come. The most important feature of the early stages of Islamisation in Southeast Asia was that it came in the wake of the region's Indianisation and subsequent Brahmanisation, and that many of the bearers of the message of Islam hailed from the same land as their Brahmin predecessors: India.

Historians have noted that the first stage of Indianisation in Southeast Asia occurred at a time when the Hindu-Buddhist kingdoms of India were at the peak of their powers and achievements. It was thanks to the power and prestige associated with the Hindu-Buddhist kingdoms of India that Hinduism and Buddhism held such attraction for the rulers of Southeast Asia, who saw in it a discourse of legitimation and authority that could be used to fortify and consolidate their own power at home. From the age of the Sailendra kings to the time of the Majapahit dynasty in Eastern Java, India had been a source of inspiration for the Hindu-Buddhist rulers of Southeast Asia. But the Hindu-Buddhist kingdoms of India would experience their own decline thanks to a combination of internal problems as well as invasions by the Mongols and Muslims from the north, and this would have a corresponding impact on the fate of the Hindu-Buddhist kingdoms of the Indon-Malay archipelago.

Muslim incursions into India began as early as the seventh century, but most of these attacks came in the form of sporadic raids that were aimed at gaining wealth rather than conquest. In time however the Muslim empires in the Arab world grew stronger and the centre of gravity of the Muslim world moved eastwards to Baghdad with the rise of the Abbasid dynasty. As a result of these geo-political shifts India came closer within the orbit of Muslim interests. By the 8th to 9th centuries, the Muslim world was faced with the threat of the Mongols from the steppes of Central Asia.

The Islamised Mongols then turned to India and launched a number of military incursions there: Punjab was conquered by Sultan Mahmud Ghaznawi in the tenth century. Later in the thirteenth century the Turkish chieftain Muhammad Ghauri invaded the Punjab and laid the foundations for what would become the Dehli Sultanate. In 1297 Hindu rule finally came to an end in Gujerat, Bengal. Then in 1398 the Mongol *khan* Timur the Lame (Tamerlane) invaded Northern India from the west and utterly destroyed Dehli. These Mongol-Indian kingdoms would later be overcome themselves by the invasion of the great Moghul ruler Babur 'The Tiger', who would lay the foundations of the Moghul dynasty in India.

The spread of Islam across South Asia mirrored the spread of Islam across Southeast Asia, and just as their predecessors had done before them the rulers of Southeast Asia from the 10th to 14th centuries turned to India for both inspiration and help when it came to governing their communities and managing their economies. The rise of Muslim power in India meant that the Hindu-Buddhist rulers of Southeast Asia were forced to negotiate with new actors on the stage of global politics, and once again the face of Southeast Asia would be altered as a result of this transnational contact and interaction. The Mongol-Muslim invasions of India meant that the long-established links between the Hindu kingdoms of Northern India and their Hindu counterparts in Southeast Asia were weakened, and subsequently broken in time. As a result, the socio-cultural and political development of Southeast Asia was to be altered for good: Mainland Southeast Asia would subsequently turn to Southern India and Ceylon (Sri Lanka) for inspiration, while maritime Southeast Asia remained beholden to the coastal trading centres of Northeastern India.

The Indonesian-Malay kingdoms of maritime Southeast Asia maintained their economic and political links with their closest trading partners in the coastal region of Northeastern India out of necessity, which meant that they were in turn exposed to the arrival and consolidation of Muslim power there. Both Indian and Chinese records show that Indian Muslims were already present in mainland Southeast Asia and the Malay archipelago by the tenth century, but like the Hindus who came from India centuries earlier most of them were itinerant traders who had come simply to trade and would later leave when the Monsoon winds changed direction to help them make the westward journey home.

In time, however, the Muslims coming from India began to settle in greater numbers in the Southeast Asian kingdoms, exactly like their Brahmin predecessors had done before them. Arabic inscriptions in *Kufic* script found in the region of Champa show that a Muslim settlement had existed there by the middle of the tenth century.[13] Other similar findings all over the archipelago suggest that Muslims had begun to settle in region the around the same time. The very first trace of the presence of Islam in Java is an Islamic inscription on the gravestone of a Muslim woman in Leran, whose date is either 1082 or 1102.[14] The fact that it was the grave of a woman seems to suggest that a sizeable Muslim community had been established there, for it is quite unlikely that many Muslim women would have been present in the early Muslim trading settlements had the settlements not been well equipped and protected. The inscription on the gravestone also indicates that the woman – named Fatimah – was not a new convert to Islam but rather came from a family of Muslims with some history.

The arrival of Islam and the Islamisation of Java coincided with the Islamisation of other parts of the Indonesian-Malay archipelago and it has to be remembered that the ruler of Malacca Paramesvara had himself converted to Islam and taken on the Muslim title of Sultan Megat Iskandar Shah before his death in 1424. In Sumatra Islam first made its presence felt in the northern part of the island and was soon established in the kingdom of Samudra-Pasai, which R. O. Winstedt claims was the first Indon-Malay kingdom to embrace Islam.[15] One of the earliest sources of evidence that points to the coming of Islam to the island is the gravestone of Sultan Malik as-Salih of Pasai, who died in either 1297 or 1307.

By the 13th to 14th centuries, Islam had spread well beyond the Bengal region and was making its presence felt in the Bay of Bengal as well as the Indon-Malay archipelago. Prominent Indian Muslim merchant-adventurers had established themselves in many of the newly Islamised Malay-Indonesian kingdoms, with some of them – such as the Bengali Malik as-Salih – rising to positions of such prominence that they even able to establish their own kingdoms, such as the kingdom of Samudra-Pasai. Malik as-Salih was certainly not the only Bengali Muslim ruler who had established himself further to the East and brought Islam with him: During his travels at the time the Moroccan Muslim traveller Ibn Battuta encountered a Bengali Queen – Sultanah Khatijah – ruling over the Maldive islands. Her father, Sultan Jalal ud-din Umar, and grandfather Sultan Salah ud-din Saleh of Bengal, had ruled the islands before her.[16]

Between the 14th to 15th centuries Islam spread across the Malay Archipelago and many of the Hindu-Buddhist rulers of the region made the conversion to Islam with the help of Muslim missionaries and scholars from India. Numerous courtly texts describe the world of the Malay-Muslim court in detail, and in many of them we see that the figure of the Indian-Muslim *Sufi* or *Ulama* – eternally vigilant and on the lookout for traces of Hindu-Buddhist influence from the not-too-distant past – was also present. In time the impact of Islam could be seen and felt on the discursive, sartorial and normative level: The era of the Hindu-Buddhist *Devarajas* finally gave way to the age of the Sultans, and Indon-Malay political culture was altered as a result.

Two factors account for the ease with which Islam penetrated and eventually consolidated its hold across Southeast Asia:

The first was undoubtedly the familiarity of Indian Muslims who were seen as the inheritors of the mantle of Indianisation that was pioneered by their Hindu-Buddhist counterparts long before their arrival. It is clear that the arrival of Islam to Southeast Asia followed exactly the same trade routes as the arrival of Hindu-Buddhist culture centuries before, and the primary agents of the Islamisation process who were themselves traders, scholars and mercenaries were no different in terms of their occupational concerns to the Hindu-Buddhist traders, scholars and mercenaries who came before them. It is for this reason that when mapping out the process of early Islamisation across the Malay Archipelago we see that the first Muslim settlements were primarily commercial coastal entrepots that were already well-established and connected to the transoceanic trade routes with India and China.

The second factor that accounts for the easy and rapid conversion of the Archipelago was the medium that was used by the Indian Muslim traders and missionaries in the spread of Islam then: By working through the discourse and praxis of popular folk Sufism, many of the early Indian Muslim preachers were themselves of a mystical bent and this allowed them to develop a localised and syncretic idiom via which they managed to spread and inculcate the ideas and ideals of the new faith easily to the local Indonesian-Malay converts. Scholars like Bruinessen (1994) and Alatas (1963) have commented at length about the form and content of Sufi praxis in Southeast Asia, and have duly noted the continuities in style and discourse to the more popular Sufi brotherhoods that were extant in India and Central Asia then.

By the 17th to 18th centuries Islam was well and truly entrenched in many parts of Maritime Southeast Asia, and it still maintained its cultural linkages with the Indian Muslim communities of South Asia. This is party due to the patterns of trade and trading networks that had existed for centuries before and were not completely severed despite the coming of the West European colonial powers that sought to re-direct the pattern of trade and trading networks towards the metropolitan capitals of the West instead.

Then by the 19th century Indian Muslim merchants and preachers were instrumental in the development of local commercial centres all over the Malayan Peninsula, Sumatra and Java, and the Indian diaspora community was well and truly settled as native 'Peranakan' communities as well. Through these diasporic communities the Indian Muslims of Southeast Asia managed to inter-marry with locals and to root themselves in the social and economic networks of the region. (Noor, 2009.a, 2009.b, 2007) They played a key role in the development of local economic, and later political, awareness among the peoples of Southeast Asia and their impact was felt with the rise of the first anti-colonial nationalist movements in the region as well.

Nor can it be said that the Indian Muslim community was a homogenous one, for the form and content of Indian Islam that had come to Southeast Asia was as diverse as there were many schools of contemporary Islamic thought and praxis in South Asia as well. Many of the sectarian and communal differences among the Indian Muslims of South Asia were later transplanted and reproduced among the Indian Muslim diaspora communities in Southeast Asia too, and communities such as the Shias, Ismailis, Bohras and both the Qadiyani and Lahori Ahmadis were very active in the development of both Islamic thinking as well as Muslim political and economic development in both British Malaya and the Dutch East Indies (later Indonesia). (Noor, 2009.a.) The Lahori Ahmadis, for instance, were among the pioneers of modern Islamic education and Muslim political activism in Indonesia at the turn of the century, and the madrasas built by the Lahori Ahmadis in places like Jogjakarta were among the first to introduce modern subjects such as political theory, economics and the arts and humanities. Later the Lahori Ahmadis would gain greater prominence in Indonesia as many of their leaders would be instrumental in developing the first anti-colonial Indonesian Muslim movements such as the *Sarekat Islam* and the *Muhamadiyyah* reformist-modernist movement as well.

The origins of the *Tablighi Jama'at* go back to the Indian Deobandi movement that was started by Maulana Muhammad Qassim Nanotawi and Maulana Rashid Ahmad Gangohi at the Deoband seminary in 1867. Like the Deobandis, the Tablighis were conservative fundamentalists who were inspired by the reformists of the *Wahhabi* movement from Saudi Arabia. Unlike the Deobandis who were educationists, the Tablighis were missionary-activists who sought to transform Muslim society and bring Muslims back to the path of true Islam. The movement was formed in the late 1920s by Maulana Muhammad Ilyas Kandhalawi (d. 1944), whose family were closely linked to the Deobandi leadership and its sister school the Mazahiru'l-Ulum in Saharanpur. The *Tablighi Jama'at* was formed at a time of intense rivalry and hostility between Muslims and Hindus in India. The movement sought to purify Indian Islam of Hindu and Christian influence, and it tried to win back Muslims who had been converted by the Hindu revivalist movements in the country. For this reason it was often criticised and attacked by radical Hindu fundamentalist groups who regarded it as a subversive force that intended to weaken the Hindu community from within. In order to deflect criticism from its activities, the *Tablighi Jama'at* rejected the use of violence and opted to remain apolitical. Unlike the Deobandis, the members of the movement avoided direct confrontation with Hindu or Christian groups. Metcalf (2002) notes that the *Tablighi Jama'at* could be compared to the Western Alcoholics Anonymous movement that started around the same time: both organisations sought to reform their followers from within and sought to improve their moral qualities while regulating their public behaviour.[4] Rejecting politics and political activism of any kind, the movement emphasised its peaceful (*sukun*), passive and gradualist approach instead. Members of the movement were expected to take part in communal activities and join in their missionary efforts. They were expected to spend one night a week, one weekend a month, forty days a year and 120 days at least once in their lives with the members of the movement.[5] This was seen as part of their *jihad* (struggle) for the sake of God and their religion. The movement spread all over the world from Europe to Asia and was held together by its close internal linkages and networks. In time it penetrated into many guilds, business communities and elite networks as well. In most cases, however, its members were ordinary Muslim males from the lower levels of society. The movement has always been able to attract such followers thanks to its emphasis on the egalitarian ethos of Islam. By the end of the 20th century the regular congregation of Tablighis in Raiwind, Pakistan and Tungi, Bangladesh, could attract several million followers, making it the second biggest gathering of Muslims after the annual pilgrimage to Mecca. Like the Deobandis, the Tablighis also had an ambiguous relationship with Sufism. They rejected many of the traditional practices and beliefs of the Indian Sufi *tariqas* on the grounds that they were contaminated by alien Hindu practices and ideas, but also sought to use Sufi methods and rituals when it suited them. Metcalf (2002) notes that 'among the Tablighis the holiness associated with the Sufi *Pir* was in many ways defused into the charismatic body of the *jama'at* so that the missionary group itself became a channel for divine intervention.' (p. 11) Like the Deobandis, the *Tablighi Jama'at* attempted to reproduce the strong *Pir-Murid* bonds in the Sufi *tariqas* within their own organisational structure, making it a very strong and intimately-linked organisational network that would be able to straddle enormous geographical distances. The Tablighis also adapted another feature of the Indian Sufi *tariqas*: the (sometimes extreme) veneration of the Prophet Muhammad and his life history. In *Tablighi Jama'at* circles, *Hadith* and *Seerah* literature concerning the Prophet was and remains of great importance.

Among all the Indian Muslim movements and networks that had spread to Southeast Asia, however, the one that had the closest links to India was undoubtedly the *Tablighi Jama'at.*. Elsewhere we have looked at the role played by the *Tabligh* in Malaysia and Indonesia as a popular movement for faith renewal that draws heavily on its cultural origins and transnational linkages to India and beyond. (Noor, 2009.a, 2009.b, 2008, 2007, 2003.) What is clearly evident in the workings of the *Tabligh* is how its own normative praxis of popular religiosity draws heavily on its cultural origins and historical linkages to South Asia, and how this history of long transoceanic contact between South and Southeast Asia also serves as the conduit via which the ideas and norms of the movement are easily spread to its new converts in Southeast Asia, who in turn see India and South Asia in general as the fountainhead of their newly re-discovered faith and commitment to Islam. (Noor, 2008, 207.)

If movements such as the *Tabligh Jama'at* and the Lahori Ahmadis are able to find a home for themselves in Southeast Asia today, one of the factors that account for this has to be the long historical contact between South and Southeast Asia that dates back to long before the demise of the Gupta civilisation thousands of years ago. This, then, is the secret that accounts for the success of early Islamisation and the subsequent conversion of Maritime Southeast Asia to Islam: That Islam came to Southeast Asia dressed in the familiar garb of the itinerant Indian, for whom Southeast Asia was an extension of Greater India, and who was not consequently regarded as an alien or foreigner.

Islam's arrival to Southeast Asia was a less a case of the imposition of the alterior and the new, but rather a turning of the page of the familiar and known. Southeast Asia was, after all, the second home to South Asians by then, and Islam's arrival was simply a case of a (belated) homecoming...

Conclusion: Re-Appraising the Arrival of Islam to Southeast Asia as a Case of Continuity Rather than Dislocation

Let us conclude by re-stating some of the premises that we began with: History, it has to be remembered, is never a closed text and the writing of history – despite its political considerations – is never a totalised enterprise that can bring us to any degree of hermetic closure. The open-ended nature of historical narratives means that all events that have and will happen in the course of time will be exposed to a myriad of contesting perspectives and interpretations, which in turn ensures that the discursive terrain of history and history-writing remains likewise open and unsutured.

This historian might, of course, wish to close the text so that some degree of sedimentation and consensus can be reached albeit momentarily and where conclusions can be drawn. A snapshot of the past offers us such a momentary escape from contingency, and we quickly draw from the well of historical data whatever tentative conclusions that can be drawn at the moment. But these conclusions can only be, at best, tentative and momentary; for with the future discovery and revelation of more and more data, the historian is once again recalled to his/her task and made to work upon the terrain of historical facts yet again.

Rather than view this state of affairs as a constant irritant in the side of the historian, we should seize upon it as an instance of productive ambiguity that allows us to critically revise and perhaps even deconstruct and reconstruct our accounts of the past with an open-minded and inclusive frame of mind. Our contention in the earlier part of this paper was that the writing of South and Southeast Asian history has, for too long, been an enterprise limited by the overriding concerns of nationalism and national history-writing, that in turn compels the historian to write a national history that is somehow meant to cater to the subjective needs and interests of his national audience.

Revisiting the shared and complex histories of South and Southeast Asia during the period of Islamisation between the 13th century to the present allows us to interject the somewhat staid narrative of Islamisation that has over the past decades gained some degree of currency in our midst: By emphasising and re-foregrounding the dimension of cultural continuity during this period of transmigration of ideas, we effectively succeed in doing several things.

Firstly, we can and should de-bunk the notion of a linear development of national history that somehow leads us to the conclusion that the modern postcolonial nation-state was a determined fact of history. The period of transcultural migration and transoceanic transfer of ideas would suggest to us that no community or nation had a monopoly on the values and symbols of cultural and religious identity, and that our forebears once lived in a world that was far more cosmopolitan, opened and exposed as it was to the external variable factors of trade and the traffic of ideas. Islamisation between South and Southeast Asia took place at precisely such a moment in our history, long before the peoples of both regions were limited by the circumstances and demands of modern citizenship and national belonging. It was an era where individuals could entertain and harbour multiple identities at the same time, long before this became a trend associated with the current wave of post-structuralist and post-modern identity politics.

Secondly, the long period of Islamisation was and should be seen in the context of a longer process of Indianisation of the Malay-Indonesian archipelago, which in turn reminds us of the long shared cultural, religious, linguistic and economic legacy that bound the two regions together. Islam's arrival to Southeast Asia, as we mentioned above, was rendered all the more easy because it came in the guise of the familiar; and this in turn should remind us of the fact that during the pre-colonial era both parts of the world were hardly strangers to each other.

Thirdly, contemporary historians of Southeast Asia should take this episode as a case of fluid history in motion and reconsider how our 'national' histories can be written in the future. To date, there are few attempts to write a comprehensive history of South and Southeast Asia that centres the Indian Ocean as the conduit and transit point for ideas, goods and cultural-religious praxis that it really was. It is as if history requires solid ground as the basis of its writing, and we forget to note the vital importance that the Indian Ocean played as the interface of ideas and beliefs. In itself, the Indian Ocean was the centre of this greater transoceanic civilisation and consequently deserves to be studies as an oceanscape in its own right. Hinduism, Buddhism and Islam all thrived and prospered across the maritime lanes and routes of this oceanscape, and the Indian Ocean played as important a role in the development of all the peripheral cultures and societies that stood on both sides of its shores as any other actor on the stage of history.

Assessing the continuity and development of both South and Southeast Asian societies and cultures during this long period of cultural and religious conversion will therefore have to be a new historical project that rejects some of the more exclusive and limiting premises of conventional, linear and determinist history while adapting alternative notions of space, time and identity instead.

Can such an endeavour meet with any degree of success? One should hope so, and to that question we can add one final observation: Writing history in the post-modern era has become a rather trendy enterprise where the wheel is invented time and again to demonstrate the permanence of the obvious and mundane. Yet at the same time, such an enterprise is still needed for it is also through such repetitive deconstruction of the narratives we use to describe our past that we can reach to some rather important observations about the present.

Re-Appraising the Arrival of Islam to Southeast Asia as a Case of Continuity Rather than Dislocation is a moot point that needs to be stated again and again in the context of the geo-political realities of today. The mundane-ness of the Islamisation process that took place between South and Southeast Asia from the 13th to 19th centuries may strike the historian as an instance of stating the obvious once too many times. Yet by emphasising the shared history between nations and communities and the commonality of fluid, open identities we are still engaged in the perennial struggle to keep the pages of history open and to prevent the monopoly and sedimentation of history-writing lest it falls into the hands of demagogic forces bent on rendering our histories absolute, total and exclusive. At a time where the rise of ethno-nationalism across many parts of the world has led to the casual murder of history for the sake of exclusive nationalist agendas, and when cultural continuity is deemed anathema for exclusive nationalists and communitarians, such an effort to reconnect our shared histories is not simply an academic endeavour, but a political one as well. For this sake, and for the sake of keeping history alive, such a critical and deconstructive reading and writing of history can never be abandoned.

REFERENCES

1. Joseph J. Ellis, *Founding Brothers: The Revolutionary Generation*, New York: Vintage Books, 2002, pp. 4–5.
2. K.K. Aziz, 1993. p.1.

3. Sylvain Levi, *L'inde Civilisatrice: Apercu Historique*. Paris, 1938. p. 30. The French Orientalist scholar Sylvain Levi (b. 1863-d.1935) was famed for his study of Sanskrit texts and ancient Indian history. His earliest works were on Indian Classical literature and drama, and he later became the Vice-President of the *Société Asiatique* that was based in Paris, France.
4. See: Sylvain Levi. *Les Marchands de Mer et leur role dans le Bouddhisme Primitif*, in *Bulletin de l'Association Francaise des Amis de l"Orient*. Paris, October 1929. (pp. 19-39); K. A. Nilakanta Sastri, The Beginnings of Intercourse Between India and China, *Indian Historical Quarterly*, Delhi, XIV, 1938, pp. 380-389; and Wang Gungwu, The Nanhai Trade: A Study of Early Chinese Trade *in Southeast Asia*, JMBRAS, XXXI, 2. Kuala Lumpur. 1958.
5. For a more detailed explanation of the symbolism detailed explanation of the symbolism of Buddha Dipankara, see: Pierre Dupont, Les Buddhas dit d'Ararmavati en Asie du Sud-est, *Proceedings from the XXIII International Congress of Orientalists*, Cambridge University, Cambridge, 1954.
6. For further readings on the cultural impact of Hinduism and Buddhism on the arts, architecture and culture of the Indon-Malay archipelago and mainland Southeast Asia, see: Farish A. Noor, From Majapahit to Putrajaya: The Kris as a symptom of civilisational development and decline. In *Journal of Southeast Asia Research*, Vol. 8. no. 3. School of Oriental and African Studies, London. November 2000; Nicholaas J. Krom, Antiquities of Palembang. In *Journal of Greater Indian Studies III*, London, 1931. pp. 24-37; Ananda Coomaraswamy, *History of Indian and Indonesia Art*, London. 1927: and *The Influences of Indian Art*, London, 1927; A. J. Bernet Kempers, *The Bronzes of Nalanda and Hindu-Javanese Art*, Brill. Leyden, 1933; Devaprasad Ghosh, Migration of Indian Decorative Motifs, *Journal of Greater Indian Studies II*, London, 1935. pp. 32-47; James Hornell, The Origins and Ethnological Significance of Indian Boat Designs, in *Memoirs of the Asiatic Society of Bengal VII*, Calcutta, 1920.
7. See: George Coedes, *The Indianised States of Southeast Asia*. (Ed. Walter F. Vella, Translated by Susan Brown Cowing). University of Hawaii press, East-West Centre, Honolulu. 1968; *The Making of Southeast Asia*, University of California Press, 1962; and *Sriwijaya History, Religion & Language of an Early Malay Polity*. Malaysian Branch of the Royal Asiatic Society. (M20) Kuala Lumpur, 1992.
8. Coedes (1968) argues that "the coming of the Indians to Southeast Asia cannot be compared to the arrival of the Europeans to America, for in this part of the world the newcomers were not strangers discovering new lands. At some time that we must try to date, following circumstances

that we can attempt to imagine, the sporadic influx of traders and immigrants became a steady flow that resulted in the founding of Indian kingdoms practising the arts, customs and religions of India and using Sanskrit as their sacred language." (pp. 14-15.)

9. Coedes (1968), pp. 16, 19.
10. Coedes, 1968. pp. 18. Coedes notes that "none of these findings can be dated before the time of Ptolemy (second century A. D.). Ptolemy's geographical nomenclature for trans-Gangetic India was full of place names with Indian-Sanskrit correspondences." (ibid.)
11. See: B.A. Hussainmiya, The Malays in Sri Langka, in *Borneo Bulletin*, 4 August 2001. pp. 1-2.
12. Brian Harrison, *Southeast Asia: A Short History*. MamMillan, London, 1957. p. 43.
13. This claim has been made by Paul Ravaisse, who deciphered the Arabic inscriptions found in Champa between 1902 and 1907. Ravaisse claims that the Muslim settlement received the protection of the Cham rulers and that it enjoyed a certain degree of autonomy in its internal governance. See: Paul Ravaisse, Deux Inscriptions coufiques du Champa, in *Journal Asiatique*, Paris, XX, 1922. p. 247.
14. G. Coedes, 1969. p. 241.
15. See: R. O. Winstedt, The Chronicles of Pasai, *Journal of the Malaysian Branch of the Royal Asiatic Society*, JMBRAS, XVI (2), 1938.
16. Fatimi, 1963. p. 22. n. 61.

PART–II. TRADE AND COLONIALISM

CHAPTER 7

China and South-East Asia in the Fifteenth Century AD

Dr. Haraprasad Ray

Throughout history South-east Asia is known to have remained a zone of peace negotiating the regions lying to its west, north-west and north-east. Its rich natural resources have been the source of supply to the foreign countries.

The East, South-east and South Asian countries should be thankful to the ancient and medieval historians of China who have taken great care to record the happenings in these countries and their inter-state relations with China. The earliest evidence of which is recorded in Chinese only. This was a sea-land-sea route described in the Huangzhi passage in the *History of the Former Han Dynasty* by Ban Gu (AD 32-92). The work vouches that as early as 1st century A.D. the Chinese traders sailed into the South China Sea in merchant ships of the foreigners' called Yue (from whom the name Vietnam originates). The Austronesians took these traders to the south-eastern coast of Thailand (Yilumuo) and from there across the Malayan peninsula through the Isthmus Kra to its west coast. Around this time the Singapore Straits (Longyamen) was also used occasionally for the return trip to China. Rhinoceros horns, elephant tusks, tortoise shells, pearls and jades, silver, copper, fruits and cloths were the items exchanged.

A survey of the period from 2nd and 1st century. B.C. to early 5th century A.D. (the Jin dynasty of China, AD 265-420) shows that the China trade was characterized by the predominance of Yue and Indian merchants who controlled the shipping. Later, the region witnessed the rise of Funan as the first maritime empire of the Nanhai.

A second phase, when the demand for religious objects and relics like joss-sticks and the like, surpassed the demand for jewels and perfumes, was characterized by the coming of the Bosi (Persians), Kunlun traders known to be the sailors of the Nanhai, and by more intimate contacts with Java-Sumatra and Sri Lanka. This period spanned the two centuries of the Southern Dynasties of China from 5th to 6th century AD[1].

The third phase, the period of trade in medicines and spices lasted through the Tang and Song dynasties i.e. from 7th century AD to 13th century, and was marked by the rise to commercial power of Srivijaya and by domination of the Persian, Arab and Indian middlemen and sailors. South-east Asian states with a substantial Indian population dominated the trade (specially the Indian trade) through their settlements which spread from South-east Asia to South-east China at the port cities of Guangzhou and Quanzhou[2].

Primary focus of trade until the 11th century AD was the China market. Many of the commodities reveal the identity of their production centres. Those of West Asian origin included higher quality aromatic essences, exotic animals and glassware. South-east Asia provided forest products like benzoin, fine resin, dragon's blood (from *daemonorhops* blame, or climbing rattan), camphor, nutmeg (*jatikosa* in India, *pala* in Malayan and *roudou kou* in Chinese) and clove[3]. Later accounts, especially the 15th century travelogues repeatedly mention that many of these natural products were being harvested and processed in the forest area of India, particularly in Kerala.

Cinnamon of southern Indian was one of the best species. Zhao Rugua of the thirteenth century A.D. ascribes the home of cardamom to a variety of centres like Cambodia, the northern region of the Malay Peninsula, Java, Sumatra, Sri Lanka and the Indian Coromondel (Cholomandalam).

Among dye-stuff, a red dye with greater affinity for silk than cotton, was native to Pegu (Myanmar), Thailand and Assam, the Pegu product being the best quality, and being in demand in both India and China. The Timor and Samban white sandalwood famous for its fragrance, did get exported to China along with the Indian red variety, used for colouring, construction and medicinal purposes. The black pepper (*piper nigrum*), the most important commodity exported to China was indigenous to Kerala from where it also appears to have been introduced into Java[4]. For export of cotton textiles Southeast Asian countries depended mainly on India for their trade with China, the region's own product being limited.

The cotton trade must be mentioned in connection with India-South-east Asia –China trade. In Chinese the term cotton that is *karpasa* was known as *jibei*. Chinese records report that the Gupta king presented jibei that is cotton products to the Chinese emperor in early 6th century A.D. When China-Southeast Asian trade increased, China acquired another term for cotton, that is *gubei* which was in all probability derived from the Malay word *kapas* which is itself a local form for Sanskrit *karpasa*.[5]

The Chinese were not a maritime nation as the Arabs or the Indians were during the Han and Tang dynasties (3rd century BC to 10th century AD); but they succeeded in their efforts to be one after 1127A.D. (during Southern Song dynasty) when the capital was shifted to the coastal city of Hangzhou which was exposed to attacks from the sea[6]. The possession of a huge naval force enabled the Chinese to maintain control over trade with a piratical fringe in the high seas in the Pacific Occan adjoining China. Towards the end of the thirteenth century and the beginning of the fourteenth century the Chinese became known in Europe through the accounts of Marco Polo, and by early Ming period (late 14th to 15th century A.D.) China was a naval power capable of extending its sphere of activity from the Eastern Sea routes to as far as the Indian Ocean shores of East Africa in the West. Their activities during this period has been discussed by the present writer in various articles in all the dimensions of the Chinese demarche into Indian and Pacific region. The first Ming emperor (Hong Wu, Zhu Yuanzhang) had a keen appreciation of naval power. The third emperor Yongle (Zhu Di), further strengthened it and employed it as an instrument of his expansive overseas policy. Thus, an efficient navy was built up comprising 3500 ships for operation in the coastal waters of China. Of these, 2700 were warships, half of them combat vessels and the other half patrol boats, of the guard stations on the sea coast; 400 were warships of the fleet based at Xinjiang Kou near Nanjing, 400 were armed transports of the grain conveyance fleet. Already around 1393 each Ming warship was required to carry four guns with muzzles the size of rice bowls, twenty guns of smaller calibre, ten bombs, twenty rockets (of crude nature), and a thousand rounds of shots. Thus, from a defensive arm the Chinese navy developed into an instrument of expansion and political domination, and from the East Chine Sea the naval power of the Chinese advanced to the South China Sea and into the Indian Ocean.[7]

It was against this background that the third Ming emperor, Yongle, desptached a series of six naval expeditions between 1405 and 1422 (1404-07, 1407-09, 1409-11, 1413-15, 1417-19, 1421-22), and a seventh one was sent between 1431-1432 under the regime of Xuanzong (Hsuantsung). All the voyages were under the direction of a 'grand eunuch' named Zheng He, a Mushim by birth with the family name of Ma He. Known as *Sanbao Taijian*, the Three-jewelled Grand Eunuch, an epithet applied to Buddhist grand monks, he was catholic in belief. He made these voyages over a period of twenty years, calling at ports in more than thirty countries. On each voyage he had a fleet of 100 to 200 ships, of which 40 to 60 were huge 'treasure ships'. The fleet carried over 27,000 men. The vessels, built at Nanjing were assembled at the port of Liujiagang in Taicang county, Jiangsu province, before sailing into the sea. The treasure-ships were about 150 metres long from stern to stern, their rudder posts 11.07 metres long, each carrying 12 sails. These were the flat-bottomed sand ships.[8]

The first three voyages did not venture beyond Calicut (Kozhikode = Guli). Envoys from Samudra (in Sumatra), Calicut, Malacca, Quilon and Aru were sent to China in Zheng He's fleet returning at the end of the first voyage in 1407 A.D. These envoys were sent back home during the second voyage when the Calicut memorial stone from the emperor was erected in the heart of the then Calicut city.[9] The adventurous Zheng He started manipulating South and South-east Asian polities. He had found a loyal ally in Shi Jinqing, a rival of the ruling king of Palembang (Jiugang), one Chen Zuyi. He attacked the latter, took him to Nanjing as prisoner where he was beheaded. It may be noted that both these princes were refugees from China.[10]

During the third voyage, while visiting Sri Lanka on the outward run, presents were offered at a temple presumably of Nayanar, and a tablet thanking the Buddha for safe journey was set up in 1409 (This stone tablet with inscription has been discovered and studied). But while in 1411 on the return journey, Zheng He captured the refractory king (or his minister and may be the King's rival) named Alagakkonara and brought him to China The prisoner was released afterwards in Nanjing.[11]

The fourth expedition extended upto the Persian Gulf, and the first officially acknowledged Chinese maritime contact with Harmuz (Ormuz) was established. But while returning home in 1415, Zheng He captured Suganla (Sekandar or Sukarna), a pretender to the throne of Samudra which legally belonged to Zaynul Abidin. The ill-fated usurper was beheaded later in the Chinese capital.[12]

The fifth (1417-19) and sixth (1421-22) voyages took the Chinese as far as Aden, Mogadishu and Malindi, and exotic creatures like giraffe, zebra, lions, spotted leopards, camels and ostriches were acquired for the Court.[13]

The seventh and last voyage was undertaken during the reign of the fifth emperor Xuanzong (Hsuanzong, reigned, 1426-35) and contact was established with Mecca for the first time, and obviously for the last time.[14]

The first four voyages were marked by military and political gains, and they set the stage for the later phases from 1417-1432 when China had already gained vast knowledge of South and South-east Asia, and enough intelligence about other foreigners, especially the Arab traders who were obviously charging abnormally high prices for their products in the China market by creating artificial scarcity.[15]

During these voyages, China demonstrated an astute sense of realpolitik in manipulating South and South-east Asian polities. They put their loyal allies in power in places of strategic and commercial importance like Palembang and Samudra (Semudera) and Sinhala. The South-east Asian waters were thus free from all human hindrances. The Chinese fleet sailed the waters like the lords of the sea, each time comprising a large number of huge boats, full of cargoes, indigenous and those marketed at ports en route, creating awe among the littorals while providing passage to the traders who might be vying with each other for getting their exotics, curios, etc. exchanged or sold in China through imperial patronage.[16]

III

No maritime trade between India and China could be transacted without touching the fringes of the South-east Asian region, that is, Malacca, Palembang, Thailand and Cambodia. Analysis of medieval trade, especially 15th century trade, bears ample proof of this. The Chinese Muslim interpreters in Persian (and possibly also in Arabic) listed nine types of textile products. Most of these names were previously rejected as ambiguous or meaningless; but through persistent research and analysis of different texts these terms have now been deciphered. They are *bafta* (*beide* in Chinese), *pachadi* (*manzheti* in Chinese), *shanbaft* (*shanabafu* in Chinese), *jhamartali* (jhin-bartali, in Chinese = *Chhinbailedali*), *Chautar* (*chhaoda-er* in Chinese), makhmal (moheimoluo), *sakalat* (sahala in Chinese), sof (also written as *suf*)(zhefu), and so on.

Bafta was a trade item from Semudera (Samudra), Palembong, Danba and Malacca, as well as from Bengal and Calicut in India. This white cloth called pavu in Malayalam, was used as garment for the lower part of the body. The Chinese required huge quantity of white cotton cloth for uniforms for the troops serving in hot and dry regions in north and north-west China, while cloth was also accepted as tax and used for payment to the imperial officers and soldiers, just as pepper was. The Ming vocabulary list of Sino-Foreign words used for training interpreters in various foreign languages even including Bengali of the time, gives *kainpha* as the Thai word for bafta cloth. Kain in Malayan language means cotton cloth and kain putih "white cloth". Its fame and value can be understood from its high cost which was fifteen strings of copper coins for one bolt which was equal to the price of an ounce (*liang*) of pure silver. This means that the Indians used to carry the cloth to South-east Asia on the way to China, while the Indians and the South-east Asian countries re-exported it along with other commodities to China.[17]

The names shanbaft, makhmal (Indian cotton velvet known in China as *douluo mian* (tula-cotton i.e. soft cotton), *sakalat* and sof make it clear that these were introduced into India from Persia (Iran) and Arabia, from where they found their way to South-east Asia for export to China. We may note here that the word for *sakalat*, called *sakalata* in India and sahala in China, is named *sakalat* in Malayan language signifying the same stuff, that is "a scarlet cloth (the name scarlet itself being the corrupt torm of *sakalat*; in medieval Bengali it was known as "a costly woven stuff". Moreover, the Malayan language confirms the prevalence of sof in South-east Asia since ancient times, the term meaning "camlet" from where *kambal* developed, and also "a species of fine woollen stuff" in Malaya and Bahasa Indonesia.[18]

Participation of South-east Asia in both Chinese and Indian trade, as the conveyor of trade items, is thus proved beyond doubt. By the medieval period the entire region came within the commercial network operated by the Arab, Indian and the Chinese traders. Not only was South-east Asia involved in the trade but the dominant trade language of the time was also a mixture of Tamil, Persian and inflected Malayan spoken language. Use in Malayan language of such words as kajang (date-plam wine) and *gendang serunai* (*shahnai* and *tabla*), *sakalata*, *sof*, *shanbaft* and *bafta*, to take a few examples from the Perso-Arabic family, stand testimony to our statement.[19]

REFERENCES

1. Haraprasad Ray, "The South-east Asian Nexus in Indo-Chinese Trade" in the author's, *Trade and Trade Routes between India and China, c. 140 BC-A.D. 1500*, Kolkata: Progressive Publishers 2003, p.159 (henceforth *Trade and Trade Routes*).
2. *Ibid*, pp. 159-60.
3. *Ibid*, p. 160.
4. *Ibid*. p.161 ; also O.W. Wolters, *Early Indonesian Commerce*, New York, 1967, pp. 136-7.
5. Ray, loc. Cit.
6. Ray, "An Analysis of the Chinese Maritime Voyages into the Indian Ocean during early Ming dynasty and their Raison d'etre", in *Trade and Trade Routes*, p. 177.
7. *Ibid*.
8. *Ibid*, p. 178.
9. Feng Chengjun, ed., *Yingyai Shenglan jiaozhu*, 1934, reprinted, Taipei, 1970, pp. 42-43.
10. Ray, "Chinese involvement in the geopolitics of the Pacific and the Indian Ocean region prior to the advent of the Portuguese" in *Trade and Trade Routes*, p. 227-8, 230.
11. *Ibid*, p. 178.
12. *Ibid*.
13. *Ibid*.
14. *Ibid*, p. 179.
15. *Ibid*, p. 219.
16. *Ibid*, p. 230.
17. Haraprasad Ray, *Trade and Diplomacy in India-China Relations, A study of Bengal during the Fifteenth century*, London – New Delhi : Sangam Books, Radiant Publishers, 1993, pp. 83-5.
18. *Ibid*, pp. 87-92.
19. Ray, *Trade and Trade Routes*, p. 163 ; see also Ray, 1993, pp. 126 where a detailed discussion will be found on the subject.

CHAPTER 8

Commerce, Circulation and Consumption: Indian Ocean Communities in Historical Perspective

Prof. Lakshmi Subramnian

This paper is an attempt to look at the dynamics and processes of identity formation among trading communities whose social profile was predicated upon cultural and commercial practices within the Indian Ocean. The Indian Ocean functioned as a trans-national zone of interaction with connections extending far across discrete civilisational units from which migrant merchant communities were drawn and thrown together to negotiate cross cultural and commercial interflows and overlaps. The temporal dimensions of these interactions were important; the world of Islam generated one set of conditions for dialogue while the intervention of western political domination served to introduce a very different set of demands and variables in the region. Equally influential was the assertion of nationalist aspirations and its accompanying cultural dynamics that at a later date inflected very distinctly, the processes of community definition and aspirations. Documenting these processes as an empirical exercise, especially in the context of the more recent debates on Diaspora models and regimes of circulation in the Indian Ocean, and how the latter served as sites of nationalist and trans-nationalist imaginings forms some of the concerns of this paper. It locates important social processes within the larger site of interaction between southern India and Southeast Asia and relates to some of the themes that this conference addresses.

While some of the empirical research is drawn from communities based in and operating from southern India, I hope to make some general formulations that an attempt is made for a broader conversation with certain thematic issues pertaining to the notion of an Indian Ocean and competing ideologies and practices. Among the communities that have been chosen are the Muslim trading communities from the Coromandel – known as the Marakkayars, of whom the Chulias formed one sub-section and who dominated the external or overseas trade of southern India in the eighteenth and early quarter of the nineteenth century. The second case study looks at the Chettiars, or more specifically the Nagarathars or Nattukottai Chettiars, a Hindu mercantile group whose presence in Southeast Asia was integrally connected with the colonial trading structure and whose ties with southern India were mediated through cultural practices, community networks of marriage and kin and also through consumption markers. Just how these became constitutive of complex and cross-cultural identities is the focus of the paper. The profiles of these two communities, their rise and evolution encompass two significant if not defining moments in the history of the Indian Ocean; one that saw the working of cross-cultural transactions across the Indian Ocean at a time when the world of pre-modern global trade fostered a particular form of cosmopolitanism predicated upon religious and social networks that trade generated, and the other which was a direct off shoot of colonialism that introduced new elements coming in the wake of capitalism, bourgeois modernity and nation state aspirations. If one contributed directly to the blurring of boundaries and to the making of a genuine Indian Ocean subject, the other produced a deep and growing angst about recovery from homes, languages and cultures left behind.

Looking at a unitary notion of a diaspora especially in the pre colonial period, it is argued that the majority of Indians were temporary residents and also that the community of migrants was differentiated in terms of class and occupation. There was in fact, no long-term separation from a real or originary homeland and that the invocation of the nation was only one and often provisional strategy in the formation of identities.

For the seventeenth and eighteenth century, Islam played a decisive role in community formation as it integrated a set of cultural and social practices across the Indian Ocean and served to position communities like the Chulias in a very significant way within the polities of Southeast Asia. Here, we need to especially factor in the influential scholarship of Enseng Ho, whose outstanding work on the Hadrami diaspora suggests very innovative ways of understanding the experience of early modern trans-national communities.

Chulias: Before and After Empire

The expanding presence of the Chulias in the trading world of the Indian Ocean, especially in the Bay of Bengal segment was particularly marked in the seventeenth century, which constituted the golden period for Indian overseas trade. South Asia, by virtue of its location and commercial and manufacturing potential enjoyed a particular pre-eminence in the Indian Ocean trading system – Indian merchants of different denomination enjoyed an unprecedented visibility as peripatetic carriers of staple as well as short term residents in the ports of the Indian Ocean[1]. Gujaratis, by and large tended to concentrate in the ports of the western Indian Ocean while Tamils from the Cormandel region were oriented to the Southeast Asian archipelago. Tamil merchants included Chettis and Chulias who in different capacities were active agents in overseas trade and made up the category of Kling mentioned in Portuguese as well as subsequent European documentation[2]. As late as the first quarter of the nineteenth century, Indians in Southeast Asia were referred to as the Klings and Chulias who T.J. Newbold described as 'traders and settlers, both Musalmans and Hindus from the Cormandel Coast'. He observed that these names had been given to them by the Malays since times of early commercial intercourse, that Kling was a corruption from Teling or Telinga[3]. John Crawfurd writing two decades earlier also commented on the frequency of communication between the Coromandel and Southeast Asia, dominated largely by the chulias whose trading enterprise persuaded them 'to seek their fortunes in a country richer by nature than their own, less occupied and the natives of which are easily circumvented'[4].

The coherence of the Chulia presence in the trading segment of the Bay of Bengal is generally dated to the expansion of Arab maritime contacts with the peninsula from the eight century. The centrality of the Coromandel in the international trade linking South Asia with southeast and west Asia brought increasing numbers of Arab merchants to Indian Ocean ports where they intermarried with local women, built networks of commercial, religious and personal contacts, and maintained relationships with local rulers supplying their requirements from war horses to spices. A testimony to the success of these networks was their importance in local courts all through south and Southeast Asia, the vitality of their religious life largely serviced by Sufi lineages and the vibrancy of the chain of coastal towns that they developed[5]. Most of these towns at least in the Coromandel were dominated by the Marakkayars an endogamous body of Tamil speaking merchants and ship owners who maintained contacts with the Arab centres of pilgrimage on the one hand and developed new ties in Southeast Asia on the other. The Marakkayars belonged to the Sh'afi order and maintained a distance from other Tamil speaking Muslims called the Labbais who were Hanafis. Marakkayars maintained the division by marrying with fellow Sha'fis from the Malabar Coast and Southeast Asia in preference to Tamil speaking Hanafis. They prized their Arab connection, claimed that knowledge of Arabic was non existent among Labbais and that these converts had deviated from proper Islamic domestic custom by adopting murai or cross cousin marriages of the kind prevalent in south India. The Marakkayars adhered to a particular lifestyle that emphasized acts of public piety, of promoting religious knowledge and scholarship and building centres like madrasas, dargahs and mosques.

Historians working on maritime India have commented on the extensive dealings of the Marakkayars, their networks in Southeast Asia and their resistance to the attempts of the European trading companies in the seventeenth century to engross the major proceeds of the country trade in the Indian Ocean. Merchants from the Coromandel – Pulicat, Nagore, Nagapatnam – had since very early times maintained regular connections with Southeast Asia. Malacca, the great sixteenth century emporium, as we know from Tome Pires' account housed an extensive Kling settlement – the Portuguese writer Duarte Barbosa referred to them as 'men of great taste and owning many great ships' and to the corpulent Chettis with great big bellies[6]. Both these groups were identified as different from peripatetic itinerant traders and seen to have substantial stakes in local society. Of the two groups, Chulias seem to have responded vigorously to the rise of new Malay ports in the late fourteenth and early fifteenth century, notably the rise of Malacca as an important emporium. The arrival of the Portuguese and their attempts at monopolising the traffic of the Indian Ocean did not seriously deflect or undermine Chulia enterprise, which opted for new ports that did not fall under formal Portuguese dispensation.

Subsequent developments, related to the internal reorganisation of states in Southeast Asia in the seventeenth century benefited and enabled merchant networks to regroup effectively; Chulias in fact fared well during these years of political transformation and expanded their operations, consolidated their presence in regional courts and even assumed administrative functions. We hear of substantial Marakkayar investments in shipping; of their close connections with local Malay rulers and of their preponderance in the textile trade of the Coromandel that continued to retain its vitality until the early eighteenth century. The succeeding decades introduced new pressures and strains in the situation; conditions of political insecurity in South Asia combined with the expansion of English private trade eroded the foundations of Chulia enterprise and caused a major jolt to the existing networks. However, this was not entirely irreversible - in fact the Nagore Acheh trade route remained the most important route in the Bay of Bengal in the eighteenth century largely as a consequence of the Chulia Southeast Asia connection. Recent research suggests that the Chulia connection remained more enduring than was previously thought and that their activities remained robust well into the closing decades of the eighteenth century. According to Bhaswati Bhattacharya for instance, a considerable part of the trade between Coromandel ports and Kedah, Acheh, Malacca was in the hands of the Chulias or their counterparts on the other side of the Bay. The trade peaked in the 1770's and was principally in textiles and enjoyed the encouragement and patronage of local Southeast Asian rulers.

The main centres of Chulia activity on the Coromandel Coast were Porto Novo and Nagore, which directed the traffic with Southeast Asia. Chulia merchants settled in the archipelago focused on Nagore and emphasized its importance. Local Southeast Asian rulers as a result endeavoured to keep this channel of communication as open as possible and even mounted a partial offensive when English private trade threatened to alter the existing arrangements[7]. Chulias were also important court officials: contemporary Europeans had occasion to comment on the close linkages between rulers of Acheh, Johore and Perak with Chulia merchant networks, some of the Chulias becoming important court officials. The rulers along with their clients resisted the strong-arm tactics of English private traders, partly in response to their own increasing involvement with trade and partly in deference to the demands of the local networks of trading interests, notably the Chulias.

The Chulias were to be found in virtually all the major courts in the archipelago in the capacity of prime ministers and senior officers. In 1783, the Kedah ruler's minister was a keen Chulia called Jemmal. Chulia enterprise dominated the trade of Acheh. Thomas Forrest in 1792 had occasion to remark, 'in India, vessels fitted out and sailed by natives alone sail at much less expense even less than one half of what they do when fitted out by Europeans although sailed by an Indian crew. Such is the frugal management and among these islands, the lascars could merely maintain themselves with fishing from inexhaustible stores and find many articles to fill up their vessels that Europeans would never think of[8]'. He noted the regularity with which Chulia vessels arrived every year at Acheh from Porto Novo. These were medium sized vessels and brought piece goods of all kinds, chiefly long cloth white and blue, chintz with dark grounds and a great deal of long cloth unbleached. The merchants sold at leisure and according to Forrest, were not above deception, as they showed their 'goods to the natives in as dark a part of their shop' as they could. It was their frugality and the cheapness of their prices that made it impossible for Europeans to compete with them[9]. The ramifications of Chulia enterprise were in full display in the states of Kedah, Perak, and Johore. Even in the nascent English settlement of Bencoolen, English private enterprise failed to deflect Chulia enterprise for the greater part of the eighteenth century, at least until the very closing decades of the eighteenth century, when the political geography was entirely redrawn

What actually accounted for Chulia success? We need not take Forrest's observations too seriously who like other Europeans saw local commercial practices as inimical to the pursuit of free trade, or local strategies as irrational. A closer reading in fact yields a very different picture of mobility and diaspora formation that was able to take on universalist aspirations The modalities of Marakkayar interaction between South India and Southeast Asia and their linkages, symbolic as well as real with Arabia, enabled them to operate very much on the lines that the Hadramis pursued and function as a composite diaspora that Ho likens to what he calls the British model as against the Jewish one. He suggests that just as the British diaspora never became ethnic minorities in the lands they colonised but took on universalising aspirations, forged loyalties around institutions such as private property, free trade and protest according to law, and organised the diaspora in the form of an empire, the Hadrami Arabs too expressed their universalist ambitions in the form of a religious mission[10]. It brought together not just people from the homeland but from through out the Indian Ocean as well. They married into the local population and became locals while at the same time, the men and their off springs continued to move through out the oceanic space for trade, study, pilgrimage and politics through out the space. In the arc of ports around the Indian Ocean, a skein of networks arose in which people socialised with foreigners and locals as kinsmen and as Muslim. Like the British model, the movement in the Hadrami diaspora brought together separated peoples not in an empire but in a religion.

Religion in this case was not only a spiritual space but a civil and political one as well. As bearers of Islamic knowledge and prestige, Hadramis were creators of Islamic knowledge; Hadramis were everywhere potential creators of public spaces and institutions. Not surprisingly Hadramis were welcomed in the new port cities and states where they made local alliances and functioned in important capacities. What is fairly remarkable about the Hadrami experience is that they were able to retain a distinct identity at one level, and at the same time create a completely new one.

From this perspective it is tempting to see the Chulias experiencing the trans-regional Indian Ocean network of peaceful trade and social exchange as an extensive domestic realm that was simultaneously local, global and Muslim. The Arab connection as mentioned before was central to the Chulias as indeed was their commitment to scholarship and the public urban expression of Islamic life style. Their facility with language was an important cultural asset that they deployed to advantage. Trade, local marriage alliances and linguistic adeptness became important strategies in configuring the Chulias who were part of the hadrami circle, and yet were local Tamils at one end and Malays at the other. The intersection of multiple identities, of practices and networks proved to be extremely important in stabilising Chulia presence in southeast Asia and in enabling some sections of the community to negotiate European political and commercial influence.

The importance of social strategies and cultural practices adopted by the Chulias is especially important to recall in the eighteenth century context when, they had to renegotiate their operations and transactions. As traders, they were not unused to sudden contingencies or having to respond to changing circumstances and stimuli; they had for long demonstrated a level of cosmopolitanism that characterised certain other trading networks in the Indian ocean like for example the Armenians. However, what made the eighteenth century experience especially striking was the intensity and rapidity of change that the trading structure underwent in the aftermath of formal European colonial control and the resilience displayed by Chulia networks in the changing circumstances. Their communication skills, penmanship and local contacts were substantial assets that they put to use in developing political contacts and in expanding their operations amidst conditions of competition and aggression. This combination of cultural integration and linguistic cum communication skills would appear to have featured as a central organising principle of the Chulia conglomerate.

Chulias and the new colonial dispensation

Chulia networks had to readjust to the radical transformation of the trading world in the aftermath of formal European colonisation. The making of the Anglo-Dutch maritime empires introduced new elements in the existing equation compelling indigenous groups to come up with new strategies. The thrust of British private trade meant new even if limited opportunities for informal partnerships. At the same time, the shift towards new commodities, especially the movement of exotic southeast wares for the growing China market downsized Indian textile trade, which faced constraints even at the level of production in south-eastern India. The traffic did not die out entirely; going by trade estimates of Penang, it would appear that Indian piece goods continued to be a major item in the trade and that Chetties and Chulias continued to be principal exporters of cloth along with English private traders. Even though British piece goods had made an appreciable dent by the 1820's, the quantity of Indian piece goods imported into Penang was still larger than that of the Europe article. John Anderson in 1846 estimated that exports of cotton and cloth from the Coromandel continued to be high even though he argued that the figure given by an earlier writer of its value at Rs. 25, 000,000 annually was somewhat inflated. Betel nuts were another important item of trade. He estimated the export of betel nut at not less than from 150000 to 160000 tons. Anderson specifically referred to 10 to 12 ships coming every year from the Coromandel bringing in piece goods of all kinds, white and blue, longish cloth, chintz and salt. During the season in June, July and August, there were seldom less than 12 or15 ships and brigs, which proceeded to Pedir for cargoes, and these along with Achenese Prahus provided the country with a variety of Europe, India and China imports[11].' Anderson was in many ways confirming the observations of Crawford, when he wrote about the numerous vessels of the Chulias. "The numerous vessels of their nation bring annually with the setting in of the western monsoon, shoals of these people literally to seek their fortunes in a country richer than their own, less occupied and the natives of which are strictly circumvented[12]." The Chulias were shrewd, supple, unwarlike, and mendacious according to Crawford and carried cargoes of cloth in their vessels that were around 200 tons dead weight.

The continuity of commercial exchanges facilitated the operations of older Tamil networks that persisted at middle and lower levels. At the same time, some of them would appear to have moved with the expanding presence of the English and taken up permanent residence in the new settlement of Singapore while continuing with their operations at Penang, Perak and Malacca. In the new centre at Singapore, they opted for newer functions that were largely ancillary to English and Chinese enterprise. The dominance of European and Chinese carriage in the transportation of European cloth and a variety of Chinese and Southeast Asian ware inevitably meant that the Chulias concentrated increasingly on lower levels of retail trade in Indian cloth and of port functions related to the handling of cargo and boat building. The terms of trade had changed; the political dispensation was no longer the same, staple Indian calico had made way for the cloths of Lancashire. The Chinese emerged as the new distributors of British goods displacing the older Asian groups. Thus in the new centres of Penang and Singapore, Chulias became small time shop owners handling a minor proportion of retail trade. They had perforce to dovetail their operations to suit the imperatives of the new economy and in the process opted for lower levels of retail trade or for collaboration with the English authorities as dependents and not partners. The perceptible decline in the trade of Indian textiles whose marketing and sourcing had been the basis of their economic success in the earlier centuries, undermined their operations and resulted in a downgrading of their reputation. It is likely that their commercial practices that came in for sharp criticism by locals and Europeans alike manifested their basic weakness in adjusting to a new situation and was in the nature of a desperate strategy in keeping afloat their small ventures. They catered to the local population whose consumption of Indian textiles would appear to have continued. But this was maintained at a lower level as contemporary observations indicated.

Multicultural negotiations: The Chulias as a diaspora

These details help us reconstruct the residual nature of Chulia trade dealings at a time when European maritime aggression had dismantled the existing political and commercial regimes in Southeast Asia and British textiles displaced Indian textiles from Asian markets and transformed existing channels and conduits of distribution. Under the colonial dispensation, new groups came into prominence – the Chinese being a notable instance, while old networks had to reinvent themselves outside the formal apparatus of empire and thereby remaining obscure in the colonial archive.

There were some exceptions like for example the narrative of Munshi Abdulla, the secretary to Sir Stamford Raffles whose account offers us a fascinating insight into the emergence and functioning of creole Muslim communities in Southeast Asia of which, Chulias were a notable case study. Abdullah's account captures the complexities and nuances of what it meant to be part of a trading network in the eighteenth century. What is even more fascinating about the narrative is how in the process of operating as a cosmopolitan, trans-national community, Hadramis and Chulias became in fact entrenched local Malays. The process was marked during the pre-colonial period; cross cultural negotiations do not seem to have been viable or possible after the formalisation of colonialism and the new labour and commercial flows it supported. In fact we hear of Chulias and Klings coming in from India under the category of indentured labour working within an assigned and somewhat lower rung of commercial society and whose existence and profile was no longer predicated on the older trans-national cultural space the Ocean represented. Likewise the Arabs coming into Southeast Asia in the nineteenth century were described as pirates and slave drivers who had to be repressed ruthlessly by the British if their aspirations of free trade and order had to be worked out. "It is seldom that the east is visited by Arabian merchants of large capital but there are numerous adventurers who carry on a coasting trade from port to port and by asserting the religious titles of sheikhs and Sayyids claim and generally obtain an exemption from all port duties in the

Malay states; they are very frequently concerned in acts of piracy and great promoters of the slave trade. This class of adventurers it will be our object to repress but a regulated trade with any of the commercial state of Arabia as Muscat, Mocha and Judda may prove extremely advantageously to the Malay countries[13]"

It is in the context of the early modern period of transition in the Indian Ocean, that we shall analyse the narrative of Munshi Abdulla (born 1797) to reconstruct the older world of multi cultural negotiations that made the chulia a trans-national subject in the most comprehensive sense of the term. I cannot resist quoting J.T. Thomson here, who writing of the 40's, when Abdullah had already reached middle age, says, "In physiognomy, he was a Tamilian of southern Hindustan: slightly bent forward, spare, energetic, bronze in complexion, oval faced, high nosed, one eye squinting outwards a little. He dressed in the usual style of Malacca Tamils. Acheen seluar, check sarong, printed baju, square skull-cap and sandals. He had the vigour and pride of the Arab, the perseverance and subtlety of the Hindoo – in language and national sympathy only was he a Malay'[14]. The biographical details of Munshi's family bring to life the ramifications of Hadrami diaspora and of the Chulia component within it. Reading his Hikayat[15] closely it is evident that not only was he born in a period of great change, but also that the linguistic resources of his community combined with their commercial contacts were especially valued assets. Munshi Abdullah came from a family of Arab traders and scribes who had married into local Tamil and Malay society in the Coromandel and Malacca respectively. His great grandfather Abdul Kadir was a Yemeni Arab who had migrated to Nagore in south-eastern India, where he married a local Tamil. He had four sons, three of whom settled in Java, Sumatra and Amboina. His fourth son took up residence in Malacca, where he married Peria Achi, the daughter of a Tamil Labbi merchant. Their son Abdul Kadir took up trade and combined it with religious instruction to supplement his income and forge deeper connections with local society. He went on to marry an upcountry Malay woman, whom he later divorced after the birth of two children. Subsequently, he married a Malacca born half Indian called Selama, whose fifth surviving child was Abdullah. Abdul Kadir was a man of enterprise and worked with the European traders in several capacities – as scribe preparing contracts and petitions, as harbour master and even as a local contact for accessing manuscripts that Europeans were interested in. The family was held in respect as they performed vital religious functions of familiarising the locals with the scriptures – Abdullah mentions his grandmother organising classes for young children in the study of the Koran. Their skills as scribes held them in good stead as merchants flocked to their chambers to arrange for documentation. Abdullah in fact mentions that good scribes were not easy to come by. "In Malacca of those days, it was very hard to find people who could do letter writing. There were four or five who altogether practiced it as a profession. There was first Khoja Muhammed, the son of a Malacca Tamil who became the Company's tolk, second Jamal Muhammed bin Nur Muhammed of Surat, third my father Abdul Kadir bin Muhammed Ibrahim, fourth Mahidin Ahmed Labbai"[16].

While it is clear that Abdulla's family belonged to the larger Hadrami diaspora which forged a local Tamil- Malay identity, it is also clear from his account how central the Tamil Muslim network was in southeast Asia and how knowledge of Tamil as an important commercial language was prized by his family as well as local merchants. Abdulla mentions time and again the attention he paid to learning Tamil. His own father spoke Tamil fluently, read and wrote accounts in it and insisted on his son acquiring fluency in Tamil and a whole range of other languages. As he observed, 'soon after having learnt Arabic and my Koran lessons well, my father sent me to a teacher to learn Tamil, an Indian language because it had been the custom from the time of our forefathers in Malacca for all children of good and well to do families to learn it. It was useful for doing compilations and accounts and for conversation because at the time Malacca was crowded with Indian merchants. Many were the men who had become rich by trading in Malacca so much so that names of Tamil traders had become famous[17]'.

Commercial skills, literacy and linguistic proficiency, networks of sociability and religious sentiment combined to give Tamil Muslims a special niche in the trading world of the Indian Ocean right until the middle decades of the nineteenth century. Thereafter, it would seem that some among them were completely integrated into local society becoming the kind of Malays as Munshi Abdulla's family represented functioning as part time scribes, part time traders and part time teachers writing contracts, moving residence and collecting local manuscripts for their European associates. The Munshi's experience was undoubtedly an exceptional one in that he made the transition from a pre-modern world into the modern with great facility and thereby positioned himself in the new trading order of Southeast Asia with an easy elegance.

At the heart of the cosmopolitanism that Abdullah's enterprise reflected, lay language and literacy networks, marriage connections and a readiness to respond to new changes. Penmanship was especially valued in Malay society and in its commercial environment, it was extremely useful for earning a living by writing letters and bills of contracts. Religion and communication were equally important qualifications and it was in the simultaneous deployment of these practices that the family demonstrated its receptivity to change. Admittedly, Abdullah veered towards the European dispensation and earned the disapproval of his critics for being 'unpatriotic', but the fact remains that his response was part of an older and embedded social strategy that the community had embraced in its pursuit of a universal cultural space charted at a personal and intimate level, through wives and relatives and at a larger one through religion and representations. Religion and pilgrimage were significant in cementing the world of trade and traffic and in creating a genuinely cosmopolitan space at least before the mid nineteenth century; later representations decrying the religious zeal of the Arabs testify not so much to religious militancy among Arabs as to the anxiety of the British in clearing the maritime channels of competition and rivalry. Not surprisingly, British observers including Raffles wrote of Arabs as intolerant and sycophantic who managed to hoodwink natives and secure high offices, which they held 'as robbers' and 'cover all with the sanctimonious veil of religious hypocrisy[18]'

The Chettis: Home and the World

On the other end of the spectrum were the Chetties whose location, response and aspirations remained more local even as they operated in an expanding global trading system. In 1879, J.D. Vaughan describing the Chetties in the Straits settlement observed that they 'may be regarded as mere visitors who have the command of fabulous sums of money it is true, but are not as a rule rich individually. They are agents of wealthy men at Madras, they take very little interest in the colony and hasten back again to their country as quickly as they can'[19].

Vaughan's observations at one level, demonstrate the fundamental difference in between the profiles of the late nineteenth century Chetty immigrants and the earlier Chulia-Hadrami diaspora in Southeast Asia. In part this was to do with the nature of the business undertaken by the Nagarathars and their commercial and religious practices that tied them very strongly and integrally to the hinterland in Tamil Nadu. The connection also meant that their political and social identity in the twentieth century was determined very closely by developments in South India. Yet this was not a mere expression of an extended overseas nationalism; a close examination of the practices of the Tamil Hindu diaspora and within it the Chettiar component in Singapore and Malaysia is enough to reveal the complexities accompanying the formation of new circulating groups within the Indian Ocean under a formal regime of colonialism. The identities of new migrant merchant groups configured differently around the issues of language, religion and reform and cultural performance. Additionally, there was a sense of material advancement that was potentially possible in the diaspora outside the home and one, which invested the community with a different sense of empowerment that distinguished them from their kinsmen at home. The case of the Chettiars in fact would appear to reinforce Markovits' suggestions about locating merchant networks in a local-global continuum, wherein the sense of common religious mission with its secular and philanthropic dimensions gave the diaspora a very distinct identity.

The Nattukottai Chettiars or Nagarathars of the nineteenth century were not part of the old mercantile groups of Beri and Balija Chetties mentioned in

European factory records. This community would appear to have emerged in the late seventeenth century as small-scale itinerant traders in salt. By the eighteenth century, some of them had extended business operations as far south as Ceylon even as they became prominent as moneylenders to the zamindari estates of Ramnad and Sivaganaga[20]. This connection gave the community not only its clear and identifiable territorial basis but also its initial capital stock which they employed in their subsequent business ventures in Ceylon and Southeast Asia. Propelled by the British connection, they moved into these areas where they deployed their distinct accounting and partnership system in undertaking the marketing, financing of agricultural produce and thereby determining the bazaar rates of interest and exchange[21]. What enabled the Nattukottai Chettiars to expand was their system of agency, whereby trusted caste members were sent out as triennial agents to conduct loan operations in overseas British colonies. By the late nineteenth century, they were an established community and identified as an influential class of merchants engaged in money lending. They assiduously maintained their connections with their ancestral base and closely participated in politics articulating their views through several newspapers that they ran.

Identities in flux: beyond the Nation?

How were these connections maintained over time? Did the community transform itself in course of the twentieth century when the experience of being nationalist, Indian and Malay figured significantly in the making of the community's identity? How far did the new symbols of nationalism alter the traditional sources of community formation? We know from David Rudner's work on the Nagarathars, that investment in rituals and traditional forms of religious offering was a critical determinant in the expansion and consolidation of their networks in Tamil Nadu. From the late nineteenth century, investment in temple endowments was followed by large-scale involvement in secular philanthropy that provided an illustration of the dynamic quality of investment in the symbolic quality of elite-hood, the social relationships it created and the social changes it affected.

The community's profile in the port towns of the Indian Ocean would not appear to have been substantially different from that in the natal base. In contrast to the chulias, the community seemed distinctly more insular inspite of their very close integration into local economic exchanges. However, they had to accommodate a double set of pressures developing from within their own community and from within the larger situation of modernization they found themselves in. This was clear in their adherence to the larger campaign for social reform and language patronage, both fo which were key elements in the community's redefinition.

Thus what distinguished the Chettiar's cultural profile in Southeast Asia was not so much cosmopolitanism, as an engagement with religious practices and performance, which was in fact a traditional means of accumulating and demonstrating symbolic capital. Following the footsteps of their counterparts in Madras, the community assumed the lead in forming urban associations to sponsor cultural performances and to take the lead in the reform of religious and social practices that no longer conformed to their appreciation of tradition. The reform interventions were also seen as absolutely vital in providing a solid base for reconstituting Indian identity in Malaysia, for retaining their links with the homeland and yet consolidating their special identity as Malay Tamils. This was not a continuation of the older heritage of being an Indian Ocean subject where the various identities were melded to form a third one. The case of the Malacca Chetties was frequently cited to make the point that they had lost their language, dress and customs and now spoke and dressed like Malays and followed only a few select customs in relation to death ceremonies. This was not seen as ideal and associations continued to insist on retaining links with India, promoting cultural activities and building up a sustainable base for the community.

It was in this connection that the circulation of cultural practices, of music, dance and drama within the diaspora became an object of overriding importance from the 1930's. As staunch advocates of Tamil, the community felt compelled to keep in step with developments in India; this could be ensured only by investing substantially in the promotion of theatre in the diaspora. Drama troupes and musicians from Madras were regularly invited. This had important consequences. On the one hand, it fed into important networks of sociability, mediated through a number of cultural associations that sprang up in the 1930's. This in turn reinforced the sense of belonging to a larger community of speakers but with a difference that arose out of being located outside the nation and within the diaspora. Like theatre, music too was considered as an important cultural resource. The pleasures of listening to music and learning it constituted part of a process of self-definition on the part of Indian elites and which tended to be replicated by certain groups, Chetties being an important case in point. The self definition of the community was organised around the biographies of great men like Annamalai Chettiar whose services, wealth and involvement with Tamil scholarship and culture were frequently invoked by both Chetty associations in Kuala Lumpur and Singapore as well as by the Malay Indian Association which had a strong Chettiar presence. At the same time, the associations in keeping with the reformist temper that characterised their politics in southern India pressed for reform of temple management and eradication of caste privileges. Here the Malay experiment was interesting in that the orthodox opinion did not have the same weight or even presence as in India. The Malay Indian association in fact stated that the reforms relating to temple management did not meet with opposition and that resistance to change in Malaya was not especially marked as the Malayan Tamils felt it was doubly necessary to carry them out in consideration of their self image in the country. In fact it would seem that even in those temples where the responsibility for management lay with labouring castes, the resistance to reform was not marked – in fact one may well see the making of a new identity that was contingent on improved economic status, and on a more considered appreciation of public space where religious practices had to be reworked. The image that we have of the proud agent showing off his household effects to new arrivals indicates just how perceptions of better lifestyles were factored into the new self perceptions of the diasporic community. And yet in the advocacy of religious practices, cultural tastes and even dress, it is clear that the community clung to notions of what constituted the appropriate subject. To this was added an appreciation of their commitment to business ventures that integrated them into local commercial society as well. As Leong Yew pointed out in his address to the farewell ceremony of Alagappa Chettiar in 1946, "Speaking as an old resident (in Singapore) if I were asked which two classes of people who have contributed most to the material wealth of this land, I would unhesitatingly say the Chettiars and Chinese sundry shopkeepers. These two classes of people are bankers and financiers of the poor[22]"

There was obviously more than an element of exaggeration in the statement. However, what is noticeable is the distinct subjectivity that coalesced around the new diaspora subject, wherein the continuity of an older inheritance was transformed by a growing sense of what the new situation demanded in terms of politics, social and cultural practices that included language in a big way. If the Chulias and Hadramis worked within the contours of a poly-lingual domain of cross cultural and commercial transactions, the Chettiars would appear to have operated within a narrower domain of linguistic and cultural politics that collapsed the nation, the community and the diaspora into a less inclusive continuum.

Resisting Conclusions

This paper has hopefully raised more questions that it has answered. I began with the premise that the story of Asian networks in the Indian Ocean in the nineteenth and twentieth centuries requires to be retold with an emphasis on the transformation of the Indian Ocean merchant subjects, some of whom like the Chulias maintained a curiously dual profile of the peripatetic with the sedentary. For the nineteenth century merchant, the world had changed but with some space left for him to articulate his sense of profit and affinity. Arabs interacted with Malays and Tamils to form a dynamic interface between pre modern commerce and that of colonial power regimes. The cumulative aspects of pre-modern commercial experience grounded in a variety of religious practice, commercial techniques and marriage networks were deployed with full effect enabling the formation of complex conglomerates that could also make a partial transition to the European dispensation. Implicit in the narrative I ahev attempted is the assumption that we need to look more closely at the processes of interaction between southern India and Southeast Asia and that these require an alternative conceptual paradigm. This could be in the form of trans-nationalism and the way it evolved before and after empire and how these trans-national links were mediated through Islam and other networks of cultural and social practices not to speak of colonial institutions and compulsions.

REFERENCES

1. Ashin Dasgupta, '*Indian Merchants and the trade of the Indian Ocean, c.1500-1750*', *The Cambridge Economic History of India* Vol. I c.1200-1750, ed. T. Raychaudhuri and I. Habib. Cambridge University Press, 1982.
2. John Crawford observed in 1820 that trade between India and Southeast Asia had always been conducted from the ports of the Coromandel and by the nation called the Kalinga or Telinga and that the shipping in which the trade was carried on by the people of the peninsula was on small vessels of 100 to 200 tons and manned by Indians generally Muslims. See John Crawfurd, *History of the Indian Archipelago* containing an account of the manners, arts, languages, religions, institutions and commerce of its inhabitants. Vol. I 1820. P. 133ff.
3. *Political and Statistical account of the british settlements in the Straits of Malacca* by T.J. Newbold in two volumes. London, 1839. Vol.I pp. 9-14.
4. *History of the Indian Archipelago containing an Account of the manners, arts, languages, religions, Institutions and Commerce of its Inhabitants* in three volumes, by John Crawfurd. Edinburgh, Archibald Constable & Co. London: Hurst, Robinson & Co. Vol. I 1820 p.133ff.
5. Susan Bayly, *Saints, Goddesses and Kings Muslims and Christians in South Indian Society*, Cambridge 1989 pp. 78-79ff.
6. *The Book of Duarte Barbosa.*
7. Bhaswati Bhattacharya, 'The Dutch East India Company and the Trade of the Chulias in the Bay of Bengal in the late eighteenth century', in K.S. Mathew (edited) *Mariners, merchants and Oceans Studies in Maritime History* Manohar 1995. PP.348-350 For a brief historical overview of Chulias see Kenneth McPherson, 'Chulias and Klings Indigenous Trade Diasporas and European penetration of the Indian Ocean littoral' in G.Borsa (ed.) *Trade and Politics in the Indian Ocean Historical and Contemporary Perspectives*. Manohar, 1990.
8. *A Voyage from Calcutta to the Mergui Archipelago lying on the East side of the Bay of Bengal* by Thomas Forrest. London, J.Robson, 1792. pp.24. 37-40, 41-42.
9. *Ibid.* pp.41-42.
10. Enseng Ho, 'Empire through Diasporic Eyes: A view from the Other Boat'. *Comparative Studies in Society and History*, 2004 pp.210-246.

11. Anderson, John, 1840, *Acheen and the Ports on the North and East Coasts of Sumatra with Incidental Notices of the Trade in the Eastern Seas and the aggressions of the Dutch.* W.H. Allen & Co. London. pp.160-161.
12. Crawford, John, 1820, *History of the Indian Archipelago Containing an Account of the Manners, Arts, Languages, Religions, Institutions and Commerce of its Inhabitants* in three Volumes. Edinburgh.
13. Archibald Constable & Co. London, Hurst Robinson &Co. Vol. I. *Asiatic Society*. Vol. XXII Part I 1949. pp. 162-65.
14. Introduction to the Hikayat Abdullah by A.H. Hill, 1954. See p. 5.
15. *The Hikayat Abdulla*. An annotated Translation by A.H. Hill, *Journal of the Malayan Branch of the Royal Asiatic Society*, (Singapore, Malayan Publishing House Ltd.) Vol. 28 Part III, 1955, No.171.
16. *The Hikayat Abdulla*. An annotated Translation by A.H. Hill, *Journal of the Malayan Branch of the Royal Asiatic Society*, (Singapore, Malayan Publishing House Ltd.) Vol. 28 Part III, 1955, No.171, p. 41. "It happened that at that time in Malacca", Abdulla writes, "my grandmother on my mother's side became a great teacher at Kampong Pali. Some two hundred children learnt the Koran".
17. *Ibid.* pp. 48-50.
18. "Under the pretext of instructing the Malays in the principles of the Mohemedan religion they inculcate the most intolerant bigotry and render them incapable of receiving any species of useful knowledge', see J.A.E.Morley, The Arabs and the Eastern trade' in *Journal of the Malayan Branch of the Royal Asiatic Society* Vol. XXII, 1949. Singapore. pp. 143-44.
19. J.D.Vaughan, *The Manners and Customs of the Chinese of the Straits Settlements* Oxford in Asia paperbacks. Singapore, 1970 Reprint. First printed at the Mission Press, 1879 pp.1-2.
20. For an account of the Chettiars in Colonial India see David Rudner, *Caste and capitalism in Colonial India* The Nattukottai Chettiars University of California Berkeley, 1994.
21. Rajat Kanta Ray, 'Asian Capital in the age of European domination: the rise of the bazaar 1800-1914', *Modern Asian Studies* Vol. 29, no. 3, 1995 pp. 449-454.
22. Leong Yew's address.

CHAPTER 9

Textile Trade from the Coromandel Coast to Indonesian Archipelago: Role of the Chettis, the Marakkayars and the Dutch East India Company, AD 1612-1704

Prof. Jeyaseela Stephen

Using the Dutch archival sources and the published records this paper attempts to examine the nature and pattern of the trade in textiles conducted from the Coromandel Coast by the Tamil and Telugu Merchants and the Dutch East India Company with various ports of Indonesian Archipelago during the Seventeenth Century. Scholars have so far mentioned that the Dutch purchased various types of the textiles without actually naming the variety of cloth. Further, various ports such as Pulicat, Devanampattinam and Nagapattinam from where the Dutch exported cloth had not been properly highlighted. We also find the role of the Tamil and Telugu traders who signed the textile contracts had been largely ignored. The available literature on Coromandel trade mentions in general terms of the textile exports without pin pointing to the various markets in the three islands of Indonesia such as Java, Sumatra and the Spice Islands (Moluccas, Makassar).[1] The volume of Dutch textile trade and the value in florins had swelled up from 1617 to 1650 and the purchase and selling prices had also increased. Owing to the demand the Dutch began to purchase cloth from various places in Coromandel and they exported to Aceh, Jambi and Palembang, the three main Sumatra markets and it thrived on well from 1625 to 1678. We also need to explore the textile trade of the Chettis and the Marakkayars who had been continuously carrying on their cloth in their ships to Banten and Aceh. We shall therefore explore how the trade from the Coromandel moved its direction from bartering cloth for spices to exchanging cloth for Minagkanbu gold and import of bullion from Japan and China to Jakarta to finally reach Coromandel.

Textiles of Pulicat and the Dutch Trade with Java and Moluccas, 1612-1650

Textiles formed the main commodity of the Dutch trade in Pulicat. As early as 1612 Hendrik Brouwer mentioned Pulicat as the left arm of the Moluccas (known as spice islands, with a group of islands such as Amboina, Ternate & Tidore in the eastern extremity of Indonesian archipelago producing nutmeg, clove, cinnamon, cardamom and cumin) since without the cotton textiles from Pulicat trade is dead in the Moluccas. Regarding the various types of textiles produced in the Pulicat region, *goulong* is described as the best variety of cloth. It was patterned in a loom and usually incorporated with gold thread. It was mainly produced for the Malay market. The other types of textiles included *tapi* which was a general name used for naming all coloured piece-goods used as skirts by both men and women in South East Asia. This *tapi sarassa* was a well known variety, patterned with birds and foliage. *Sarassa* was a cheap strong calico either plain or striped. *Patta* was a cheap dyed cotton usually striped cloth. The Dutch also exported slaves from Pulicat to Batavia. From there they were sent to other places. It is reported in 1624 that 630 salves sent from Pulicat and 45 of them died on the way. The Dutch also exported cloth needed by the slaves. Striped dungarees were ordered for the use of company's slaves in Banda and Amboina.

The Dutch often had financial problems for conducting trade at Pulicat. Due to shortage of capital in 1617 it was only possible to send 110 packets of *goulongs* to Banten against the orders for 300 packets. *Goulongs* from Pulicat were exported to Jakarta @ Jayakarta, the victorious town (Batavia) too. On 22 November 1617 a ship from Jakarta sailed to Pulicat called The Gouden Leeuw and on 5 August 1619 another ship from Jakarta sailed to Pulicat called The Eenhoom. Thus direct shipping activities had developed between Jakarta and Pulicat. Adolf Thomasz, the Dutch official in Pulicat was ordered to remain careful while accepting the textiles from the merchants since several pieces of cloth were dyed with false dye. The Dutch factor in Pulicat was also requested to purchase red *beatilhas* and other textiles for Java, Moluccas and Tennaserim. When enquired about the details of three packets of clothes that were sent from Pulicat to Jakarta the Dutch officials were not in a position to state anything regarding the quality of clothes. In some of the goulongs, the red colour was found faded. Therefore Jacques Lefbrve, the Dutch official at Pulicat was urged to be very careful while accepting the clothes from the Tamil and Telugu merchants.[2]

The quality of Pulicat cloth came to be defined by the Dutch in terms of tightness and evenness of weave, thread count, uniformity of twist, alignment of warp and weft, degree of finishing applied and the use of a lead seal to designate that a cloth has passed inspection. The Dutch purchased *percalles* and *sarasse malayu* that were meant for the markets in Amboina and Makassar. 20,000 pieces of *percalles* were exported. A sample of 200 pieces of *salempores* had been also sent. *Palempores* textiles with the flowering tree type made their way to Indonesian markets. *Tapis sarass* costing 6½ to 7½ *pagodas* per 20 pieces were sent to Jakarta. These were painted very well and so fetched 30 to 35 rials per piece at Java. Pulicat weavers and artisans were unwilling to manufacture eleven types of textiles at the old price offered by the Dutch Company. Therefore the Dutch also increased its prices.

The Tamils and the Telugu Cloth Traders in Pulicat, 1614-1641

The textile trade of Pulicat was mainly in the hands of the *chettis* and *marakkayars*. They used to carry on a large scale trade all along the Coromandel Coast. They took sailing permits from the Dutch factor but their overseas trade was unsafe. In one case we find that the Portuguese had burnt two ships belonging to the *marakkayars* of Pulicat.[3] It is said in the Dutch records that the natives of Pulicat scrupulously followed the advice given by the Dutch to conduct maritime trade. Therefore it is stated that there was a lot of scope for development. De Haze, the Dutch official was interested to make available the ships of the Dutch company for the native merchants when they wanted to use it for their trade in 1614.

The Dutch took the help of many native traders especially the *chettis*. Chief merchant appointment was the Dutch innovation to conduct their textile trade smoothly. The first chief merchant of the Dutch was Achyuthappa Chetti. Dutch records mention Raghava Chetti at Pulicat was put into prison in 1627 because he refused to discharge his debts either to the Dutch company or to the merchants of the company. He had also managed to escape from Pulicat to Durgarajapattinam and placed himself under the services of the English seeking protection.[4]

Chinnana Chetti, the brother of Achyuthappa Chetti continued to help the Dutch in Pulicat. It is mentioned in Dutch records he was the revenue farmer and owned the right to collect taxes at Pulicat in 1644. He is also mentioned as a broker. It is also stated that the Dutch were his tenants and they paid taxes. It is learnt that Chinnana Chetti who was very powerful became hostile to the Dutch in 1645 because of some problem. It was at this time Lakshmi Chetti in Pulicat was appointed as the broker of the Dutch to help in their trade.

Various names of the *chettis* are mentioned in records. Malayya Chetti was a resident of Pulicat. Koeri Chetti is another resident mentioned in the dagregister of Pulicat in 1640-41. Chinanna Chetti also lived in Pulicat. They all had helped the Dutch company's trade in textiles. Their trading activities were confined both to urban centres and rural areas fostering inter-regional trade. The VOC had a chief merchant who arranged cloth for export and he was mainly held responsible by the Dutch. They gave money in advance to him and he distributed cash advances to the weavers to manufacture cloth. On delivery the balance was paid and settled. Commerce, conflict and competition became the order of the day among the Telugu and Tamil merchants. Fluctuating fortunes had to be spelled out in the event of the death of the chief merchant. The Dutch always found it difficult in textile purchases for lack of knowledge, language and expertise.

Role of the Chettis and the Marakkayar Traders: Textiles of Porto Novo, Nagore, Tranquebar and Pondicherry Exported to Banten: 1651-1681

It is well known that under Pangeran Rana Manggala (1608-24) the port of Banten in Java emerged as an international mart. Tamils and the Telugu traders in large number traded there by exporting cloth which was used for exchange of nutmegs.[5] A Dutch official was appointed in 1609 there mainly to direct trade. The *shahbhandar* and *lakshamana* in Banten were *chettis* appointed by King Rana Manggala.

Banten continued to receive its textile supply from the ports of Coromandel. Abdul Fath Abdul Fattah Agerg (1651-82) the Sultan of Banten himself entered into business partnerships with the Coromandel merchants. The Sultan encouraged Bantenese traders and licensed them with permits to sail to the ports in Coromandel. He himself traded with his ships that sailed to Porto Novo, Pulicat and Nagapattinam. His commercial partners were the *marakkayars* who acted as textile agents in the Coromandel Coast. This had facilitated the development of textile trade. Dutch free burghers at this time therefore came to Banten to buy the Coromandel cloth. In 1663 Bantenese market was short of the textiles of Coromandel as the cargoes were sold away. In 1667 A new ship built by the Sultan at Renbag sailed to Coromandel. It returned with adequate quantity of cloth that was required for sale in Banten. Many Coromandel merchants began to stay in Banten since 1670 and they did not return to the Tamil Coast, but their family members continued sail and conduct trade from Coromandel to Banten in the subsequent period. The Sultan of Banten sold his ship to a trader from Porto Novo called Naina Marakkayar in 1675. The *shahbhandar* in Banten appointed was Sulaiman Dawood in 1682.

Table 1
Recorded Shipping from the Ports of Coromandel to Banten, 1675-81

Name of the Port	1675	1676	1681
Porto Novo	4	1	1
Nagore and Tranquebar	4	1	1
Pondicherry	-	-	2

Table 2
Recorded Shipping from Banten to the Ports of Coromandel, 1675-81

Name of the Port	1675	1676	1681
Porto Novo	1	6	1
Nagore and Tranquebar	4	1	-

The *Marakkayars* of Nagore extensively participated in the textile trade. They sent their textile cargos in the ships that sailed from the Danish port of Tranquebar. The Portuguese ship owners at Porto Novo also took the bales of textiles of these private traders in their ships to Banten. Some of the *Marakkayars* of Porto Novo took the help of the French in Pondicherry and they exported textiles to Banten in the ships that sailed from Pondicherry. Mohammed Lebbai the trader of Porto Novo became the business agent of the Sultan in Banten. He was also the agent in-charge of opium trade in Java. It is stated that he had six assistants and one such name found mention was Mohammed Nayinar Marakkayar.

Nagapattinam Textile Trade with Makassar and Jakarta, 1660-1701

Coromandel cloth was in high demand at Makassar and the Dutch used it for buying cloves. The VOC flooded the Makassar market with Coromandel textiles between 1645 and 1652. Textiles trade continued to flourish even during 1660-1662. The Dutch who wanted to have a monopoly over the trade in textiles and cloves approached the ruler for favourable terms of trade and they successfully accomplished it through the treaty of Bangaya signed in November 1667. Sultan Hansanuddin at that time was compelled to agree to expel all non-Dutch traders from his kingdom. The cloth exported from Pulicat in Coromandel had to be sold only the VOC there.

The *dagregister* of Jakarta reports that the Dutch exported many varieties of textiles from the Tamil Coast to Jakarta. The Indonesian and Malay traders flocked there to purchase these textiles from the Dutch in Jakarta. They exchanged many varieties of goods. The proportion of textiles in the total value of the cargo in Jakarta sent out by the Indonesian and Malay traders went on increasing between 1659 and 1673. The Dutch mainly exported (*guinees lijnwaad*) guinee cloth from Coromandel to Jakarta. It was mainly used for the slaves.

The Dutch continued to export textiles from Coromandel to Jakarta with the exception of the years 1691 and 1697. The value of textiles exported during the 1690s approximated a million *florins*. Later we find textile exports had increased to 1.7 million *florins* in 1701. An important feature characterizing the development was due to the growing shift in the area of textile procurement by the Dutch from Pulicat to Devanampattinam, Porto Novo and Nagapattinam where cloth was at low price and in abundance. Further, textile markets in the Coromandel hinterland such as Salem and Thanjavur provided a large proportion of textiles. The textile investment in these two places by the Dutch was reported to have been 1.4 million florins. It is also mentioned that the Dutch had invested 1.7 million florins in other areas under their direct supervision in the Coromandel Coast for the supply of textiles. But the total supplies that the Company was able to get hold of were still considerably short of the orders.

Import of Bullion into the Coromandel by the Dutch, 1618-1704

The monetary system of the Coromandel Coast in the Sixteenth Century remained firmly based on gold.[6] There was no financial crunch in Coromandel at that time without supply of silver. The standard coin was the *pagoda* (52.40 grains) that had the image of Vishnu on the obverse. The *pagoda*'s subsidiary coins were the half *pagoda* and the *panam* (five grains) in gold. The latter was one of the smallest gold coins that had been heavily alloyed and used extensively for ordinary commercial transactions. A copper coin weighing between twenty five and thirty grains was in use known as *kasu*. A centrally controlled minting structure was absent under the Vijayanagara rulers who ruled the Tamil Country during the Sixteenth Century because the state favoured decentralization.

When the Dutch arrived at Pulicat on the Coromandel Coast they found that minting was free and it was open to anyone to go to the mint to get his bullion converted into coins at a very nominal charge. These charges amounted to about 5.6 per cent of the value of the coins minted. According to records the Dutch for the first time imported gold from the Netherlands to the Coromandel Coast in 1618. Gold that was received from the Netherlands by the Dutch in 1624 was sold at Pulicat at a profit of five per cent. The Dutch later understood that by minting gold in the local mints they could earn more profit and so the gold which was received from the Netherlands on 5 December 1625 was minted to pagodas at Pulicat and it rendered an extra profit of eleven to twelve per cent. On 27 June 1627 we find that 1948 ½ rials weight gold received from the Netherlands was also minted at Pulicat and a neat profit of 2680 florins was made. One Pulicat *pagoda* was fixed at eighty four *stuivers* as late as in 1634.

In the meanwhile the Dutch also began to explore the possibility of bringing gold to Pulicat from the ports of Asia rather than importing from the Netherlands. According to records Dutch ships sailed from Formosa to Pulicat on the Coromandel Coast for the first time in 1641 carrying gold. Coromandel thus received gold in bullion in Japanese *koban*. This gold brought to Pulicat in 1641 was also minted into coins and fetched a profit of three per cent to eight per cent. In 1641 the Shogun imposed a ban on the export of gold by the Dutch in Japan. The VOC therefore brought gold from the Netherlands to Pulicat. In 1652 the VOC imposed a new set of money conversion rates at which the rix dollar was made equivalent to only fifty two *stuivers*, the rial to fifty *stuivers*. It may be said that earlier a rix-dollar was equivalent to 2½ florins and one rial was fixed at forty five *stuivers*.

Gold in bullion in Japanese *koban* was imported by the Dutch to Pulicat since in 1664 ban on export of gold in Japan was withdrawn. But in 1668 ban on the export of silver came into vogue. As a result the VOC could not import much silver bullion to Coromandel. The Dutch Company began to obtain gold ducats from Persia at that time and it continued to import to Pulicat till 1696 when the gold content was reduced from 85.69 to 56.41 percent. The Dutch continued to import gold from West Asia and Japan to Coromandel. It must be mentioned that after the decline of the Vijayanagar Empire in the second half of the Seventeenth Century we find the emergence of several political authorities in the Coromandel Coast. Multiplicity of such political authority led to the opening up of new mints causing varieties of new coins. reflecting regional variations affecting the uniformity of coins in the region. However, the multiplicity of mints established along the Coromandel Coast and hinterland is an indicator of the growing volume of trade and the increasing need of money supply.

Japanese silver was called Schuitzilver in Dutch records and this was obtained by the Dutch partly from Japan and partly from Canton. As early as 1646 we find bar silver among the species which the VOC imported to Pulicat on the Coromandel Coast. In 1647 the Japanese silver bars and rials which were brought to Pulicat were sold to merchants.

Copper was imported by the Dutch from 1624 into the Tamil Coast and it was coined. The Dutch recognised the seriousness of copper coins exported from the Tamil Coast to Sri Lanka by the Tamil and Telugu traders in 1682. Therefore a regulation was issued on 3 July 1682 against the bringing of copper coins from the Tamil Coast. Almost 2.3 million ponds of copper bars were sold in 1683-84. It is reported that more than sixty per cent of the total gross profit in that year had originated from the sale of copper in the Coromandel Coast. It is calculated that in the Seventeenth century Coromandel received twenty six per cent of Dutch Company sales of copper bars. The view of Fernand Braudel that the great world depression of the Seventeenth Century had severely affected the flow copper to India and cowries temporarily took place of copper in the transactions may be called into question. We find the Tamil Coast not at all affected by the flow of copper and cowries were not at also used at all in the transactions.

Dutch Mint in Pulicat, 1647- 1696

The Dutch desired to obtain the minting rights in 1610 from the local ruler but it was only allowed to operate a mint in 1647 to coin *pagodas* in the fort Geldria at Pulicat. It was stipulated at that time that of the 0.75 per cent seigniorage on minting due to the government, the VOC was allowed a concession of fifty per cent on the metal minted on its own account and thirty three per cent on the account of the local merchants and others. The main currency was the *pagoda* which exerted a major influence on commercial transactions between the Dutch and the Tamil and Telugu merchants. Mints coining the *pagodas* had more or less a uniform standard. The subdivision of the *pagoda* was called *panam* or *fanams*, as the Dutch called it began to gain wide usage during the Seventeenth Century. The native mints brought out coins which were not always comparable in weight and fineness across the different mints and so the monetary system of Coromandel in the Second half of the Seventeenth century was more complex than any other region of India. The Dutch continued to produce coins at Pulicat when minting rights were again reconfirmed to them in 1657 by Mir Jumla. The coins were known popularly as Pulicat *pagodas* and they were widely used in circulation. The Dutch Governor of Pulicat in 1679 by beat of tom-tom forbade the traders and the public to circulate *kasu,* the English copper coins in Pulicat. The reason was that the English *kasus* were passed at forty two for one silver *panam* of Madras while the Dutch gave forty five *kasus* for one silver *panam* of Pulicat a higher value i.e., was equal to 1 1/4 *panams* of Madras. However, the Dutch copper coins *of kasu* had the same weight of the English.[7]

The VOC's profit by having *pagodas* minted in Pulicat was greater than the profit from silver in Bengal in 1680s. The pagoda gold coin in 1680s was rated at 120 light *stuivers* and a *stuiver* of nine quantity gold of 189 marks, five ounces and eighteen *engels.* In 1683 the company had changed the rate of conversion from 105 to 120 light *stuivers* for the pagoda. Japanese gold was brought in huge quantities to the Coromandel Coast and it is said that the Coromandel had absorbed 3.03 million florin in money and bullion between 1680 and 1685. In January 1687 gold brought by the ship's cargo that arrived from Melaka to Pulicat was minted and a total of 13,620 *pagodas* to a value 81,724 *florins.* It is stated that a profit of twenty nine to thirty four per cent was made. The Japanese in 1696 debased their silver and gold coins. The new debased gold *koban* contained less gold than the old ones but kept the same weight. This meant that *koban* which yielded a profit at the sale on the Coromandel coast now involved a loss of about fifteen per cent. Thus coins needed for advancing money to the weavers were met with from the Pulicat mint. The Spanish rial rate was fixed at fifty four *stuivers* in the Dutch settlements of Pulicat and Nagapattinam.

Dutch Mint in Nagapattinam, 1658-1704

The Dutch were allowed to mint gold coins called *varahans* (*pagodas*) and establish a mint in 1658 at Nagapattinam for three years. The profits of the mint were to be shared at fifty per cent of the usual duty between the Nayak and the VOC. In 1661 Vijayaraghava Nayak granted the privilege of coining silver *panams* and copper *kasus* besides gold coins for three years subject to the condition that the net proceeds of the mint were to be shared equally between VOC and the Nayak. It was again renewed in 1674. When Ekoji became the ruler in 1676 he granted the approval for minting the silver *panams* of 3/2 mattu current in Thanjavur and gold coins called *varahans* then in circulation by the VOC with the stipulation that net profits were to be shared equally.

The Dutch in 1690 approached the Maratha ruler of Thanjavur to permit them to mint Dutch coins such as guilders and stuivers for their trade purposes in Sri Lanka. This was also allowed by the Nayak but he insisted more coins needed for circulation in his kingdom in the Tamil Coast to be minted at Nagapattinam. This made the Dutch to mint gold, silver and copper coins then current in Thanjavur kingdom. Their mint records of 1694 furnish details including the cost of minting. It is noticed that Aariyappa, one of the Dutch Company's Telugu interpreter along with six others in Nagapattinam had been engaged in producing a large quantity of substandard *panams* in the name of VOC and they were caught by the Dutch. The VOC officials took stern measures to stop it and they also ordered for a thorough enquiry at that time. Some of them were arrested in this connection. In the records of the VOC we find the statement of deposition given by Vedaranyam on 26 November 1691 concerning the coining and issuing of false *panams* done at Nagapattinam. Another statement of deposition made by Periya Pillai on 8 December 1691 regarding the same issue is also found. However, the final report of enquiry and the outcome of it such as punishment if any meted out is not found mention in the records of the later period. Dutch records show that the Dutch continued to import gold and silver to Nagapattinam.

The Dutch used the coins minted by them for the purchase of textiles in the region and cash flew in to the weaving villages in the hinterland of Nagapattinam. During the period of 1701-1704 the VOC exported a total of slightly below 300, 000 *kobans* from Japan to Nagapattinam. This was chiefly needed because gold coins meant a supply of cash to Coromandel from where they needed to procure textiles for export.

Tapan Ray Chaudhuri opines that the Dutch carried Coromandel cloth valued roughly to one to two million Dutch guilders to Jakarta between 1620 and 1650 equivalent to ten or twenty tons of silver. Based on Ruurdje Laarhoven study we find that the Dutch exported textiles from Coromandel to South East Asia in 1641 to the tune of 3,57,000 pieces and Anthony Reid had estimated it to the value of 1,43,000 Spanish reals (dollars). But it is necessary to look into minutely the actual number of bales exported and the types of cloth purchased and profits made at each final destination than generalizing the whole. The VOC attempted to monopolise the supply of cloth from Coromandel to South East Asia and so transported volumes of textiles to Jakarta. The amount of cloth shipped from Coromandel to Jakarta dropped steadily from a peak of two million guilders worth each year in the 1660s to less than 8,00,000 guilders in the late 1680s. The reasons could be seen well in the Dutch records itself. The Javanese as early as in 1684 began to weave cloth by themselves and it was not only for their own use but also produced abundantly for sale in the local markets. The Javanese cloth began to appear for sale in the 1660s began to replace the Coromandel cloth in the markets of southern Sumatra. A Dutch record dated 8 December 1693 mentions that the Javanese who earlier bought Coromandel cloth for their daily use had stopped buying and only the elite cloth of Coromandel had continued to be purchase for the use of the wealthy in Java. The Dutch in order to protect the trade in the import of Coromandel textiles had commissioned in 1684 the Coromandel weavers to copy Javanese batik but the product turned out to be five times as expensive and it was of low quality. Further in 1686 the VOC continued to toy with the impractical idea and so it prohibited the import of bees wax into Java. All the attempts of the Dutch to monopolise the textile trade did not work out properly.

To conclude it may be said that as early as in 1603 we find names of twenty eight varieties of textiles exported from Santhome of Mylapore, Nagapattinam Krishnapattinam and Durgarajapattinam to Java, Jambi, Moluccas, Banten, Amboina and Seeram in South East Asia which had been mentioned in the report of November 1603 prepared by Stalpaert van Wide. However, in 1617 only seven varieties of textiles were exported by the Dutch in Pulicat.[8] In 1619 only six varieties by them from Pulicat to Moluccas and Java and in April 1631 eleven varieties were only exported. The Dutch in Devanampattinam exported only five varieties of cloth in 1618. It is significant to note that many varieties of textiles were not exported by the Dutch in Coromandel to Indonesia and the cloth varieties were very limited when compared to the earlier period.

As the Dutch made Jakarta the headquarters of the VOC the *Chettis* and the *Marakkayar* cloth traders avoided Jakarta and so they sailed in their ships carrying textiles from Porto Novo, Nagore, Tranquebar and Pondicherry to places such as Aceh and Banten the non-Dutch ports from 1651 to 1682. The Sultans of Aceh and Banten also encouraged these Tamil traders very much and so they even settled down with their families but conducted trade with their own families and relatives. These Tamil traders proved to be strong competitors in textile trade in Java and Sumatra. After the conquest of Melaka in1640 although the Dutch became a powerful force in the Melaka Straits yet they could not control and exercise monopoly over the textile trade. Various treaties signed by the Dutch with the rulers of Palembang and Jambi were only short lived. It is no doubt that since 1644 textiles were ordered from Coromandel for more than one crore and thirty lakhs value in florins to Indonesia, Dutch textile trade began to decline from Coromandel to Jakarta in 1680s. Local textile production in Java affected the Dutch trade and thus we find changes in the pattern of use of textiles also led to decline in textile trade from Coromandel to Indonesia. Textile demand to the Netherlands coincided with this development and so the Dutch exported Coromandel cloth to Europe.

REFERENCES

1. S. Arasaratnam, *Merchants, Companies and Commerce on the Coromandel Coast*, Delhi, 1980; Kankalatha Mukund, *The Trading World of the Tamil Merchant: Evolution of Merchant Capitalism in*

the Coromandel, Hyderabad, 1999, Tapan Raychaudhuri, *Jan Company in Coromandel*, The Hague, 1962; Sanjay Subrahmanyam, *The Political Economy of Commerce, Southern India, 1500-1650*, London, 1990; S.P. Sen, "The Role of Indian Textiles in South East Asia Trade in the Seventeenth Century", *Journal of South East Asian Studies*, Vol.3, No.2, September 1962, pp. 92-110.

2. Jan Pietrsz Coen, *Bescheiden ... op;cit,* Vol. II, pp. 304-305 (22 November 1617); See also, NA, VOC 1067, fl. 37.
3. NA, VOC 1066, fls. 170-17v, See the letter of Adolf Thomasz at Pulicat to the Directors in Amsterdam on 8 May 1617.
4. BL, OIOC, *Letters from India 1600 to 1694, Kolonial Archief Letters*, cclviii, dated 27 June 1627. The Dutch records are available from volume 32 to 86 of which up to 58 are in translations.
5. G.P. Rouffaer en J.W. Ijzerman, *De Eerste Schipvaart der Nederlanders naar Oost-indie Cornets de Houtman, 1695-1697*, The Hague, 1915, Vol. I, p.74.
6. Coromandel was a gold zone and silver coins of the nayaka rulers of Tamil country under the Vijayanagra empire had been very rare. There is only one example of a silver coin having been known so far. See, *Indian Antiquary*, Vol. XXV, p. 318. How far the Portuguese trade in the Tamil coast had affected the Tamil coinage system has been studied and it has been concluded that it meant no change. S. Jeyaseela Stephen, *The Coromandel Coast and its Hinterland: Economy. Society and Political System, 1500-1600*, Manohar, Delhi, 1997.
7. RFG, *Diary and Consultation Book 1679*, See the entry dated 16 October 1679. One English *panam* was equal to 36 *kasus* in the Dutch settlement of Pulicat. The English in Madras gave 42 *kasus* for one Dutch *panam*. Hence the English Governor forbade the traders to receive the Dutch *kasus* from Pulicat in 1679.
8. Naational Archief, The Hague, Mss. "*Memorie van November 1603 over den toenmaligen handel, voor name Sykmet lijnwaden, in Voor Indie, uitgezonderd Cambay en Chaul (Tjasel), op. het Maleische Schiereiland, en in den Maleischen Archipel*", under 'Kamer van Zeeland 4! G'. On the parchment is written, *'Artikelen ende instructien op de Schepen*'. The whole Memorie has been carefully reproduced in G.P. Rouffaer and H.H. Juynboll, *De batikkunst in Nederlandsch-Indie en haar gexchiedsnis*, Utrecht, 1914, Bijlage 111, pp. xi-xxv. This was partly published by J.K.J. de Jonge, ed., *De Opkomst van het Nederlandsch Gezag in Oost Indie, 1595-1610*, The Hague/Amsterdam, 1875, Vol. III, p.149. F.W. Stapel has used this Memorie in ex-plaining some textile terms in F.W. Stapel, ed., Pieter van Dam, *Beschryvinge van de Oostindiscke Compagnie*, 's-Gravenhage. See also Ishrat Alam, "A Dutch Memoir of 1603 on Indian textiles" in Irfan Habib, *Akbar & His India*, Delhi, 1997, pp. 294-297.

PART–III. MULTI-CULTURALISM AND RISE OF FUNDAMENTALISM

CHAPTER 10

The Colonial Experience of India and Indonesia: Some Comparisons

Prof. Aditya Mukherjee

This paper seeks to look at the Indian and Indonesian experience in the context of the economic impact of colonialism on these countries from the 16th to 20th century. I may mention at the outset that the revisionist view of colonialism which seeks to portray colonialism in a positive light has now once again become very fashionable. This is particularly true for countries which in recent years have been doing well, that is countries such as South Korea, Indonesia and India. Surprisingly, the view that is now being argued is that the current success of this region is closely connected with the colonial experience. It is suggested that it is the colonial opening up, which created the conditions for the economic take off in these countries.

A peculiar argument has emerged which tries to claim the credit for the current success of this region and India to their colonial past. By a virtual sleight of hand the two processes of globalization one under colonialism, between the 16th and the 19th century, and the other after the Second World War are conflated. The fact that in the colonial period there was an enormous movement of labour and capital, and an enormous expansion of trade is being conflated with a similar expansion. In fact in some ways there is an even larger expansion, of trade and movement of capital that was witnessed in the 20th century especially since the 1960s. No mention, of course, is made of the fact that in the later phase labour did not move as easily as it used to move in the early colonial phase or of the fact that the earlier process occurred under colonial hegemony for colonial purposes while the latter process was essentially mediated through independent nation states in a vastly changed global capitalist system.

The basic position argued is that colonialism had a positive impact on the colonies and that particularly the expansion of trade under colonialism was very beneficial for the colony and created positive initial conditions in the post colonial situation.

I have shown how the modern debate on colonialism got sparked of in the mid-19th century with the early writings of Marx.[1] In two journalistic articles written by him for New York Tribune in 1853, Marx talked of the *destructive* and *regenerative* role of colonialism. What Marx had meant was not that there will be a destructive phase and then a regenerative phase, an understanding which even R.P. Dutt had. For Marx they were a simultaneous process. The destruction of what (on the basis of knowledge available to him at that time) he characterized as the stagnant, unchanging 'Asiatic Societies' by colonialism would lead to their regeneration. In other words the understanding was that colonialism, however painful it may be (and Marx described the pain of colonialism very eloquently) *on a historical scale* it had a positive role.

This view Marx puts forward in one article in August 1853 and never repeated it. Subsequently, in whatever he wrote, including in late 1853, and very clearly in the first volume of capital in (1867) there was no question of his ever talking of the *regenerative* role of colonialism, instead he began to identify some key structural features of colonialism which played a destructive role for the colony. However, this one article was picked by people like Morris D. Morris on the Right and Bill Warran on the Left to argue that colonialism creates the condition for the development of capitalism, and they sight Marx for this position.

Marx himself gave up this position once he actually studied a colonial situation, that of Ireland. But I must highlight the fact that the early Indian Nationalists, people like Dadabhai Naoroji, Ranade, etc. were among the first in the 1860s to make a breakthrough in making a detailed, multi-pronged and sophisticated critique of colonialism at the same time as Marx, decades before Hobson, Lenin or Rosa Luxemburg deepened the critique of colonialism over nearly a century.

Let me at the outset state few major generalizations about colonialism widely accepted by its critics.

First, colonialism under-develops and it structurally disarticulates the colonial economy in a manner that, rather than facilitate the transition to capitalist development, makes the transition to capitalism more difficult. The point one in making is that it is wrong to assume that if one moved on the colonial path then one would eventually reach capitalism however slowly, in however restricted a manner. Colonialism and capitalism are not even parallel paths which can never meet. They are actually *divergent* paths. If you move on the colonial path then the shift from colonialism to capitalism becomes more and more difficult. The longer the colonial experience the more difficult is the transition.

Second, colonialism under-develops by appropriating surplus in all stages of colonialism. It is not as if some parts or some phases of colonialism are good while other parts or phases are bad. This in fact was often the self perception of the colonialists themselves in the later, the so called liberal imperialist phase of colonialism. They saw the first, the early mercantile phase of colonialism as grossly exploitative and claimed to bring in the second, positive phase under the slogan of a so called "modernization" programme (in Indonesia this phase came in the name of the 'ethical policy') which saw the establishment of railways, communication systems, etc., and other such 'benefits.' So convincingly was this position argued for nearly a century that even now some of our academics as well as political leaders reiterate this position.

Claiming to be liberal and fair they argue that while undoubtedly colonialism was very exploitative and took immense economic advantage of the colony nevertheless it left behind some *residual benefits* such as the railways, an education system, a modern bureaucracy, etc. There is a major fallacy in this understanding. The very *instruments* of colonial suppression and exploitation, the Railways, the colonial civil service, etc., which subverted modern capitalist development in favour of colonial structuring, cannot be taken as the 'residual' or partial' benefits of colonialism. The opportunity cost of failing to use the same resources alternatively, to suit the national interests of the colony, for over centuries of colonial domination is mind boggling. To relay the same railways now, a hundred and fifty later in a manner that suit the colony's interests would cost many many times what it would have a hundred years ago. As for the civil service, etc., India more than sixty years after independence is still trying to get its bureaucracy and police to act like civil *servants,* i.e., committed to the service of the people rather than as the exploitative rulers, a role they had performed in the colonial period.

Third, though colonialism appropriates surplus from the colony and under-develops it throughout all its stages, the *nature of surplus appropriation* may change over time and space. The mode of surplus appropriation is a function of a complex set of factors such as the specific need of the metropolitan country and the capacity of the colony at different stages of world capitalism over time. When, for example, in the pre-industrial revolution era, *labour* was the key factor of production in world capitalism, one witnessed either labour being transported away as slaves or indentured labour, or the produce of labour working in the colony being taken away for free. When, aided by the above transfers the process of industrialization begins in the metropolitan countries and *capital* becomes the key factor of production in late 18th and early 19th century one witnesses major transfer of capital from the colony, what we call the drain or tribute or unrequited transfer of produce of the colonial people, from the colonial empires to the metropolitan countries. This period also saw the capturing or monopolization of the colonial markets for the capitalist production of manufactures of the metropolitan countries. And, similarly, now when knowledge is becoming the key factor of production in the so called post industrial society what is being transferred is not labour or capital but primarily knowledge. That is why a country like India for nearly the last half a century (from the mid 1960s onwards) has been losing its top brains consistently. This is something that is globally seen. In other words, colonialism is not always the same thing. What is constant is that there is a transfer of surplus. The manner in which it occurs varies over time. It also varies between countries and that is what will become evident when we compare the colonial experience of India and Indonesia.

In both India and Indonesia the original colonial intervention occurs in the mercantile period, the early phase of capitalism when mercantile capital dominated in Europe from the 16th century onwards. This is not true of all colonies. Many colonies, like Egypt got colonized only in the 19th century. That is the early mercantile period is virtually missed out.

Indonesia got colonized much earlier than India. The Portuguese arrived in the early 16th century followed by the Dutch, Spanish and the English. The Dutch East India Company formed in 1602 seized control over Indonesia by the middle of the 17th century. The English East India Company on the other hand seized control over parts of India only in the middle of the 18th century.

The Merchantile Phase

The commonality of both these countries in the mercantile phase was that the colonial powers were interested in picking up colonial produce. They were at this stage not interested in the colonial markets. In both cases, originally the metropolitan country had nothing to sell to the colony in return for the colonial produce. When the Dutch came, or the English or the Portuguese came to Indonesia, they had nothing to sell. And that is where India came in to some extent. It was Indian textile from the Coramandal which would be taken and exchanged for the spices from this region. That is what would then be re-exported globally. In the Indian case, it was identical. There was nothing that the British had to sell in India. Therefore, India had been acquiring bullion in return for the textile and spices that was taken from India.

This situation was intolerable to the respective colonial masters in the long run, and therefore in both the countries one sees a shift from trade to tribute. Tribute from conquered territories now replaces trade. The element of exchange virtually disappears and there is constant pressure to acquire political control over larger and larger territories. Colonial commodities were now picked up for free or virtually free as tribute or payment for being 'Governed' or 'civilised'. However, how tribute was picked up varied enormously between countries. In the Indian case tribute was largely cash land revenue. The peasant had to pay land revenue in cash which was then used to pick up the colonial produce (textile, opium, food, raw cotton, etc.) which was then exported abroad. In the Indonesian case that was not the case. That is, it was not cash that was being demanded of the peasantry as tribute but it was either a substantial proportion of the peasant's produce or it was in the form of compulsory labour. The issue was not how the surplus was picked up but the fact of the surplus being picked up. It could be directly through labour charges, labour services or through produce or through cash.

Also, the commodity that would be picked up or exported from the colony to constitute the tribute could vary vastly between countries and change over time for the same country. It shifted from spices to coffee to sugar to oil and rubber in Indonesia and from textiles or cloth to opium (once Industrialized Britain did not want India to export cloth) to food, indigo, raw cotton, pig iron, etc. in India.

While comparing the mercantile phase of colonialism in India and Indonesia it is to be noted that though the Dutch East India Company which controlled Indonesia gets dissolved in 1798, nearly *half a century before* the English East India Company which controlled India is dissolved in 1858, yet in Indonesia this first stage type of colonialism involving direct appropriation of surplus where colonial monopoly trade essentially constituted the tribute, *continued for nearly fifty years after it stops in India.*

In Indonesia, monopoly trade continues till the Culture System introduced by Van den Bosch ends in 1870. After formally the Dutch East India Company was dissolved there was a brief, about fifteen year long, 'liberal' experiment when Holland was under French occupation, and Java under English occupation till 1815. This liberal experiment was tried intermittently and half heartedly for another fifteen years even after Dutch supremacy was re-established. The 'liberal' experiment involved changes like freer trade replacing monopoly trade and withdrawal of forced labour. The experiment did not suit Dutch interests as the chief beneficiaries of liberalization were the industrialized parts of Europe like Britain whose trade with Indonesia began to grow rapidly. Also, the tribute to Holland in the form of direct appropriation of colonial produce fell drastically.

The Free Trade, Industrial Phase

Holland did not experience industrialization till late into the 19th century. The industrialized part of Holland, which was Belgium, seceded in 1830 and therefore, for the Dutch, the primary interest from her colony, Indonesia, remained the mercantile stage interest of seizing colonial produce as direct appropriation of surplus rather than capturing the colonial market.

The Dutch therefore reverted to essentially the Company phase type of system though the Dutch East India Company was dissolved. Dutch monopoly control over what was produced in Indonesia, and what proportion of that produce was forcibly appropriated as tribute as well as monopoly trade in that produce was reintroduced through the NHM (Netherlands Trading Company) under the Culture System introduced by Bosch in 1830. Immediately the tribute, *Batig-slot,* which Holland could raise from Indonesia, shot up once again.

Indonesia, thus experienced a very short period of what has been called the second stage of colonialism where the industrial interest of Holland could dominate by ending the first stage type of exploitation. Within a very short period of the end of the first stage in Indonesia the third or the Finance Capital stage involving huge foreign investments was ushered in and it grew under the so called 'Ethical Policy".[2]

The Indian situation was somewhat different. Britain being the first Industrialized country had a very important and prolonged second stage interest of capturing and retaining the Indian market for its industrial produce and acquiring Indian primary produce in the form of food, raw material etc. A change was required from seeking only colonial produce to seeking colonial markets. This led to Britain whittling down the monopoly of the English East India Company's in the early decades of the 19th century much before it was formally abolished. The company after all exported textiles from India, precisely what Britain wanted to *import* into India.

The introduction of the so called "free trade" in India destroyed India's traditional industry and prevented the rise of modern Industry. Britain in this stage harvested not only the benefit of having a captive market and an agricultural hinterland but also appropriated surplus through the process of *unequal exchange* that occurs even when there is 'free' trade or exchange of commodities between countries with widely divergent productivity levels as the socially necessary labour time used in commodities produced by the colonial, un-industrialized, low productivity country is much higher than that used in commodities produced by the metropolitan, industrialized, high productivity country.[3]

The Financial Phase

Also, the third finance capital stage in India was different from Indonesia in certain respects. India did not receive large foreign investments as happened in Indonesia and many other colonies from the late 19th century onwards when the world witnessed the scramble for colonies and large foreign investments being made in the colonies. India was in fact a *net exporter of capital* to Britain. India fitted into the third stage of colonialism by enabling Britain to capture new colonies by providing men and materials and also by, to a considerable extent, 'funding' British investments abroad. It has been calculated that Indian tribute, i.e., capital transfers from India in the late 19th century helped Britain balance its balance of payment deficit with the rest of the world to the tune of about 40 per cent[4] when the British deficit was in part due to the huge investments it was making in the colonies at that time.

However, despite the differences in the manner in which the three stages of colonialism unfolded themselves in Indonesia and India it is very important to highlight certain common features witnessed by both the colonies.

First, the direct appropriation of surplus or collection of tribute, associated with the mercantile phase of colonialism, *continued throughout colonial rule* in both the countries even when subsequent stages of colonialism had come in critiquing the first stage and claiming now to 'modernise' the colony through building up transport and communication and foreign investments in other areas. In fact the size of the tribute actually *increased* over time. The tribute from Indonesia called *Batig-slot* which had fallen drastically in the early 19th century rose dramatically with the introduction of the Culture System. The massive Indonesian tribute to Netherland which had ceased in the early 19th century rose to an annual average of 18 million guilders between 1831 to 1877.[5] Another estimate put it at $ 8 million of tribute per year in that period. With the introduction of the 'Ethical Policy' in 1900 the tribute was said to have risen to $ 150 million per year by World War II.

The tribute or unrequited transfers were possible only if the colony had a consistent net export surplus. All colonies transferring tribute therefore necessarily had a large trade and a huge export surplus. In Indonesia, like in India, foreign trade and an export surplus grew dramatically even after the demise of the respective East India Companies. The export surplus in commodities was 5 million guilders in 1830 when the Culture System was introduced and it rose sharply to a peak of 64 million in 1870 when the system was ended. Thereafter, as a result partially of the excessive bleeding of the colony the export surplus (and consequently the tribute) shrunk to 57 million guilders annually between 1896 and 1900. Then with the launching of ethical policy in 1900 the export surplus (and the tribute) once again shot up from an annual average of 78 million guilders between 1901 to 1905 to more than 600 million guilder between 1916 and 1925![6]

The same can be seen in the case of India. The revenue (mainly Land Revenue) that the British could raise from India increased rapidly over the 19th century compared to second half of the 18th century and innovative ways were found to convert the revenue into remittance, first through a triangular trade with China and export of Opium[7] and later through a multi lateral trade with large number of countries involving export of agricultural and mineral produce from India..[8] The twentieth century saw a rapid expansion of the financial transfers from India to Britain which was facilitated by a growing Indian export surplus. The value of India's export surplus in merchandise increased by more than three times between 1871-76 and 1921-26 from Rs. 200.8 million to Rs. 617.4 million.[9] Thereafter the fall in the export surplus during the Great Depression years was fully compensated by massive exports of Gold from India to maintain the level of the tribute transfer to England.[10]

Second the tribute which took away anything between 5 to 10 percent of the GDP of the colonial countries[11] prevented the process of primary accumulation which was a necessary condition for the transition to industrial capitalism for any economy. Nine percent of the GDP of the British territories in India were drained out through tribute in 1801 when Britain was investing only seven per cent of its GDP as the first country undergoing industrialization.[12]

The tribute however played a critical role in the industrialization of the metropolis. It has been calculated that tribute from British colonies in Asia and the West Indies was 84 percent of British capital formation out of domestic savings in 1801.[13] Indonesian tribute led to an addition of around 8 per cent to the Dutch domestic product.[14] Thus, to the extent the Dutch and the English were able to appropriate tribute from their colonies to fund their process of primitive accumulation, necessary to make a transition to industrial capitalism, to that extent they did not have to do it on the backs of their own working class and peasantry.

Third, it must be pointed out that just as increase in trade and a growing export surplus did not benefit the colonies and was in fact a critical instrument of colonial exploitation similarly foreign capital that came in both in India and Indonesia also did not benefit the colonies. Foreign capital of the colonial period is vastly different in impact from the capital transfers that were seen in East Asia in the 60s and 70s which transformed the region. These are not to be conflated. While one occurred in a situation of colonial dominance the other occurred in the context of Independent nation states. Besides, the nature of world capitalism, including the nature of foreign capital had under gone substantial changes over this period rendering them incomparable in many respects.[15]

As discussed above India did not receive large amounts of foreign capital in the colonial period and was a net exporter of capital. The little capital that came, went in areas which strengthened the colonial structure. It went to Government borrowing to pay shortfalls in Home Charges or tribute, plantations, extractive industries, and transport etc. Less than 1 per cent of foreign capital that came to India before World War I went into industry![16] Even the capital that India received, for example in the building up of the railways, had their multiplier effect in the metropolitan country and not in the colony. The backward linkages of the railway investment went to Britain as virtually the entire investment had to be spent in Britain to buy steel, wagons, locomotives, etc. The forward linkage of the railways in the sense of what use it was put to, also went to Britain as it was used to carry raw materials to the ports and British manufactured good to the interiors.

In case of Indonesia, while she received huge amount of foreign capital from the late 19th century onwards its impact was similar. Most of it again went to export oriented plantation and extractive industries, with industrial investment being negligible. These investments helped create the export surplus necessary for meeting a rapidly growing demand for tribute. There were hardly even any external economies that occurred in favour of the colony as result of the massive foreign investments. Clifford Geertz has shown how a very highly developed, capital intensive foreign capital based sugar plantation sector could co-exist with a primitive rice cultivation system in the same region employing the same peasants, one having no positive impact on the other![17]

Conclusion

In both the cases of India and Indonesia despite a lot of growth of trade and even foreign flow of funds these countries emerged as poorer, disarticulated, backward, structurally colonial economies. (One must note that a movement along a production function which can occur with increasing trade etc. can occur simultaneously with the production function itself shifting inwards that is the overall economy shrinking). At independence, after centuries of so called benefits of colonial rule (what in India used to be called *Angrezi Raj ki Barkhaten*) in both countries industry contributed less than 5% of their GDP. They inherited distorted, unbalanced economies with little inter-sectoral exchanges occurring, say between agriculture and industry or between consumer good and capital good industry within the country and each sector being linked to the metropolitan country. It is this extroversion and lack of inter-sectoral exchanges within the economy which chiefly distinguishes a peripheral dependent economy from a core or central developed economy.[18]

In both cases the growth that we witness in recent years is not a function of what was left behind by their respective colonial experiences but of breaks from their colonial legacy. At independence both countries had similar problems to face. Whether it was Nehru or Sukarno, the first task was to unstructure colonialism so that conditions could be created whereby these countries could participate in the globalization process not merely as victims but as partners, who with the help of the independent national state could wrench major economic benefits for it.

Colonial structuring had meant as Angus Maddison's figures show that India which was the largest economy in the world contributing 25 per cent of the global GDP (more than eight times that of the U.K.) in the early 18th century was reduced as a result of 200 years of colonial rule to contributing a mere 4.2 per cent in 1950.[19] It is after several initial hard decades of colonial un-structuring done under the Nehruvian paradigm (not the wasted 40 years) that India is only now beginning to claw her way back into improving her share of the global GDP. The Indonesian experience after independence has followed a similar trajectory.

REFERENCES

1. "The Return of the Colonial in Indian Economic History: The Last Phase of Colonialism in India," Presidential Address (Modern India), *Indian History Congress, Sixty-Eighth Session*, 28-30 December, 2007, New Delhi, reprinted in *Social Scientist*, Vol. 36, Nos. 3-4, March-April, 2008 and in *Social Science Probings*, June 2008.
2. The Indonesian colonial experience is brilliantly detailed by J.S. Furnivall in two major works, *Colonial Policy and Practice*, CUP, 1948 and *Netherlands India*, CUP, 1939.
3. See Aditya Mukherjee, *Imperialism, Nationalism and the Making of the Indian Capitalist Class*, Sage, 2002, p.39 and Presidential Address, op.cit. and Michael Baratt Brown, *Economics of Imperialism*, Harmondsworth, 1974.

4. See Eric J. Hobsbawm, *Industry and Empire,* Harmondsworth, 1969.
5. Furnivall, op.cit.
6. See Amiya Kumar Bagchi, *The Political Economy of Underdevelopment*, Cambridge, 1982, table 4.1 p. 74.
7. See Irfan Habib, "Colonisation of the Indian Economy 1757-1900", in *Essays in Inidan History: Towards a Marxist Perception,* Tulika, 1995.
8. See A.K. Bagchi, *Private Investment in India1900-1939,* Cambridge, 1972.
9. Amiya Kumar Bagchi, *The Political Economy of Underdevelopment, Cambridge*, 1982. table 4.2, p. 89
10. See S. Subramanian and P.W.R. Homfray, *Recent Social and Economic Trends in India,* New Delhi, 1946 and Aditya Mukherjee, Presidential Address, op. cit.
11. Angus Maddison calculates the Dutch remittance from Indonesia during 1921-38 to be 10.6 percent of Indonesian domestic product adding 8 per cent to the Dutch domestic product. "Dutch Income in and from Indonesia 1700-1938" *Modern Asian Studies*, 23, 4, 1989, p.646.
12. Irfan Habib, op.cit.
13. Utsa Patnaik, "New Estimates of Eighteenth-Century British Trade and Their Relation to Transfers from Tropical Colonies in *The Making of History: Essays Presented to Irfan Habib, New Delhi, 2000.*
14. Angus Maddison, op.cit.
15. E.J. Hobsbawm, *Age of Extremes: The Short Twentieth Century.* Harmondsworth, 1994.
16. See Arun Bose, "Foreign Capital", in V.B.Singh, ed., *Economic History of India,* 1857-1956, Allied, Bombay, 1965, p. 494.
17. Clifford Geertz, *Agricultural Involution, The Process of Ecological Change in Indonesia,* Berkeley, 1963.
18. See Samir Amin, *Accumulation on a World Scale,* New York, 1974 and "Accumulation and Development: A theoretical Model" *Review of African Political Economy,* 1974.
19. Angus Maddison, *The World Economy: Vol. I A Millennial Perspective and Vol. II Historical Statistics,* OECD, 2006, Indian Edition 2007, Table 8b. p. 641.

CHAPTER 11

Evolution of Islam as a Socio-political Force in Indonesia (1500-1950)

Dr. Dilip Chandra

The scope of this paper is limited to the advent of Islam in southeast Asia, more specifically to Indonesia and its impact on the social, cultural and political life of the people of the area. An extensive discussion of this wide-ranging topic is beyond the scope of this paper and it is intended only to highlight the major developments during the period, i.e. 1500 to 1950. In the first part, the spread of Islam to the area is traced. The important point here is that Islam was spread in this area mainly by traders from the western coast of India initially, and it was the port areas that first came under its impact. Only gradually it spread to the interior, a fact that greatly influenced the nature and extent of its influence on the local populace The second part deals with gradual conversion of the masses through a slow process of acculturation. This was what gave Indonesian Islam its unique syncretistic character. Various Pre-Islamic traditions and rituals were allowed to be continued which helped a rapid conversion of the people The third important point dealt with here is the impact of modernist movements in Islam in the Middle East on the Indonesians that gradually led to the formation of different Islamic reformist organizations in the country and influenced the process of Islamization greatly in last two centuries.

Finally, the impact of colonialism or rather interaction with the Europeans (Christians) and the emergence of Islam as a political force has been briefly touched upon An understanding of the role of Islam as a rallying point is an essential pre-requisite for a proper comprehension of the political behavior of the Indonesian Muslim parties. In the final analysis, it may be stated that though the impact of Islam on Indonesian society was indeed deep and far-reaching, a certain continuity from the past, specially in the social life of the people, has ensured the prevalence of a very tolerant faith that seeks to compromise, rather confront other sets of beliefs and traditions. India, having a similar multi-religious and multi-ethnic population, has a lot in common with Indonesia, and together they could contribute greatly towards initiating dialogue among nations and be the voice of sanity that is urgently required in the present day strife torn world.

Advent of Islam

Historians are generally in agreement that Islam came to the Indonesian archipelago around the 15th century and its early torch bearers were traders from the western coast of India.[1] Trade contacts had existed between the ports ofthe Gulf area and China over the centuries, long before the advent of Islam. Malacca played the most vital role in this process and greatly influenced the spread of Islam in the whole region.[2] In fact it was the trader who was instrumental in spreading the new religion.[3]

As it happened in India, specifically in Gujarat, it was the rulerwho got converted first, and the masses took up the faith later, and this process was gradual. However, in the initial phase, the foreign merchants played a very significant role. They were not allowed to carry out trade without the permission of the native ruler and the main link between the ruler and the foreign trader was the *shahbandar*, who himself was often a foreigner, since his job required proficiency in foreign languages. So, once the trade passed into the hands of the Muslim traders, many foreign Muslims came to occupy the position of the *shahbandar* and thus became channels through which Islamic influence could be carried to the royal courts. They also introduced Muslim scholars in the courts of the native kings, who later played the most vital role in propagating Islam among the masses.[4]

Since the traders brought Islam to the region, it were the coastal towns that were initially Islamized. In the island of Java, some of these towns were Demak, Gresik, Tuban etc. However, the first island of the archipelago that felt the impact of Islam was Sumatra, where it arrived in the first quarter of the 15th century following the Islamization of Malacca in 1414.[5]

When the Portuguese eventually conquered Malacca in 1511, Islam had already made deep inroads into the archipelago. The Muslim traders who had been driven out of Malacca by the Portuguese, settled in the northern Sumatran state of Aceh which later became a leading centre for Islamic studies and subsequently the foremost Islamic centre in the whole region.[6]

By the middle of the 15th century, Islam had already spread to many of the northern ports of Java which were also important trading centers during the rule of the Hindu-Buddhistic Majapahit empire of Java. When Majapahit declined during the latter half of the 15th century, it came under attack from its recently Islamized vassals and eventually, power passed for a while into the hands of the Muslim kingdom of Demak.[7]

However, political chaos prevailed almost till the latter part of the 16th century till a new and powerful kingdom of Mataram emerged from the ruins of the Majapahit. The ruler of the new kingdom was converted to Islam and this greatly fostered the spread of Islam to the interior of Java.[8] So by the 16th century, Islam became the dominant religion in the region. However, the spread of the new faith from the coastal towns and royal courts to the interior parts of Java was a gradual and by and large peaceful process, carried out mainly through acculturation.[9]

Spread of Islam

As mentioned earlier, the process of Islamization of the archipelago specially in the interior parts of the islands, was a slow one and took several centuries.Some have opined that the process is an incomplete one.[10] Traditional sources like *Babad Tanah Jawi* mention that Islam was spread among the masses in Java through the efforts of Wali Songo (Nine saints)[11] They are called Wali (saint in Arabic) and Sunan (in Javanese). These saints were mostly of foreign origin, some of Chinese descent, others central Asian, Arab and so on. It is worthwhile to mention here some of the prominent ones, and specially the way they spread the message of Islam among the masses.[12] Some of the prominent ones are as follows:—

(i) Sunan Bonang (Raden Maulana Makdum Ibrahim).He was born in Tuban in 1465 and was of Chinese descent. He is said to have used the famous traditional Javanese orchestra-Gamelan and Javanese songs to spread the message of Islam.

(ii) Sunan Kalijaga (Raden Mas Said). Born in Tuban in 1460, he was one of the main disciples of Sunan Bonang and also used art and culture as his medium for preaching. His teachings were more Sufistic. Being very tolerant of local traditions, he followed a step by step approach to conversion and used the traditional Wayang Kulit, Gamelan, songs etc for this purpose. He is traditionally regarded as the most revered saint and carried deep influence among the masses in Java.

(iii) Sunan Ampel: He was father of Sunan Bonang and said to be the descendant of great Hadramaut saint, Ahmad Al-Muhajir, who had migrated from Basra. However some others claim that he was of Chinese origin and had come to Java in 1445.

(iv) Sunan Kudus (Jafar Shadiq).He was founder of Kudus and is one of the Wali Songo, who is said to be of Egyptian origin. He founded the Masjid of Kudus and also adopted the methods of Sunan Kalijaga for conversion. Buddhist-Hindu symbols were used by him, specially in the architecture of mosques and in rituals etc.

(v) Sunan Gunung Jati (Syarif Hidayatullah). Also one of the saints of Egyptian origin and was born in Java in 1448.

(vi) Sunan Maulana Malik Ibrahim: He was of Central Asian origin (from Uzbekistan), who is said to have arrived in Gresik in 1404 and was son of Maulana Jumadil Kubro of Samarkand.

These and several other saints, religious scholars were the principle agents of propagation of Islam among the masses in the heavily populated island of Java. As is obvious, they all had to adopt a conciliatory and accommodative attitude towards the prevailing beliefs and practices, which had existed since even before the Hindu-Buddhistic practices were introduced in the island. In fact Hinduism itself had earlier been accepted as one of the layers of beliefs and rituals in addition to what prevailed before it, suitably adapted to the age old beliefs and practices. Hence, when Islam was introduced, it too mostly meant taking on new names for the old ones.[13] The new religion, especially in Java, therefore, took on a syncretistic character as large number of conversions were achieved by showing essential similarities between Islamic and Hindu-Buddhistic beliefs and practices.[14] In many cases, an Islamic preacher would simply ask a gathering of people to recite the confession of the Muslim faith, and apparently no one seriously objected to it.[15] This slow process of Islamization was in progress when the Dutch arrived in Indonesia at the beginning of the 17th century. An external factor which had helped Islamization earlier was also the advent of the Portuguese in the region. The wars against them led many native princes to convert to Islam as it served as a rallying point for them.[16] This was true specially in places like Ternate, Aceh etc.

However, as explained earlier, at the social level, the progress of Islamization was quite slow and compromises had to be resorted to. This led to significant social and cultural differences among people of different regions. Java, specially has witnessed an intense struggle between the syncretistic and the orthodox Muslims ever since Islam was introduced in this island.[17]

Impact of modernist movement and Dutch policy towards Islam

The nineteenth century saw some major developments taking place both inside and outside Indonesia which had far-reaching consequences and a special bearing on Islam in Indonesia. First was the emergence of reformist ideas in Islam in Egypt, developed by Muhammad Abduh (1849-1905). The starting point of Abduh's thinking was the 'inner decay' of Islam and the need for its revival.[18] Basically, two schools of thought emerged under the impact of western civilization in 19th century Egypt. One was the old religious school which resisted any change, while the other was the modern school of thought that accepted changes.[19] Abduh sought to prevent any breach between the two schools by accepting the need for change (but not every change) and showing that these changes had been prescribed in the Quran. From this it followed that Muslims should first give up Taqlid (imitation) and try to understand Islam as it was understood before dissension had crept into it.[20] Abduh and his Syrian pupil, Rashid Rida founded the journal Al-Manar (the Lighthouse) in 1897, which served as their doctrinal organ.[21]

The Manar declared that true Islam accepted all progress for those who did not stand by the four schools of the Muslim Law.[22] In short, it started a movement to bring Islam into conformity with the modern scientific age. At the same time, it sought to extricate those elements from Islam which had come to be associated with it during the course of time and had 'confused the simple tenets of the religion.' Hence the call "back to the Quran". A number of Indonesians who went to study at the University of Cairo brought back these ideas with them. At the same time, the large number of Hadjis who went to Mecca for pilgrimage also became a strong channel of communication between Indonesian Muslims and their counterparts in the Middle East. Geertz maintains that with the increase in the number of Hadjis, "more orthodox practices and ideas began to penetrate the Indonesian Islamic community ..transforming it into something less.. 'indic'"[23]

The influence of militant Wahabis of Arabia on many Hadjis also helped strengthen Islam all over the archipelago in the 19th century.[24]

The second important development was the establishment of Dutch colonial rule in Indonesia and its impact on the socio-political life of the people. Though initially, the Dutch rulers followed a policy of non-interference in the social and religious activities of the people, subsequently they got more and more involved in it, specially during and after the 'Padri War' which has been even termed as the "watershed of Islamic modernist movement in Indonesia."[25] The movement took an anti-Dutch character after the colonial rulers intervened on behalf of the conservative Adat (customary law) followers in the Menangkabau society in West Sumatra.[26]

This was followed by other anti-Dutch uprisings during the 19th century in Bantam, Palembang, Banjarmasin and Aceh. These events led to the demand for an Islamic policy, since the number of Indonesian Hadjis continued to grow and in fact there was a regular "Jawah" colony in Mecca inhabited by the Javanese pilgrims. This fact was pointed out by Christian Snouck Hurgronje, the first Advisor in the newly created department on Arabian and Native Affairs in 1889. Hurgronje,who was the first Dutch expert on Indonesian Islam had a first hand knowledge of the Jawah colony of Mecca.[27] He confirmed that the Indonesian Muslims there took part in Pan-Islamic activities but also asserted that not all of them should be regarded as fanatical Muslims. He stressed on the need for the Dutch government to identify the moderate and the fanatical elements among them and also to be aware of every new development that took place there.[28]

Based on his theories, Snouck formulated his Islamic policy which was adopted by the government. This policy entailed a vertical division of Islam i.e., (a) religion in the sense of a personal faith and (b) religion which regulated social relationships among the followers of Islam. While the former remained free from governmental interference, the latter was not considered entirely personal and therefore complete freedom was not allowed in this sphere. The government reserved its right to interfere here, even by force of arms, if required.[29] In other words, Islam could not be left alone in so far as it had a political character.

Snouck Hurgronje's policy may have had a temporary success, but eventually it led to unfavorable consequences for the Dutch. Their pre-occupation with curbing Pan-Islamism led them to underestimate the modernist movement which was developing in Indonesia. At the same time, their efforts to create a class of western educated group who would support the Dutch colonial regime, led to just the opposite consequences. In fact the new elite later became the chief spokesmen for the Indonesian people in their demand for political freedom.

These significant developments in the 19th century had a direct bearing on the growth and development of Islamic organizations and parties around the beginning of the 20th century.

Growth and Development of Islamic organizations and parties

The socio-political impact of reformist ideas of Abduh and Al-Manar upon Indonesian Muslims was profound and had far-reaching consequences. This impact was felt both at the rural as well as the urban level. It was the Santri group in urban areas which was more influenced by these ideas. Clifford Geertz writes" while Islam in the countryside remained focused in isolated mosque-school complexes, a demand arose in the cities and towns for a wider and more closely knit religious movement which could harmonize new economic and political interests with an unadulterated Islamic tradition."[30] The economic interests of the traders led to the formation of the first Islamic organization, the Sarekat Dagang Islam (Islamic Traders Union) in 1909 by Raden Mas Tirtoadisurjo followed by another organization with the same name in 1911 in Solo, founded by Haji Samanhudi.[31] Though, the Union was essentially an economic movement, strated by Indonesian Batik traders to protect themselves against aggressive local Chinese competition, the word Islam subsequently proved to be the most important factor in bringing together all sections of the Islamic community on a common platform against the Chinese and later all Europeans. In 1912, the word "Dagang" was dropped and Islam came to assume greater significance in the newly formed "Sarekat Islam" under the leadership of Haji Omar Said Tjokroaminoto, a western educated employee in a Surabaya commercial firm from a noble family, who was also known for his anti-Dutch views.[32] The movement spread rapidly, and one of the reasons was the identification of Islam with nationality by many people.[33]

Another Islamic organization that came up was the Jong Islamieten Bond (JIB-Young Muslims League) founded by another prominent SI leader, Haji Agus Salim, in 1925. JIB included those western educated Muslims who had not been able to adapt themselves to the process of political modernization and gradually grew into a training school for providing an Islamic leadership, distinct from the 'secular' westeren—oriented Indonesian intellectuals.[34]

However, the impact of modernist ideas was nowhere more in evidence that in the Muhammadiyah (literally followers of (Muhammad), a socio-religious organization founded by a religious, Mecca-returned businessman from Yogyakarta, Kijaji Haji Ahmad Dahlan in 1912.[35] The organization drew its membership mainly from the middle class, the urban traders and to an extent also from among the rural traders. The Muhammadiyah emphasized the rational character of Islam. The two major factors that led to its rise were: deviation of Muslims from the real teachings of Islam and also the increasing Christian missionary activity in Indonesia.[36] Hence the Muhammadiyah, right since its inception, laid emphasis on the increase of knowledge and comprehension of the Islamic faith. Its main activities were in the religious, educational and social fields. So, 'purification. reformation and defence of Islam against external influence and attacks' were the main objectives of the Muhammadiyah.[37] Though the Muhammadiyah itself did not take part in politics, it left its members free to do so. Most of the Islamic leadership in the subsequent political parties in fact came from the Muhammadiyah.

An equally important Islamic organization which came up almost at the same time and in fact as a reaction to the ideas and activities of the Muhammadiyah was the Nahdatul Ulama (NU), which was founded in Surabaya in 1926, by two orthodox Muslim scholars (Ulama), namely, Kijaji Hashim Ashari and Kijaji Wahab Hazbullah.It was set up primarily to counter the rapidly growing influence of the modernists and also for protecting the traditionalists. The main aim was to defend the authority of the four orthodox schools of law (Madhahib) of Islam against reformist attacks.[38] The NU emphasized strict adherence to one of the four Islamic schools of Law (Indonesian mainly followed the Syafi school), the authority of which was questioned by the Muhammadiyah.[39]

Apart from this issue, the Ulamas were also regarded as the preservers of ancient traditions of Java, since they insisted upon keeping the old traditions intact. They accepted the incorporation of Javanese mystic elements in Islam. The Muhammadiyah did not approve of Muslims indulging in non-Islamic practices. Consequently; the NU movement has been regarded by many scholars as an effort to preserve the Javanese way of life.[40] In this context, it is necessary to keep in mind the high esteem in which these rural kijajis were held by the masses, especially due to their superior knowledge of the religious scriptures. Over the years, the Kijaji had come to acquire the top position in the social and religious hierarchy.[41]

At the same time, many of the Kijajis, over the years, came to possess considerable amount of landed property and engaged in agricultural trade. through which they became quite wealthy. Hence, they also felt a threat to their interests by the attack of the reformists.

However, the NU and Muhammadiyah, remained essentially socio-religious movements in pre-independence days and their main concern, though perceived differently, was the promotion of Islam in Indonesian society. They also served as rallying point for the Muslims against the Dutch during the nationalist movement.

Summing up the events of this period, it could be said that though Islam as a political ideology made itself manifest on several occasions, for most part, it remained dormant. The various Islamic parties and organizations came together for the larger cause of independence, and their inherent differences surfaced only after the country became independent. In between however, the Japanese occupation period (1942-45) saw Islam gaining ascendancy and also formation of federations, which served to further mobilize and strengthen the Islamic groups.

It has been observed that the period of Japanese occupation provided 'political articulateness to Indonesian Muslims'[42] Of course, behind this creation of political articulateness among the Muslims was the Japanese assumption that Islam could be used for mobilizing the local population to work for the Japanese war efforts. The keystone of the Japanese Islamic policy in Indonesia was to win over the Islamic leadership of all sections by offering them important positions, thereby enlisting the support of the masses. However, the Japanese authorities banned political activities and allowed only non-political Islamic organizations to function.[43]

The Islamic organizations had earlier formed a federation in 1937 in Surabaya, which brought the NU, Muhammadiyah and SI and later other Islamic organizations together to bring about unity among the Muslims, specially in face of the increasing Dutch actions which were perceived to be inimical to the interests of Islam. The number of organizations participating in it had risen to 21 by 1941. Now in the initial years of Japanese occupation, this federation, called MIAI (Supreme Council of the Muslims) was revived and its headquarters were moved to Jakarta.[44] In this way, the Islamic federation was able to keep itself out of the other federation, Pergerakan Tiga A, which was formed by the Japanese to enlist the support of all groups. The Japanese seemed to support the Muslim organizations against the nationalist ones, in order to drive a wedge between the two. The Japanese continued to make concessions to the Muslims in several ways, specially by honoring their important leaders. For instance, in 1943, Dr. Husein Djadjadiningrat was appointed as the Head of the Religious Affairs Office and Kijaji Mas Mansur as its adviser.[45] Later in the same year, Muhammadiyah chairman Hadikusumo was flown to Tokyo along with Soekarno and Hatta to be honored by the Emperor. The Religious Affairs office itself was expanded in mid-1944 and many Muslim leaders were appointed to key positions. Muslim leaders were also appointed in large numbers in important bodies like The Central Advisory Council etc. When eventually a volunteer corps for the defence of Java was formed by the Japanese in October 1943, the Muslims joined it in large numbers. Leaders of Muhammadiyah and JIB became senior officers in this body called PETA.[46]

By far the most significant development of this period from the viewpoint of Islamic organizations was the formation of the Masjumi (Consultative Council of Indonesian Muslims), which was established under the aegis of the Japanese in November 1943, after the earlier MIAI was forced to dissolve itself. Though its creation was a kind of victory for the Japanese, the Masjumi enjoyed greater prestige than its predecessor and also greater support from all sections of the Muslims. Its position was further strengthened after March 1944, when the Japanese Administration decided to create branches of the Religious Affairs Office. The Masjumi leaders came to occupy important positions in them.[47] However, all this happened under strict supervision and control of the Japanese.

Eventually, however, with the decline of the fortune of the Japanese in the Pacific War in early 1945, the Administration announced the formation of a Body called BPKI in March 1945, which was work out the details for the administration of an independent Indonesian state. The Japanese had no specific plan concerning the place of Islam in the new government, and in fact the secular nationalists stole a march over the Islamic organizations as 55 out of the 62 members of the BPKI were from among the secular nationalist groups. This was a major setback for the Islamic organizations which became evident during the first session of the BPKI which was dominated by the secular nationalists and where Sukarno propounded his concept of Pancasila (five principles) as the guidelines for the independent Republic of Indonesia.[48] In an elaborate speech on 1st June 1945, Sukarno spelt out the five principles which were based on Nationalism, Internationalism, Democracy, Social Justice and Belief in God[49]. Of these principles, Belief in God was the one, which later became the main point of conflict between the Islamic and the Nationalist groups. But at the time of the first session of BPKI, a sub-committee was formed under Sukarno to receive and formulate suggestions for the future Indonesian Constitution. There was heated debate in this Body regarding the basis of the new Indonesian state, i.e. whether it was to be Islamic or Secular. Subsequently, a joint meeting of the sub-committee and the BPKI was called on 22nd June 1945 where a nine member committee was formed to draft a preamble for the future constitution of Indonesia. Four of these committee members were from the Islamic group.

On the specific issue of Belief in God, a compromise was temporarily achieved by stating including the lines "Belief in God, with the obligation of practicing the laws of Islam for the adherents of that religion, in accordance with the principles of just and civilized humanity."[50]

The clause was deliberately left vague and nobody wanted to force the issue at a time when the Dutch were trying to re-occupy Indonesia. Sukarno's personal influence also helped shelve the matter temporarily.[51]

Islamic parties in the newly independent Republic of Indonesia

So, at the time of the proclamation of Indonesian independence on 17th August 1945, Islamic parties, though strongly organized, had not been able consolidate the gains that they seemed to have made during the Japanese occupation period.

The Masjumi was revamped in November 1945.Its first congress was attended by nearly all important Indonesian Muslim leaders of the day and it decided that it would be the sole Islamic political party with its headquarters in Yogyakarta.[52] It enrolled all political and non-political Islamic organizations of the pre-war days. The Masjumi declared its aims to be twin fold, i.e. to uphold the sovereignty of the Republic of Indonesia and to uphold the Islamic faith and realize Islamic ideals in the affairs of the state.[53] Masjumi wanted the establishment of a democratic government in an "Islamic society and state" and pleaded for early general elections.

The period of the Indonesian Revolution, ie 1945 to 1949,was marked by sharp differences between the leading Islamic party and the secular nationalists, supported by socialists like Sjahrir, who headed many of the cabinets. The Masjumi specially criticized what it perceived as the 'conciliatory attitude' of the newly formed government towards the Dutch. The period also exposed some inherent weakness in the Islamic community, when the PSII (partai Sarekat Islam Indonesia) broke away from the Masjumi in July 1947 in order to join the Amir Sjarifuddin cabinet.[54] This was because the PSII, though had joined Masjumi, had preserved its organizational structure as before. This example was emulated by the NU also in 1952, when it broke away from the Masjumi.

The period also witnessed the rise of the Darul Islam movement in 1948 after the Renville Agreement in January 1948.[55] S M Kartosuwiryo, who led the movement called the Agreement as a "betrayal of the people of Indonesia.." and urged the Islamic militant groups like Hizbullah and Sabilillah in West Java to continue resistance against the Dutch. Kartosuwiryo, erstwhile member of the Masjumi party left the organization and decided to carry out fight on his own in the Ciamis area of West Java.

Soon afterwards, following the Second Military Action by the Dutch, he declared 'Holy War' against them and in early 1948, proclaimed a Negara Islam Indonesia(NII) led by him. He called himself the Imam-Head of the State and created a Dewan Fatwa (Council for Decisions on Canonical Law), appointed Muftis (Judges) and constituted an Army called Tentara Islam Indonesia (Indonesian Islamic Army). The DI movement, though put down later on by the Indonesian Army (TNI) was significant in the sense that it promoted the idea of an Islamic state and in later years have also continued to motivate some sections of the radical Islamic groups.

By the time the Dutch finally left Indonesia in December 1949, the Islamic parties were still grappling with some of their inherent problems. The secular nationalists had consolidated their position in the government, and even though prominent leaders of the Masjumi like Sukiman and Natsir headed the initial cabinets, the Islamic parties were far from achieving the united front that they intended to project when the Masjumi was formed. Lack of western educated leaders, dissensions and also political opportunism frustrated the efforts of the Masjumi to build up the unity which was required to carry out its political struggle in the democratic system. They desperately looked forward to the general elections which were held subsequently in 1955. However, the Masjumi failed to emerge as the single largest party (since the NU which had got 45 seats, had already broken away from it). Even though the Islamic parties together got the largest number of seats in the parliament, they failed to put up a joint front due to their basic differences and also Sukarno's opposition to the Masjumi.

The fractured mandate meant prolonged controversies between the secularists (supported by the Communists) and the Islamic (mainly Masjumi) on several national and international issues.

The Constituent Assembly which also was elected during the election debated the issue of the new Constitution for three long years without being able to achieve consensus. The Islamic parties again failed to get their agenda implemented (ie of the state being declared Islamic) and eventually the Constitution of 1945 was adopted. Here again, the clause of Belief in God remained but God was mentioned as Tuhan Yang Maha Esa and not Allah. At the sametime, it also did not make it obligatory for Muslims to practice the Islamic Law, as had been earlier agreed upon. Frustration grew among the more radical elements in the Masjumi, which eventually led to the breakaway movement called PRRI, that was put down by the government and the Masjumi banned in August 1960.

Conclusion

An analysis of the growth and development Islam as a socio-political force in Indonesia since its advent till after independence lead us to certain broad conclusions. First and foremost is that the majority of Indonesian Muslims (mainly in the most populated island of Java) are syncretistic in their beliefs and practices and this has continued till date. It is perhaps the singe most important factor that has worked against the interests of those wanting an Islamic state or the imposition of Sharia(Islamic law) on the Muslims. The continued influence of the NU is a clear proof of the fact that the Javanese are by and large advocates of the "home grown Islam" which ensures a continuation of the Javanese way of life. The recent writings of an important section of the Ulamas, led by Kijaji Hadji Abdurrahman Wahid (Gus Dur as he is refreed to), erstwhile President of the country show that a large section of them actually feel that radical Islam is a threat to the unity of the nation. The Wahid institute set up by Gus Dur seeks to promote pluralism and the concept of a democratic secular state, which they feel is compatible with Islam.

Secondly, history and struggle of Islam in Indonesia, also reveals that Islam has always been a rallying point for the masses, and it is likely to remain so. In recent time, specially during the later years of the Suharto regime, most political agitations were backed by Islamic organizations. It has been observed that in recent years, the efforts of the political parties and organizations have been to create a state based on Islamic values which are of universal nature. No wonder, eradication of corruption is highest on the agenda of the new Islamic party, PKS (Partai Keadilan Sejahtera). Agitations have also been carried out against issues like gambling, pornography and so on. These are likely to continue in future too.

Finally, the activities of militant Islamic groups, which have raised many eyebrows in different quarters, deserve some mention. It is indeed true that some of the radical militant Islamic groups with international links have been active since the closing years of Suharto regime. This has been caused as much by the laxity and corruption in the political bureaucratic circles as anything else. It can also been seen that such militancy is not a new phenomenon. The history of the Darul Islam movement is as old as the Republic itself. However; it is also true that such movements are by and large rejected by the masses.

The new era of Reformation that has started in Indonesia since the fall of Suharto has witnessed a genuine desire by the people to establish democracy. The recent elections also show that stability and development, which are sought to be realized through a genuine democratic process, receive greater mass support than religious ideology. After decades of struggle, the Islamic political parties and organizations seem to realize that their best chance of realizing the 'Islamic values' in a majority Muslim state is through 'Musyawarah' ie Consultation and not Confrontation. If the current elections are any indication, one is likely to witness a period of greater cooperation among parties and less hostilities. However, the government needs to be more watchful and take prompt action against the militant groups in order to restore the confidence of the international community regarding future of secular democracy in Indonesia.

REFERENCES

1. For the details of Islamization of Java, see "*A History of Southeast Asia*" by DGE Hall, Macmillan Asian Histories Series, London, 4th ed. 1981, 1070 pp.
2. Java was converted in Malacca observes R A Kern. See *Ibid* 229.
3. *Ibid* p. 217.
4. B.Schrieke, "*Indonesian Sociological Studies*" (The Hague and Bandung, 1959), Vol 2, p. 238.
5. B H M Vlekke, "*Nusantara, A History of Indonesia*" (The Hague, 1959), p. 444.
6. See Hall, n 1, pp. 209-19.
7. See Theodore G Pigeaud and H J De Graaf, "*Islamic States in Java*". 1500-1700 (The Hague, 1976) p. 8.
8. *Ibid.*
9. See, Robert A Jay, "Religion and Politics in rural central Java", cultural report series no 12, *Southeast Asian Studies*, Yale, 1963) p. 120.
10. See Harry J Benda, "*The Crescent and the Rising Sun*" (The Hague/ Bandung, 1958) p. 9.
11. See Jay, n, 9 p. 6.

12. The information on Wali Songo is based on the writings of Ricklefs, "*A History of modern Indonesia since c. 1300*", Macmillan, London, 2nd ed.1991, pp. 9-10. Also see Mulyono, Prof. Dr. Slamet in "*Runtuhnya Kerajaan Hindu-Java dan tumbuhnya Negara-negara Islam di Nusantara*" Yogyakarta, LKis, 2005. pp. 86-101. yes.
13 See Jay, n 9, p. 713. See R Kennedy, "Contours of Culture", *Far Eastern Quarterly*, Vol. II, no. 1, November 1942, p.13.
14. See Jay, n 9, p. 7.
15. See The Voice of Indonesia (monthly, Djakarta) Vol. 3, March 1955, p.1.
16. See W F Wertheim, "*Indonesian Society in Transition*" (The Hague/ Bandung, 1964) ed. 2 p. 199.
17. See Ckifford Geertz, "*The Religion of Java*" (Illinois, 1960. sp pp. 126-30 for the essential differences Between the 'Santris' and 'Abangans'.
18. See Albert Hourani, "*Arabic Thought in the Liberal Age* (1798-1938)" (London, 1962. 403 p. see esp. p. p. 136.
19. *Ibid* pp. 137-38.
20. *Ibid* pp. 140-41
21. H.Lemmens "*Islam-Belief and Institutions*" (London, 1968). 268 p.
22. *Ibid*, pp. 212-213.
23. See Clifford Geertz, "Modernization in a Muslim Society: Indonesian case" in *QUEST* (Bombay) no. 39, Oct/Dec 1963, pp. 9-17.
24. Anthony Reid, "Nineteenth Century Pan-Islamism in Indonesia and Malaysia" in *Journal of Asian Studies* (Ann Arbor, Michigan USA) Vol. 26, No. 2, Feb. 1967, p. 272.
25. A H Johns, "Muslim Mystics and Historical Writing" in DGE Hall ed. "*Historians of Southeast Asia*" (London, 1961) p. 42.
26. See Taufik Abdullah, "*Adat and Islam: an axaminantion of conflict in Minangkabau*" in Indonesia, Modern Indonesia Project, Cornell Uni.Ithaca, NY, 2 Oct. 1966).
27. See C Snouck Hurgronje, "*Mekka, in the latter part of the Nineteenth Century's*" by J H Monahan (Leyden/London, 1931). sp. Ch IV, pp 215-92.
28. *Ibid* p. 291.
29. See Dr. W H Van Helsdingen and Dr H Hoegenberk eds "*Mission Interrupted: A Symposium*" (Elsevier, 1945) p. 97.
30. See Clifford Geertz "Religious Belief and Economic Behaviour in a Central Javanese town" in *Economic Development and Cultural Changes* (Chicago, USA) Vol. 4,1955-56, pp. 134-58.
31. See J S Furnivall, "*Netherlands India: A study of plural economy*" (Cambridge, Mass. 1944) p. 243-44.
32. See Deliar Noer, "The Rise and Development of the Modernist Muslim Movement in *Indonesia During the Dutch Colonial Period*" (Cornell Univ. NY, 1963) pp. 170-71.

33. *Ibid*, p. 7.
34. See Benda, n 10, p. 127.
35. For details, see Solichin Salam, "*Muhammadiyah dan Kebangunan Islam di Indonesia*, Djakarta, 1965.
36. *Ibid* pp. 56-57.
37. (Woking, England) Vol. 53, no. 2, Feb. 1965 p. 30.
37. See *Ibid* pp. 57-60. Also A Mukti Ali "Modernism in Islam in Indonesia" in *Islamic Review* (Woking, England) Vol. 53, no. 2. Feb.1965 p. 30.
38. B J Boland, "*The Struggle of Islam in Modern Indonesia*" (The hague, 1971) p. 49.
39. Bernard Dahm, "*History of Indonesia in the 20th century's*" by P S Falla (London,71,) p. 75.
40. See Boland, n 38. p. 50.
41. See Ken Ward, "The 1971 Elections in Indonesia: An East Java case study" Monash paper on *S E Asia, No. 2*, 1974, Monash Univ. pp. 90-113 for Kijajis role in the Pesantren.
42. See Harry J Benda, "Indonesian Islam under Japanese Occupation, 1942-45" in *Pacific Affairs Qtly*. Vol. 28. no. 4, Dec 1955. p. 353.
43 See Harry J Benda "*The Crescent and The Rising Sun*" (The Hague, 1958) pp. 74-76, 112 for the Details of the Japanese policy.
44. See, C A O Van Nieuwenhuijze, "*Aspects of Islam in post-colonial Indonesia*: Five essays" (The Hague, 1958) pp. 117-142.
45. See Benda, n 43, p. 136.
46. *Ibid* p. 139.
47. *Ibid* p. 162.
48. Occupation: 1944-45, *Interim Report Series*, SEAsia Prog. Cornell Uni. Ithaca, 1961 pp. 2-25.
48. *Ibid*, pp. 24-25 See Benedict R O'G Anderson, "Some Aspects of Indonesian Politics under the Japanese Occupation: 1944-45, Interim Report Series," *SEAsia Prog*. Cornell Uni.Ithaca,1961 pp. 2-25.
49. *Ibid*, pp. 24-25.
50. *The Indonesian Revolution: Basic Documents and the Idea of Guided Democracy* (Dept. Of Information, RI, Dec., 1960) p. 54.
51. See Anderson n 48 p. 174.
52. See Noer, n 32 p. 43.
53. For the details see *Ibid*, 44-69.
54. Kahin,G M, *Nationalism and Revolution in Indonesia* (Ithaca, NY 1970) p. 210. See *Illustrations of the Indonesian Revolution*, 1945-50 (Min. of Information, Jakarta, 1954. See Kahin, G M, *Nationalism and Revolution in Indonesia* (Ithaca, NY 1970) p. 210.
55. See *Illustrations of the Indonesian Revolution*, 1945-50 (Min.of Information, Jakarta, 1954).

CHAPTER 12

Problems of Multiculturalism in Southeast Asia—A Case Study of Malaysia

S. Utham Kumar Jamadhagni

The countries of South East Asia are multicultural in nature. However, there have been problems of policy and practice. Using Malaysia as an illustration the article looks at three instances that call into question the policy of multiculturalism in this region. Freedom of religion one of the basic guarantees in a multi-ethnic society has been undermined in the case of Lina Joy a muslim-converted to Christianity. The majoritarian policy of affirmative action unique to Malaysia subserves the interests of the minorities and the events that have led to the emergence of HINDRAF to protect their rights further throw light on the fissures that could divide a multi-racial society. The threat of fundamentalism and the process of islamisation could lead to further marginalisation of minorities plunging states like Malaysia into a vortex of violence. The article evaluates Malaysia with regard to lina respecting all cultures within its confines.

Introduction

Southeast Asia consists of the mainland and maritime regions with the countries of Laos, Cambodia, Vietnam, Myanmar and Peninsular Malaysia forming the mainland and the island countries of Brunei, Indonesia, Philippines and Taiwan comprising the maritime section. The countries of Southeast Asia like many countries in Africa and Asia boast of a multicultural mix of population.

Multiculturalism entered sociological discourse in the postcolonial period. It has come to mean the state accommodation of minority cultures differing in nationality, ethnicity or religion. J.S. Furnivall the British administrator and political writer identified the Southeast Asian countries as the most striking examples of plural societies.[1] However the process of assimilation is far from complete or peaceful. He was also of the opinion that Asian nationalism instead of bridging the divide within societies would only result in "pitting one ethnic community against another".[2] We would take a look at the state of Malaysia as a case in question regarding the issues related to multiculturalism as a policy in that state.

Malaysia is populated by Malays, Chinese and Indian immigrants with a little more than 50% being Malays and ethnic Chinese making up a quarter of the population and the Indians comprising nearly 8% of the total. The tribal people called the "orang asli" are mostly found in the Borneo island part of Malaysia in the provinces of Sabah and Sarawak. The British colonizers in the early nineteenth century brought the Indians as labourers to work on rubber plantations. The immigrant Chinese community flourished in businesses and this has been the cause for dissatisfaction among the impoverished Malays in the early years of independence leading to inter-ethnic riots. Though the state of Malaysia was declared a multicultural society with Indian and Chinese populations apart from the tribes, there are indications that it is leaning towards an Islamic set up. In keeping with the Orwellian tenet that 'some are more equal than others', Malaysia follows affirmative action for the Muslim Malays and other "indigenous" groups. The disparity in treating different sections of society could give rise to inter-ethnic and inter-religious conflict. But this has been tactfully avoided by Malaysian authorities through semi-democratic acts which possess a "distinct tilt towards the Malay muslim side"[3].

The dilemma was put poignantly by Yang di-Pertuan Agong Tuanku Mizan Zainal Abidin, 13th King of Malaysia, at his installation ceremony on 26 April 2007 when he said, "*I admit it is not easy for a multi-racial population to live in peace and harmony. Look around us. Not many are successful; more have failed. We must maintain this precious unity to the best we can.*"[4]

A multicultural society encompasses many religions, races and other distinctions that are accepted, recognized and respected by the state. In the case of Malaysia, the multicultural fabric has been called into question by the rising religious fundamentalism and the active government support in the way of policies that aid one section to the disadvantage of the other. This is being illustrated in this article using three examples. The first being the case of Lina Joy. The next is the "bhumiputera" concept and its associated issues. Finally, we look at the HINDRAF movement and how a multicultural state is being threatened by Islamism and other divisive tendencies.

Islam *vs* the rest

Azlina Jailani, a Malaysian Muslim converted to Christianity. She managed to change her name to Lina Joy in her Malaysian identity card (MyKad). However the religion was still listed as Islam. Her repeated attempts at removing the word "Islam" from her card proved futile. She made several applications between 1998 and 2000 all of which were rejected. When she sought legal redress there were more reversals. She lost the case both at the High Court (2001) and Court of Appeal (2005). Finally she approached the Federal Court where it was decided on May 30, 2007 that the word could be removed only after a certification by a Shari'a court (Islamic court) of her renouncement of the religion of Islam. The National Registration Department's interpretation left her with little to turn to. Thus, though the right to adopt a religion of one's choice is a constitutional right guaranteed by the article 11 of the Malaysian constitution, in practise it does not apply to Malays. On the other hand an apostate or one who abandons Muslim faith is punishable under Malaysian law with a sentence of three years in a faith rehabilitation center. The apostates could undergo an additional six years of "rehabilitation" if they don't show signs of repentence in the first place.[5] It is highly unlikely that any shari'a court would agree to a change of religion. Thus in this case, the "right to religious freedom" a principal tenet of multiculturalism as a concept, has been undermined.

There have been other cases where Indians have either converted to Islam or wished to abandon it just before death. This was time and again rejected and in some extreme cases they were buried as muslims even without the knowledge of their family. A case in point is that of M. Moorthy Muhammad Abdullah a Hindu who was the first Malaysian to scale the Mt. Everest died in December 2005. Claiming that he had converted to Islam shortly before his death, the Federal territory Islamic Council insisted on giving him a burial. The widow of Moorthy approached the Kuala Lumpur high court which ruled that the matter was not under its jurisdiction. There have been many other cases of alleged conversion of Hindus to Islam

This has brought into question the very basis – multiculturalism of the Malaysian state. It is seen by many as evidence of "how religious politics is cleaving a nation".[6] More worrisome is the fact that such judicial decisions "setting aside constitutional protection in favour of the sensibilities of Muslim believers"[7] can only strengthen the process of Islamisation that would threaten the very fabric of multiculturalism.

Affirmative action

The next issue is that of the concept of *bhumiputera* and the preferential treatment they entail from the state of Malaysia. The article 153 of the Malaysian constitution grants the king responsibility to protect the Malays and the indigenous peoples of Malaysia collectively called *bhumiputera* (Sanskrit for "sons of the soil"), a term coined by the father of Malaysia, Tunku Abdul Rehman. It allows for the establishment of quotas for *bhumiputera* in educational admissions, obtaining scholarships and even stock options in business. It is an unusual public policy in that the majority of the population benefit from preferential actions. The *bhumiputera* policy was intended to "redress imbalances in the educational and economic position of the ethnic Malays"[8].

The new economic policy or NEP which was based on the bhumiputera idea was introduced after the Chinese-Malay riots of 1969 aimed at restructuring society to reduce poverty. Some of the provisions of the NEP included a compulsory 30% equity share of bhumiputras in businesses. It was designed to increase their 2% share of the economy earlier. The NEP offered government construction contracts, approved permits (APs) to import cars and even real estate privileges.[9] The majority Malay community was further empowered by nothing short of a constitutional amendment in 1970 that termed any challenge of the terms of the affirmative action policy and the special status of the Malays a "seditious criminal offence".[10]

Though the policy was initially time-bound there have been at least two extensions. The finding of independent research institutes that the *bhumiputera* share of economy is much higher than the targeted 30% has met with government denial[11].

More and more evidence points to the fact that the policy has not benefited the native population, instead it has resulted in lack of efficiency and even corruption. The concessions in educational admissions have not led to increase in the employment of Malay students. It has also been reported that the Malay students do not choose employable subjects and rather stick to simple subjects.[12] The wealth is getting concentrated in the hands of a few while many languish in poverty. The incessant brain drain has resulted in qualified non-Malays including Chinese and Indian immigrants "migrating to greener pastures"[13]. Policies that have a strong Muslim and Malay leaning have been implemented – sometimes affecting the non-Malay and non-Muslim communities. Many government schools, and state-run colleges and universities have rules regarding dress code. These are in line with the precepts of Islam. For example, girls or ladies are banned from wearing short-sleeved blouses and hemlines must get lower than the knee; boys and even men are compelled to wear longs and track bottoms all the time during physical education lessons. Such practices "do not lend credence to the avowed stance of the government on multiculturalism"[14]. The former Prime Minister Mahathir Mohammed was among those who stressed that the Malays need to stop depending on preferential treatment to gain entrance in higher education.[15] Many Malays themselves wish to have a merit-based rather than a race based policy.[16]

Alienated Indians

The last issue in consideration is the indefinite detention of HINDRAF members since November 2007. The Hindu Rights Action Force (HINDRAF) is a coalition of 30 Hindu non-governmental organisations formed to preserve Hindu community rights and heritage in Malaysia. The Hindu community was alarmed by the "relentless destruction" of Hindu temples across Malaysia that took place over a period of six months in 2006. While the authorities cite construction rules and development projects as reasons for demolition, the Hindus fear that the increasing Islamisation of the legal process could mean undermining the rights of this minority.

The building of the Kuala Lampur-Damansara-Hulu Klang expressway has led to the demolition of the 60-year old Aum Sri Siva Balakrishna Muniswarar temple in Sepatak, northeast of the capital, Kuala Lumpur as it was found to be "in the way"[17]. The Hindu community was deeply disturbed at the destruction of more than six temples in a span of six months in 2006 and was alarmed at the 'unlawful and indiscriminate manner'[18] in which the demolitions had taken place.

Century-old temples that had come up even before Malaysian independence and have continued to exist for so long have systematically been demolished. The list of temples that have been erased from the Malaysian landscape include the Sri Ayyanar Sathiswary Alayam at Jalan Davies; the Malaimel Sri Selva Kaliamman temple in Kuala Lumpur; the 107-year old Sri Maha Mariamman temple, Padang Jawa – the oldest Hindu temple in Malaysia; Sri Kaliamman temple in Midlands Estate, Seksyen; and the Gangai Muthu Karumariaman temple in Kedah. These temples came up in plantation and settlement areas much before development of any proportion had taken shape in Malaysia. The incidents have galvanized the Indian community to protest against the destruction of their cultural heritage and more importantly has turned into an assertion of minority rights.

Beginning with a class action suit filed against the UK government demanding compensation for exploiting indentured Indian labourers demanding compensation and failing to protect minority rights, leaving them to the mercy of the Muslim Malay rule, the Hindu community began to express its displeasure and protest in a peaceful way. The government warned of dire consequences if the peace march was conducted. The HINDRAF leaders were arrested as a preventive measure under the Sedition Act a couple of days before they had planned to march to the British High Commission to hand over a petition to request the appointment of a Queen's counsel to fight their case.[19] In fact the then Prime Minister Badawi himself personally signed the order for the arrests. Riot police were pressed into duty. The participants marched with huge portraits of Queen Elisabeth II and Mahatma Gandhi to show their peaceful intent. In spite of a court acquittal on the grounds of lack of evidence, the HINDRAF leaders were rearrested under the draconian Internal Security Act on December 12, 2007. Their alleged links with the LTTE and other militant organizations were cited as reasons. Under this law, the detention could be indefinite and without trial. The detention without trial of the HINDRAF leaders has evoked criticism from around the world.

The ethnic Indian community went on to organise a novel march to the Malaysian Parliament to offer roses to the Prime Minister to exhibit their peaceful intent in February 2008 with children in the vanguard. However, the Malaysian government cracked down heavily on the peaceful march and used tear gas and water cannon on several hundred protesters.[20]

The latest development is the release of two HINDRAF leaders in the first week of April 2009 by the new prime minister Nazib Tun Razak "in a spirit of reconciliation".[21] However three other leaders still languish in prison.

The alleged neglect of the interests of Indians by the largest party the Malaysian Indian Congress (MIC) that is supposed to work for their cause is perhaps the most perplexing.[22] The demand for a change in leadership that has remained the same for more than thirty years and an increased focus on Indians and their rights and interests has become more vociferous recently. Over the years the leaders of the MIC have been accused of lack of unity, initiative and assertion on issues like language, citizenship and representation.[23]

Conclusion

These three examples illustrate the threat faced by multiculturalism in Malaysia. The case of Lina Joy brought forth the undermining of one of the most basic of human rights, namely freedom to choose one's religion. The very fact that a non-Muslim cannot present his or her case in a shari'a court cuts at the very root of justice. In addition, the constitutional guarantee of respect for all faiths is rendered void by referring cases to the Islamic court, which does not entertain the possibility of apostasy.

The effect of race-based affirmative policy that too for the majority has not paid much dividends. It has built a class of wealthy bhumiputera and diminished the chances of nourishing skills in the indigenous population by making them complacent with government doles and employment. This removes the imperative for capacity-building and produced unemployable people in a globalised economic milieu. Like in many other cases the policies cannot be terminated, as beneficial parties would resist it.

Finally, the blatant disregard for the rights of the religious sentiments of the minorities does not augur well for a modern democratic state. Demolition of temples – considered the symbols of religious beliefs – is sure to strike a discordant note. The move has been useful in bringing together the Hindu minorities under a single fold and struggle for a much larger cause than protection of religious rights. Repressive laws can harden the resolve to fight the system and resort to violence instead of peaceful means of protest and disagreement.

Contrary to the Malaysia's national motto of "unity is strength"; Malaysian multi-ethnic fabric seems to be under stress. It is now challenged by the forces of fanaticism and majoritarianism. The projection of Malaysia as a moderate Muslim country priding its multicultural background rings hollow in the wake of the above discussed illustrations. The governments themselves have moved away from defining Malaysia as a multicultural country to declaring it an Islamic state. The erstwhile Prime Minister Abdullah Ahmed Badawi promoted a theory of government based on the Islamic principles known as Islami hadhari (civilisational Islam).[24]

The attempt by the government to view Isalmic hadhari as an anti-dote to the tide of extremism as also to project Malaysia as a modern, democratic, tolerant and economically competitive Muslim country may be appreciable on the surface. However it has to counter the undercurrent of Islamic fundamentalism at home. Public schools are becoming more islamised. More women are wearing the headscarves. The influence of the *ulema* or religious teachers is growing. The muslim moral police also known as JAWI detain hand-holding couples and threaten "deviant" muslims to be sent to rehabilitation centers.[25] There has been tacit assistance to separatist tendencies in the region. Though there has not been any major terrorist activity in Malaysia, there have been reports of leaders of regional outfits residing in Malaysia.

Government policies to alleviate the conditions of the majority have only led to further alienation of the already suppressed minorities. The rise of Islamic fundamentalism in the Southeast Asian neighbourhood together with the process of Islamisation could soon destabilize the much-touted multiethnic social fabric. Violence and separatist tendencies could increase leading to stern government action, which could lead to a deadly spiral of force and counter force. The accommodation of the rights of non-Malay groups, the assurance of rule of law and not bowing down to the religious sentiments of the majority can restore the prestige and respect of Malaysia being a truly multicultural entity that could lead the way to progress and prosperity in the region.

REFERENCES

1. Robert Hefner ed., *The Politics of multiculturalism : Pluralism and citizenship in Malaysia, Singapore and Indonesia*, University of Hawaii Press, 2001 p.4 http://books.google.co.in/books?id=mhgzRW8NlfoC&dq=multiculturalism+in+malaysia&printsec= frontcover&source=bl&ots=xu6oZYdA QW&sig =LR3lNe_m3Jv22oShabNAweXeIA0&hl=en&ei=FlffSYLxHYK NkAXHn7DNCw&sa=X&oi=book_result&ct=result&resnum =9#PPA4,M1 (accessed April 10, 2009).
2. *Ibid* p. 6.
3. I respect your articles of faith - will you respect mine?, The *Guardian*, Feb 16, 2006, http://www.guardian.co.uk/world/2006/feb/16/religion.uk1.
4. As quoted in Timo Kortteinen, Islamic resurgence and the Ethnicization of the Malaysian State: The Case of Lina Joy, *Sojourn*, Oct. 2008. http://findarticles.com/p/articles/mi_hb3413/is_2_23/ai_n31059714/?tag=content;col1(accessed April 11, 2009.
5. Sarah Page, Malaysia: woman fights for right to convert, *Religioscope*, 21 Oct. 2004 http://religion.info/english/articles/article_110.shtml (accessed April 10, 2009).

6. Hannah Beech, Malaysia's crisis of faith, *Time*, May 30, 2007 http://www.time.com/time/world/article/0,8599,1626300,00.html (accessed April 10, 2009).
7. Angela Wu, Show of bad faith, *Wall Street Journal*, June 1-3, 2007 http://www.becketfund.org/files/c8589.pdf (accessed April 10, 2009)
8. William A.Stoever, Malaysia, the bumiputra policy, and foreign investors: An evaluation, *Studies in Comparative International Development (SCID)* Volume 20, Number 4/December, 1985 p. 86 http://www.springerlink.com/content/75933263517147h3/
9. http://www.observerindia.com/cms/export/orfonline/modules/issuebrief/attachmen ts/malaysia_1203067850658.pdf
10. N.Ganesan's Liberal and structural ethnic political accommodation in Malaysia in Will Kymlicka, Baogang He, ed., *Multiculturalism in Asia*, Oxford University Press, 2005 p.143 http://books.google.co.in/books?id =RW4krJ7SYvkC&pg=PA137&lpg=PA137&dq=multiculturalism+in+southeast+asia&source=bl&ots=IAYz33s-7h&sig=zEZ_2XxoZISb1BWOAQThDoF_lhg&hl=en&ei=T1ngSc-Problems of multiculturalism in Southeast Asia – A case study of MalaysiaL9WLkAWIrZ3XCw&sa=X&oi=book_result&ct=result&resnum=5#PPA136,M1.
11. For a detailed discussion on various estimates refer Peter Searle, *The Riddle of Malaysian Capitalism*, University of Hawaii Press, 1998 p.68 http://books.google.co.in/books?id=yBKFEea3nT0C&dq=Peter+Searle,+ The+Riddle+of+Malaysian+Capitalism,&printsec=frontcover&source=bl&ots=UGIn5uekmW&sig=5QjW5CkzxpLeX_ppKUzvEf8fcXI&hl=en&ei=lkJYSu_0LZb06AP0hrCVCw&sa=X&oi=book_result&ct =result&resnum=1.
12. http://avideditor.wordpress.com/2009/03/11/this-day-march-12/
13. Coscan Gant, *Different Approaches to multiculturalism* http://www.helium.com/items/696795-multiculturalism-in-malaysia-and-singapore (accessed April 11, 2009).
14. Chu Chin Wok, multiculturalism in Malaysia and Singapore, http://www.helium.com/items/1404098-multiculturalism-in-practice-the-malaysian-and-singapore-experience?page=2 (accessed April 11, 2009).
15. Stacy Wong, *Multiculturalism in Malaysia and Singapore*, http://www.helium.com/items/81482-multiculturalism-in-malaysia-and-singapore/print.
16. Poll shows most Malaysians want NEP to end, *The Malyasian Insider*, http://www.themalaysianinsider.com/index.php/malaysia/10233-poll-shows-most-malaysians-want-nep-to-end (Accessed July 11, 2009).
17. Vinay Lal, Multiculturalism at risk, *Economic and Political Weekly*, Sep 2, 2006 p.3765 http://www.sscnet.ucla.edu/southasia/Diaspora/IndiansMalaysia.pdf (accessed April 11, 2009).

18. 'Temples in Malaysia under threat', *Times of India*, June 11, 2006 http://timesofindia.indiatimes.com/articleshow/msid-1637380,flstry-1.cms (accessed April 11, 2009).
19. For a report see, Police arrest HINDRAF leaders, *The Star*, November 23, 2007 (accessed April 11, 2009) http://thestar.com.my/news/story.asp?file=/2007/11/23/nation/20071123123403&sec=nation.
20. Hindraf's 'roses campaign' thwarted, *The Hindu*, February 17, 2008 http://www.thehindu.com/2008/02/17/stories/2008021750180100.htm (accessed April 11, 2009).
21. 2 Hindraf leaders released by new Malaysian PM, *Times of India*, April 4, 2009 http://timesofindia.indiatimes.com/World/2-Hindraf-leaders-released-by-new-Malaysian-PM/articleshow/4358328.cms (accessed April 12, 2009).
22. http://thestar.com.my/news/story.asp?file=/2009/4/17/focus/3715464&sec=focus.
23. Rajeshwari Ampalavanar Brown's The Contemporary Indian Political Elite in Malaysia in Kernial Singh sandhu, A.Mani eds., *Indian communities in South east Asia*, Institute of Southeast Asian Studies, 2006, pp. 237-265 gives an excellent insight into the gamut of issues. http://books.google.co.inbooks?id=TeExjdWUmJYC&pg=PA237&lpg=PA237&dq=mic+and+indians+in+mal aysia&source=bl&ots=PULVGzHiQc&sig=rBe2774KBXGeW-KRf7hoQMIYO8M&hl=en&ei=5EdYSsCKG 4fU6QPU98CWCg&sa=X&oi=book_result&ct=result&resnum=9.
24. See Prime Minster of Malaysia's official website www.pmo.gov.my for a detailed understanding of the concept.
25. For a comprehensive analysis of the issue refer Ioannis Gatsiounis, "*Islam Hadhari in Malaysia*"in Hillel Fradkin, Husain Haqqani and Eric Brown ed., Current trends in Islamist Ideology, Vol.3, Hudson Institute, 2006, pp.78-88. http;//www.futureofmuslimworld.com/docLib/20060217_TRENDS3_complete.pdf (accessed April 11, 2009).

CHAPTER 13

Creeping Intolerance in Plural Societies of Southeast Asia

Prof. Baladas Ghoshal

History, geopolitics and millennium-old interactions with other peoples and their cultures have endowed Southeast Asia with a uniqueness that involved harmonious blending of different ethnic communities, religious groups, their customs, belief systems and practices allowing inter-ethnic and inter-faith coexistence. That is however changing in recent times under pressures of globalization, political compulsions and opportunism, and ideas and money flowing from the external world. This is particularly true of Islam, a religion of majority people in Southeast Asia. A fundamental transformation is taking place within the Muslim community all over the world – an identity formation based on a world view taken from early Quranic precepts and a code of conduct resembling a way of life that was prevalent in the Arab world in the mediaeval period in the formative stage of Islam. This form of identity is premised on an understanding and a belief that to be a true Muslim one has to be different from 'others' in every aspect of life and that there can not be a meeting ground between Islam and other religions. Adaptation of other customs, traditions and cultures in its path toward the expansion of the religion had only led to aberration and corruption of original and pristine ideas of Islam. It is only through the practice of mediaeval Arab traditions and way of life that the evil eyes of other religions can be kept at bay. Such a world view based on Arabization of Islam may not be the most predominant among the Muslims of the world yet, but is surely gaining slow and steady ground.

Fuelling this new Islamic identity is the steady process of transformation from a secular, inclusive and an adaptive Islam to a more textual, ritualistic and exclusive one by exogenous forces, as ideas, practices and finances flow from the Arab world. The transformation brings about conflicts – not only within Islam as to its correct interpretation and desirable way of life, but also among Muslims and others in otherwise tolerant and harmonious plural societies like Malaysia and Indonesia, where Islam once arrived, mostly peacefully, through trade. This process of homogenization or what I prefer to call "Arabization" of Islam emphasizes rituals and code of conduct more than substance and Islam's universalism. It stems from the "the Wahabi creed,".a rigid branch of Islam exported from and subsidized by the government of Saudi Arabia. Wahhabism is distinct in its destructive nature when religion is used by the state for political ends. Unlike other traditions that accommodate dissenting views, the Wahhabis claim to possess an undebatable version of 'true Islam". Arabization of Islam is a trend that somewhat obscure many Muslims from the real divine value of Islam.

Arabization of Islam

The use of the term 'Arabization' begs clarification. Since the original Muslims were mostly Arab, everything associated with them - their culture, names, and family structures - has been associated with Islam. But this presents a problem since the vast majority of Muslims in our current world are not Arab. There is not even an Arab monolithic form of Islam and culture. Some might even suggest that passing off Arab culture as Islam in this regard is inaccurate, exclusionary, and disrespectful of other Muslims' cultures evolving through a blend of religious and local traditions and customs. This is where my use of the term 'Arabization' gains salience. Everywhere in South and Southeast Asia, among the Muslim community there is a growing trend of imitating and replicating Arab cultures and customs to prove their true Islamic identity at the expense of their own rich syncretic cultures that allowed not only Islam to spread in the whole region but also harmonious inter-faith interactions.

Converts to Islam illustrate the issue poignantly. Having an Arab name makes one seem more "Muslim," because of the way Arab culture is seen as synonymous with Islam. In Indonesia, India and what is now known as Bangladesh it was quite common to find Muslims having pre-Islamic local names side by side with Arabic names. The name of the Indonesian prime minister during the Bandung Conference, Ali Sastroamidjojo is an excellent example of this blending. While there are still many Indonesian Muslims who have Sanskritized names, there is now an increasing trend toward naming younger ones with Arabized names. Another excellent example is clothing, which mostly affects Muslim women. The 'niqab' (the face-veil), also known as 'hijab', 'zilbab' or 'tuding' in Malaysia, was rarely seen outside of the Arabian world until recently. Most Muslims see the niqab as a byproduct of Arab culture. The urge for a Muslims to wear veils can be traced from a Quranic perception "to wear their veils over their bosoms". The prescription need to be understood within the socio-cultural environment. It was given at the time of Rasullulah, who saw Arab women wearing veils — not due to any religious motives but rather due to the harsh and dusty desert climate — but let their bosoms wide open. He then urged the women "to wear their veils over their bosoms." He was urging modesty, not necessarily a particular dress-code. It is only recently that the veil has been interpreted as religiously authentic instead of a cultural expression and therefore a must for all Muslim women. "What is troublesome about all this," to quote a

Muslim scholar from South Asia: "is that most Muslims who are non-Arabs complain that they're not seen as Muslims because they're not Arab (or ethnically Middle Eastern, in some cases). But when non-Arab Muslims take Arab names or wear Arab clothes under the guise of 'Islamic authenticity,' we're all reinforcing the idea that we're not really Muslims unless we have some link to Arab culture."

Arabic language has an important role in the diffusion of this process. James Coffman, while doing research in Algeria in the mid-1990s on differences between students schooled primarily in Arabic and primarily in French, found Arabized students seeing the world in a far more Islamic fashion than do their French-oriented peers. He argues that language inevitably imposes cognitive categories that force an individual into a particular symbolic order in thinking, communicating, and the ordering of his experience. Arabic's highly charged sacred character increases its coercive power, making it what Benedict Anderson, the renowned scholar from Cornell University, calls a "truth-language." Arabic is the language of Islam, the language chosen by God to speak to mankind, influences how a person perceives the world and expresses reality. This, in turn, has a profound impact on a society's outlook. Arabic and Islam are complementary and mutually reinforcing. Arabization and Islamization are inseparable parts of a single cultural ideal that now pervades the Arab world. In their drive toward authentification, and uniformization of Islam, the transmitters (Saudi Arabia and other Arabic countries) and the recipients (non-Arab Islamic societies) are equally emphasizing 'Arabization' as the norm of pure and ideal form of Islam to be followed by Muslims all over the world.

History of Islam in Southeast Asia

Islam's expansion into Southeast Asia came about only in the 1300's, some seven centuries after the death of the Prophet Mohammad in 632 A.D.[1] It rested on a relatively thin layer of Hinduism and Buddhism that local ruling classes had adopted one thousand years before from 600 B.C. to reinforce and legitimate their rule. However, the deepest layer in local culture was then and remains the traditional animist folk religion, strongly influenced by deferential superior-inferior feudal political culture. Islam went to Southeast Asia mainly from two sources: India where it had already undergone transformation moderated by its centuries of co-existence with Indian culture and was far more tolerant and easy going than the austere, ascetic, strictly observant and orthodox Islam that reached the region from Yemen and Saudi Arabia. Indian cultural influences reached much earlier than the Yemeni or the Saudi Arabian and formed the main thrust of religious customs and practices among the larger majority of Muslims in the region. Thus, the most appealing feature of Islam before the process of Arabization was its ability to blend with local traditions and practices, which gave it a syncretic and inclusive character, allowing tolerance and respect for other religions. Blending of indigenous beliefs and customs with Islamic faith allowed for the evolution of folk theatre, like the '*wayang*' shadow plays, drawing stories from the Hindu epics, turning them into indigenous traditions. Over the past three decades, however, the nature of Islam changed dramatically in Malaysia and to a certain extent in Indonesia *Wayang* was banned for a number of years in Kelantan under pressure from the conservative Parti Islam SeMalaysia (PAS); on the ground the stories are 'unIslamic'. Under popular pressure, the Wayang has been revised again, but with different stories, and using Islamic characters, shorn of its original flavour and appearing more a caricature of its earlier form. In Indonesia, the 'wayang' is still a part of the Javanese culture despite pressures from the more conservative Muslims. Indonesia's very diversity – in terms of ethnicity, culture and religious beliefs together with a fractious Islam – has allowed that country to practice secularism amid pressures from more fundamentalist groups to adopt 'syariah,' or Islamic law.[2] Yet Islamic orthodoxy and creeping intolerance towards other faiths are slowly taking root among the grassroots Islamic society in Indonesia.

Arabization of Islam

This process of homogenization or identity formation based on institutions, beliefs and practices that were associated with the evolving and expanding early Muslim community in Arabia in the years after the death of the Prophet seeks to rid all aberrations in Islam that came to be adapted in its century's long encounter with the customs and beliefs of other societies. In the absence of a better term, I prefer to call this process an "Arabization of Islam", a rigid branch of Islam exported from and subsidized by the government of Saudi Arabia. The use of the term 'Arabization' begs clarification. Since the original Muslims were mostly Arab, everything associated with them - their culture, names, and family structures - has been associated with Islam. But this presents a problem since the vast majority of Muslims in the current world are not Arab. There is not even an Arab monolithic form of Islam and culture. Some might even suggest that passing off Arab culture as Islam in this regard is inaccurate, exclusionary, and disrespectful of other Muslims' cultures evolving through a blend of religious and local traditions and customs. This is where my use of the term 'Arabization' gains salience. Converts to Islam illustrate the issue poignantly. Having an Arab name makes one seem more "Muslim," because of the way Arab culture is seen as synonymous with Islam. In Indonesia, India and what is now known as Bangladesh it was quite common to find Muslims having pre-Islamic local names side by side with Arabic names. The name of the Indonesian prime minister during the Bandung Conference, Ali Sastroamidjojo is an excellent example of this blending. While there are still many Indonesian Muslims who have Sanskritized names, there is now an increasing trend toward naming younger ones with Arabized names.

Another excellent example is clothing, which mostly affects Muslim women. The *niqab* (the face-veil), also known as *hijab*, *zilbab* or *tudung*, was rarely seen outside of the Arab world until most recently. Most Muslims see the *niqab* as a by-product of Arab culture. The urge for a Muslims to wear veils can be traced from a Quranic perception "to wear their veils over their bosoms". The prescription need to be understood within the socio-cultural environment. It was given at the time of Rasullulah, who saw Arab women wearing veils - not due to any religious motives but rather due to the harsh and dusty desert climate - but let their bosoms wide open. He then urged the women "to wear their veils over their bosoms." He was urging modesty, not necessarily a particular dress-code. It is only recently that the veil has been interpreted as religiously authentic instead of a cultural expression and therefore a must for all Muslim women. "What is troublesome about all this," to quote a Muslim scholar from South Asia: "is that most Muslims who are non-Arabs complain that they're not seen as Muslims because they're not Arab (or ethnically Middle Eastern, in some cases). But when non-Arab Muslims take Arab names or wear Arab clothes under the guise of 'Islamic authenticity,' we're all reinforcing the idea that we're not really Muslims unless we have some link to Arab culture."[3] Many Muslims held onto the past, even moving into that past, in a bid to protect themselves from a modern world that is difficult to understand. One way of coping with modernity has been moving to an Arabization of Islam Arabic language has an important role in the diffusion of this process. James Coffman, while doing research in Algeria in the mid-1990s on differences between students schooled primarily in Arabic and primarily in French, found Arabized students seeing the world in a far more Islamic fashion than do their French-oriented peers.[4] He argues that language inevitably imposes cognitive categories that force an individual into a particular symbolic order in thinking, communicating, and the ordering of his experience. Arabic's highly charged sacred character increases its coercive power, making it what Benedict Anderson, the renowned scholar from Cornell University, calls a "truth-language." Arabic is the language of Islam, the language chosen by God to speak to mankind, influences how a person perceives the world and expresses reality. This, in turn, has a profound impact on a society's outlook. Arabic and Islam are complementary and mutually reinforcing. Arabization and Islamization are inseparable parts of a single cultural ideal that now pervades the Arab world. In their drive toward authentification, and uniformization of Islam, the transmitters (Saudi Arabia and other Arabic countries) and the recipients (non-Arab Islamic societies) are equally emphasizing "Arabization" as the norm of pure and ideal form of Islam to be followed by Muslims all over the world. Hadith is the basis for the development of notions of shari'ah that are heavily influenced by early and medieval Arab cultural norms.

Emergence of Wahhabi-ism

At the heart of this transformation of Islam is the ideology of Wahhabism, a movement that seeks to return to what its adherents see as the purest form of

Islam, that was practiced by the Prophet Mohammed and the two generations that followed him. In practice, this means the rejection of unwarranted innovations (bid'ah) brought to the religion in later years. Wahhabism formed the creed upon which the kingdom of Saudi Arabia was founded. The primary doctrine of Wahhabism is *Tawhid* or the uniqueness and unity of God. Ibn Abdul Wahhab, the founder of the movement, was influenced by the writings of scholars such as Ibn Taymiyya and rejected medieval interpretations of Islam, relying on Quran and Hadith.[5] He preached against a "perceived moral decline and political weakness" in the Arabian Peninsula and condemned idolatry, the popular cult of saints, and shrine and tomb visitation. Wahhabism also denounces the practice of blind adherence to the interpretations of scholars and the blind acceptance of practices that were passed on within the family or tribe. Wahhabism is noted not just for urging Muslims to follow the religious duties of Islam, such as *Salah* but compelling them to do so. Like most Sunni Islamic fundamentalist movements, the Wahhabis advocated the fusion of state power and religion through the reestablishment of the Caliphate, the form of government adopted by the Prophet Muhammad's successors during the age of Muslim expansion. What sets Wahhabism apart from other Sunni Islamist movements is its historical obsession with purging Sufis, Shiites, and other Muslims who do not conform to its twisted interpretation of Islamic scripture. Wahhabism is distinct in its destructive nature when religion is used by the state for political ends. Unlike other traditions that accommodate dissenting views, the Wahhabis claim to possess an undebatable version of "true Islam". "Wahhabis breaks one of the cardinal rules of warfare in Islam – that Muslims should not fight other Muslims. The Wahhabis or the Salafis divide the world strictly into believers and non-believers who must be fought, writes John Esposito of Georgetown University. Arabization of Islam is a trend that somewhat obscure many Muslims from the real divine value of Islam.

During the 1970s, Wahhabi clerics encouraged the spread of this revolutionary and atavistic ideological synthesis into Saudi universities and mosques, because it was seen as a barrier to the threat of cultural Westernization and spread of corruption that accompanied the 1970s oil boom. Consequently, the royal family and their religious establishment looked for a cause with which to deflect the growing zealotry from Wahhabist theofascism, a danger highlighted by the seizure of the Grand Mosque at Mecca by heavily armed Islamic Studies students in 1979. The diversion that the royal family seized upon was the Soviet invasion of Afghanistan. According to Western observers like Gilles Kepel, Wahhabism gained considerable influence in the Muslim world following a tripling in the price of oil in the mid-1970s. Having the world's largest reserves of oil but a relatively small population, Saudi Arabia was in a position to spend tens of billions of dollars throughout the Muslim world promoting Islam, and in particular Wahhabism, which was sometimes referred to as "petro-Islam".[6] Its largess funded an estimated "90% of the expenses of the entire faith," throughout the Muslim world, according to journalist Dawood al-Shirian.[7] It extended to young and old, from children's madrassas to high level scholarship. "Books, scholarships, fellowships, mosques" (for example, "more than 1500 mosques were built from Saudi public funds over the last 50 years") were paid for. It rewarded journalists and academics who followed it; built satellite campuses around Egypt for Al Azhar, the oldest and very influential Islamic university. The financial power of Wahhabist advocates, according to observers like Dawood al-Shirian and Lee Kuan Yew has done much to overwhelm less strict local interpretations of Islam, and has caused the Saudi interpretation to be perceived as the "gold standard" of religion in many Muslims' minds.

An estimate by a former CIA director indicates that by 2005 the Saudis had spent some $90 billion to export Wahhabism globally. This is more than twice the estimated rate of $1 billion per annum spent by the Soviet Union on propaganda during the Cold War.[8] Much of this Saudi funding went towards the establishment of Wahhabi-dominated religious schools, colleges, and other social and cultural infrastructure, while in non-Muslim countries alone, the Saudis financed the construction of some 2,000 schools, 1,500 mosques, and 210 Islamic centers between 1982 and 2002. Saudi financial power also means that it can control key Muslim publishing houses, promoting Wahhabi texts and ensuring the suppression of Sufi, Shi'a, and other Muslim works now deemed non-Islamic. It also supports the training of imams and endowments to universities (in exchange for influence over the appointment of Islamic scholars). The lack of a formal ecclesiastical hierarchy within Sunni Islam renders traditional religious institutions weak in the face of well-funded Wahhabi missionary activities. Most Sunni Muslims look to their local imams for religious guidance. In poor countries, these imams and local leaders often find it difficult to resist the siren song of small amounts of Saudi aid that accompany Wahhabist missionaries in poor. Moderate imams do not have a comparable source of financial patronage with which to combat its spread. Predictably, precise information on the extent of this funding is difficult to obtain, but governments in the West are increasing pressure on Saudi Arabia to oversee, regulate and disclose information about the flows of financial support. Throughout the world, Saudi-backed Wahhabi groups control or dominate various major Muslim organizations. For example, the Organization of the Islamic Conference and its subsidiary, the Islamic Development Bank and related organizations have exported Wahhabi Islam to the rest of the Muslim world as well as to Europe and America.[9] The World Islamic League was a primary Wahhabi vehicle, exercising influence through such bodies as the European Council of Mosques and the Islamic Coordinating Council of North America.

An open manifestation of this trend towards Arabization in Southeast Asia is the way the Malaysians and Indonesians have adopted Arab greetings (*assalam aleikum*) in place of customary Malay greetings (*selamat pagi*-good morning). The Javanese, while adopting Islam in the 13th century had devised their own architectural design replicating traditional sloping roofs on mosques. Now all that has changed and one sees only Arab version of Onion domes on all mosques in Indonesia. Farish Noor, an influential Muslim scholar from Malaysia feels almost a sense of betrayal from the disappearance of such cultural manifestations. To quote him: "What irks me the most, and pains me considerably, is the loss of what used to be referred to as the Indonesian-Malay mosque. The Indonesian-Malay mosque – examples of which include the Masjid Kampung Laut in Kelantan and the mosques of Malacca – was once the norm for all the mosques of Southeast Asia. Furthermore they demonstrate their transnational character when we compare them to the Sinhalese Buddhist image houses (known there as Davatages) that are almost exact copies of the mosques of Malacca, Demak, Palembang etc. Yet today the traditional mosques are being leveled to the ground, to be replaced by Arab and Persian-styled mosques, or worse still the huge (and ugly) 'Petrodollar' mosques that we see all over the non-Arab world as well."[10]

Headscarves are slowly becoming synonymous with Muslim women's identity and a sign of pure womanhood. A Malay student of mine once told me she took to wearing the '*tudung*' (headscarf) not out of conviction but out of a fear that failing to do so might bring her a bad name as a woman of "loose character." Many men in South and Southeast Asia are also taking to Arab male dress of long robes to look more authentic Muslim. In Southern part of India, even a few years ago, one could not distinguish between a Hindu and a Muslim from either his dress or language. Once the Muslims from Southern India started going to the Gulf countries for jobs, many of them returned getting acculturated to the Arabic language, dress and customs, resulting in visual divide between the two communities. But unfortunately a push towards Arabization of culture is in evidence. So *Allah Hafiz* (May Allah protect you) is replacing the traditional *Khuda Hafiz. Khuda,* they allege, is Persian and is not equivalent of Allah. Pakistani newscasters now conclude the programmes with *Allah Hafiz.* Demands are rising in Pakistan to dislodge word *Khuda* from the national anthem.

In Malaysia, non-Muslims are concerned about the encroachment of Sharia law into civil law, particularly after the controversies surrounding the burial rights of M Moorthy, Lina Joy's conversion to Islam and the recent proscription of the usage of the term "Allah" amongst Christians. Lina Joy, a case that has become a battleground of Malaysian political and cultural identity, and of freedom of religion. The case highlights what some analysts believe are the Arabization of Malaysian Islam, a dynamic that can also be seen in Indonesia. Lina Joy tried to get herself deregistered as a Muslim and reregistered as a Christian. As a Muslim she is not allowed to marry a Christian man and any children she has must be brought up as Muslims. She appealed to the courts on the basis of Article 11 of the Malaysian constitution, which guarantees freedom of religion. Many Muslims believe apostasy - changing your religion - is not only a sin but should be punishable by death. A well conducted survey of Malay attitudes recently found that a majority of Malays think of themselves first as Muslims, rather than as Malays or Malaysians, the one civic identity that embraces all of Malaysia's races and religions. The same survey also shows that Malays tend to conceive of Malaysia as an Islamic state, and want it in the future to be more Islamic.[11] Similarly, while supporting freedom of religion, there is little community support for the idea that a Muslim has the right to change their religion. Malaysia's Prime Minister, Abdullah Badawi, himself an Islamic scholar, has pioneered the concept of Islam Hadari, by which he means a tolerant and inclusive Islam. But even Islam Hadari suggests a special role specifically for Islam in determining the constitutional relationship between the state and the citizen.

Fearing loss of religious freedom, non-Malay and non-Muslim religious groups have come together to demand that the Malaysian government protect non-Muslim rights. The demonstration organized by the Hindu Rights Action Front (HINDRAF) demanding the government to protect the welfare of the minority Indian community is a manifestation of such fears. Demolition of many Hindu temples in recent years is another concern of the Hindu community in the country. Such fears found concrete expressions in their attempt to reject the ruling the coalition and preference for the opposition parties in the recent elections in Malaysia.[12] In Indonesia, a few years ago, former president and influential cleric Abdurrahman Wahid suggested that Indonesians revert to customary greetings, and conservative Islamic leaders in Indonesia were outraged. This could be the tip of the iceberg for profound changes taking place in Islamic Southeast Asia and may have implications for other states throughout the region. Mr. Wahid in many of his writings often criticized Indonesians' incapability to embrace Islam within their own local tradition and the tendency of some to imbibe Arab attributes as a sign of inferiority complex. Wahid's understanding of Islam is something broader, deeper and better than the tradition-bound view of life imposed by traditional schools of Islamic law (all the more striking because Wahid is himself a leading theologian of the Shafi'i school). He attributes the orthodoxy in Islam as a function of Imam al-Shafi'i remodeling Islam by putting into place the mechanism of understanding everything through law [Shariah] in the second century of Islam, and to the teaching of Islam's traditional *surras* in the old way, which was rote memorization. To quote Wahid: "The teaching [suffered from] conventionalism. You were not allowed to go your own way."[13]

Even Indonesia society is slowly undergoing major transformation in terms of inter-faith societal relationships.[14] Not long ago, Indonesians of different faiths commonly participated in one another's religious ceremonies. Muslim clerics reportedly use "fatwas" against such inter-religious social mixing, even in offices. An Indonesian Christian businessmen narrated his bitter shock to me when, in mid-1990s, his Muslim employees suddenly broke with tradition and refused to appear with colleagues in a photograph for the company's New Year greeting card. While in Malaysia one cannot marry a

Muslim without conversion to Islam, such marriages were once common in Indonesia. Today, those marriages incur the wrath of the conservative Muslim groups. The goals of the most conservative Muslims in Indonesia are strict interpretations of Islamic law. Small numbers of them believe that they are called to fight the West in an ideological confrontation demanded by their interpretation of certain texts. These groups believe that the world is divided into two groups: the followers of Islam and the followers of Satan. They want *sharia* law because, they believe, life without it is worth nothing. Finally, they believe that all other beliefs are false. In numbers Indonesia's moderate mainstream - bolstered by groups like Muhammadiyah and Nahda'tul Ulema - dwarfs the radical fringe. Notwithstanding their small numbers, they were successful last November in preventing a liberal Egyptian Islamic thinker Nasir Hamid Abu Zayd of Egypt from addressing an international youth conference in East Java by putting extreme pressure on the Religious Affairs Ministry of Indonesia.[15] Abu Zayd was already in Surabaya, East Java, when he was told through an SMS by the ministry to stay away from the forum. A small minority can create havoc when the so-called 'silent majority' remains really silent for the fear of being branded as 'not true Muslims'. Since the Indonesian Ulema Council (MUI) issued its much-criticized 'fatwa' banning liberal concepts of Islam, secularism and pluralism hard-line Muslim elements have been pushing for the eviction of JIL, a cultural complex set up by progressive and moderate Muslims and headed by noted Muslim scholar Ulil Absar Abdalla, who himself received death threats for publishing articles criticizing the conservatism of some Muslim leaders in the country. For the past three years Indonesian politics have been roiled by an Islamist attempt to label anything they deem sexually arousing to be a form of "porno-action." Many moderate Indonesian Muslims see this as an assault on *pancasila*, Indonesia's secularist state philosophy from the time of its founding, as well as an assault on common sense. "[16]

The continuing violence in Poso in Sulawesi has further underlined the growing threat of Indonesia's Islamists. Far from being alien to Indonesian Islam, it is only the most recent in a long history of puritanical movements resulting from Saudi funding in its expansion in the 1980s and 1990s. As important as funding is the close communication between Indonesian Salafis and their Middle Eastern mentors, most but not all of them Saudis. It is no coincidence that leaders of most radical organizations in Indonesia, like Lashkar Jihad, (Jaffar Umar Thalib) and Front Pembela Islam (Islamic Defenders Front) Habib Mohammad Rizieq Syihab and Abu Bakar Ba'asyir, the spiritual head of Jemaah Islamia, are all of Arabic descent. Islamic radicals like these pose a direct threat to Indonesia's centuries-old tradition of tolerance and moderation. While the Lashkar Jihad has disbanded itself in 2002, the followers of FPI moves freely and mounts attack on anything they feel is against the strict teachings of Islam. The recent attack by the Islam Defenders Front (FPI) against pro-pluralism activists staging a rally at the National

Monument (Monas) in support of the Islamic minority sect Ahmadiyah, a Muslim sect that has its origins in India but now has followers worldwide, including in Indonesia, is one more instance of their crusade against any liberal and moderate discourse on Islam in Indonesia and the government's failure to protect the supporters of pluralism and soft attitude towards aggressive fundamentalist Muslim organizations in the country. Many noted Indonesian lawyers and rights activists like Todung Mulya Lubis believe that the government's decision to issue a decree in June last year banning Ahmadiyah was a constitutional violation. "Our law enforcement is too weak to punish those violating laws and the Constitution. The ban showed majority rule has prevailed over the rule of law," he said.[17] Commenting on the decree Masdar F. Mashudi, deputy chairman of NU, Indonesia's largest Muslim organization, said there was no basis in Islam to give a group's right to brand others heretical as no Islamic groups or individual could declare themselves the only truthful people.[18] Indonesia's leading English daily, Jakarta Post, was even more strident in its editorial on June 6, 2008: "Indonesia has officially stopped being the tolerant nation it has always proclaimed to be, especially when it comes to religion. The country with the world's largest Muslim population, one that has long prided itself for its diversity and peaceful coexistence between people of different faiths, is no longer a safe place, particularly for religious minorities. . . . This is the first time in the republic's history that the state, which proclaims to be neither theocratic nor secular, has interfered in the substance of the religion."

The first major challenge to the Indonesian style of Islam came in the 18th century, in the form of a movement to purify Islam by removing aberrations that had crept into the faith through local customs. A manifestation of this clash within Islam could be found in the 20th century Indonesia, in the division between the two Islamic political organizations, Masyumi and Nahdatul Ulama, the former as the advocate of purifying Islam and the latter supporting the blending of Islam with local traditions. When education was liberalized in the 1960s, more Indonesians studied abroad. Religious students went to the Middle East, where many studied Wahhabi and Salafi doctrines. Pakistani preachers arrived, offering strident Wahhabi interpretations of faith. Traditional locally trained "ulema," religious leaders, were in large part displaced or undermined by foreigners. The spread of madrassas, the conservative religious boarding schools funded by Middle Eastern money, throughout Southeast Asia has since confirmed the arrival of radical Islam. Even some "pondoks," or religious boarding schools in Indonesia, have also come under the influence of more extremist clerics. Islamists from the Middle East, Pakistan, Bangladesh and ex-Mujahideen have taken control of the mosques and madrassas radicalizing the discourses on religion and trying to win the hearts and minds of ordinary Muslims at the grassroots.

Secular dictatorship is also culpable. Other than the slow process of Arabization of Islam in Indonesia, over-representation of Christians in public positions during the Soeharto administration also contributed to the Muslim-Christian divide in today's Indonesia. In his attempt to clip the political wings of Islam, then Indonesian President Soeharto reduced space for democratic expression. Thus, mosques became the center for the expression of Islamic feelings and activities. But the diversity of Indonesian society did not allow the spread of a unified version of Islam, which could influence every Indonesian. Only a small minority of Indonesian Islamists espouses violence, but they have been very vocal and capable of attracting media attention and followers. A few cases of radical minority action like Bali bombing is enough for Indonesia to earn the distinction of hotbed of terrorism in Southeast Asia. This is more so because moderate Muslims had failed to silence radical groups taking over public spaces in the country. The majority's silence was caused by the pragmatic attitude of moderate Muslims and the government's failure to embrace them in countering radicalism and violence. But then at times of perceived threat, open-minded moderates and exclusivist fanatics close ranks and form united fronts of considerable clout, pursuing objectives that are not necessarily constructive. The rumor that Christian organizations were sending guns to the Moluccas to boost the Christian force in the raging conflict a few years ago swiftly mobilized the Islamic jihad and, people say, the moderate Muslims in the armed forces, too. Across Java, Christians complain of church burnings and intimidation by homegrown local militias. In Sulawesi three teenage school girls were beheaded as a warning to the Christian community.

As Muslims became more exclusivist and fundamentalist, the impact spread to other religious groups. After the Bali bombing, the region experienced a rise in Hindu rituals and evangelical Christian appeals. In recent years, a demand that Indonesian Muslims follow syariah law has resurfaced, despite having been dismissed by the country's founding fathers at independence in 1945. In 2003, seven districts had faith-based laws in place including bans on alcohol or women going out alone at night. Today, 53 districts, or more than 10 per cent of all Indonesian regencies, live under some form of Islamic-inspired law. More places are expected to implement similar initiatives this year. But the very diversity of Indonesian society did not allow the spread of a unified version of Islam, which could influence each and every Indonesian. A distinction needs to be made between those Islamic radicals who advocate an Islamic state and would like to see the followers of the faith to pursue an Islamic way of life, but eschew violence and terror in achieving their goals, and those groups that believe that end justifies the means and would not hesitate to make common cause with even international criminals.

Under the influence of Arab ideas and finance, even in countries like, the Philippines, Thailand, Cambodia and Myanmar Islam, which is only a minority religion and had an indigenous flavour in terms of customs and practices, has now assumed a much more conservative character. Stories about growing violence and appeal of radical Islamic ideology among the Muslims in these countries are daily news. According to Ziauddin Sardar, a South Asian

Muslim scholar based in the United Kingdom, many Muslims held onto the past, even moving into that past, in a bid to protect themselves from a modern world that is difficult to understand. One way of coping with modernity has been moving to "an Arabization of Islam".[19] Lee Harris, the author of "Civilization and Its Enemies: The Next Stage of History" explains Islamic fanaticism as a "defense mechanism," shielding Islam from the pressures of the changing world around it and allowing it to expand into territories and cultures where it had previously been unknown.

Apart from the impact of the Islamic revolution in Iran in the 1970s and the rise of the "Dakwah" (encouraging people to be Muslims by revealing the good of Islam) movement in both the countries in the 1960s and 1970s, this transformation of Islam in the region is also influenced by the globalization of political Islam. The internet has helped encourage uniformity of opinion in Islamic world. Transnational linkages facilitated by globalization and the revolution in information and communication technology spawned the emergence of such groups who believe in an ideology that any one who is perceived to be an enemy of Islam need to be annihilated. In the World Wide Web radical Muslims have found their most congenial method of communication. It satisfies their need for secrecy and concealment more effectively than any other medium, and allows them to transmit messages around the globe instantaneously. Al-Qaeda itself, as well as other terrorist groups such as Hamas and Hizballah, operates websites that not just to issue threats and other public statements, but to, in the words of the Net watchdog site Internet Haganah, "distribute official messages and communiqués; recruit and indoctrinate new members' communicate with forces that are distributed globally; and train in methodology and educate in ideology. *Maktab Al Jihad* (www.maktab-al-jihad.com), *Daleel Al-Mojahid, Jihad Unspun* (www.jihadunspun.net), *Clear Guidance*:(www.clearguidance.com)., *Islamic Awakening* (islamicawakening.com) are some of the Muslim radical websites that portray Islam under seize and call upon the Muslims all over the world to fight against its enemy and annihilate them.

Implications: social, cultural, political, economic

Many Muslims in Southeast do not fully subscribe to Arabization and view the rise of a fundamentalist form of Islam as a threat to their way of life and social harmony. In an international conference on 'Challenges facing the Muslim Ummah in the modern world', organized by the Hamdard Foundation, Pakistan, on September 3, 2004, Mahatir Mohammad, the former Prime Minister and architect of Malaysia's modernization and economic prosperity, declared: "There is nothing to say that Muslim societies and Muslim countries should recreate the life and the environment that existed at the time of the Prophet (S.A.W.) before it can be considered as Islamic or before it can survive and prosper," adding that Islam is for all times, not just for the Seventh Century of the Christian Era or the First Century of the Hijrah. The attempt to recreate the environment of the Seventh Century denies the relevance of Islam in terms of time and environment. It only weakens the ummah and renders Islam irrelevant except for the performance of religious rituals.[20] "Because of all these deviations from the teachings of Islam, because of the differing interpretations and the confusions that they cause, the Muslims have become backward, weak and unable to deal with the multitude of challenges they now face," he said. Not surprisingly one sees the emergence non-political Islamic groups, the so-called liberals and moderates, competing for influence among the elite and the students in almost all the Muslim countries in Asia.

While the battle for the hearts and minds are welcome in a vibrant society, the growing influence of Islam and the attendant communalization of politics in Indonesia have planted seeds of social turmoil that threatens world's largest Muslim country, Indonesia's stability and affect neighbours of Southeast Asia's largest country. Even if terrorism and violence are combated through socio-economic measures to deal with the root causes of poverty and social violence, and through gathering and coordination of intelligence, the very process of Arabization of Islam poses a threat to future social and political stability in South and Southeast Asia. As Islam undergoes major transformation at the grassroots in Malaysia and Indonesia, pressures for 'sharia' and introduction of more rigid Islamic way of life in these societies will mount further impinging on the character of the state and inter-faith relationships. If the character of the state changes from a plural and secular to an Islamist Indonesia, world's largest Muslim country, it will have far-reaching consequences not only on social, political and economic stability of Southeast Asia, but also on the strategic environment in the region with an Islamic Indonesia and Malaysia sitting on the mouth of the Straits of Malacca, controlling bulk of the Asian trade and commerce. That will tear the whole of Asia-Pacific region apart on religious lines along Islam-Buddhist divide. China and Thailand are two predominantly Buddhist countries in the region, which are facing challenges of Islamic extremism, the former in the Xinjiang province and the latter in the Southern part of the country. Both these areas border other Islamic countries.

Its economic impact on the region will be equally disastrous, for social instability will undoubtedly impinge on political stability and in turn on economic development. Asia Pacific's process of economic integration had been more a function of globalization and the activities of trans-national finance and production networks promoting intensity and regularity of intraregional processes than of regionalism growing out of conscious and deliberate attempts by national states to create formal mechanisms for dealing with common trans-national issues, alone. Social and political instability will drive the foreign capital, an essential element in the region's economic success and growth, out of the region, as is evident in Indonesia following the Bali bombing and other terrorist incidents in the country.

Conclusion

Arabization poses a threat to all Muslims who believe in Islam's divine character and universalism, and can be combated only by them. It is not a crisis between civilizations as Huntington would have us believe, but a crisis within civilization and need to be fought from within. Arabization's major appeal emanates from Islam's millenary expectations and the unfounded utopia of a just and prosperous society under Islamic rule. This is also fed by the silence of the moderates in the face of the more vocal minority trying to hijack Islam for their perverted gain. Christianity has passed through this phase and the contradictions between the sacred and the profane was resolved by separating the church from the state during the period of renaissance and reformation. If the powerful, modern, ideas of 'jehadi' Islamism are not met in the marketplace of ideas with an equally vigorous, contemporary, articulation of peaceful, syncretic and inclusive Islam, then 'the center of gravity' of public discourse will inevitably slide towards those ideas that appear most powerful and relevant to the modern world. The progressive interpretation of Islam developed by late Nurcholish Madjid and his friends, such as former president Abdurrahman Wahid in Indonesia, Anwar Ibrahim and Chandra Muzaffar in Malaysia, and Surin Pitsuan in Thailand, who is now the current secretary general of ASEAN, represent a powerful alternative to 'jehadi' Islamism. The need of the hour for the Muslims in Asia is to de-Arabize Islam from its exclusivist mould and promote a more inclusive Islam based on their own indigenous cultures and traditions blending with universal message of Islam, as were case in India and Indonesia in the period before the inroad of the Islam of the desert. There is also an urgent need for the moderates to break their deafening silence against tyranny of the small minority who are bringing shame and bad name to the religion and shed their inertia and fear of being branded as not 'good Muslims' by their perverted radical minority. In this project Indonesia and India, the two largest Muslim countries in the world, can make a positive contribution in projecting their composite culture manifested in Borobudur and Prambanan in the former and Ajmer Darga Shariff and Fatehpur Sikri in the latter.

REFERENCES

1. On Islam in Southeast Asia, see, Ahmad Ibrahim, Sharon Siddique and Y. Hussain (Comps), *Readings on Islam in Southeast Asia* (Singapore, Institute of Southeast Asian Studies, 1985).
2. Peter G. Riddel, *Islam and the Malay-Indonesian World: Transmissions and Responses* (University of Hawaii Press, 2001).
3. Fatemeh Fakhraie, "The Arabization of Islam," *altmulim*, 8 January 2008. htto://www.altmuslim/a/a/print/2648.
4. James Coffman, "Does the Arabic Language Encourage Radical Islam?" *Middle East Quarterly*, December 1995. http://www.meforum.org/article/276.

5. Hamid Algar, "Wahhabism: a Critical Essay," *Islamic Publications International*, Oneonta, New York, 2002; Also see, Rentz, George S. *The Birth of the Islamic Reform Movement in Saudi Arabia.* London: King Abdulaziz Public Library, 2004.
6. Kepel, Jihad, pp. 69-75.
7. Dawood al-Shirian, 'What Is Saudi Arabia Going to Do?' *Al-Hayat*, 19 May 2003.
8. Quoted in David E. Kaplan, "The Saudi Connection: How billions in oil money spawned a global terror network", *US News & World Report*, 12 July 2003.
9. John Esposito, *Unholy War: Terror in the Name of Islam* (Oxford: University Press, 2002), p.108.
10. Farish Noor, "Malaysia: Still Looking for an Islam to Call Our Own," *Malaysia Today*, 21 February 2008. http://mt.m2day.org/2008/content/view/3161/84.To quote him further: "If in the past Muslim preachers were happy to preach the universal values of Islam using an idiom and discourse that was replete with local cultural references, what we are seeing today is more than simply the Islamization of Malaysia: it is the Arabization of our Asian society."
11. Quoted in Greg Sheridan, "Death of Religious Tolerance in Malaysia," *The Australian*, 26 December 2006.
12. Dilip Lahiri, *Malaysian Indian Community: Victim of 'Bumiputra' Policy*, Issue Brief 12, Observers Research Foundation, New Delhi, 15 February 2008.
13. Quoted in Bret Stephens, "An Interview with Abdurrahman Wahid," *Wall Street Journal*, 7 April 2007.
14. Baladas Ghoshal, "The Rise of Extremism – Part II," *Yale Global Online*, 3 April 2007.
15. *Jakarta Post*, 16 November 2007.
16. See *Jakarta Post*, 8 December 2008.
17. *Jakarta Post*, 21 June 2008. A series of articles in the newspaper running throughout the month deplored government's soft attitude toward Islam.
18. *Jakarta Post*, 21 June 2008. "The fact that we must pray 17 times a day so that God can show us the right way tells us that no Muslims can claim they are already in the right," Masdar said. Muslim scholars and political observers said on the occasion that as major moderate groups, the NU and Muhammadiyah should have prevented the recent attacks by the Islam Defenders Front (FPI) against a pro-pluralism rally, and the subsequent issuance of a joint ministerial decree against Jamaah Ahmadiyah. Most commentators were unanimous in their assessment that moderate Muslims had failed to silence radical groups taking over public spaces in the country.
19. Quoted in Trisha Sertori, "Muslims should 'hold up the mirror', says writers in Ubud," *Jakarta Post*, 2 October 2006.
20. *Dawn* (Lahore), 4 September 2004.

PART–IV. ECONOMIC DEVELOPMENTS

CHAPTER 14

ASEAN—Prospects and Problems

Amb. Sudhir Devare

ASEAN concluded its 14th summit on 1st March, 2009 in Thailand and came out with a joint statement which, inter alia, called for a coordinated approach to deal with the current financial meltdown, stressed the need for reform of the international economic system while remaining firm against protectionism. The Summit which was earlier postponed due to the political disturbances in Thailand is the first one after ASEAN adopted its Charter in December 2007. The 42 year old regional grouping acquired the status of a full-fledged legal entity with the adoption of the Charter even as ASEAN declared its commitment to become a Community, a common market by 2015. ASEAN aims at evolving a Security, Economic and Social Community by this date. Clearly, the ASEAN leaders had in mind the ambition of moving in the direction of the European Union (EU), the regional grouping regarded most successful so far.

After four decades where does ASEAN stand on the path of regionalism? Is it a cohesive, well integrated grouping of countries of Southeast Asia or a mere conglomerate of countries loosely bound together by the considerations of expediency and convenience? Has the organization over the years made serious efforts to overcome the principal constraint of sovereignty? ASEAN has steadfastly supported the principles of sovereignty and non-interference in internal affairs. This has been brought to bear from time to time when there were bilateral disputes or serious violations of human security within an ASEAN country.

Last year, the dispute between Thailand and Cambodia on an ancient Buddhist temple located near their boundary brought the two countries to a military conflict. It was averted at the last minute; but the tension between the two countries on this issue continues to fester. Significantly, ASEAN itself could do little to bring the conflict under control. Indonesia and Malaysia had come close to an armed clash in the Ambalat Sea off Sulawesi over the question of rights for oil and natural gas four years ago. There are several bilateral issues among ASEAN members which remain unresolved that have the potential of disrupting peace and security in the region. And there is no effective mechanism within ASEAN (though the General Council has the powers, in principle) which can deal with such inter-state issues.

The question that is often asked even within ASEAN today is that can ASEAN find its reliance on 'consultations and consensus' adequate enough to address all intractable issues? If sovereignty or non-interference in internal affairs is going to be upheld in bilateral disputes, how can ASEAN aspire to become a security community? Hasn't ASEAN reached a stage after 42 years where it could dare to go beyond the norms of respect for absolute sovereignty and non-interference? If regionalism has to acquire credibility then the regional organization should have the powers to act for the unity and strength of the organization which could go beyond the interest of an individual member state.

As to the principle of non-interference in other's internal affairs which ASEAN has scrupulously followed there has been much criticism from outside powers and lately even from within. The Myanmar situation has become a test-case on this score which is often cited as ASEAN's inability to influence or shape the course of events in Myanmar where the pro-democracy forces have been put down by the military and the popularly elected leader, Aung San Suu Kyi detained for years. Of course, there are opposing views within ASEAN and outside as to the need to conform to the norms which the West regards as essential in regionalism. For that matter, the whole debate on 'Asian values' was centred on different perceptions towards human rights, freedom of expression, state role etc. Though ASEAN continues to adopt a neutral line on the Myanmar issue-as it did again at the just concluded Summit there is now a clear indication of discontent within the grouping over a fellow member state's refusal to defer to the winds of democratization and human rights protection that are blowing across most of ASEAN countries. It was significant that the ratification process of the ASEAN Charter was held up in the Philippines and Indonesia for several months where the elected parliaments roundly criticized the lack of clear and adequate provision in the Charter for some action in the event of failure of a member state to safeguard individual freedom and human rights. Human security is becoming a principal plank which ASEAN states are now stressing across their grouping. Setting up of a human rights body in the ASEAN by July 2009 is a key agenda item before them. Several issues such as migration, especially illegal migration at the intra-ASEAN level is causing considerable friction among the member states. Indonesian workers in Malaysia and Singapore, the Philippines maids in Singapore and Malaysia; Lao and Cambodian fishermen on the Thai trawlers and the current plight of the Rohingyas from Myanmar in Thailand and Indonesia are some of them. While the Thai authorities want the Rohingya boat people to be treated as 'economic migrants' , some others ask them to be regarded as 'refugees'.

Democratization in Indonesia has become an important element in the dynamic of ASEAN. Indonesia, the largest country (nearly half the population of ASEAN) has been regarded as a leader of this regional grouping. The advent of democracy in 1998 and subsequent stability and relative peace is leading to a further assessment of Indonesia's role in ASEAN. Some thinkers in that country are also asking if Indonesia shouldn't be playing a larger role beyond ASEAN. Indonesia is now a member of G-20. The country has had a peaceful democratic election this year and is also hoping to have a GDP growth of appr. 4%, respectable enough as compared to negative growth in South Korea or Singapore. In the view of Indonesian strategists, a regional architecture would be necessary to address the issues of security, peace and economic development in the Asia-Pacific in which major nations of the region and beyond would have to be represented. The 'Concert of Powers' that is necessary for the purpose should, in their eyes, include eight large powers namely, the U.S., China, Japan, India, South Korea, Russia, Australia and Indonesia with ASEAN as an associate member represented by its Chairman and Secretary General.

ASEAN's relevance is also often being questioned by scholars and academics from ASEAN. They ask: can ASEAN handle the challenge created by the rise of China and India? Can ASEAN continue to offer a credible platform for all major powers (such as in ARF) in maintaining security and peace in the region? After all, the north Korean nuclear issue was taken out of ARF and assigned to the Six Party Talks. Will EAS (East Asia Summit) which ASEAN successfully crafted in 2005 as a larger grouping of 16 countries in the Asia-Pacific endure and evolve into an economic community? It was reported at the time of the formation of the EAS that it was at the insistence of some of the ASEAN members, namely, Singapore, Indonesia and Vietnam, and Japan that India, Australia and New Zealand were included in the grouping and as a result the group was expanded to 16. In the meanwhile, the ASEAN +3 arrangement which has received much encouragement and support from China continues to meet regularly and has made considerable progress. The +3 countries, namely, China, Japan and Korea constitute nearly 80% of trade and investment in the ASEAN +3 grouping. As a result, ASEAN's belief that the three northeast Asian giants, because of their own mutual differences need a common platform (namely, ASEAN) to come together is also increasingly proving to be overstated. The three powers, China, Japan and Korea met at the summit level at Fukuoka in Japan in December 2008 and reviewed their cooperation and future plans. This was significant considering that till recently the three found it very difficult to put aside their historic rivalries and hold talks.

The ASEAN countries' new concern is the current financial slowdown which they no doubt share with the rest of the world. Most countries of Southeast Asia, especially the economically advanced ones among them as well as Vietnam are predominantly export-oriented economies. With global demand sharply declined these economies will find it very difficult to recover soon. This would put considerable pressure on the countries, especially the less developed CLMV (Cambodia, Laos, Myanmar and Vietnam) states. Any plans of raising economic competitiveness through additional investments may have also to wait. Modernization of security and defence forces which most ASEAN countries are in need of might also have to be deferred. This will no doubt result in the Southeast Asian states lagging further behind in military preparedness as compared to some of their large neighbours like China, Japan or India. In the coming months, one of the major issues confronting the countries of Southeast Asia would be the problem of migration as unemployment in the region continues to increase. With economies like Singapore already in recession (-5% growth) and Malaysia as well as Thailand in similar situation job prospects for a large number of workers from neighbouring countries like Indonesia, Myanmar, Cambodia or the Philippines are going to substantially decline. This will result in social unrest which can have severe political consequences as well. Within a span of just ten years or so after the Asian financial crisis, Southeast Asia is again faced with a harsh socio-economic reality. How to address this is a major challenge before them.

With regard to security aspect too, it seems that security of ASEAN states cannot be taken for granted. Although ASEAN have succeeded in keeping the region free of inter-state military conflict, particularly after the end of the Cold War, they continue to remain vulnerable to outside pressures and influences. No doubt ASEAN have persuaded major powers to sign the Treaty of Amity and Cooperation. The only major non-signatory country, namely, the United States is also expected to join this treaty soon. The U.S. which has military alliances with Thailand and the Philippines, as well as with Japan, South Korea and Australia continues to be the preponderant military and economic power in the region. With the visit of Secretary Hillary Clinton to the largest ASEAN member, Indonesia, in late February, 2009 the U.S. has signified its renewed interest and commitment to the region. President Obama's childhood connection with Indonesia is also known. He is expected to visit the country early in his administration. The U.S. appointed a special ambassador to the ASEAN last year. (A number of powers in the Asia-Pacific including India have also taken this step.) All this notwithstanding, it is evident that the U.S. lack of interest in the region during the Bush administration has led to the situation of a security space, at least a perception to that effect, which China, the rapidly growing power has sought to fill. China follows a dual approach in dealing with Southeast Asian countries. On the one hand, under its New Security Concept it follows friendly and cooperative relations. On the other hand, it does not let outstanding issues be forgotten. China recently protested to the Philippines when the latter passed a law about its ownership of Kalayaan Islands, a part of the Spratlys. China continues to claim sovereignty over all islands in the South China Sea.

Several security concerns continue to cast their shadow over Southeast Asia. They relate to both, traditional as well as non-traditional areas. While ethnic and separatists' insurgencies continue in many parts of the region, jihadi terrorism has emerged as a major threat. Southeast Asia has become a new frontier of Al-Qaeda terror. Indonesia has had major terrorist incidents a few years ago. Threat of Jemaah Islamiah continues to loom over a number of countries. Indonesia and Malaysia as well as the Philippines and southern Thailand have seen a sharp rise in fundamentalism.

Another concern is maritime security. The region is home to some of the world's most critical waterways such as the Malacca Straits. The adjoining states, Indonesia, Malaysia and Singapore have undertaken to safeguard the security of this important Sea Lane Communication (SLOC); but will need considerable assistance to ensure its full safety. The threat of piracy in Southeast Asia can also not be ignored. The question of energy security is yet another major issue facing ASEAN countries. With most of them (Indonesia became a net importer of oil 2 years ago) becoming energy deficient and dependent on imported oil, the issue of energy acquires a new dimension in the previously energy-exporting region.

Conscious of its strategic vulnerability and military weakness, ASEAN have worked out over the years a web of interlocking arrangements with neighbouring powers and those from outside the region which they perceive as a security assurance. These include, besides their own ASEAN Community, Dialogue partnerships with major countries around the world, ASEAN+ summits, ASEAN Regional Forum (ARF), ASEAN + 3, East Asia Summit (EAS) etc. These mechanisms have enabled regular exchanges among the major powers of the world with ASEAN as a pivot. In that sense, this whole effort is itself a substantive CBM (Confidence Building Measure) which has served ASEAN well so far and is expected to contribute to the maintenance of stability and security in the turbulent Asia-Pacific region.

For India, too, this arrangement has been of strategic benefit. It is for this reason, India's 'Look East policy' is anchored in deepening ties with ASEAN. While this policy has helped India to secure engagement with the dynamic region of the Asia-Pacific in which the contribution of ASEAN is by no means insignificant, the latter has also drawn advantage in having a large, stable and rapidly developing economy like India in its engagement matrix. India also provides a strategic ballast on ASEAN's west side. In recent years ASEAN has found it useful to ride India's fast economic growth and expanding market as also its IT and service sector. For India, ASEAN has become an important hub in promoting trade and investment in the wider Asia-Pacific region. India can also leverage the brand-name of Singapore or Thai or Malaysian companies in doing business in China, Japan or the U.S. There are more than 2000 Indian companies based in Singapore doing business all over the world from there. Besides, Indian companies also learn best business practices followed in ASEAN, some of which are top class in the world. Thus there is a natural fit, complementarity between India and ASEAN which both recognize and seem to value today.

As India-ASEAN relationship started developing in the early- mid 90s, it had to be put on a strong economic footing which is being done through bilateral and ASEAN-India level trade and investment arrangements. With liberalization and greater private sector involvement in business, bilateral trade between the two has seen a sharp increase. The two-way trade crossed $37 billion in 2007 with ASEAN exports amounting to $ 24.6 billion and Indian exports at $12.4 billion. Similarly, investments on both sides have rapidly grown. Indian investment in ASEAN amounted to U.S $1.56 billion in last 10 years. Tourist arrivals in ASEAN from India are expected to touch 1 million by 2010. With India having a Comprehensive Economic Cooperation Agreement (CECA) with Singapore, and a partial FTA with Thailand , and now an ASEAN-India FTA, already negotiated and expected to be signed at the time of the EAS in April 2009, India and ASEAN are poised to become major economic partners in the near future.

All this augurs well for an interdependent and mutually beneficial relationship between the two which have a combined population of nearly 1.7 billion. On the path of the overall economic integration in Asia which both ASEAN and India are interested in this will be an important step.

As seen above, ASEAN states are today at the crossroads. They are faced with numerous challenges, security, economic or social. For these countries, which have unfortunately been victims of extra-ordinary natural disasters in the recent past, a period of stability and sustained growth is a sine qua non for progress and prosperity. Political cohesion in ASEAN is still an on -going process. ASEAN is still a long way from what the European Union has achieved. In any case, the two have a different historical background and context and therefore cannot be compared. At the present time, ASEAN states are faced with serious consequences of the global economic downturn. In the circumstances, the march towards a credible regionalism in ASEAN will be anything but gradual and far from being spectacular. However, it should be mentioned that the policy framework that ASEAN have put in place is in the right direction. That includes their several cooperative arrangements with major powers of the region and outside world. With their own Charter having been adopted ASEAN have now a roadmap before them. They may appear to meander on the path but it is fairly certain that they will attain their objective of an ASEAN Community by 2015. A union, howsoever loose and informal, of 570 million or more people in the strategically important area in the Asia-Pacific will be reality which its western neighbour India would need to take a close note of.

CHAPTER 15

India—ASEAN Economic Relations: Opportunities and Challenges for Asian Economic Integration

Dr. Amita Batra

Rationale of India-ASEAN and Asian Economic Integration

Regional economic integration in Asia was triggered in the 1990s in response to the emergence of continent – wide trade blocs in the north-significantly the European Union (EU) and the North American Free Trade Agreement (NAFTA), and eventually the Free Trade Area of the Americas (FTAA)). There was a desire among the East Asian economies to counter the differential treatment that was inevitable on account of the preferential arrangements created by the EU, NAFTA and other preferential agreements and strengthen their negotiation leverage against these regional groups. This East Asian aspiration has steadily strengthened over time as the trend toward regionalism expanded geographically as well as functionally. The rise of India and China as global economic powers and the consequent shift in the global centre of gravity to Asia has given a new phillip to the process of regional economic integration in Asia.

This process of economic integration has also been fueled by a prior process of market forces in the region, as firms construct production chains across the area to exploit the comparative advantage of its individual countries. The East Asian financial crisis in 1997-98 acted as a catalyst in the process by underscoring the need for East Asia to institutionalize its cooperation to solve similar issues and prevent new ones. The Asian financial crisis was also instrumental in bringing to the fore the imperatives for ASEAN to regain its economic dynamism as also its position as a viable regional institution.

Among other developments in the region that have contributed to this momentum is the rise of China. Due to its size and huge market potential, China has led to a restructuring of the pattern of regional economic integration. Based on the restructuring, new regional production and services networks have been gradually established. Also, after its accession to the World Trade Organization (WTO) China developed a free trade agreement (FTA) with

ASEAN, which has recently been extended to cover some services. This led to a domino effect in the region with Japan and Korea announcing their own bilateral FTA deals with the ASEAN.

India ASEAN Economic Relations

India's association with ASEAN member nations has been long standing, though the formal beginning can be traced to the adoption of the 'Look East Policy' that was officially launched in 1991. The 'Look East Policy' had its genesis in the end of the cold war and a strategic shift in India's vision of the world and India's place in the evolving global economy. Simultaneously, it was also the outcome of the process of economic liberalization initiated in India in June 1991. The initiation of the LEP signaled the end of India's pursuit of self reliance based on an inward looking growth strategy and the start of an era when India opened up to the opportunities from Globalization, in terms of both international trade and investment. The LEP also sent out strong signals that the region had come to acquire a significant positioning in India's foreign policy and in economic terms it would be regarded as a new source of business opportunity while also becoming an inspiration for economic development. Closer economic ties with ASEAN, it was assumed would provide momentum to India's reform programme as it would require lower trade barriers and liberalized investment regimes. As India's economy continues to grow the LEP has acquired an added dimension of regional economic integration. The slow progress in the process of integration within South Asia has made it necessary for India to extend its economic vision beyond the confines of its traditional policy and the South Asian region.

A clear institutional framework for operationalizing economic cooperation between India and ASEAN is already laid out. India became a sectoral dialogue partner of ASEAN in 1992 with a focus on cooperation in trade, investment, tourism and science and technology. The relationship was upgraded to full dialogue partnership in December 1995 at the fifth ASEAN summit in Bangkok. India became a member of the ASEAN Regional Forum in 1996. The ASEAN – India relationship was upgraded to summit level in 2002. India is now an ASEAN summit partner along with Japan, China and South Korea. An important milestone in the ASEAN-India association was the hosting of the first ASEAN – India summit 2002 in Phnom Penh. The first India-ASEAN Business Summit was also held in 2002 in New Delhi and has now become an annual feature prior to the India-ASEAN Summit as a forum for networking and exchange of business experiences between policy makers and business leaders from ASEAN and India.

The framework agreement (FA) for an India-ASEAN FTA was signed during the second India-ASEAN summit held in Bali in October 2003. Discussions on the Rules of Origin have been finalized and a 35% value addition norm in addition to change in tariff heading has been agreed upon.

The tariff elimination will be undertaken in a phased manner and completed by 2015. Import duties on 71 per cent of products will be removed by December 2012 and on another 9 per cent by 2015. For about 10% of additional tariff lines on the sensitive track, the tariffs will not be eliminated but brought down to 5%. India has 489 items, mostly farm products, on the sensitive list which will not be subject to tariff cuts[1].

In addition, India has entered into several bilateral initiatives with ASEAN member countries. India signed an FTA with Thailand in 2003 and the two countries are working on Investment Cooperation Agreement. A Comprehensive Economic Cooperation Agreement (CECA) between India and Singapore was signed in June 2005. The agreement which came into effect in August 2005 includes liberalization of trade in goods, services, bilateral investment promotion treaty that ensures national treatment, a double taxation avoidance agreement and an air services agreement in addition to an FTA. Already Singapore is among the top 5 investors in India and has invested in sectors like infrastructure development, especially port development and in knowledge economy sectors like telecom. Other sectors where scope for cooperation is visible and desirable are banking, automobiles, SME, pharmaceuticals and energy as also architecture, accounting, science and technology, education and tourism.

India has entered into a number of bilateral treaties and agreements for cooperation in the fields of trade, finance, science and technology, agriculture, tourism and culture, air services and visa exemption with Laos, Cambodia and Vietnam. India has some major projects in Cambodia in the areas of education, entrepreneurship development and information technology. India is also considering entering into FTAs with Malaysia and Indonesia.

As part of its 'Look East Policy' India has strengthened cooperation with Myanmar, the only ASEAN country with which India shares both land and maritime boundaries, in a number of sectors by extending a number of general and project-specific credit lines to Myanmar in the last few years.

India is also improving its relations with ASEAN through other elements like offers of lines of credit, better connectivity through air (open skies policy), rail and road links and by entering into some other agreements with ASEAN like the Treaty of Amity and Cooperation (TAC).

The improvement in India – ASEAN ties is reflected in the increasing bilateral trade. India's trade with ASEAN, which was US$ 9.7 billion in 2002-2003 has increased to more than US$ 30.64 bill. in 2006-07. India's exports to ASEAN that were US$ 10.41 billion in 2005-06 have increased to US$ 12.56 billion in 2006-07, registering thus a growth of 20.67 % in this period. India's imports from ASEAN accounting for US$ 10.88 billion in 2005-06 have increased to US$ 18.08 billion in 2006-07, implying thereby a growth of over 66 per cent. Despite the sustained improvement in India ASEAN trade, India's trade with ASEAN constitutes only 9.6 per cent of its global trade while ASEAN's trade with India makes up only 2 per cent of its global trade, indicating thus the huge trade potential that is yet to be explored between these two regions. Further, given the geographical contiguity and proximity as also cultural affinity, and economic dynamism of the two regions, formal analysis using the Gravity model estimation (Batra, 2006) technique is similarly indicative of a high potential of trade between ASEAN and India.

India's Trade with ASEAN

(US $ billion)

Year	*Exports*	*Imports*
2003-04	5.82	7.4
2004-05	8.42	9.11
2005-06	10.41	10.88
2006-07	12.6	18.08
2007-08	16.37	22.66
% share in India's total	9.8	9.45

The 'Look East Policy' that was primarily directed towards improving relations with ASEAN in the initial years has now progressed to encompass other nations of the region such as China, Japan and Korea. India-China relations have entered a phase where economics is taking precedence over other issues. A Joint Study Group was set up in 2004 to explore opportunities for economic cooperation in trade and investment. Feasibility studies for an FTA are being undertaken. The two economies are already members of the Bangkok Agreement[2]. India has recently signed a CECA with Korea. A Joint Study Group was set up in 2005 to explore opportunities for economic cooperation in trade and investment. Work on the India-Japan comprehensive economic partnership agreement (CEPA) is on the fast-track. In fact, the submission of India-Korea joint study group report and the beginning of final rounds of negotiations for an economic partnership pact influenced Japan to accelerate preparations for the India-Japan agreement.

These initiatives reflect India's evolving perspective on and the growing acceptance of the tremendous potential for creating synergies in the Asian region.

Institutional Mechanisms for Asian Economic Integration

Notwithstanding these developments in ASEAN and India-ASEAN relations, the process of regional cooperation in Asia is yet not well-defined and the search for an institutional mechanism that can carry the idea forward continues. While proposals like the ASEAN+3 have been logical outcomes of the trade led market integration that the region has experienced over the last couple of decades, this configuration of 13 countries has not been able to go beyond formalizing financial cooperation. The rise of India and its likely influence along with China on the economic landscape of the region has in fact forced reconsideration of the existing institutional configurations. Not only is there an existing economic rationale for a regional arrangement in East Asia that is inclusive of India but the convergence of economic policies in Asia today has in fact led to a rethinking on the earlier strategic assumptions that influenced the emergence of particular regional groupings in Asia. The new world order provides scope for redefining the territorial compass of the groupings of the future. Hence, attempts at the establishment of an institutional identity thus far restricted to the 'ASEAN+ Three' and the creation of an East Asian Community have been more recently extended to a more inclusive East Asia Summit (EAS) process. It has opened up ideas about the value of more comprehensive cooperation possibilities in Asia initiating thus a new and exciting beginning of a process that could evolve into an Asian Economic Community. The first EAS summit was held in 2005. At this summit, 16 nations, ASEAN, the +3 economies of China, Japan and Korea; and India, Australia and New Zealand in acceptance of their growing economic interdependence and linkages agreed to the creation of a harmonious economic community and proposed to work towards this objective through instruments of deeper integration.

Alongside the East Asia Summit process there are ongoing individual ASEAN+1 processes of economic cooperation among the member nations of the Summit. As discussed earlier in the paper the ASEAN-China FTA triggered a series of FTA agreements with ASEAN by Japan, Korea and India. The deal towards the India-ASEAN FTA have been finalized over a period of five years. Japan and Korea are still negotiating the terms of their FTA with ASEAN. A convergence of these ASEAN+1 FTA deals into a single harmonized regional agreement is a proposal that often finds mention in the literature. Credence to the proposal is lent by the fact that these FTAs are yet on the negotiation path and it may therefore be possible to subject them to harmonized constituent elements that would be suitable for convergence. While the above highlights the potentially ripe opportunity for these nations to move ahead with a regional economic community that can aptly counter the preferential biases inherent in the already established economic union and FTAs in the North, there remain issues that may pose a challenge in this process and hence need to be resolved for forward movement. These issues are discussed in the paragraphs that follow.

ASEAN Centrality and Integration

Irrespective of which one of the above is the chosen mechanism, it is clear that ASEAN is the most acceptable centerpiece of Asian economic integration. Given this fact, it is only appropriate that an assessment of the suitability of ASEAN as an institutional mechanism for the desired objective and role is undertaken.

ASEAN is still an association of ten diverse nations that has yet to achieve the objective of its own integration i.e., the ASEAN Economic Community. The process has been given a reasonable push forward at the

ASEAN 2007 summit when the ASEAN charter issued a declaration for the implementation of the ASEAN Economic Community by 2015. The Charter is a blueprint for the ASEAN Economic Community aimed at transforming ASEAN into a single market and production base, a highly competitive economic region, a region of equitable economic development, and a region fully integrated into the global economy. While the objectives outlined are noble, it is to be realized that the Charter is aimed at ASEAN integration process and hence, it may actually prove to be a setback for the argument that ASEAN Plus Six is an optimum mechanism for realizing gains for economic cooperation and signaling to the rest of the world that Asia can create inclusive forums to enhance its voice in global affairs.

In addition, the ASEAN integration experience has thus far been slow and the ASEAN FTA that was implemented in 1992 with the constituent elements of the common effective preferential tariff (CEPT), Agreement on the ASEAN Investment Area (AIA) for investment liberalization (1998), and the ASEAN Framework Agreement on Services (AFAS) for services liberalization have not been fully utilized or implemented. Some studies estimate that only 3% of the intra-ASEAN trade has availed of the CEPT rates (Baldwin, 2006). The rather limited ASEAN integration therefore provides weak benchmarks for regional integration in Asia. Few mechanisms are in place to propel integrative forces in trade in goods as also in investment and services liberalization. And many ASEAN members are already engaged in bilateral deals, seemingly more as a consequence of the 'convoy problem' rather than as contributory elements of competitive liberalization in the region.

To take the process of ASEAN integration forward strong political will and leadership is the foremost requirement. This is particularly important given the development gap among the member nations. The issue of national sovereignty is another sensitive issue that needs to be sensibly dealt with in bringing the economies under a common institutional arrangement. Individual ASEAN members may not all be agreeable to transfer sovereignty to a supranational authority. In addition, the economies, in being a part of the overall regional supply chain are actually competing in their export markets. In the face of these competing interests it will be a challenge to make the ten members identify common interests under a collective singular identity. The given institutional mechanism is certainly not equipped to handle this. The 'ASEAN way' of consensus based decision making while making for peace and regional stability has done very little for the cause of regional integration. This needs to change. The small secretariat of the ASEAN has to acquire the status of a regional organization with staff that is capable in terms of number and expertise to handle the delicate national issues as well administrative tasks in the process of regional economic integration.

The alternative mechanism that as earlier suggested finds favor with some experts, that is, convergence of the ASEAN+1 FTAs also has some prior requirements that would need to be satisfied for its success. These are as discussed below.

Merger of the ASEAN+1s – Necessary Contributory Factors

Compatibility of the ASEAN+1s: Only if the ASEAN+1 agreements of the plus four economies are compatible with each other would there be hope of linking these agreements to constitute a regional economic entity in Asia in future. Compatibility is possible as the elements of the 'plus one' agreements are still being negotiated. A greater focus on harmonization and consistency within ASEAN is required-say for e.g. with respect to the rules of origin that at present may be scattered and inconsistent with one another.

Compatibility with WTO: As the individual agreements with ASEAN are pursued the aim of a Pan Asian FTA should be paramount throughout the exercise for all involved. This is required as even though bilateral arrangements provide necessary strategic access to markets they are ultimately and inherently protectionist in nature. Unlike unilateral and multilateral trade liberalization they allow protectionism through a process of liberalization that is conditional upon reciprocity and restrictive rules of origin. As East Asian integration has been largely 'market driven', this should continue to be so and the commercial logic of the market should continue to guide the process. For this the prime responsibility of all governments is to create domestic conditions that will facilitate the market flows. So that as unilateral economic reform and trade liberalization remain the priority focus areas for Asian economies and specifically for India, the bilaterals should be undertaken in a manner that they can promote multilateral trade liberalization limiting the discriminatory effects.

India and China – Competitive or Complementary in Asian Integration Process?

Another aspect that needs due clarity is the presence of India and China in Asian integration. The economic consequences of the emerging new regional architecture in Asia comprising both India and China need to be reviewed. Both India and China have signed an FTA agreement with ASEAN. The ASEAN–China Free Trade Area (ACFTA) is due to be up and running by 2010 for the more developed ASEAN-6 and by 2015 for Cambodia, Laos, Myanmar and Vietnam. The ASEAN–India FTA (AIFTA) as per the agreement is to come into effect in 2011 for the developed members and in 2016 for the Philippines and the new members of ASEAN. India and China are both members of the East Asia Summit and are hence co-participants in the formation of the Asian Economic Community. While the oft quoted context for India's participation, rather inclusion in the forum is stated to be as a counterweight to China, the economic rationale may prove otherwise. Given the differential degree and nature of integration of the two economies in the global and regional economy it may be hard to justify clubbing of the two economies as competitors and hence a counter to the other. Some aspects of the development process underlying the stated differential between these two economies are highlighted below so as to place in context the India China relationship – competitive or complementary – in the efforts towards economic integration in Asia.

India and China relationship in the last decade has evolved on lines of pragmatism and can today be characterized as a successful economic partnership. While the India China FTA/RTA is under study, the two countries have surged ahead with bilateral trade of the magnitude of around 40 billion. In 2007-08 India's exports to China were of the order of $11 billion and imports from China totaled 29 billion. China has emerged as India's largest single country trading partner. However India and China have traversed a differential path towards growth and global integration and so it may not so easy to look at these two economies within the same global or regional context. Some evidence towards this is presented below.

India and China in the Global Economy

India and China are two of the most dynamic economies of the world, having registered sustained high growth rates over the last few years. India's average real growth rate between 1995-2004 was 6.1%, while that for China was 9.1%. However, the contribution of the two economies to world growth is significantly different. Between 1995-2004, China's average contribution to world growth was almost 13% in comparison with India's, which was only 3%. Again, while India and China have both undertaken economic reforms and liberalized their economies, the pace of integration is different in each case. For both exports and imports of goods India's share in the growth of world economy total exports and imports over 1995-2004 is less than 2% in contrast with that for China in which case it is about 8-9%. Overall, India's share in world trade – exports and imports- is only about 1% while China's share is around 5-6%.

Gross Domestic Product in Six Large Economies

Economy	*Share of world GDP:2004*	*Average real growth rate: 1995-2004*	*Average contribution to world growth: 1995-2004*
China	4.7	9.1	12.8
India	1.7	6.1	3.2
US	28.4	3.3	33.1
Japan	11.2	1.2	5.3
Germany	6.6	1.5	3.0
Brazil	1.5	2.4	1.5
World	100	3.0	100

Source: Wnters and Yus uf, 2007.

Global Integration: International Trade

Exports of Goods and Services			*Imports of Goods and Services*	
Economy	*Share (2004)*	*Share of growth 1995-2004*	*Share (2003)*	*Share of growth 1995-2003*
China	5.7	8.9	4.8	7.8
India	1.2	1.8	1.1	1.8
US	11.2	10.7	16.5	24.1
Japan	5.4	-3.7	4.7	-0.8
Germany	9.1	7.7	8.2	3.6
Brazil	1.0	0.5	0.7	0.3

Source: Wnters and Yusuf, 2007.

As for financial integration India has attained the status of an attractive investment destination and has made large strides in capital account liberalization. Despite this progress India absorbs less than one percent of the global FDI flows while China corners almost 8%. The figures for portfolio investment and foreign exchange reserve accumulation may be more encouraging but it is clear that even though India's participation in the world economy is increasing it is yet not close to the levels attained by China. It may not be fair then to really posit India and China as competing economies in the world. This fact is further reinforced when we undertake a detailed analysis of the global/ regional comparative advantage of these two economies.

India and China: Global and Regional Comparative Advantage

When the global comparative advantage of the two economies is analyzed, the picture appears to be very similar as both India and China have maximum comparative advantage in unskilled labor intensive goods followed by technology and human capital intensive goods. Seemingly, the two economies may appear as competitors.

India China: Global Comparative Advantage

FI	*China*	*India*
Human Capital	334	293
Natural resource	94	95
Technology	600	412
Unskilled labour	660	489
Unclassified	45	49

Source: Batra, 2007a.

But this is only the broad picture. The detailed picture presents contrasting information. When a commodity level analysis of the possible competitive threat that India and China may pose to each other in the global or regional market (ASEAN) is undertaken, it is observed that there are very few commodities for which either India or China pose a direct threat to each other. In fact, there are very few commodities, among their top ten best performing sectors, where the two countries share their comparative advantage regionally or globally. If we trace the trend development in the manufacturing sector of the two economies, it is easy to discern that both India and China are moving along divergent paths. There is increasing divergence between the Indian and Chinese structure of comparative advantage (See figures 1&2). India and China have been specializing in different product lines within each product category. There are fundamental differences in the development strategies followed by the two economies. China, during the process of development and trade liberalization, has made greater investment in manufacturing. China's manufacturing sector accounts for more than 41 percent of its GDP, with manufacturing goods constituting 93 percent of its exports. This is in contrast with India's trade in manufacturing not being remarkable to date with the sector's share being just about 20 percent of GDP. India is not a major force in international manufacturing, except in textile and clothing, pearls, precious stones etc, glass and glassware, miscellaneous manufactures and other unskilled labor-intensive (ULI) commodity categories given abundance of low-cost labor which makes it acquired specialization and comparative advantage. In contrast, China has experienced dynamism in its manufacturing skills, specialization pattern and consequently export structure. From specializing in ULI sectors like toys, footwear, apparel and light manufactures in the last decade it has in this decade advanced to office machinery, electrical and electronic equipment and appliances. China today is the manufacturing hub of the world. (Batra, 2007a).

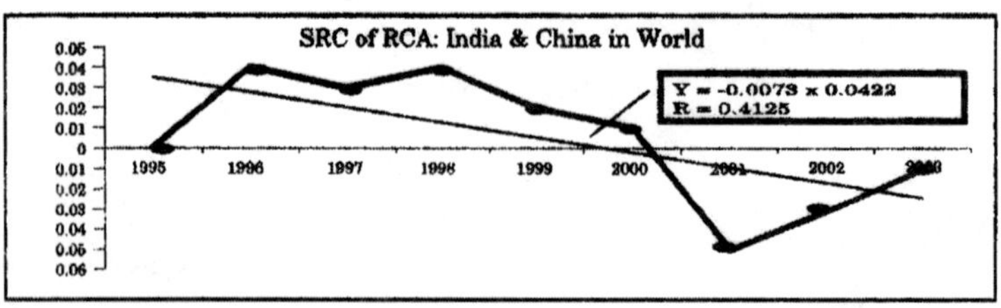

Fig. 1: Negative Trend: Correlation of Manufacturing Sector Global Comparative Advantage.

Source: Batra, 2007a

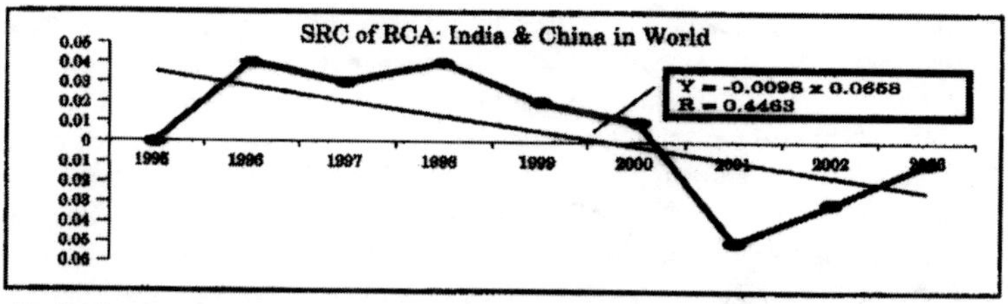

Fig.2: Negative Trend: Correlation of Manufacturing Sector Comparative Advantage in ASEAN .

Source: Batra, 2007a

Given this background analysis it may be appropriate to re-assess the India - China paradigm in the context of Asian integration. India and China need not be viewed as competing nations, they may in fact complement each other, and it is the latter force that may be worth exploring rather than the 'counterweight' argument positioning of India in the regional context.

The Global Context for Asian Economic integration

Notwithstanding these challenges and regional developments the process of Asian economic integration is in the current context likely to receive the necessary momentum from global developments. While regional integration in Asia may not be propelled forward by common threats, the common benefit of regional stability that regional integration is likely to yield in the current scenario of global downturn is far greater and may prove to be the necessary trigger factor. The global crisis with its contagion spreading to Asia may prove to be second awakening for the region to come together in a formal institutionalized manner so as to prevent them being swept away in the wake of a crisis that is not of their own making.

Some evidence of the recognition of this opportunity by the regional leaders is already evident. In the wake of rising western protectionism, ASEAN leaders at the 14th Summit Meeting held recently made an appeal for coordinated action. In one voice the region is seeking bold and urgent reform of the international financial system to make it more equitable, comprehensive and inclusive representing interests and voices of the emerging market economies. The ASEAN leaders have grasped the opportunity to take forward the existing regional financial cooperation mechanism through multilateralization of the Chiang Mai Initiative (CMI) as also in exercising the option of creation of a regional reserve pool. The other options that though available have not been sufficiently developed can now be taken up with renewed vigor. Among these the important ones would be Asian Bond Fund, the Asian Bond Market Initiative which on account of lack of market liquidity and relative stability of the region's currencies against the US dollar have had limited attractiveness as a diversification strategy in the past. Another aspect that the region needs to focus upon collectively is achievement of closer exchange rate cooperation as excessive exchange rate volatility needs to be avoided. It is also time to seriously look at the option of evolving an Asian currency unit. The Asian Development Bank has done much work on this issue already. Some other steps like establishing transparency and regulation for development of efficient capital markets are also essential. Now, time is also ripe for some bold initiatives like setting up the Asian Infrastructure Finance Corporation given the significance of cross border infrastructure in the connectivity of the region and its implications for regional integration and the potential that may be inherent in such schemes for the revival of the regional economies.

South Asia – East Asia: Pan Asian Economic Integration

Finally, it needs to be noted that the regional integration process that is on in the region and that is inclusive of India has potential spillover effects for South Asia and consequently for a wider Pan Asian integration process. The process of integration in South Asia has been slow, plagued as it is by historical baggage as also by economic asymmetries. However, now, as India moves ahead on a decisively higher growth path, it may be opportune for South Asian countries to embark collectively to take advantage of the gains of India's globalization and regional alignments.

While SAFTA has taken the process of regional economic integration in South Asia forward in the last two years, India's successful integration with East Asia may help provide another window of opportunity for the region. For the South Asian economies for which India is the predominant trade partner, this should lead to an acceleration in their pace of integration with India as this will give them a direct and easy access to the 'Arc of Advantage' reflected in the coming together of the sixteen member nations of the East Asia Summit. And, till the India-ASEAN or EAS processes bear fruit, it may in the meanwhile also be useful to explore two existing agreements that have the potential to give a concrete shape to the South Asia – East Asia trade bloc particularly given the economic advantage of an Asian bloc that spreads across sub-regions of South and East Asia. These agreements are the BIMSTEC and the Bangkok Agreement. To be more useful for the purpose of regional integration both the Agreements call for a review of scope – both in terms of member nations and sectoral coverage. It may be an even better idea to work on these two aspects of the Agreements while simultaneously considering the merger of BIMSTEC and the Bangkok Agreement. A brief description of the Agreements in the present form is given below (Batra, 2007b).

BIMSTEC: At the sub-regional level, the major initiative is BIMSTEC. BIMSTEC comprises Bangladesh, India, Myanmar, Sri Lanka, Thailand, Bhutan and Nepal. This initiative includes countries from both SAARC and ASEAN and in fact acts as a bridge between the two. The first ever summit-level meeting for BIMSTEC was held in July 2004 when it acquired its new incarnation - the Bay of Bengal Initiative for Multi-sectoral Technical and Economic Cooperation. This Bay of Bengal initiative is dynamic and offers the prospect of widening the network for outward oriented growth in this part of Asia. It can emerge as a bridge between the more inward oriented South Asia, and the more outward oriented South East and East Asia. Through this route India, followed by SAARC can reach out to the South East Asian region and beyond to the Asia-Pacific community. The BIMSTEC Agreement therefore holds prospects for a much larger Pan-Asian economic cooperation in the long run. The second BIMSTEC summit meeting was held recently in New Delhi.

Bangkok Agreement: Bangkok Agreement was signed in 1975. Members are Bangladesh, China, India, Republic of Korea, Laos and Sri Lanka. The Agreement is at present limited in scope as it covers only tariff concessions on goods. The Agreement has been revitalized in 2001 with the entry of China. This agreement is a more potent instrument than the BIMSTEC as a facilitator for South Asia – East Asia economic integration. That China, India and ROK are already members of this agreement is indicative of the huge market potential inherent in the agreement. Further, the agreement is open to all developing member countries of ESCAP and is consequently the only truly regional trade agreement in Asia. In terms of its potential membership this is the only agreement that has the potential to develop into a regional trade agreement leading to regional economic integration in Asia.

Ultimately it needs to be realized that an Asian bloc will not just benefit the region and its economies as analyzed above[3] but it can be a potential instrument of changing incentives for the trade blocs in the Americas and Europe and actually make possible multilateral freeing of trade.

REFERENCES

Baldwin, R. (2006). "*Managing the Noodle Bowl: The Fragility of East Asian*".

Regionalism". *Discussion Paper Series*, No. 5561. Center for Economic Policy Research, UK.

Batra, Amita, 2006, "India's Global Trade Potential: The Gravity Model Approach", *Global Economic Review* (Routledge), September, Vol. 35, No. 3.

Batra, Amita, 2007, "Asian Economic Integration - ASEAN+3+1 or ASEAN+1s?", *ASEAN Economic Bulletin*, August, Vol. 24, No. 2.

Batra, Amita, 2007a, "The Structure of Comparative Advantage of China and India: Global. and Regional Dynamics", *China and World Economy* (Blackwell) Vol.15. No. 6 November 15.

Batra, Amita, 2007b, "South Asia's Free Trade Agreement: Strategies and Options", *Economic and Political Weekly*, Vol. XLII, No.38, September 22-28.

Winters, Alan, and Shahid Yusuf (ed.), 2007, Dancing with the Giants: China, India and the Global Economy, The World Bank, Washington DC and Institute of Policy Studies, Singapore.

1. Simultaneous to finalizing the FTA deal India now needs to take proactive measures to ensure that the competitiveness of tea, coffee and pepper economy is bolstered so as to meet the low-cost competition from plantation crop producers like Vietnam. Measures to cushion the impact of post-FTA regime with ASEAN for Indian plantation sectors that are also employment-intensive need to be taken and some initiatives in this direction are already underway.
2. Now the Asia Pacific Trade Agreement.
3. This Asia wide FTA will have many efficient and competitive countries thereby minimizing the extent of trade diversion relative to SAFTA.

CHAPTER 16

India—ASEAN FTA Blues

Dr. N. Chandra Mohan

The ongoing recession in the world economy is triggering protectionist, beggar-thy-neighbour trade policies that are reminiscent of the 1930s. The fate of the Doha Round of WTO multilateral negotiations hangs in the balance even as member countries scramble to sign bilateral free trade agreements (FTAs). India is not too far behind in this veritable stampede for inking these agreements – 8 are currently in operation, 1 has been signed, 12 are under negotiation and at least 11 more are proposed as of June 2009, according to the Asian Development Bank.

Economists specialising in trade are extremely skeptical that these FTAs have anything to do with free trade. Far from it, they form an unruly mass of crisscrossing strings that Professor Jagdish Bhagwati of Columbia University called a "spaghetti bowl" [1] that hampers rather than facilitates free trade for those left out. Such FTAs entail different rules of origin and preferences that benefit only member countries. Whether the trade creation for such member countries is welfare-enhancing for their stakeholders like farmers and local industry is also far from certain.

Trade economists, for their part, believe that politics and non-economic factors are the main drivers of the rush to conclude FTAs. Bureaucrats and politicians, especially the so-called reformers in their midst, are susceptible to the need to showcase that India has arrived on the world stage! Bhagwati has written that the short tenure of bureaucrats and politicians predisposes them towards immediate results: the "spaghetti bowl" of bilaterals is easy to negotiate and regret perhaps.[2]

India's experience in Asia is instructive as it entered into a framework agreement for an FTA with Thailand. It has sought greater cooperation with the Bay of Bengal grouping of countries BIMSTEC — Bangladesh, India, Myanmar, Sri Lanka and Thailand. A comprehensive economic cooperation agreement (CECA) with Singapore is operational. More recently, an economic partnership agreement with South Korea was signed followed by an FTA that was inked with the Association of Southeast Asian Nations (ASEAN) on August 13, 2009.

Most if not all these trade agreements face domestic opposition, including from the ruling political party. During the first term of the Congress-led United Progressive Alliance during 2004-2009, there was a realisation at the highest levels that such bilaterals must be carefully scrutinized for their costs and benefits.

The India-ASEAN FTA is likely to be the country's most important and ambitious trade agreement. ASEAN's GDP of $1.5 trillion is not very different from that of India's GDP of $1.2 trillion. An FTA is bound to open up a substantial market for our goods. India, too, can benefit from services trade with ASEAN. An FTA, thus, will spur the globalizing drive of India Inc eastwards as it forms partnerships, alliances and joint ventures to leverage the bustling business potentiality of this region during the 21st century.

Despite its evident importance, however, India's stance in its negotiations with ASEAN has been defensive in nature. To safeguard the interests of farmers and domestic industry, a huge negative list of 1,414 tariff items — including palm oil, toilet seats, chewing gum — was originally included for exemption from free trade with ASEAN. This list has since been pruned down to 489, but ASEAN members weren't amused. What was the point of the FTA if the negative list included palm oil, tea, pepper and textiles that would affect 80 per cent of their exports to India!

Indian industry, for its part, also nurtures a deep-seated ambivalence over the benefits of such bilaterals, including the one with ASEAN due to the persisting domestic handicap of inverted duty structures. This contributes to a skewed pattern of trade tilted against India. There is also concern over the prospect of diversion of foreign direct investments (FDI) from countries like Japan, whose companies can use their bases in countries like Thailand as a staging ground for their assault on India's domestic market in automobiles and consumer electronics.

Nevertheless, closer economic engagement with ASEAN cannot proceed without a greater degree of self-confidence on the part of stakeholders like India Inc. If India desires to be a part of the broader Asian community, a degree of openness is called for. Is India Inc ready for a greater degree of openness? After having experienced decades of tariff protection, it is certainly not easy to be prepared for accelerated reductions in import duties. But being defensive about one's market is not the best way to gain from two-way trade.

The Pan-Asian Vision

India's closer engagement with Asia is of relatively recent vintage — the early 1990s to be precise when we became a sectoral dialogue partner of ASEAN. A decade later, a framework agreement on comprehensive economic cooperation with this grouping was concluded in 2003 at Bali, Indonesia. India's ambitions of looking eastwards acquired a firm foundation with the signing of a bilateral framework agreement for an FTA with Thailand in 2004 and CECA with the city-state of Singapore on June 29, 2005, both of which are currently in operation.

The CECA with Singapore is much broader in scope than the Indo-Thailand trade agreement that has only seen the implementation of an early harvest scheme (EHS) for tariff concessions for 82 items. By contrast, the CECA includes an agreement on investment promotion, an improved double taxation avoidance agreement, a liberal air services agreement and a work programme for cooperation in healthcare, education, tourism etc. Clearly, this FTA-plus agreement is intended to serve as a template for India's growing engagement with ASEAN and East Asian countries.

Although it was considered important, India's CECA with Singapore took 26 months to come to fruition. Negotiations for this bilateral began in May 2003 and was a brainchild of former Singapore's premier Goh Chok Tong. The deadline was April 2004 but these talks had to be put on hold as national elections were called in that country. The government also changed in India. Goh stepped down, paving the way for Lee Hsien Loong to take over as premier of the city-state. But for the interest taken by Dr. Manmohan Singh, this state of affairs may have drifted indefinitely.

Dr Singh's forte is economic diplomacy and he has articulated a strong vision statement for India's Look East policy. He envisioned, in fact, a pan-Asian community encompassing ASEAN, China, Japan, Korea and India. At a time when the WTO trade talks are going nowhere, the effort to put in place a regional bloc rivaling the European Union in terms of income and the North American Free Trade Area in trade commends itself. Such an ambitious vision is, no doubt, responsible for the bilaterals that India has signed with countries in the region.

However, this worthwhile diplomatic effort of working towards a larger community encompassing ASEAN, China, Japan, Korea, India, Australia and New Zealand will not bear fruition unless there is connectivity. Without connectivity, pan-Asian integration is inconceivable. Unless India is linked with the region through road, rail, air and shipping services, freer trade will be sub-optimal. China's trade with ASEAN is already 7-times that of India's and if the latter wants to ramp up trade with the region to $50 billion by 2010, connectivity is crucial.

To its credit, India recognises this problem and is involving the ASEAN in its north-east region where south-east Asia really begins. Connectivity with Thailand entails establishing road, rail and other linkages traversing through Bangladesh and Myanmar. India, for its part, has proposed to the Myanmar government that it will rebuild the Settwe Port and make the Kaladan river navigable to provide an alternative access into Mizoram and the north-east. The idea is that the north-east will then be integrated via Settwe with the rest of south-east Asia.

Participation in China's Kunming initiative that integrates Yunnan Province, Myanmar, northeastern India and Bangladesh is also worthwhile in this regard. Manishankar Aiyar who was India's petroleum minister during the first term of the UPA government, had proposed the Iran-Pakistan-India gas pipeline be extended to China via Bangladesh, but given the difficulties he considered re-routing it through the north-east. To forge road linkages, the opening up the Stillwell Road from the north-east into China's Yunnan province.

Better connectivity is vital for greater pan-Asian integration. Towards this end, transport infrastructure in north-east India must undergo a transformation beyond improving only airline connectivity. The old sea-faring links also must be re-established if India is to seriously look eastwards as it has done throughout history.

India Inc's fears

Leveraging trading opportunities with Asia is also a major challenge. Even though India's trade flows to Asia-Pacific region have been booming of late, even surpassing the value of its trade with the US and western Europe, the country must develop greater self-confidence to engage with this region. India Inc, for its part, nurtures a deep-seated diffidence over the benefits of the FTA with Thailand, CECA and prospective FTA with ASEAN largely due to internal cost disabilities that hamper its competitiveness vis-à-vis imports from these countries.

For starters, India Inc's ambivalence has been fueled in large measure by the skewed pattern of trade in favour of Thailand after the FTA came into effect in September 2004. Recent trade numbers indicate, in fact, that much of the gains have accrued to Thailand for the 82 items that form part of the EHS, which includes items like colour picture tubes, auto parts and electronic goods. From 2004-05 to 2007-08, Thailand's exports to India under EHS trebled to $470.5 million while India's exports to Thailand rose by only 87 per cent to $90.7 million.

India Inc fears are not entirely misplaced as Thailand's exports of items like epoxide resins, polycarbonates, aluminum alloys, window and wall air-conditioning machines, reception parts for colour TV sets, cathode ray TV picture tubes, including video monitoring tubes surged while there were no gains from trade for India. India's bilateral trade deficit in these EHS items ballooned 16-fold from $23.29 million in 2003-04 to $379.8 million in 2007-08. In this milieu, Indian companies might be tempted to outsource or even shift their bases to Thailand.

From a macroeconomic standpoint, there is also concern over the prospect of diversion of FDI as a consequence of bilaterals like the India-Thai FTA. Japan is a case in point. With its love affair rapidly souring with China, the major beneficiaries of its FDI in the future are likely to be countries like Thailand rather than India — unless, of course, the latter aligns its duty structures in line with the former and significantly improves its attractiveness as an investment destination for Japanese capital. Clearly, much depends on India's environment for doing business.

Considering the experience of trade in EHS items, the Indo-Thai FTA is in deep trouble and is unlikely to be formalized in a hurry. The Thai side, for its part, has also refused to budge from its demand of making the rules of origin (ROO) norms for the agreement less stringent than the norms being followed under the EHS. India, which is already taking a beating after reducing import tariffs on 82 items under EHS, naturally is unwilling to make the ROO less harsh as it could lead to a higher flow of imports due to third country imports coming into the country.

An Indo-Thai trade negotiating committee has already been constituted and 17 rounds of discussions for the FTA on goods have so far been held. Negotiations for an FTA in services and investment have also begun. But against the backdrop of the EHS trade imbalances, it is most unlikely that the FTA on trade in goods will be concluded this year as planned. But Thai authorities, for their part, like the Board of Investment of Thailand, remain somewhat more optimistic of enhanced levels of bilateral trade and investments between the two countries.

CECA Concerns

India Inc has similar concerns over the CECA with Singapore. Here again, the fear is that foreigners (read China) will misuse such agreements as a staging ground for cheaper exports to India. They consider the city-state to be mainly a trading rather than manufacturing hub although it hosts 7,000 plus MNCs in that country. Although the CECA allays these concerns with clearly laid out ROO and value addition norms of 40 per cent, India Inc's doubts persist although there are huge potential gains from using Singapore as a base to expand in Asia.

What then are the benefits, if any, of CECA? When Singapore's former premier, Goh, was asked this question, he quite simply replied investments! For all the doubts that India Inc harbours, leading groups like the Tatas, Mahindra and Mahindra, TVS among others intend to or have already established facilities in the city-state to secure a bridgehead to the ASEAN region as a whole and China. The CECA enables such corporates to access Singapore's interlinked equity capital and debt market to meet their growing need for diversified sources of funding.

Singapore already has a sizable exposure to India and is currently the second largest foreign direct investor, with investments cumulating to $7.93 billion between April 2000 and April 2009. The state-owned Temasek is also one of the largest private equity companies with investments of $5.1 billion (inclusive of Pakistan) as of March 31, 2008. It has broadened its partnership with telecom giant Bharti as a lead investor in a spin-off venture that manages telecom tower assets, besides partnering the Tata Group and STAR in their direct-to-home TV distribution venture.

For such reasons, the post-CECA expectations that foreign investments from Singapore will boom have proved self-fulfilling. Another benefit of CECA is that it will enable India to leverage vast pools of Islamic funds — pegged at $250 billion plus with annual growth of 15-20 per cent – that have headed to Singapore post 9/11. The list of potential investment benefits is a growing one as the agreement is basically a win-win situation for both India and the city-state. However, to harness its full benefits, India Inc must shed some of its hesitancy towards such agreements.

Post-CECA, bilateral trade volumes, too, are up by 41 per cent to $12.4 billion in April-December 2008 according to India's commerce ministry. India's trade numbers, however, are presented in a different format than Singapore that differentiates between the city-states' domestic and overall trade. Unlike India's EHS trade imbalances with Thailand, the experience with Singapore is more positive as it has registered a surplus of $733 million with the city-state in April-December 2008.

In contrast to the experience of EHS trade with Thailand, the bilateral trade pattern with Singapore is much more diverse. India is registering surpluses by exporting topped crudes, motor spirits, aluminum goods, jewellery, non-industrial diamonds, benzene, telephone and cellular network equipment, ships and aircraft bunkers, among others. Imports, too, are equally diverse ranging from topped crudes, parts and accessories for printing machinery, electronic circuits, parts and apparatus for transmission, reception of voice and data, styrene etc.

Trends in bilateral commercial services trade, however, are not encouraging as the advantage currently being in favour of Singapore. In 2008, the city-state's exports of commercial services to India grew faster than that to the rest of the world. The important bilateral commercial services were transportation, trade-related and travel services, communication and other services and financial services, including insurance.

However, growth in bilateral commercial services trade volumes has moderated significantly post-CECA when compared to the pre-CECA period. "This is a clear indication that despite the potential, bilateral trade in commercial services has failed to take advantage of the preferences and concessions garnered in CECA negotiations" argued Ms Karmakar.[3] Unless India swiftly concludes mutual recognition agreements of professional services that it is interested in, among other measures, Singapore's gains will continue to be relatively greater.

Indo-ASEAN FTA Woes

However, the biggest setback to the Prime Minister Dr. Manmohan Singh's economic diplomacy in looking eastwards might well be the persisting domestic opposition to the Indo-ASEAN FTA. As noted earlier, this opposition emanates from the ranks of his own Congress party, segments of which feel that such FTAs don't translate into electoral support in states like Kerala.

The latter has a vibrant plantation economy and fears are rife that it might be impacted adversely by such agreements. The refrain is that the Indo-ASEAN FTA might benefit India but not Kerala!

Attention is drawn to the problems being faced by Kerala's plantation farmers due to imports of tea, pepper and cardamom from Sri Lanka. Thanks to the Indo-Sri Lankan FTA, signed in 1998, spice and plantation products from ASEAN countries have allegedly found their way into India as they were claimed to be of Sri Lankan origin. Similarly, while palm oil is being imported into India at a duty of 80 per cent, the finished product enters duty free. Vanaspati or hydrogenated vegetable oil imports, thus, have been booming of late into the Indian market.

At the First ASEAN-India Summit held on November 5, 2002 in Phnom Penh, Cambodia, the then Prime Minister of India announced that India will extend special and differential treatment to ASEAN countries based on their levels of development to improve their market access to India. More importantly, he also stated that an FTA will be concluded within a timeframe of 10 years. Under the bilateral framework agreement on CECA signed at the Second ASEAN-India summit on October 8, 2003 at Bali, Indonesia, the FTA was to be finalized by June 30, 2005.

This deadline kept receding as negotiations encountered serious difficulties. The bilateral discussions ground to a halt in June 2006 when India released its huge negative list. For a sense of perspective, the ASEAN-India trade negotiation committee has met as many as 21 times to resolve the various contentious issues. There are no prizes for guessing that disagreements were sharp over the number of items that India wants to keep tariffs high on — palm oil, pepper, coffee and tea that impact the livelihoods of farmers in Kerala and Bengal.

The UPA government has sought in vain to appease Kerala's politicians by stating that India's commitment for tariff by 2019 would entail a tariff of 37.5 per cent for crude palm oil by the end of this period from levels of 80 per cent prevailing in 2005. Similarly, for refined palm oil, coffee and tea the tariffs would reach a level of 45 per cent by 2019. For pepper, the tariff would be at a level of 50 per cent by 2019. It has also been pointed out that rubber plantations have been provided protection by placing natural rubber in the negative list.

The Indo-ASEAN FTA provides for elimination of tariffs in a phased manner by 2016 on 80 per cent of the 5,000 traded products that include industrial and agricultural goods like consumer electronics, farm products, metals and chemicals. Ten per cent or 500 items have been placed on the sensitive track in which tariffs will be brought down by 5 per cent by 2016. Highly sensitive products like crude and refined palm oil, tea, coffee and pepper face duty cuts of 30 to 45 per cent by 2019. Around 489 items are on the negative list and will not be subject to tariff cuts.

Dr. Manmohan Singh has forcefully argued "A free trade agreement with the ASEAN is an international political commitment and is also part of the Look-East policy," during a cabinet meeting on July 29, 2009. Other cabinet colleagues chipped in by highlighting the diplomatic embarrassment India would risk if it were to pull out of negotiations and expressed the fear that if ditched, the ASEAN might get into a tighter strategic clinch with China on the rebound. "We will lose southeast Asia to China," one of the ministers reportedly argued.

For all these dismal tidings, India's trade with ASEAN constitutes only 9.3 per cent of its global trade during April-December 2008-09, while ASEAN's trade with India is only 2 per cent of its global trade — pointing to a huge upside trade potential that can be tapped with an FTA. Formal analysis using gravity models by researchers like Dr Amita Batra of the Jawaharlal Nehru University also points to a high potential of trade between India and ASEAN considering the geographical contiguity, cultural affinity and economic dynamism of the two regions.

According to gravity models, the flow of trade between a pair of countries is proportional to their economic mass (national income) and inversely proportional to the distance between them. Bilateral trade, thus, is positively a function of national income and negatively a function of distance. Dr Batra's work found that among ASEAN nations, high trade potential was indicated for Philippines, Vietnam and Cambodia.[4] No doubt, these are countries whose share in India's trade with ASEAN is much lower than Singapore, Malaysia, Indonesia and Thailand.

The good news is also that the Indo-ASEAN FTA is expected to kick in after a sustained improvement in bilateral two-way trade. India's trade with ASEAN, which was $ 9.8 billion in 2002-03 has grown more than three-fold to $34 billion during April-December 2008-09. India's exports to ASEAN rose three-fold from $4.6 billion to $13.8 billion, while its imports from ASEAN increased four-fold from $5.1 billion to $20.2 billion over this period. With this quickening tempo, bilateral trade volumes can easily cross $50 billion by 2010.

India should leverage its free trade agreement with the 10-member ASEAN if its ongoing efforts to forge pan-Asian integration, linking the Himalayas to the Pacific, are to bear fruit. Even if these are considered second-best options to a multilateral WTO trade agreement, the basic point is that India will only derive benefit from them if important stakeholders are less ambivalent regarding the potential gains. India Inc needs to exhibit greater self-confidence as leading two-wheeler manufacturers have already set up facilities in some ASEAN countries[5].

Addressing FICCI's AGM in January 8, 2007, Dr Singh forcefully appealed to India Inc that it "can no longer seek excessive protection through tariffs and must prepare for the brave new world of global integration." Indian business must also be prepared for a more fast-track economic integration in

South Asia. As the region's largest economy, we must be more open to our neighbours, he added. This also applies to the BIMSTEC grouping and ASEAN if India's to successfully integrate with the populous and prosperous economies of Asia, including China.

The success of smaller Indian companies like Professional Couriers, a parcel service company, that made Singapore its South-east Asian logistics hub, indicates the way forward. India Inc must form joint ventures or alliances with local businessmen in ASEAN countries like Malaysia and Indonesia. No headway is possible unless it deals with the Bhumiputras in Malaysia and Indonesia. A fast-globalising India Inc, thus, must seize the opportunity thrown up by the FTA with a sizeable economic entity with a combined GDP of $1.5 trillion and trade of $1.7 trillion like ASEAN.

REFERENCES

1. *Free Trade Today*, Oxford University Press, New Delhi, 2002, pp. 112.
2. *Free Trade Today*, p. 116.
3. "India-Singapore CECA – Limited gains in services", *The Hindu Business Line*, May 8, 2009.
4. Batra, Amita, "India's global trade potential: The gravity model approach", *Global Economic Review* (Routledge), September, Vol. 35, No 3, 2006.
5. Bajaj Auto Ltd. and TVS Motors entered Indonesia in fiscal 2006 and 2007 respectively.

CHAPTER 17

Comparative Management Systems in India and Southeast Asia

Prof. Vinayshil Gautam

Introduction

The study of "Comparative Financial Management Practices of India and South East Asia" is based on secondary as well as primary data collected from 101 manufacturing PSEs and 36 service PSEs for the post-liberalization period of 13 years (1991-2003).

As far as capital expenditure activity is concerned, the sample manufacturing and service PSEs have made substantial investments in acquisition of new assets.

The study found that maximizing return on total investments in assets (ROTA) has been consistently identified as the most popular measure in India, the United States and the United Kingdom.

With respect to financial decisions pertaining to new investments, the bottom up approach was found to be more popular in US and Japan, whereas the top-down approach found greater receptivity amongst the top management in Indian firms. Survey results showed that a significant number relies exclusively on traditional methods of investments appraisal, namely, the payback (PB) period and the average rate of return (ARR). The sample corporate firms in India and SEA preferred the PB and NPV methods due to their simplicity, saving in time and cost and easy understanding to top management.

Also according to the study, some of the firms continued to treat-equity funds (both equity share capital and retained earnings) as 'cost-free' sources of finance. As a matter of fact, equity funds, in general are costlier than any other source as equity investors are to be compensated for additional risk borne by them compared to lenders.

For financing of investment and designing of capital structure, the Indian corporate firms have shown a marked preference for debt.

According to "Pecking Order Hypothesis" firms follow a financing hierarchy with retained earnings at the top, followed by debt and external equity. The study showed that the Indian firms consider retained earnings to be more important source of funds than their counterparts in Southeast Asia, especially, Malaysia and Singapore. The flip side of retained is the dividend payout (D/P) ratio. Indian companies also seemed to have a stable dividend policy: their payout ratio declined in the post liberalization period.

As far as financing of working capital is concerned, matching approach followed by aggressive approach was more popular with Indian corporate firms.

Finally, study concluded that the wedge between theory and practice of financial management is not as wide as generally perceived. It is indicative of the maturity and professionalism in management of corporate finance function in India as well as southeast Asian region.

Information Systems, Organizations and Comparative Management

For achieving long term prosperity, the research on "Information Systems, Organizations and Comparative Management" emphasizes on discouraging international loans, which is an instrument of neo-slavery. This is evident in case of Africa which has been under high debt repayment obligations for a long time, and as a result its economic prosperity has been adversely affected.

There have been many concerns for the Asian region in recent times, which include security issues and mounting education, technology and healthcare costs. However, hence for the evolution of the region, learning the exchanges from comparative experiences of Africa and Latin America and at the same time the entire world is necessary.

The Asian companies lag behind their global counterparts in sharing information. While only 60 percent of the Asian organizations share company goals and vision, more than 80 percent of the Western organizations do so.

Though the Asian organization impart training and development to their employees, but trail behind in imparting skills like team problem solving and decision making. However, the rewards and compensation programs for employees are well established.

Therefore, going forward, the Asian region requires greater accountability in public expenditure and higher investment in infrastructure. The region needs to invest effectively and look to import technology from the rest of the world. The prudent controlling by the central banks, that limited impact on the economies during recessionary times, should be carried forward.

It can be concluded that Asia has a role to play in management in particular and creation of new world order in general.

International Competitiveness: Evaluation and Enhancement

The study on "International Competitiveness: Evaluation and Enhancement" proclaims that with the liberalization winds sweeping across continents in the last two decades. Darwin's theory of "survival of the fittest" has become more relevant to business world. The book also highlights the importance of country level competitiveness.

The research is based on an enormous amount of quantitative and questionnaire data about the comparative performance of three industries – Auto component, Construction and Telecom in India, Japan, Korea and the US. The report provides a comprehensive coverage of the competitiveness at the industry level.

Competitive industries often require a competitive environment to flourish and sustain their competitiveness. It is rare to see many sophisticated competitive firms and industries in countries, which are not very competitive. Considering the importance of country competitiveness for the competitiveness or industry and firms, competitive performance of India was reviewed by different approaches.

The key symptoms of India's poor competitiveness were identified, which are mentioned below:

- Stagnation and slow progress on issues like income disparities, population explosion, illiteracy and lack of infrastructural support
- Lack of aspiration among the Indian firms to be world class and compete globally
- A sense of collective paralysis, helplessness and a feeling of inferiority
- Lack of vision and strategy for future
- Looking to the West for validation of ideas and strategies and neglecting successful examples in the East and developing countries.

To validate the above points, more direct measures of corporate and industry competitiveness are required.

At the country level, India's standing on various parameters like infrastructure, people, management has been quite low as compared to Asian nations like China, Japan, South Korea and even Malaysia.

The evaluation of telecom industry's competiveness of India vis-à-vis Japan and China's telecom sector produces expected results. India fares poorly in both technological and human resources aspects. The lack of systemic policy and strategy of continuous improvement on criteria where there is a wide gap between local and global performance standards is cited as the main problem.

The results are similar for automotive and construction industry. All three Indian companies have been found on the negative end of the spectrum with Japanese companies being the most competitive.

To conclude, poor competitiveness of India means that companies and industry need to make efforts to overcome their weakness. Taking lessons from the success of Green Revolution and Operation Flood, the industry needs to focus on imagination of coping with resource constraints. The business models needs to be indigenously developed along with having strong leadership to provide vision for the future. The firms should develop their own understandings, approaches and strategies and implement them to enhance their competiveness. Hence, to develop competiveness. firms need to ensure a customer driven approach and develop a strategic outlook. They need to build quality processes in their organisational structure. An effective use of the technology is a must along with designing of an appropriate Human Resource system.

Digital Imperatives

The research on "Digital imperative" talks about achieving competitive advantage by performing better than competitors on existing dimension of competition and establishing new dimensions on which to compete by creating a new product/market combinations. Creation of viable futures would not be possible without taking into account the Mandarin, Japanese, India and South East Asian intellectual traditions.

Competitive advantage can be achieved in different ways:

1. Performing better than competitors on an existing dimension of competition
2. Establishing a new dimension on which to compete
3. Creating a new product/market combination

The ICT experience in South and Southeast Asia is explored in great detail. In the case of Singapore, the government took special interest in developing the sector by acquiring equity stakes and direct financial subsidies to the ICT companies. The same in not true in the Indian context. The role of Temasek Holdings of developing the teleco, Il infrastructure in the country has been tremendous. The birth of Singapore ONE as a part of the National Computer Board IT-2000 plan did a great deal to enhance Singapore's broadband networks. .

In Myanmar where the telecom sector is riddled with inefficacies, the government dominates the telecom scene completely with a state company, Myanmar Ports and Telecommunications being the largest telecom provider.

In Indonesia on the other hand the telecom sector has seen liberalization and has attracted foreign investment. The regulatory regime, though, has several limitations in terms of tariffs and universal service obligations. IPR protection too is a major challenge. IMF (International Monetary Fund) played a significant role in de-controlling Indonesian telecom.

Telecom services in Thailand are at par with international standards in urban areas, with a mix of private and government-run players.

Against this backdrop, the study of the Indian telecom sector has been undertaken.

Tele-density in India at the time of independence was extremely low (e.g. in 1948 it was only 0.02 %). However, the real efforts to boost this sector were started as late as mid 1990s with the initiation of liberalization in 1994, An independent regulator TRAI was set up in 1997.

Due to these efforts, the Indian telecom industry, today, is amongst the fastest growing industries in the country as well as in the world.

The point of significance is that the Information and Communication Technology (ICT) plays an important role in providing economic benefits to the society. The ICT helps in higher effectiveness in value chains operations and helps in exploring greater opportunities in E-business and global marketing opportunities. It enables creation of complex transactional business alliances with accelerated, standardized business practices and soaring international trade in services.

Conclusion

ASEAN has played an important role globally both as a trade bloc and in political terms. In the last 40 years since its inception, it has evolved into one of the largest trade blocs in the world and more importantly as one of the most promising regions for fuelling growth.

The political challenges of the 1990s and the Asian financial crisis have helped it emerge stronger and resilient, helped build strategic frameworks to counter such problems collectively. The Tsunami that rocked the region helped strengthen the coordination in disaster management system, another important upshot.

Promoting a common identity of ASEAN, expanding its network to make the efforts towards AStAN+6 a priority would help increase its clout in the global arena.

The research on Comparative Management Systems in Asia conducted at IIT Delhi through a series of publications draws learning from a variety of sectors ranging from telecommunication, information technology, automobile to name a few and throws light on future directions for organization development in the region. It notes how, financial managements systems and their evolution, especially post the Asian Financial Crisis, have brought about significant changes in the macro and micro economic policies in the region. A cautious prudent approach to financial liberalization has indeed benefitted the region as has the increase in intra-regional trade flows.

With a common ASEAN identity, which is unique, distinct and involves neighbouring trade partners, ASEAN could add more meaning into the lives of millions that inhabit the region. The arc of prosperity could be a reality, sooner than is envisaged.

REFERENCES

1. Gautam, Vinayshil; 1997; "*Organisational Futures: A Comparative Management Perspective*"; Hindustan Publishing Corporation; New Delhi.
2. Jain, P.K. Kumar, Manoj; 1997; "*Comparative Financial Management: Practices of Indio and South East Asia*"; Hindustan Publishing Corporation; New Delhi.
3. Kanungo, Shivraj (Ed); 1997; "*Information -Technology at work: A collection of Managerial Experiences*"; Hindustan Publishing Corporation; New Delhi.

4. Gautam Vinayshil; 2000; "*Information Systems, Organisations and Comparative Management*"; Hindustan Publishing Corporation; New Delhi.
5. Join, P.K., Yodav, Surendra S.; 2000; "*Economic Crisis in South East Asia: A Study of Implication for Global Economy*"; Hindustan Publishing Corporation; New Delhi.
6. Jain, P.K. Yadav, Surendra S.; 2000; "*Financial Management Practices in select private corporate : A comparative study of India , Thailand and Singapore*"; Hindustan Publishing Corporation; New Delhi.
7. Momaya, Kiron Kumar 2001; "*International Competitiveness: Evaluation and Enhancement*"; Hindustan Publishing Corporation, New Delhi.
8. Join, P.K. Join, P.K., Yadav, Surendra S.; 2005; "*Financial Management Practices - A Study of Public Enterprises in India*"; Hindustan Publishing Corporation; New Delhi.
9. January 2005; "Experiences Gained by New Partnership Initiatives and Possible Means to Improve Coordination at regional Level: ASEAN Committee on Disaster Management (ACDM)".
10. Gautam, Vinayshil; 2006; "*Digital Imperatives*"; Hindustan Publishing Corporation; New Delhi.
11. Kamal, Adelina; Coordinator, Environment and Disaster Management ASEAN Secretariat; November 2007; "ASEAN's Initiatives on Disaster Risk Reduction".
12. Simon, Sheldon W.; August 2007; "ASEAN and its Security Offspring: Facing New Challenges"; http://www.strateqicstudiesinstitute.army.mil/pdffiies/pub 793. pdf.
13. 2007; "Ten as One: Challenges and Opportunities for ASEAN Integration"; United Notions Economic and Social Commission for Asia and the Pacific Bangkok; http://www .unescap .orq/unis/asean/ten@one.pdf.
14. "Indio and A.SEAN"; IBEF; December 2007 (Online); http://www.ibef.orq/india/indiaasean.aspx.
15. "Emerging Asian regionalism A Partnership for Shored Prosperity"; Asian Development Bank; January 2008. (Online) http://aric.adb.·:xQ/emerqinqasianreqionalism/odfs/Final_ear_ chapters / final%20report.pdf.
16. Francis, Smitha; Kallummal, Murali; June 2008;The New Regionalism in Southeast Asian Trade Policy and Issues in Market Access and Industrial Development: An Analysis of the ASEAN-China Free Trade Agreement"; http://www.networkideas.org/working/aug2008/06_2008.pdf.
17. February 27, 2009 "Intra-ASEAN trade vital in tough times" Inquirer.net; http://www.inquirer. net / specialfeatures/ thefinancialcrunch/view. php? db= 1 &article=20090227 -191335.

PART–V. ARC OF PEACE AND PROSPERITY

CHAPTER 18

Some Thoughts on the 'Arc of Peace and Prosperity'

Amb. Rajiv Sikri

The idea of such an 'arc', as far as I am aware, emerged in discussions, conversations and meetings that were held between the leaders of Japan and India a few years ago. What is the region covered by this 'arc of peace and prosperity'? This 'arc' encompasses the region from South Asia up to the Pacific, covering all the East Asian and the South East Asian countries, plus Australia and New Zealand, which are on the periphery of this 'arc.' If one considers all the countries of this region from Himalayas to the Pacific, it is obvious that this region has in abundant measure all the key elements, whether it is population, GDP, economic growth rate, foreign exchange reserves, or trade volume that goes to make it a dynamic region. Both Prime Minister Manmohan Singh and former Prime Minister Atal Behari Vajpayee have publicly spoken about the enormous potential of this region. Prime Minister Manmohan Singh has said that his vision is that there should be free movement of people, goods, capital and ideas across this vast space. This is a very bold and farsighted vision that deserves to be commended. One must admit that when this was put forth four or five years ago it sounded a bit unrealistic and idealistic. Today, when the relative weight of the West in US and Europe has declined and that of Asia is increasing, I think it compels greater attention.

The question is: what are the countries of this region going to do? Are they going to come together or is Asia going to remain divided? After all, let us not forget that Asia was deliberately divided by the colonial powers. We have not really fought as many wars among ourselves as those that have been imposed on us. For centuries, the West cut up and divided Asian countries and augmented mutual antagonisms among Asians. The skeptics say that there is no 'Asia', that Asia is a figment of the imagination. To these people, my answer is: Well, if you can have the concept of a 'Europe', why deny the concept of 'Asia'? It is well known that Europeans have had a centuries-old history of divisiveness and conflict, and have fought innumerable bloody wars and butchered hundreds of thousands of people. Yet today, people are prepared to accept the concept of 'Europe' based on Graeco-Roman civilization and Christianity. Why then should it be difficult to accept that 'Asia' is a similar unit based on commonalities of thinking and culture across the continent, derived from Buddhism and Hinduism. Even Islam in Asia, including the whole of South Asia, Indonesia and Malaysia, has a distinct, and much more tolerant, character in tune with these native traditions.

Even as there are developments in Asia that brighten the prospects of this 'arc of peace and prosperity' becoming a reality, one should not ignore some real problems that are likely to be encountered in this path. One fundamental problem, of course, is that while many countries do share India's vision outlined above, there are differences among Asian countries on how to realize this vision. These differences came out most graphically in the setting up of the East Asia Summit (EAS), where, as you probably know, India had a difficult time to become a founder member. However, a long-term vision combined with successful Indian diplomacy ensured that India was a participant in the inaugural EAS summit. The East Asia Summit process is continuing, perhaps a little slower than was originally thought, but I think the EAS train is on the rails. Against this is the competing vision of the ASEAN+3, which brings together ASEAN, Japan, China and South Korea, being pushed primarily by China, which thinks that through this mechanism it would be able to dominate the region. It is precisely because of such fears that countries like Japan, Vietnam, Indonesia and Singapore have been keen to involve India so that there is some kind of balancing factor to Chinese hegemony over East and Southeast Asia. Now as the process of building a community in East Asia gets under way, the ongoing struggle that can be expected to intensify is about the nature of this 'arc of peace and prosperity.' Would it be centered on the EAS, or the ASEAN+3?

Other knotty questions will also have to be tackled. Although it is a global player and has significant interests and presence in East Asia, the United States is not a member of the EAS. Apart from the Shanghai Cooperation Organisation, this is the only other organisation, what is more a major organisation, of which the United States is not a member. When the EAS was set up, the United States was too distracted by its preoccupations with the wars in Afghanistan and Iraq, and the rising tensions with Iran. However, today the United States realises that it cannot and should not neglect this region. US Secretary of State Hillary Clinton's recent visits to China, Japan, Korea and Indonesia bring out clearly that this part of the world will be once again a priority area of US foreign policy priorities. The United States also understands that this part of the world has an increasing global weight. Of course, one cannot envision an 'arc of peace and prosperity' without factoring in what the United States will do and what kind of pressures it will bring upon the countries to make sure that it is included. I am not saying that the United States cannot or should not be included. But there is little doubt that US membership of the EAS will undoubtedly change the balance and the dynamics of the EAS.

Russia too has been very keen on joining the EAS, but has not succeeded so far. As a country that also has an East Asian character, Russia does have a legitimate claim to membership. However, politically, it would be difficult to include Russia in the EAS without also including the United States. Another, bigger, question is: what would happen to Taiwan and North Korea? After all you cannot have any 'arc of peace and prosperity' that ignores these two sore thumbs sticking out in East Asia.

From the Indian perspective, it is obviously to India's advantage that it is a member of this grouping. At the same time, if India integrates with East Asian and South East Asian countries, how does India handle its South Asian neighbours? Are they going to be left behind? What happens to Bangladesh? Are we going to have 50 million Bangladeshis migrating to India? These are real questions. As India evolve its 'Look East' policy, and its integration with this part of the world, it has to factor in its immediate neighbours too. Some mechanisms like BIMSTEC serve precisely this purpose. In my own discussion with Bangladeshi interlocutors I have found that they are keen to get involved in India's initiatives with its eastern neighbours because they see the opportunities for themselves through linkages with East and Southeast Asia. Moreover, from India's long-term point of view, it is desirable that Bangladesh should feel a little more reassured if it is part of a larger framework and not so dependent on India; perhaps then Bangladesh may be more responsive to India's concerns.

Let me deal with some of the other mechanisms that could be potential building blocks in the process of building an East Asian community. ASEAN is at the core of Asian community building. But a big and legitimate question is: where is ASEAN headed? There is already a two-speed ASEAN. One comprises the more developed members of ASEAN namely, Indonesia, Malaysia, Philippines, Singapore, Thailand and Brunei. The other is the CLMV group of less-developed countries of ASEAN comprising Cambodia, Laos, Myanmar and Vietnam. Over the last three years, ASEAN has been forced thrice to reschedule its planned annual summit. Will ASEAN be able to retain its central role as a grouping that brings together the major powers? In this respect it plays a role similar to the role that Luxemburg or Brussels plays in Europe. But it is unclear whether ASEAN will be able to indefinitely continue to do this.

Another existing organisation is APEC. While the Americans are committed to APEC, it seems to be going nowhere. Its future as a serious regional organisation remains uncertain. Moreover, India is not a member of APEC. So should India be interested in APEC? For many smaller countries APEC is quite important since, among other things, it provides their leaders an annual photo opportunity with the US President. For India this may not be a relevant consideration.

Then there is the ill-conceived and short-lived 'Quad' that brought together India, Japan, the United States and Australia a couple of years ago.

However, as a result of vehement opposition from China, and also because of a change of governments in both Japan and Australia, the Quad has been given a quiet burial. Australian Prime Minister Kevin Rudd has been pushing the idea of an Asia-Pacific Community, comprising the United States, Japan, China, India, Indonesia, and unspecified 'other states in the region'. No doubt Australia expects that it would be included. Without specifically mentioning, much less endorsing Kevin Rudd's idea, some influential and well-connected Chinese scholars have been trying to gauge reactions in the region to such an idea. It is not ruled out that it is the Chinese who have put up Kevin Rudd (who is unabashedly pro-Chinese) to float this idea. If so, what could be the Chinese game? It is possible that this is a Chinese attempt to prevent the emergence of the India-Japan-US- Australia 'Quad'. What they are doing is essentially to try to spike the idea of the 'Quad' by expanding it to include China, as well as Indonesia that, because of its geographical location and size, is a very important country for China's trade and energy SLOCs. Another problem with the Rudd proposal is that it divides ASEAN and all the ASEAN countries (other than Indonesia) that have been left out of the proposed grouping will oppose this proposal tooth and nail.

Anyway, these are some of the ideas being floated around the world. Just as there is some thinking under way on this issue in other countries, there should be similarly be some thinking within India too. I am sure that within the Government there are ideas on what should be the elements of the new Asian cooperative mechanism that would ensure that this area really becomes an arc of peace and prosperity.

I will not elaborate on the defence relationship that India has with the various countries in this region because Vice Admiral Chauhan has talked on this subject very eloquently and in detail. But I would like to raise a couple of issues. It is very important that India's defence ties with all the countries of the region should expand. India's objective national interests necessitate this. After all, a significant proportion of India's foreign trade is with these countries. In addition, we also need to develop both a psychological and a real counter to ongoing Chinese activities in the Indian Ocean. India needs to be more active in this regard. This can be done bilaterally, through exercises, training or other cooperative activities with individual countries. It can also be through confidence-building regional mechanisms like the Indian Ocean Naval Symposium (IONS), the MILAN exercises, the ASEAN Regional Forum (ARF), and Track II mechanisms like CSCAP and the Shangri-La dialogue. Japan is obviously going to be a key player and India has rightly been giving considerable attention and focus to engaging Japan. Japan has the second largest economy in the world and very formidable, if well masked, military capabilities that can be unleashed at a short notice. The problem, however, is that Japan has a somewhat inconsistent view of India that appears to be considerably dictated by the state of its relations with China. As you know, under Prime Ministers Abe and Koizumi, the relationship between China and

Japan was a little frostier than it is today. In addition to engaging Japan, we also need to continue to engage South Korea.

The 'arc of peace and prosperity' is only one of the 'arcs' that matter to India. Vice Admiral Chauhan has brought out the importance of another 'arc', namely the 'arc of communications.' As India sits at the centre, or at the head, of this 'arc of communications,' this gives India additional importance. In addition, there are two additional 'arcs' involving India that intersects with the other 'arcs' already mentioned. One is the 'arc of energy' extending from the Persian Gulf through the Caspian Sea and going on to Siberia and the Far East. India is a large power that is most proximate to the Persian Gulf, and India will inevitably have to play a role in securing not only its oil supplies but also its trade with the region. It is not ruled out that in a decade or two from now, or even earlier, the United States may reduce its military presence in the Persian Gulf region. In such an eventuality, who would take on the security responsibilities of the Persian Gulf region? From India's point of view, if the Chinese and other powers establish a presence in a big way in the Persian Gulf region, or the Gulf of Aden off the Somalia coast, India would understandably get a little nervous. Thus India has to take a hardheaded security view of the Persian Gulf because of India's enormous energy dependence on the Gulf region, as well as the reality that about 5 million Indians are living and working in the Persian Gulf region. As a result of the recent economic downturn, a not insignificant number of people who have lost their jobs in the Persian Gulf states are coming back to India. This is creating problems back home. Thus instability in the Gulf will have domestic fallout within India for which India has to be prepared. What would happen if a shooting war were to break out in the Persian Gulf? The Indians living there would panic. However, what to talk of the Indian Air Force, even the Indian Navy candidly acknowledges that it is beyond its capabilities to transport stranded Indians in the Persian Gulf back to India. We did a small relief operation in Lebanon in 2006 and evacuated a fairly substantial number of Indians in 1991 at the time of the First Gulf War. But if there is any major problem our five million Indians will remain stuck there, and it will not be long before many Indian State Governments, particularly in south India, are destabilised. Thus India has to do some forward planning for difficult and tricky scenarios and to give serious thought to the security aspects of the Persian Gulf region.

The final arc, perhaps the most difficult one, is the 'arc of instability. 'From Pakistan, right up to the Mediterranean is a very unstable region and one of the most turbulent and problematic areas of the world. The whole region – Pakistan, Afghanistan, Iran, Iraq, Lebanon, Syria, Israel, and Palestine – is a virtual tinderbox. Now the fire is spreading towards India. We are rightly worried about what is going to happen to Pakistan. Will instability in Pakistan affect India? In any case, we cannot ignore it. Our history tells us that this has been the area from which all the threats to Indian security have emanated. Once again we are confronted with a challenge to India's security from this region. Thus, while we look at the opportunities of the 'arc of prosperity and peace' to our east, we should not forget that the real troubles are to our west to which, therefore, India must give much greater attention and focus.

Finally, I would just like to flag a couple of issues on the naval side for consideration. One, the US navy is the dominant navy in the Indian Ocean — indeed across the world. It is well known that the US Navy has more manpower strength and firepower than all the other navies combined in this region. India has to take a view whether it can, or indeed whether it should, piggyback on the US? Or are India's interests better served if it engages in cooperation with the US on a more need-based basis? The reason why it is essential to answer this question honestly is that there is no free lunch with the Americans – or indeed with anyone else. Therefore, ours must be a very carefully weighed and considered decision in this regard. It should not be an ideological or a motivated view. It is possible that the senior naval officers here know it better than I do about what the US naval presence in Diego Garcia means for us. What were the security imperatives that led India to send its military to Sri Lanka in 1987? Are all those considerations now absent or no longer relevant? What happened in 1971 when the USS Enterprise sailed into the Bay of Bengal when India was conducting its military operations in Bangladesh? These and other questions must be squarely and honestly addressed. If India's economy grows at 8-9% per year, or even at a more modest and definitely realistic 6-7%, after 10-15 years India will become a formidable power. Will India then be a target for containment by outside powers? These are some of the questions that we must seriously address.

Finally, linked to this is another key question: how does India have a strategic relationship with the US when India's naval fleet as well as the development of India's naval equipment and systems is so heavily dependent on Russia? India is looking primarily at Russia for all its future major high-technology naval acquisitions, whether it is nuclear submarines or an aircraft carrier. Other countries will not let India even sniff at these products. Admiral Roy and others who have lived in Russia and worked with the Russians, would probably know better, but I do believe that at a time when US and Russia are again entering a period of strategic competition, the Russians will hardly be inclined to give India their hi-tech products if India is entering into a strategic relationship with the United States.

CHAPTER 19

India, ASEAN and Asia-Pacific

Prof. P.V. Rao

Europe's departure from Southeast Asia and the subsequent passing of the region under American-led cold war alliance system, sustained the wedge between India and the newly emerged nations of Southeast Asia. Jawaharlal Nehru's efforts to bring together the Asian nations into a common fold and build an Asian identity was devoured by cold war politics as Southeast Asia passed under the SEATO. Domestic politics of these states and their nation-building strategies like Malaysia's *bhoomiputra* marginalized the Indian communities. Indian business communities and the indentured workers who followed them to build the colonial economies were ill-treated, including confiscation of their properties as by the post-colonial Burmese regime. The Indian government was not inclined to address their grievances at official level, and Nehru advised the Indian diaspora to reconcile to the local political regimes. Such hands off approach distanced diasporic Indians of Southeast Asia from their ancestral land.

Eclipse of cold war and the loss of Soviet Union as India's close strategic partner drove New Delhi to rethink her frozen relations with Southeast Asia. No less, India's opening up to the global market forces and the drive to attract foreign capital provided a strong economic impulse to forge closer synergies with the tiger economies of the east. New catchwords such as 'Rediscovering Asia,' 'Look East,' 'Asian Century partnership' frequented Indian official and semi-official lexicon since the decade nineties. Building bridges with the East assumed part of the prioritised domain of Indian diplomacy evidenced by well-programmed and publicized visits by the political leadership to the Southeast Asian states. The early phase of India's look east policy centred on ASEAN. During its first phase, look east I, New Delhi had to strenuously exert its diplomatic skills to persuade the skeptical Southeast Asian countries of India's genuine interest in the region. Historical and cold war hangovers had long distanced the regions on either side of the Malacca Straits, a chasm deepened by the Southeast Asian sensitivities over India's naval 'expansionism' in the Indian Ocean. Nor were the ASEAN countries impressed with India's economic policies, despite recent economic reforms.

Thus there was hardly a positive attribute in the ASEAN outlook that proved attractive to invite India's involvement in the region. Certainly, on balance, India was no match to China and Japan who had far greater economic potential to share with ASEAN. Hence, India was allowed a graduated access – sectoral to full dialogue partnership – which culminated after a decade in Summit Partnership in 2002 (Asean+1). A year later the India-ASEAN Framework Agreement on Comprehensive Economic Cooperation, commonly called free trade area (FTA) agreement, was signed which envisaged investment facilitation and tariff elimination on goods and services by 2007 between India and the ASEAN countries. However, the FTA failed to meet its timeframes as serious differences developed over the details, with ASEAN insisting on the inclusion of larger number of goods under FTA coverage and higher duty cuts by India on the goods entering from Southeast Asian countries. As FTA failed to meet the deadline of coming into force, trade level between the both parties too did not register good progress. It was just about $40 billion per annum, not an encouraging figure. On the other hand, bilateral free trade area pacts reached by India with Thailand and Singapore are in force and are more promising in increasing trade volume than the multilateral FTA.

India-ASEAN economic relations carry a sub-regional development promise in the sense that their trade route would contribute to the development of India's northeastern region (NER), contiguous to Southeast Asia. In fact, NER has been conceived as India's gateway to the ASEAN region. The region is accorded an inclusive role in the country's economic engagement with the Southeast Asian countries in which Thailand figures prominently. Emphasizing that "high priority" needs to be given for development of highways, railways, airways, shipping services and energy linkages between India and ASEAN countries, the *ASEAN-India Vision 2020* notes that these linkages will "contribute significantly to the overall development of India's northeast region which is the gateway to ASEAN."[1] It may be recalled that ancient trade and religious contacts between India and the Indo-China passed through the northeastern region. South and Southeast Asian societies conducted their trade through the adjoining territories as well as the sea routes.

Today, in the era of globalization, there is an effort to restore the ancient caravan routes to build trading networks. In fact, plans to develop transnational transport linkages to this end are already in place. Already, a 1300 km.India-Myanmar-Thailand trilateral highway connecting the NER is under construction. India's business group, ASSOCHAM proposed to build an optical fibre telecommunication link alongside the highway. A 135 km. road linking the Moreh town in Manipur with Myanmar was completed recently and an India-sponsored Asian Motor Rally was flagged off from Guwahati, passing through Myanmar and Thailand and terminating at Hanoi. Yet, such efforts to link India through the NER to the ASEAN region notwithstanding, there is least evidence of the region in any way benefited by them, the main reason, not difficult to guess is the insurgency in NER. A senior official of India's foreign ministry in charge of the east Asian affairs, Rajiv Sikri expressed this pessimism in saying that the look east policy "is intended to benefit the northeast. So far there are no visible effects of the policy in any of the seven states. The northeast is already burning."[2]

India's current eastward drive attempts to synthesize the cultural past with the present. Buddhist communities in Thailand, Indonesia, Singapore and the CLMV (Cambodia, Laos, Myanmar, and Vietnam) are expected to reconnect the cultural bridges between India and ancient Farther India, if their passage to Indian Buddhist sites is made easier. The *ASEAN-India Vision 2020* says: "The shared history and culture dating back to several centuries provides a base for tourism exchanges. A large number of tourists from Southeast Asia come to centres of Buddhist pilgrimage in India every year."[3] To this end relaxation of visa regulations, concessional admission fee to enter the pilgrim sites and comfortable accommodation are planned.

A 'Buddhist Circuit' encompassing the holy sites of India and Nepal is the tourist blueprint. In fact both parties signed an 'open skies' agreement which would increase air traffic by granting greater access to the airports of each of the signatories. Yet, there is not significant tourist flow into India, while, on the contrary, greater number of Indians are attracted by Southeast Asia's well developed holiday resorts.

The Indian diasporic entrepreneurs in Southeast Asia – scions of Klings, Chulias, Chettiars, Kanganis, etc. – are today wooed by market-driven India to join her trade and investment regime. Policy measures to encourage engagement with Indian business world include investment incentives, tax concessions, property ownership and dual citizenship, which are part of India's general PIO (people of Indian origin) policy. Though Singapore and Malaysian Indians have shown interest to invest in India, prospects from other Southeast Asian communities of Indian origin are limited.

By the end of the decade nineties, India's canvass of look east policy was widened beyond Southeast Asia. While ASEAN would obviously be in focus, under phase II of look east, sustained efforts were made to gain access to wider Asia-Pacific region through the ASEAN structure. India's strategic periscope, in the post-Soviet and post-cold war era, was redefined to address the dynamic strategic and economic changes that were fast underway in the Asia-Pacific, a region which symbolised the Asian Century. Such an articulation of India's widened interests was expressed in several official pronouncements. Addressing the India-ASEAN Business Summit in 2004, prime minister Manmohan Singh said:

It is only inevitable that we take the existing India-ASEAN relationship to a higher level where we envision an Asian Economic Community which encompasses ASEAN, Japan, Korea and India. Such a community would release enormous creative energies of our people. . .This community of nations would constitute 'an arc of advantage', across which there would be a large-scale movement of people, capital, ideas and creativity....[4]

Similarly, *Indian Maritime Doctrine* (2004), the official document of the Indian Navy released in 2004 stated that the "centre of gravity is shifting from the North America-West Europe axis to the North America-Asia-Pacific rim, with Japan, China and the Asian Tigers looming large in global economic considerations."[5] And, therefore, if India has to safeguard her legitimate political and strategic interests in that dynamic region, it is imperative to project her presence and power in the Asia-Pacific rim. To this end, New Delhi joined in a number of regional multilateral arrangements such as the Asean Regional Forum (ARF), Treaty of Amity and Cooperation in Southeast Asia (TAC), Asean Security Community, Asean Summit (Asean+1), East Asia Summit, etc. The following diagram illustrates the Indian membership in various regional organizations of Southeast Asia.

India's Multilayered Engagement with East Asia

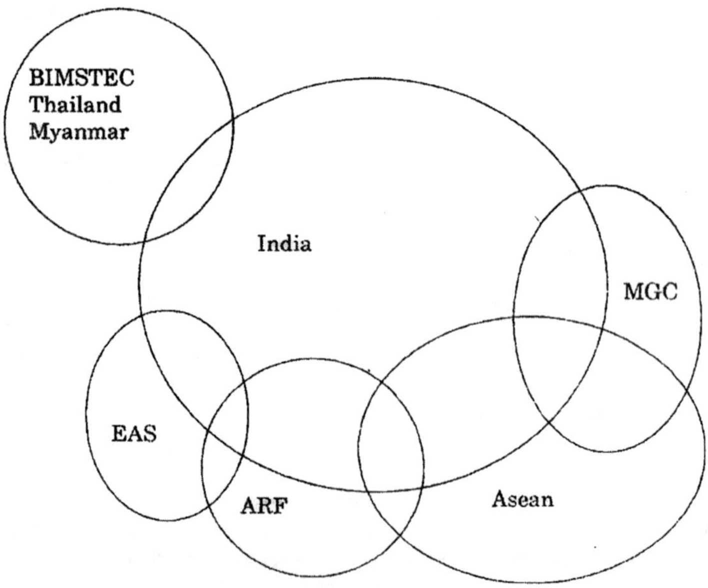

ARF: Asean regional forum; CLMV: Cambodia, Laos, Myanmar, Vietnam; MGC: Mekong-Ganga cooperation; BIMSTEC: Bay of Bengal multisectoral economic cooperation. (reproduced from, P.V. Rao, *India and ASEAN: Partners at Summit*, Knowledge World, New Delhi, 2008).

Strategic Objectives of India's Regional Involvement

Apart from the economic domain, India is a keener participant in Southeast Asia's regional strategic domain. Indian engagement with Southeast Asia and the regions beyond is motivated by her overall objective of seeking a major role in Asia. It reflects New Delhi's extension of strategic perimeter, premised on gaining legitimacy as a major partner in the Asia of twenty-first century, the Asian Century. Such a self-defined role, goaded by the post-Soviet Asian power matrix, broadly required accommodation with two overlapping regional power centres: ASEAN representing Southeast Asia and the former Indo-China; East Asia, representing China, Japan, and Taiwan. Engaging these regional formations, collectively folded into a loose interregional brand called Asia-Pacific which includes the United States and Australia too, has been the *leit motif* of India's look east policy. While the look east policy's initial phase focused on the ASEAN, toward the dawn of the millennium, reaching out to the wider Asia-Pacific was more pronounced. In other words, as this author argued elsewhere, ASEAN was used by India as a springboard to engage the wider Asia-pacific.

The Asian power structure consists of ASEAN, China, Japan, and the United States and to some extent Australia, as key players. It is a combination of global (US) and regional powers devoid of a formal structure and alliance system. Even the ASEAN as a homogenous regional body lacks a common security architecture. Rising China is a factor of common concern to all other powers, regional and extra-regional, but there is no common strategy among the players, small and big, to counter the Asian giant. Balancing China's power and moderating her regional behaviour ranges from strategic partnerships, accreditation to regional economic and security forums, trade pacts, binding treaties, defence cooperation and energy deals. In other words, Southeast Asian countries are adopting an inclusive approach to manage the threat from China.

Southeast Asian dilemma is how to cope with the big power involvement in the region, avoid conflict and ensure regional stability. All the ASEAN countries are no match to the individual military capabilities of the great powers, and hence in a very broader sense, there are two layers of power structure in the region: the militarily weak and economically vibrant Southeast Asian countries; and militarily and economically strong major powers. Between these two layers there is a wide strategic space laden with several options to engage one another, bilaterally or multilaterally, to gain individual security and ensure stable regional order. India is factored into such geo-political scenario wherein she volunteered her presence and is also co-opted by the regional powers, big and small.

Southeast Asia's geo-political landscape transformed considerably with the active involvement of China and India in the region. Conventional understanding of Southeast Asia's strategic sphere ranged from Malacca Straits to South China Sea. But, with India, a South Asian power declaring her strategic reach up to South China Sea and China (also Japan), a East Asian power en-routing the Bay of Bengal unto the oil-rich gulf (the New Silk Route), the outer limits of Southeast Asia's security domain too are enlarged. ASEAN's enlargement from six to ten also added to its geo-political space. As the regional involvement of one power tilted the power equations, ASEAN had to welcome another to balance the situation. Thus in India's eagerness to join the ASEAN system, its members saw an opportunity to balance the Chinese role in Southeast Asia. Singapore prime minister, welcoming India to the ASEAN Summit thus would remark:

> We welcome India's participation in ASEAN for two reasons: One is strategic. We do not want another big country to be actively engaged with the ASEAN, Otherwise ASEAN would be in a sense overwhelmed by their (sic) Northeast Asian countries – China, Japan. So if we have another wing in terms of constructive engagement that is India, it will make for a more stable ASEAN.[6]

The common refrain in the literature on India-ASEAN relations is that India was conceived as the western wing of the ASEAN jumbo, the northeastern powers symbolising its eastern wing. Both the Asian powers, India and China, since the end of the cold war, have been closely engaging the ASEAN for multiple purposes: trade, investment, energy, sea routes and strategic space. Both, though for historically dissimilar reasons, had to indulge in serious diplomatic persuasion to gain the confidence of ASEAN members, with considerable success. It is also noticeable that both the Asian powers are involved in competitive strategies in engaging the ASEAN countries. In economic terms, India lags far behind compared to the Chinese business, trade and investment levels in the region. But, in strategic terms, India has established considerable presence in the region by enacting defence agreements with several ASEAN countries.

The Indian Navy (IN) is the most chosen instrument of India's foreign policy toward Southeast Asia. *Indian Maritime Doctrine*, declares that the country's "maritime vision for the first quarter of the 21st century must look at the arc from the Persian Gulf to the straits of Malacca as a legitimate area of interest".[7] Even South China Sea is regarded as part of this arc of Indian strategic sphere. Such a pronouncement exactly complements post-cold war Indian definition of her foreign policy extension. Thus the Indian Navy has concluded a number of agreements with the Asia-Pacific countries aimed at maritime confidence-building through regular ship visits, fleet reviews, joint procurement and combined exercises. India is also sharing with the Southeast Asian maritime neighbours her naval soft power which includes training naval personnel, sharing naval capabilities, surveillance technology, disaster management, etc. Thus the IN's lead role in the evolution of India's post-cold war eastern drive needs to be recognized. A well-informed Southeast Asian scholar GVC Naidu would claim that the IN was responsible for opening the initial channels of communication with the Southeast Asian countries and that its CBMs formed the basis of India's Look East policy.[8]

Apart from the bilateral naval interactions with the Southeast Asian countries, IN had initiated the multinational naval exercises, beginning with the *Milan* in 1995. This biennial naval conclave in the Andaman & Nicobar islands (AN) was a true naval initiative, without a precedent. In a historical perspective, *Milan* is India's maritime counterpart of the Afro-Asian Solidarity Conference, proposed and led by India, at the Indonesian city of Bandung exactly forty years ago in 1955. Jawaharlal Nehru's dream of building an Afro-Asian forum in world politics was shattered by the emerging cold war equations which broke the Bandung spirit. Four decades later, India again took the initiative, this time a maritime one, of bringing together the Southeast Asian neighbours to assemble in her sovereign waters. *Milan* is not only an Indian initiative, but it is the first Indian Ocean attempt to assemble the regional navies on a common platform.[9]

China factor

India's recent Southeast Asian policy, underpinned by active strategic and economic involvement in the region, is naturally viewed by China with concern, even suspicion. Beijing too responded by cultivating defence relations with countries like Malaysia and Indonesia while its serious involvement in the economic and military fields of the Bay of Bengal countries of Myanmar and to a lesser extent in Bangladesh is well known. Some China observes even argue that her 'string of pearls' doctrine is to some extent linked to India's look east policy and the establishment of Andaman & Nicobar Command on the western flank of Malacca Straits.[9]

There is a significant American dimension to India's post-cold war Asia-Pacific policy. Almost since the unveiling of the look east policy, Washington and New Delhi have been shaping up their strategic partnership which, among other things, ensured a closer role for India in the Asia-Pacific region. India has been accorded a prominent role in the US dominated Eastern Hemisphere, a role hitherto preserved for America's cold war allies. Successive US Administrations continued to treat India as America's close partner in the Asia-Pacific domain. Washington sees in rising India a great potential and promise to counter the growing Chinese power, an objective shared both by Washington and New Delhi. An American senior naval officer had expressed this view in the following language: "The United States and India both view China as a strategic threat and share an interest in understanding China's strategic intent, though we do not discuss this publicly....A positive relationship with India offers a hedge against China's potential ambitions in Northeast and Southeast Asia...."[10]

The Bush Administration consolidated the positive gains made in Indo-US relations under the Clinton Administration and pledged its support to make

India a major power in the twenty first century. Among the major objectives of such policy was to help India become powerful enough to hedge China. Indian-born American Ashley Tellis who exercised considerable influence on the Bush Administration's India policy rationalized why the US should throw her weight behind India, in his report, *India as a New Global Power: An Action Agenda for the United States* (2005). In his *Agenda*, Tellis argues that the US should align with India because this growing Asian power "can be a counterfoil to China." According to him, the Bush Administration in fact had unveiled a major policy initiative which pledged to "help India become a major power in the twenty-first century," investing the energy and resources necessary to secure her untroubled ascent to great-power status.[11] The Chinese, as mentioned above, are concerned about the Indo-American *entente*. But, how far and soon such a partnership could impact on Beijing's Asian role is a subject to several ponderables: Sino-US relations, particularly in the trade field; strength and sustainability of Indo-US partnership; regional responses to Indo-US engagement in Asia-Pacific; and the regional security order in the Asia.

In the Asia-Pacific theatre, Indian and American navies are engaged in both bilateral and multilateral cooperation. Bilateral naval cooperation includes joint exercises, patrolling and information sharing. At multilateral level, both the navies are party to the quadrilateral group which consists of the Australian and Japanese naval forces, apart from the Indian and American. It is this multilateral combination which had undertaken group exercises in the Bay of Bengal and South China Sea, much to the chagrin of China. China, sensing she was the target of such naval operations, lodged a diplomatic protest by issuing a demarche to the participating countries. Japan in recent times has been emphasizing close economic and strategic relations with India. Her traditional rivalry with China and the latter's current rise as a global power have been the natural sources of concern to this East Asian power. Tokyo hence is building close synergies with India and the Indo-US strategic partnership offers a convenient multilateral framework for Tokyo to work with to advance its interests in the Asian region. As a Japanese analyst observed India and Japan could easily work in mutual interest given their diplomatic and security relations with rising China and "it is unavoidable to see a different course between India of non-alliance and Japan of alliance with the U.S."[12]

Among the East Asian powers Japan has moved closest to India in every major field since the beginning of the millennium. She is the single largest ODA contributor to India and is actively involved several investment and infrastructure projects. The visiting Japanese prime minister to India launched an 'arc of advantage and prosperity' with India as part of his India-Japan Global Partnership in the New Asian Era, in April 2005. An otherwise predominant economic relationship between the two Asian powers was complemented with a 'strategic' element leading to signing a 'Roadmap for

New Dimensions to the Strategic and Global Partnership' in 2007, the year which Tokyo declared as the *Year of India*. These exchanges "demonstrate a new Japanese approach to India for a better strategic engagement that would contribute to the Asian security, while at the same time not undermining its alliance relationship with the US."[13] (Panda,).Engaging Japan, therefore, fulfils India's millennium aspiration to join the Asian Century, in which Japan is a key player. In fact, apart from the bilateral engagement, Japan was keen to co-partner India in the five-member Asian multilateral economic forum, the JACIK (Japan, ASEAN, China, India and Korea) as also the four-power quadrilateral forum of democracies, which was floated by Tokyo.

Conclusion

Overall, India has emerged as a key actor, economically and strategically, in Southeast Asia, rather the Asia-Pacific region. Her potential to contribute to the Asian economic growth and regional security order is undisputed. India is integral to the JACIK (Japan, Asean, China, India, Korea), which is a pan-Asian group actively debating and drawing long-term plans for Asian economic integration, or an Asian Economic Community. New Delhi's importance to Asian security cooperation is recognized in equal measure as reflected by its inclusion in the Quadrilateral group, an Asia-Pacific security forum comprising Australia, Japan, United States and India. Viewed in historical perspective, India has regained her historic links with Southeast Asia. Efforts to resuscitate ancient ties, cultural and commercial, with Farther India have fairly succeeded. The great divide drawn by two historic forces – colonialism and cold war - is narrowing in favour of closer integration between the two sides. India-Southeast Asia relationship in the past was a link, dominant link, in the chain of what is called 'Oriental globalisation' or the 'Asian super highway' (Braudel). Today, both are integrating into the 'Asian Century', a rough equivalent of 'Asian superhighway.'

By subscribing to various regional trade groups, India has established her economic presence in Southeast Asia, though the latter is yet to be convinced about India's ability to deepen mutual economic partnership. Strategically, India has carved out a bigger role for himself in the Asian geo-political landscape. Through membership in fora of regional bodies, combined with sustained display of her naval power, India has staked her political claim to be a legitimate actor in the Asian power structure. Major powers like the US, Japan, China and the medium ASEAN powers acknowledge India as a dominant regional power. Thus, on balance, India's strategic presence outweighs her economic activism in Southeast Asia. Though it is a historical anachronism to search for close parallels between early Indian role in Southeast Asia and her present role therein, there is no doubt that India has gained back much of the lost ground in the region.

REFERENCES

1. *ASESN-India Vision 2020, working together for a shared prosperity,* Research and Information System for the Non-aligned and Other Developing Countries, New Delhi, 2004.
2. Rajiv Sikri and Marie Lall, "India is loosing Burma to China, *Deccan Chronicle*, August 18, 2007.
3. *Vision 2020*, p.48.
4. Quoted in, *RIS Policy Brief*, no.28, October 2006, p.3.
5. *Indian Maritime Doctrine*, Integrated Headquarters, Ministry of Defence, New Delhi, 2004.
6. Quoted in. K.Santanam and Srikant Kondapalli, Ed. *Asian Security and China, 2000-2001*, Shipra Publications, New Delhi, 2004, p. 246) 25.
7. Indian Maritime Doctrine.
8. G.V.C.Naidu, "India and Southeast Asia," *World Focus,* vol.*25,* no.9, September 2007,p.7.
9. See, Srikant Kondapalli,"China's Perspectives on India's Look East Policy," *South Asian Affairs*, Centre for SAARC Studies, Vizag, vol.1. no.2, 2008, p.67.
10. Quoted in, Julie MacDonald, *Indo-US Military Relationship: Expectations and Perceptions,* Department of Defense, USA, 2000, p.37.
11. See, Francis C. Assisi, "Indo-American Ashley Tellis Helps Evolve US-India Strategy (against China and the Islamic World), *Indolink.com*, July 6, 2005.
12. Yomiuri Shimbun, "Indo-Japan Cooperation," paper presented at the Indo-Japan Dialogue on Ocean Security, 2005.
13. Rajaram Panda, "Maritime Security: Strategic Implications in Indo-Japan Relations," paper presented at NIDS-IDSA Workshop, NIDS Tokyo, February 2009.

CHAPTER 20

India and Southeast Asia: A View from Singapore

Asad-ul Iqbal Latif

The Indian Ocean was an inter-regional and inter-civilisational area created by the free interplay of trade, religion and culture among Indians, Arabs and Chinese. Then, the intrusion of European imperialism turned the ocean into a bitter arena of naval rivalry that drew Asians into its violent orbit. European colonialism superceded the non-invasive nature of Asian interactions across the ocean's waves. However, it did not destroy these interactions entirely, nor erase their legacy in ideas, art and culture. At the heart of that legacy is the country after which the ocean is named. India is destined by geography to be the meeting point of western, northern, eastern and southeastern Asia. In making this point in March 1947, even before India had achieved independence, Pandit Jawaharlal Nehru laid the basis for its re-engagement with countries that were emerging from colonial rule. The Asian Relations Conference of March-April 1947 in Delhi was a precursor to the Bandung Conference of 1955 that expanded the sphere of re-engagement to Afro-Asia, and to the Non-Aligned Movement, which developed global agency. That we should meet in the historic city of Delhi is for me both an honour and a humbling experience. It is an honour because, courtesy of the Society for Indian Ocean Studies, I have gate crashed into such a distinguished gathering of scholars. I am humbled because we are all, in our different but related ways, re-examining India's place in the oceanic sphere of things, of which Southeast Asia is an intrinsic part. What Fernand Braudel did for the Mediterranean as a force in European history, and what K.M. Panikkar did for the Indian Ocean, was to give us a profound sense of the *longue durée*. The long term humbles mortals. However, this is also why it is so insistent in its demands on our exertions and imagination. I thank Professor Satish Chandra, Professor Baladas Ghoshal and their colleagues in the Society for having made this seminar possible.

One of the most prominent international developments to have occurred in the opening years of the 21st century has been India's appearance as a swing state in world affairs. This development has sturdy antecedents. China's role as a swing state that first broke with the Soviet Union and then turned towards the United States redefined the strategic landscape in the early 1970s. Four decades later, in different circumstances, India's role as a swing state moving towards the United States promises to rewrite the strategic script of these times. In the earlier case, the balance of power in Asia shifted decisively in favour of the United States. Today, relations between the United States, the leading keeper of the international *status quo*, and China, the primary challenger to American superiority in Asia, are likely to be affected similarly. The reasons for the two shifts are similar: China's 1964 nuclear test transformed its strategic potential for the United States during the Cold War; and India's rather longer journey to nuclear power from 1974 to 1998, from Pokharan I to Pokharan II, is doing the same today. In an article written soon after the 1998 nuclear explosions, Mohammed Ayoob noted that, as "the lone superpower and major provider of public goods in the international system, the United States has come to realize the importance of pivotal regional powers and the fact that international order can attain legitimacy and stability only if these same qualities are first achieved within regional orders." Hence it made sense for Washington to help New Delhi become South Asia's "regional security manager".[1] The recent Indo-US nuclear deal marks the culmination of a slow process of recognition, thwarted at many stages, of the international reality of India as a nuclear state. How far New Delhi's role as a regional security manager will go remains to be seen; much will depend on regional responses to such a role. However, no matter how other South Asian nations treat India's regional role, India is outgrowing South Asia. Southeast Asia is now an integral part of India's extended neighbourhood.

To be honest, India's relations with the Association of Southeast Asian Nations (ASEAN) during the second half of the 20th century were generally uneasy. They were presaged in New Delhi's dismissive reference to Southeast Asia's capital- and America-friendly states as "Coca-Cola countries". During the Cold War, Non-Aligned India refused to join any club that might alienate the Soviet Union. India's relations with ASEAN plummeted during the Vietnamese invasion and occupation of Cambodia and China's subsequent war with Vietnam. However, the end of the Cold War and the imperatives of globalisation led India to rediscover ASEAN, which was expanding to encompass the whole of Southeast Asia. The rediscovery took the form of the Look East policy that was initiated in 1991 and enunciated in 1992. Since then, India's relations with ASEAN have progressed greatly. India became a sectoral dialogue partner of ASEAN in 1992, a full dialogue partner in 1995, and a member of the ASEAN Regional Forum (ARF) in 1996. India became a summit-level partner of ASEAN in 2002 and signed the ASEAN-India Partnership for Peace, Progress and Shared Prosperity in 2004. Indian involvement in several regional initiatives – such as the Mekong-Ganga Cooperation (MGC) scheme and the Bay of Bengal Initiative for Multi-Sectoral Technical and Economic Cooperation (BIMSTEC) – added depth to the engagement. India is a member of the East Asian Summit (EAS) process, which began in 2005.

China Looks South, India Looks East

Even as we discuss India's current relations with Southeast Asia, we should not lose sight of history because the region offers much scope for reflection and analysis in terms of the *longue durée*. Southeast Asia is defined by its geographical position south of China and east of India. Historically, the Nanyang, the lands lying beyond China's southern seas, were part of the orbit of imperial China. This fact has consequences for Southeast Asia in an era of China's rise, and influences the region's expectations of India.

In some views, China's grand strategy is based on its historical self-perception as the Middle Kingdom. In this belief-system, the rebirth of the Celestial Empire, carrying the Mandate of Heaven, and its reappearance on the global stage mark the true onset of the Asian Century. The Chinese government itself makes no such claims, but scholars such as David C. Kang do so implicitly when they make a case for a Sinic Asian order today. Kang argues that relations in East Asia have been more peaceful and stable historically than those in the West because a strong and stable China preserved hierarchical order characterised by "considerable informal equality" among states. This order lasted till the intrusion of the Western powers in the 19th century introduced into Asia the Westphalian tradition of international relations, which consisted of formal equality among nation-states but informal hierarchy and nearly constant conflict among states.[2] The historical template for the restoration of China's pacifist role would be the great Ming dynasty naval expeditions of Admiral Zheng He and the establishment of a tributary system in the Nanyang.

Along with Central Asia, Southeast Asia is closest today to the gravitational pull of a 21st-century Chinese Celestial Empire, if there is to be one. Southeast Asia constitutes the immediate periphery of a resurgent China, which has launched an economic charm offensive across the region. In this offensive, the generous Free Trade Agreements that China has signed with ASEAN countries are more than economic moves: They are strategic instruments. ASEAN benefits from China's peaceful development, which makes this largesse possible, but some wonder whether it might lead to the restoration of the pre-colonial tributary system in the Nanyang, when China offered those who acknowledged its symbolic suzerainty more than it received in return.

Wang Gungwu warns against attributing historical bad faith to Chinese aspirations today. He notes that after three decades of Zheng He's "exceptional" voyages, the Ming emperors returned to the control of traditional lands and forbade foreign adventures.[3] The danger, Wang argues, lies not in China's worldview emanating from its own history but in a strand of modern Chinese historiography which, influenced by the study of modern Western history, has sought to reinterpret the notion of empire to draw comparisons with European empires in Asia. He declares that, today, there is no place for an historic empire or a tributary system. Reiterating the point that it is not China's past that is worrying but how it might respond to what other countries are doing in the present, he writes: "What would be new and alarming to the region would be a modernized China finding that it has to behave like the modern great powers of the West."[4]

The same might be said of India and a restored Indic order. Curzon's vision of India in the scheme of things was elegant, but imperial.[5] Britain maintained its empire by securing India through the exercise of naval supremacy from Aden to Singapore, turning the Indian Ocean effectively into a British lake. Writing before India's independence, K. M. Panikkar penned an elegiac endorsement of Curzon's political geography in *India and the Indian Ocean*.[6] Speaking in the long aftermath of Curzon's India, and picking up the British trail following their military retrenchment East of Suez in the 1970s, US former Secretary of State Henry Kissinger declared that there was compatibility between American interests and India's avowed desire to prevent another dominant power from emerging between Singapore and Aden.[7] Replicating Britain's legacy, Kissinger encouraged Indian Curzonians for whom India's strategic neighbourhood stretches from West Asia to Southeast Asia. Indeed, he said explicitly that he expected India to conduct its strategic Aden-to-Singapore policy in China's neighbourhood.[8]

Just as Kang's desired recreation of a tributary order is not the policy of the Chinese government, Kissinger's Curzonian flourish is not the policy of the Indian government. There is good reason for this reticence. K. Subrahmanyam cautions perceptively against a replay of Curzon's imperial thinking because it belongs in the 19th century, an age of unsteady, incompetent and contending autocracies that could be coerced into the arc of British supremacy from Aden to Singapore.[9] That era came to an end with decolonisation and the rise of nationalism. Today, ASEAN is "wisely cultivating a multifaceted security relationship with all the major powers".[10]

So should we see India in the neo-Curzonian – not Curzonian – scheme of things. As C. Raja Mohan declares, a "neo-Curzonian foreign policy is premised on the logic of Indian centrality, permitting multidirectional engagement – or "multi-alignment" – with all major powers and seeking access and leverage from East Africa to Pacific Asia". Such a forward foreign policy would see India engage actively in regional fora such as the South Asian Association for Regional Cooperation (SAARC) and ASEAN "while not shying away from potential strategic competition with neighbors such as Pakistan and China".[11]

In this context, a far better historical template for modern India than Curzon's geography is the civilisational footprint that pre-colonial India has left in the region. This footprint, which comprises the *mandala* system and the non-invasive nature of India's chief exports – trade, religion and culture – is distinguished by the fact that, unlike the Sinic tributary system, the Indic *mandala* system did not have an imperial centre back home. In the classic formulation of G. Coedes in *The Indianized States of Southeast Asia*, Indians, unlike Chinese, "nowhere engaged in military conquest and annexation in the name of a state or mother country". The Indian kingdoms that emerged in "Farther India" enjoyed only ties of tradition with Indian dynasties; there was no political dependence.[12] ASEAN would be comfortable with a rising India's reach, not to contain or to strategically encircle China, but to balance China in an Asian *status quo* in which America is the primary offshore balancer in East Asia, Japan is central to that role, and Australia plays an essential supporting role. The choices that India makes in this environment will be crucial.

One of the best choices that India could make would be to develop a coherent soft-power strategy.

India's Soft Power

Joseph Nye has made a persuasive case for the use of soft power as an instrument of foreign policy. He writes:

A country may obtain the outcomes it wants in world politics because other countries – admiring its values, emulating its example, aspiring to its level of prosperity and openness – want to follow it. In this sense, it is also important to set the agenda and attract others in world politics, and not only to force them to change by threatening military force or economic sanctions. This soft power – getting others to want the outcomes that you want – co-opts people rather than coerces them.[13]

Nye attributes to Japan, Asia's first moderniser, the greatest soft power that any Asian country possesses, with China's and India's real promise lying only in the future.[14] However, in an important article, Amit Gupta speaks convincingly of India's character as a reformist state in international relations – as distinct from both *status quo* and revolutionary states – and its "evolutionary response to the shift in power within the international system in the 1990s".[15] These reformist and evolutionary impulses provide a credible basis for India's use of soft power, which is essentially ideological attractiveness. Indeed, as a "brand state", India is associated with a remarkable degree of progress achieved indigenously; it "is internationally known as the land of Bangalore, IITs, Infosys, Jet Airways, and outsourcing".[16] Again, India's successes underscore the viability of its using soft power to influence other nations and advance its interests abroad.

While soft power becomes particularly relevant in the context of India's rise to great- power status, its fundamental sources – pluralism, liberalism and secularism – predate this rise and emanate from some of the deepest recesses of the Indian psyche. Let us look briefly at them.

There is a telling anecdote in Pavan Varma's book, *Being Indian*, in which a transsexual walks up to a shop to buy vegetables. After the transsexual has left, the shopkeeper's neighbour asks: "Was that a man or a woman?" The shopkeeper replies: *Sabji lene aaya tha, le kar chali gayi*." ("He came to buy vegetables, and she left after buying them.")[17] This ability to *reconcile* opposites, and not merely tolerate them, is a very Indian attribute. It characterises a civilisation in which pluralism demarcates the boundaries of being Indian, in which eclecticism defines, in Sunil Khilnani's expression, the very idea of India.[18] Of course, pluralism is not an exclusively Indian trait but it certainly is instinctively Indian. The notion of unity in diversity is an early Indian export that is seen, for example, in the state motto of contemporary Indonesia, *Bhinneka Tunggal Ika*. That term is derived from a 14th-century mystical poem, the *Sutasoma*, in which Mpu Tantular ponders the essential oneness lying among the surface differences between Buddhism, Saivism and the new, fringe presence of Islam in East Java.[19] This syncretism contributed immensely to the intellectual greatness of the Majapahit Empire.

The fact, extending from the mundane to the cosmic, that difference is natural leads inexorably to the political fact that democracy, in its liberal manifestation, is the best form of governance because it is only through liberalism that difference paradoxically underpins order. There would be no need for liberalism in heaven because it consists only of the community of the saved: There would be no need for liberalism in hell because it houses only the community of the damned. But in this world, where communities co-exist, overlap, communicate and interact, human consciousness is by its nature divided. Division and difference preclude a single, timeless, definitive and correct answer to the challenges of human existence. Instead, society presupposes an unceasing search for concrete and contingent solutions that, like science, are open to interrogation. Science is that which is falsifiable; so is the science of politics, to the extent that it is a science. It is based on negotiation and compromise, not finality and certitude. Consensus is situational and provisional, and is therefore temporary. It is but a working consensus that will pass with the times and be replaced by some other consensus or none at all. Consensus is a readiness to agree, or to agree to disagree; it is not a blank cheque granted in perpetuity.

This fact was driven home to me in this city last month, when I participated in the inaugural Delhi Dialogue between India and ASEAN. Since the Washington Consensus has been left in tatters by the mad excesses of neo-liberalism and neo-conservatism; and since not everyone is comfortable with the absence of democracy in the Beijing Consensus, I asked whether it was time for a Delhi Consensus that combined functioning elements of the free market in goods and services with the free market in ideas and beliefs. An Indian economist replied to me. "You are the first person in history to use the words 'Delhi' and 'consensus' in the same sentence," he said. Everybody burst out laughing at the summary death sentence that he had passed on hopes of a Delhi Consensus, but he had a point. Indians are wary of political decisions taken from above and palmed off as consensuses for mortals below. In *The Argumentative Indian*, Amartya Sen fetes India for its "long tradition of public arguments" and its "toleration of intellectual heterodoxy", so that when independent India became the first non-Western country to choose a democratic Constitution, it used not only the examples of Europe and America but "drew on its own tradition of public reasoning and argumentative heterodoxy".[20]

Secularism appears in the religious aspects of life as a direct consequence of pluralism's role in intellectual life and liberalism's place in political life. Again, its roots lie deep within Indian history. Contextualising the resilience of secularism in modern India, Amartya Sen examines the intellectual persistence of the *Lokayata* tradition of scepticism and materialism, and the inextricable contribution made by sceptics, agnostics and atheists to India's intellectual life. "Recognizing the history of heterodoxy in India is critically important for coming to grips with the cross-current of ideas, including intellectual processes and scrutinized convictions, that have survived through the turbulence and turmoil of Indian history," Sen writes.[21] Secularism can be understood in two ways: as "neutrality between different religions"; and as "prohibition of religious associations in state activities".[22] Perhaps as a reflection of the fact that heterodoxy has coexisted historically with a marked degree of religiosity, Indian secularism "has tended to emphasize neutrality in particular, rather than prohibition in general".[23]

An everyday but nevertheless poignantly telling incident comes to mind when I think about India's soft power. Five years ago, I was invited to savour the riches of the Deccan Odyssey, a luxury train that travels through the heartland of Maharashtra and Goa on a week-long trip that begins and ends in Mumbai. On that trip, in a Maharashtrian city, I found myself unwittingly in front of the branch office of a right-wing party that boasts a religious base. The fact that I tend to find myself on the left of any faith would have made me extremely unwelcome in that office. Milling around the crowded area were some party workers. I was about to move away from them when a portly buffalo sauntered up to the assemblage with a nonchalance that no Bollywood superstar could have matched. I can tell neither the faith nor the political allegiance of that buffalo; I know not whether it belongs to any party of the faithful, is an outright atheist, or is a closet agnostic. What I did witness was the instant change that came over the politics of humans, if only for a passing moment, at the sight of the buffalo. As it moved into the crowd, we scattered left and right. Several right-wing party workers found themselves on my left; a friend from the train, whom I suspected of harbouring really left-wing views, found himself deposited on the right of other party workers. The buffalo exuded supreme self-confidence as it passed neutrally through us, with that watery look of impassiveness that buffaloes unfailingly possess. Confronted by it, we transcended our religious and political differences in no time as we scattered to safety.

At its soft-power best, the Indian state is a bit like that transcendental buffalo. It stays out of sight much of the time, it is not given to making lengthy speeches, and not everybody likes it, but when it appears, it is irresistible. It is much safer to get out of its way than to resist it. In matters of pluralism, liberalism and secularism, it an astringent recognition of the truth that to live is much better than to die. India is a life-culture, a blessing in a world where death-cultures and suicide cults are trying to set the international agenda. We should not underestimate India's importance to the world.

In that world, the natural correlates of India's influence point east. In terms of its immediate neighbourhood, Indian soft power is unlikely to work in Central and West Asia. No one can teach the Taleban Bharatnatyam, nor can the greatest of multi-culturalists inspire a Wahhabi Ramayana along the lines of the Javanese Ramayana. Southeast Asia's riverine cultures possess a natural affinity to Indic civilisation, which is almost incompatible with the desert religiosity prevalent in some parts of West Asia. Hence look east. Here, I would like to acknowledge the work that Professor Baladas Ghoshal had done to remind India of the importance of Southeast Asia. [24] Among his several writings on India's Look East policy is a 100-page paper that he has prepared for the Ministry of External Affairs. It examines in detail India's strategic interests in Indonesia, Myanmar, Vietnam and Singapore. "Instead of defining its own role in the emerging regional and global economic and security architecture, India is almost depending on other powers to accord a role for itself," he complains. "One hears from our foreign policy and security establishments more of what the United States, Britain or France speaks about India's rising power and its potentialities. Status of a major power requires articulation of one's own vision and place in the world and shaping the strategic environment in a manner that moves others to accept and adjust themselves to that proclaimed world view," he adds.[25] In that spirit, he makes pointed recommendations on how India can use its soft power in culture, education and democracy to both expand its interests in Southeast Asia and underpin stability there in an era of China's rapidly growing influence in the region.

Conclusion

In conclusion, it might be appropriate to mention two concrete ways in which India could give its Look East policy greater cultural depth. First, the idea of setting up Tagore Institutes around the world is an excellent one. Although the Indian Council for Cultural Relations does good work, there is a need for Indian culture to have a permanent, instantly recognisable and iconic presence abroad. Tagore Institutes would do this and bring India into the league of countries whose cultural diplomacy fuels their formidable soft power. Examples are, of course, Britain with the British Council, France with the Alliance Française, Germany with the Goethe-Institut, and now China with the Confucius Institute. India should not lag behind them any more.

Southeast Asia, where people already have a favourable image of India's benign historical role in their societies, should form a primary focus of this important initiative.

Secondly, New Delhi should move expeditiously with the proposal to set up a revived Nalanda University on the site of what was one of the world's first residential universities. Nalanda was founded around 450 AD under the patronage of the Gupta emperors although, according to some records, it dates back to 500 BC, around the time of the Buddha. Even the latter founding date would make Nalanda precede the world's oldest extant universities, although these have been in continuous operation: the University of Al Karaouine in Fez (founded in 859 AD), Cairo's Al Azhar University (975 AD), the University of Bologna (1088), the University of Paris (1150), and the University of Oxford (1167). Nalanda existed till 1193, when the forces of Bakhtiyar Khilji sacked it. At the height of its glory, the university boasted more than 10,000 students and 2,000 teachers drawn from Korea, Japan, China, Indonesia, Persia and Turkey.[26] The Nalanda Project, which is an important initiative of the East Asian Summit process, has benefited from the labours of a mentor group chaired by Nobel laureate Amartya Sen. According to Chidanand Rajghatta, the group has decided to structure the largely postgraduate research university around six schools: the School of Buddhist studies, philosophy, and comparative religion; the School of historical studies; the School of International Relations and Peace; the School of Business Management and Development; the School of Languages and Literature; and, the School of Ecology and Environmental Studies. Singapore is privileged to be a participant in the Nalanda Project and in reviving a university "aimed at advancing the concept of an Asian community...and rediscovering old relationships".[27] The initial endowment – which ranges between US$250 million and US$1 billion – is not excessive, but its impact would be considerable in East Asia, including Southeast Asia. In the words of Neelam Deo, India's consul-general in New York, reviving the university would "emphasize the importance of eastern intellectual endeavour and ensure that human aspiration is not be dominated by (the) western imprint".[28] Indeed, reviving the university would prove once again that learning, an endeavour dear to the Indian mind, can and must survive the sword.

Ultimately, culture is the story of the mind outliving the depredations wrought by nature and man. The exercise of soft power in India's relations with Southeast Asia would have a firm foundation in that ancient promise of culture.

REFERENCES

1. Mohammed Ayoob, "Potential Partners: India and the United States", *Asia Pacific Issues*, No 42, (Honolulu: East-West Centre, December 1999), pp. 5, 9.

2. David C. Kang, "Getting Asia Wrong: The Need for New Analytical Frameworks", *International Security* 27, no. 4 (Spring 2003): 66-7.
3. Wang Gungwu, *The Chinese Way: China's Position in International Relations* (Oslo: Scandinavian University Press, Norwegian Nobel Institute Lecture Series, 1995), p. 54.
4. *Ibid*, p. 69.
5. Lord Curzon of Kedleston, *The Place of India in the Empire* (London: John Murray, 1909), p. 12, cited in C. Raja Mohan, *Crossing the Rubicon: The Shaping of India's New Foreign Policy* (New Delhi: Penguin Books, 2005), pp. 204-5.
6. K.M. Panikkar, *India and the Indian Ocean: An Essay on the Influence of Sea Power on Indian History* (Bombay: George Allen & Unwin (India), 1971). The book was first published in Britain in 1945, and a second edition appeared in 1961. However, Panikkar was right in noting that "ever since the sixteenth century, from which time the Indian Ocean became the scene of a struggle for the control of the sea, the future of India has been determined not on the land frontiers, but on the oceanic expanse which washes the three sides of India" (page 7). World War II had underscored an historical lesson. The ease of Japan's conquest of Singapore, and its control of the Bay of Bengal, showed that India could be threatened more easily from the East than from the West. Hence, the strategic area in Indian warfare was not so much the Burmese frontier as it was Malaya, Singapore and the Andamans.
7. *Indian Express*, November 16, 2004.
8. *Ibid.*
9. K. Subrahmanyam, "The Aden-Singapore illusion", *The Indian Express*, December 11, 2004.
10. *Ibid.*
11. Parag Khanna and C. Raja Mohan, "Getting India Right", February 13, 2006, *RealClear Politics*, http://www.realclearpolitics.com/Commentary/com-2_13_06_PK_pf.html
12. G. Coedes, *The Indianized States of Southeast Asia*, edited by Walter F. Vella and translated by Susan Brown Cowing (Honolulu: The University Press of Hawaii, 1968), p. 34. Among the leading proponents of the "Greater India" thesis was the Indian historian R.C. Majumdar. He describes how India's land and sea trade with the region developed into "regular colonization, and Indians established political authority in various parts of the vast Asiatic continent that lay to the south of China proper and to the east and south-east of India": R.C. Majumdar, *India and South East Asia*, K.S. Ramachandran and S.P. Gupta, eds. (Delhi: B.R. Publishing Corporation, 1979), p. 16. But even as he acknowledges the thrust

of Majumdar's thesis on how Indian culture spread to Southeast Asia, Benudhar Patra notes that the Greater India theory is not free from a "chauvinistic approach": "Kalinga in South East Asia", *Orissa Reference Annual 2004*, p. 160.

13. Joseph S. Nye, Jr., *Soft Power: The Means to Success in World Politics* (New York: Public Affairs, 2004), p. 5.
14. *Ibid.*, p. 88.
15. Amit Gupta, "India's Soft Power", *Indian Foreign Affairs Journal*, Vol. I, No. I, January-March 2006, p. 47.
16. *Ibid.*, p. 49.
17. Pavan Varma, *Being Indian: The truth about why the twenty-first century will be India's* (New Delhi: Penguin Books, 2005).
18. Sunil Khilnani, *The Idea of India* (London: Penguin Books, 2003).
19. Anthony Reid quoted in *The Jakarta Post*, cited in Indonesia Matters, January 21, 2007, http://www.indonesiamatters.com/1043/unity-in-diversity/
20. Amartya Sen, *The Argumentative Indian: Writings on Indian History, Culture and Identity* (London: Penguin Books, 2005), pp. 12-13.
21. *Ibid.*, p. 21.
22. *Ibid.*, p. 19.
23. *Ibid.*, p. 20.
24. Baladas Ghoshal, "A Fresh Look at India's Look East Policy", Paper for the Ministry of External Affairs, Government of India, from a grant from the Policy Planning Division, and prepared under the auspices of the Centre for Policy Research, New Delhi. I thank Professor Ghoshal for kindly making a copy of this paper available to me.
25. *Ibid.*, pp. 3-4.
26. Chidanand Rajghatta, "Nalanda to move from ruins to riches", *Times of India*, May 11, 2008.
27. *Ibid.*
28. Cited in Ibid.

CHAPTER 21

Cooperative Maritime Security of the Asia-Pacific Region: A View from the Indian Navy

V. Adm. Pradeep Chauhan

India's 'geo-strategic maritime-security environment' is shaped by three major factors: first, the geographical conformation of the Indian Ocean and the Asia-Pacific regions; second, by India's own national maritime interests; and third, by the interplay of the geo-strategies of other maritime powers with that of India. Today, the huge energy-resources of the Indian Ocean Region are driving particularly strong maritime connectivity between the Indian and the Pacific Oceans and consequently, it is necessary to paint the picture of maritime cooperation within the maritime-security canvas of the Asia-Pacific littoral as a whole. It must never be forgotten that the term 'Asia-Pacific' includes ***both***, 'Asia' **and** 'the Pacific' and that neither word can be either unduly emphasised or unduly downplayed at the cost of the other. Indeed, in both these oceanic spaces, trans-regional geo-strategy, as also geopolitics, are being shaped by the ongoing major — even historic — shift in the overall Asian power structure caused by the near simultaneous rise of, India, China, Japan, and, ASEAN.

Insofar as India is concerned, the terrorist attacks in Mumbai between the 26th and the 29th of November 2008 have forced all of us to take a detailed and fresh look at our maritime-security environment. Indeed, strong winds of change are buffeting the once familiar landmarks of the entire security environment, whether on land or at sea. Perhaps the most significant catalyst of change has been the rise and proliferation of malevolent non-State entities. And yet, the advent of the non-State actor has not removed the State-actor from the geo-strategic stage, nor, indeed, reduced the State to a bit-player in the global and regional geo-political play. In fact, in our immediate neighbourhood, we are witnessing a coalescing of the State and malevolent non-State entities. This has created a malevolent hybrid that we might describe as the State-sponsored non-State actor. It is this hybrid that lies at heart of our current security dilemma. Should our 'preventive', 'curative' and 'punitive' security-efforts be directed principally towards the State-sponsor or the malevolent non-State entity? How are the linkages between the two to be laid bare for the world to see, especially in cases where the world may not be 'willing-to-see'?

It seems increasingly clear that we urgently need to reshape our fundamental approach to 'security', shedding the 'Cold War' baggage of predominantly 'competitive' security-constructs and adopting, instead, multilateral, 'cooperative' constructs — such as the IONS Indian Ocean Naval Symposium and the WPNS Western Pacific Naval Symposium initiatives — that seek to provide 'comprehensive' security. These will be dilated-upon, at greater length, later in this paper.

In all these strategic considerations, there is the pervasive impact of 'geography' that must be taken into account. Indeed, 'geo-strategy' has been well defined by the Chinese analyst, Senior Captain Xu Qi of the PLA Navy, in "China Military Science", which is one of China's most prestigious military journals. He describes it to essentially be "*... a country's effort, in the world arena, to exploit its 'geographic location' and use 'geographic orientation' to pursue and safeguard its national interests...*". What this means is that each nation engages in Geo-Strategy with varying degrees of success, based upon its Geographical Position — which is a fixed factor, and, its demonstrated abilities in terms of 'Geographic Orientation' — which is a variable factor and can also be called the country's 'Strategic Culture'. This 'Strategic Culture' is a direct function of scholarship... a deep study of history and the derivation of lessons drawn from historical experience.... the ability to identify and forecast security interests and threats, etcetera. As the erstwhile US Secretary of State for Defence, Donald Rumsfeld, pithily remarked in the 2006 '*Shangri-la Dialogue*' held annually in Singapore, the essence of geo-strategy is that "*... where one stands on any given security issue depends upon where one sits*"!

As far as India is concerned, she 'sits' at the natural junction of the busy international shipping lanes that criss-cross this ocean and this determines much of our security viewpoint. In terms of shipping density, the sea area around India is one of the busiest waterways of the world, with over one-hundred-thousand ships transiting the international shipping lanes of this region every year and the Strait of Malacca, alone, accounting for some sixty-thousand ships annually. Of all the cargo that moves along the international shipping lanes of the Indian Ocean, perhaps the most critical is petroleum and petroleum-products. Almost 1,000 million tonnes of oil from West Asia passes close to our shores annually. Some part of this is destined for our own ports, to feed the increasing demand for energy to fuel our current economic growth. A much greater proportion, however, is destined for the oil-intensive economies of the USA and Europe, and, of course China and Japan. We see the Indian Navy and the Indian Coast Guard as major stabilising forces in this great movement of energy across the Indian Ocean, not just for ourselves, but for the world at large.

To return to the pervasiveness of 'change', the Indian Navy feels a strong sense of empathy with the well-respected Methodist Bishop of Washington DC, the Most Reverend G Bromely (1891-1963), who emphasised that "*Change is inevitable. The great question of our time is whether the change will be by consent or coercion*". The problem is not merely the 'changed framework' that we must contend with. The problem is that we find ourselves living within a 'framework-of-change'. Consequently, it ought to come as no surprise that the concept of security, too, has changed steadily over the years. Traditionally, security used to be thought of only in military terms. However, as we begin to incorporate the many facets of 'Human Security', we find ourselves moving away from an earlier and excessively-narrow definition of 'security' within only a military construct. This changed approach to security finds its historical moorings in the famous "Common Security" report that had been authored over a quarter of a century ago, by the "Independent Commission on Disarmament and Security Issues" chaired by the late Prime Minister of Sweden, Mr Olof Palme. This report emphatically drew attention to alternative ways of thinking about peace and security by formally acknowledging that common security requires that people live in dignity and peace, that they have enough to eat and are able to find work and live in a world without poverty.

As a consequence of this transformation in the manner in which we conceptualise security, new terms such as 'Non-Traditional Security' and 'Human Security', some drawn from the 1994 Report of the UNDP, have made their way into the Indian Navy's contemporary security-lexicon and lodged themselves within its collective security-consciousness. India's thinking about Maritime Security is now firmly established within a new construct that incorporates military, political, economic, societal and environmental dimensions, and recognises the many linkages between them. 'Military' maritime security does, of course, continue to enjoy primacy for the Indian Navy, existing as it does in a world-system defined by Westphalian concepts of national sovereignty. However, our thinking is increasingly influenced by the UNDP list of as many as seven additional components of 'Human Security': *Economic Security*, *Food Security*, *Health Security*, *Environmental Security*, *Personal Security*, *Community Security*, and, *Political Security*.

Today, there are several significant threats to human-security, including wars and international terrorism. Drugs and arms smuggling are very real threats that continue unabated. Demographic shifts — whether caused by migration or by other factors — continue to haunt security organisations. We are only now becoming aware of the extent of environmental degradation and its security overtones. Energy, food and water shortages are all moving up the ladder of security-related threats that are becoming inseparable from military threats. These have led to the formulation of new concepts such as 'comprehensive security' and 'cooperative security'. Cooperative Naval constructs such as the IONS and the WPNS are, in fact, founded upon these 'Non-Traditional' security-concepts, involving 'cooperative' rather than 'competitive' security and 'comprehensive' rather than narrowly 'military' security. Naturally, security issues within the maritime domain need to be referenced more towards common interests rather than threats. At a regional level, our common interests are, indeed, these very same 'Human Security' Issues. It is in our common interest to create and consolidate a region in which the present Ostrich-syndrome is rejected, where we jointly face-up to the common challenges that confront us, where the comity of nations is both intrinsic and assured.... where every nation, big or small, is treated as an equal... where multiple options of governance are recognised as being functions of the independent choice of the people of each nation-state... where the people of every state of the region can live in dignity and peace... where poverty stands banished and prosperity sits in its place.... where the state protects the individual and the individual preserves the state in a symbiotic relationship designed to establish and spread stability across the region.... and where malevolent non-State entities find neither spatial nor temporal room for manoeuvre.

It is, therefore, appropriate that within the maritime domain, the concept of 'Maritime Security' is increasingly being described as a condition characterised by freedom from threats arising either 'in' or 'from' the sea. These threats could arise from natural causes or from manmade ones, or, from the interplay of one with the other, as in the case of global warming or environmental degradation. Take the Maldives for instance. It has a population of a quarter of a million people. If the rise in sea-level as a result of global warming were to continue, Maldives will disappear and we will suddenly have a quarter-of-a-million 'boat people'. Where will they go? What contingency-plans have been drawn up to cater for such a scenario? On a more immediate and disturbing level, human traffickers abuse the maritime medium to cruelly exploit economic inequalities and the human yearning for betterment in the quality of life, cramming their hapless human cargo into appalling conditions of deprivation and degradation. In similar fashion, poachers, gun-runners, drug-smugglers and a variety of maritime criminals, including terrorists, abuse the freedom of the seas, bringing into question the very rationale underlying these historical freedoms.

Then again, we have the scourge of piracy, which has resurfaced from the pages of regrettably romanticised history and, along with the more enduring spectre of maritime crime, mocks the United Nations' "Law of the Sea" that we have so painstakingly formulated. For instance, off the troubled coast of Somalia rampant piracy and armed-robbery are maritime manifestations of an increasingly unhappy situation. The ease with which governments can be rendered ineffective is amply illustrated by the many incidents of hijacking that continue to be unaddressed despite express authorisation by Somalia and the UN Security Council to pursue and suppress pirates even within the territorial waters and the land-territory of Somalia. While perusing even what purports to be the latest tabulation of incidents of piracy — from the Gulf of Aden on the western flank of the maritime area under consideration, to the Sulawesi Sea on the eastern flank — it is frightening to realise that the list is very probably *already* out of date! In contrast, however, the security situation vis-à-vis the Strait of Malacca offers a striking example of the success that can be achieved through cooperative and collective security constructs. Concerted actions by the littoral states have caused incidents of piracy to dwindle very significantly and in this regard, the actions of the littoral states of Indonesia, Malaysia, Singapore and Thailand, are deserving of particular praise. And yet, even here, there is clearly much that remains to be done. The Strait remains very vulnerable to terrorist attack. At its narrowest point, the strait is less than 1.5 nm wide, and, a successful attempt to sink a ship in this bottleneck could have severely-adverse fallout on merchant traffic.

Like many of the countries of South East Asia and East Asia, India has a special interest in the safety and security within the Strait of Malacca, particularly and at the mouth of the northern funnel of the strait. The Andaman and Nicobar Islands stretch right across the mouth of the Strait of Malacca, and, Car Nicobar is a mere 86 nautical miles from the province of Aceh in Indonesia and security issues in this general area are very likely to generate immediate repercussions in the A& N Islands. In terms of trade, our interest in the Straits of Malacca and Singapore is even more compelling. China (including Hong Kong) is, today, our largest trading partner worldwide — ***ahead*** of the USA. As a regional trading-bloc vis-à-vis India, East Asia and South East Asia are way ahead — in terms of 'volume' as well as 'value' and, consequently, in terms of 'importance' — of the EU and the USA. The safety and security of this ***trade*** (it must be remembered that merchant ships flying the Indian-flag account for only some 13% of our overseas trade), brings great centrality to the Strait of Malacca and beyond, to the lesser known but far more risk-prone Strait of Makasar. Insofar as the Straits of Malacca and Singapore are concerned, India is thus both, a *'Funnel-State'* as well as a major *'User-State'* and can hardly be expected to be a disinterested bystander to developments in these Straits.

Within the Straits of Malacca and Singapore, there are three fundamental issues that impact upon the security-paradigm of the Asia-Pacific. These three issues might conveniently be considered in two separate 'groupings'. The first grouping comprises 'navigational safety' and 'environmental protection' and is a relatively benign area, in which international cooperation has made considerable progress (albeit after a fairly difficult start in the late-1960s and early-1970s). Within this group, 'policy' matters are addressed by the 'Malacca-Singapore Straits Committee' — a grouping of 'senior officials' from Malaysia, Indonesia and Singapore, while 'technical' matters are handled by a 'Tripartite Technical Experts Group' (TTEG). The second 'group' has only a single constituent, viz., 'Security' has been a more difficult area, where delicacy, tact, patience, and, perhaps most important of all, transparency-of-intent, are all required to be brought to bear. The Government has publicly declared that we are fully appreciative of the legitimate sensitivities of the three 'Littoral States', and are ready to help in whatever manner the Littoral States deem most appropriate. And yet, these two groupings are, in fact, very closely linked. Just ***how*** closely, was dramatically driven home on 6 January 1975, when the MT *Showa Maru*, a VLCCVery Large Crude Carrier of 2,37, 000 DWTDead-Weight Tonnes, ran aground in Indonesian waters within the Straits and more than 7,500 tonnes of crude oil were spilt. Each one of the several remedial measures proposed has obvious and overt security facets. It is these linkages with 'security' that prompt an inclusion of this subject within this document. Over the years, activities relevant to the first 'group' have matured significantly and India, in common with the several States of ASEAN, is intimately and constructively involved with the initiative (led by the UN/IMOInternational Maritime Organisation) known as the **'Cooperative Mechanism'**, which was established in Sep 07, after a series of meetings with the IMO, major user states and other stakeholders. A series of six focussed projects have been identified and a number of equally well-focussed organisations have been set-up to promote regular discussions, to oversee the coordination of implementation of the projects, and, to oversee the utilisation of the financial contribution received from various parties. The six 'Projects' are: (1) Removal of wrecks in the Traffic Separation Scheme'; (2) Cooperation and Capacity-building for Hazardous and Noxious Substance Preparedness and Responses'; (3) Demonstration of 'Class B' AIS-transponders on Small Ships'; (4) Setting-up of Tide, Current and Wind Measurement Systems'; (5) Replacement and Maintenance of Aids to Navigation'; and, (6) Replacement of Aids to Navigation'. India, which had committed itself to 'Project 1' and 'Project 4', has recently earmarked funding in support of these commitments.

In overall terms, the problems that confront the countries that abut the waters of the Asia-Pacific maritime spaces are not 'small' by any standards. As if the challenges identified by the foregoing paragraphs of this paper were not challenges enough, the Asia-Pacific region is also the locus of over 70% of the world's natural disasters. The Indian Navy firmly believes that these challenges can be met only through a regionally inclusive process of cooperative security. We continue to view 'Constructive Engagement' as the primary means of achieving and assuring mutually beneficial maritime security, stability, safety, and consequent collective prosperity amongst all nation-states of the Asia-Pacific littoral. We firmly believe that, for instance, 'Constructive Engagement' between navies enables the gaining and sharing of operational, and, doctrinal expertise... as also transformational experiences... the examining and imbibing of 'best-practices'..... the generation of inter-operability, and, the enhancement of Maritime Domain Awareness through a variety of information-sharing mechanisms. In order to maximise beneficial gains, it is clear that all of us need to engage in both directions along the axis of perceived maritime-capability — not just with navies that we consider to be as advanced or more advanced than our own — but equally, with navies for whom ***our*** engagement will ***build*** capacity1 and ***enhance*** capability 2. We believe that it is precisely this patient and step-by-step process of building capacity and enhancing capability, especially amongst the smaller littoral states of the region that will transform some of the security-related fragility of the Indian Ocean littoral into robustness born of self-confidence and self-sufficiency.

Cooperative mechanisms for the speedy, effective and humane application of maritime power for regional Humanitarian Assistance and Disaster Relief operations form an obvious and important aspect of this 'Constructive Engagement'. Yet, it took the Tsunami of 2004 to drive this home with telling effect. With the more recent examples of the *Jogjakarta* earthquake in Indonesia, Cyclone *Sidr* that struck Bangladesh in November of 2007, and, most recently, the devastation caused by Cyclone *Nargis* as it tore through the Irrawady delta, causing widespread death and destruction in Myanmar, the criticality of working towards interoperability right from the planning and induction process of new platforms bears no repetition to this audience. Similarly, the widespread publicity that was accorded to the regionally-inclusive evacuation undertaken in July 2006 when warships of the Indian Navy, moved as many as 2,280 nationals of India, Sri Lanka, Nepal, Lebanon, and even Greece, to safety from war-ravaged Lebanon, makes it unnecessary for me to expound unduly upon the advantages of having succour and extrication options available to non-combatants and civilians — even in distant lands.

We continue to be encouraged by the realisation that we are not alone in these efforts at Constructive Engagement. The efforts of the USNS *Mercy*, as also those of the USS *Pelelieu*, for instance, offer a vivid example of the enormous goodwill that can be generated and the succour that can be provided through multinational, maritime 'Humanitarian Assistance' missions. Thus, in response to a 2006 request from the US Navy for Indian medical augmentation and support by way of participation on board the hospital ship *Mercy* during her humanitarian mission to East Asia, a ten-member medical team from the Indian Navy, along with a second team drawn jointly from the Indian Army and the Indian Air Force, undertook a four-month embarkation — from 23 May 06 to 01 Sep 06 — to render medical succour and humanitarian relief to stricken people in the Philippines, Bangladesh, Indonesia, and East Timor. In similar fashion, ten Medical, Veterinary and Medical-Engineering specialists from the Indian Armed Forces embarked the USS Peleliu on that ship's 'PACIFIC PARTNERSHIP' mission from Jun to Sep 07, covering the Philippines, Marshall Islands, Vietnam, and Papua New Guinea. The contribution of the Indian Armed Forces medical and support personnel has been extremely well-appreciated and this year (2008) too, an eight-member tri-Service team of medical officers, paramedical and medical-support personnel have, only a few months ago, completed yet another embarkation aboard the USNS *Mercy*, (from 15 Jun to 15 Sep 08), having rendered succour to the needy in Vietnam, Timor-Leste, Papua New Guinea and Micronesia.

These deployments and embarkations provide ample evidence of the relevance and support that HADR operations enjoy across the Asia-Pacific. The construction, acquisition and induction of large amphibious, helicopter-carrying and hovercraft-capable platforms are very much the flavour of the season amongst a number of navies and these are becoming increasingly politically acceptable because of their obvious application in HADR situations. This is one of the many lessons that the *Tsunami* of December 2004 has taught us. This boom in regional naval growth thus offers a unique window of opportunity to all of us within the Asia-Pacific region. Indeed, there are many overlapping bilateral and multilateral security constructs, forums and groupings in the Asia-Pacific Region such as such as the ASEAN[3], ASEAN+3[4], APEC[5], ARF[6], the 6-Party Talks, the East Asia Summit, etc. At the Navy level, the WPNS is clearly the most important multilateral security construct. All these overlapping bilateral and multilateral security constructs are manifestations of the regional drive towards cooperative security through Constructive Engagement.

The Indian Ocean segment of the Asia-Pacific littoral is now beginning to catch up. Although a noble beginning was made over a decade ago, with the launch, in March of 1997, of the **'Indian Ocean Rim – Association for Regional Cooperation'** (IOR-ARC), this grouping confined itself purely to economic cooperation and specifically abjured security issues. It must, of course, be admitted that in 1997, the notion of security within the collective minds of the countries of the Indian Ocean was still very strongly biased towards military security alone. This lacuna has now been comprehensively addressed thanks to a very robust amount of synergy between the military-maritime establishments and the foreign affairs establishments across the Indian Ocean littoral. As many readers would be aware, in February of 2008, driven by the need to address regional vulnerabilities by capitalising upon regional strengths, the Chiefs-of-Navy of very nearly all littoral states of the Indian Ocean Region gathered in New Delhi, both in 'assembly' and in 'conclave', to launch the Twenty First Century's first significant international maritime-security initiative — namely, the Indian Ocean Naval Symposium, or 'IONS'. That the launch of so important a regional initiative was able to meet with such wide acceptance across the length and breadth of the Indian Ocean was in itself a unique phenomenon — but one representative of a region that has come into its own and is ready to evolve a broad consensus in facing the myriad security challenges within the maritime domain.

The acronym 'IONS' is particularly fitting, since the etymology of the English word "ions" is drawn from the Greek word '*ienai*' meaning '*go*' and implying movement and the fundamental concept of IONS, too, is one of 'moving' together — as a region. There are 35 littoral states in the Indian Ocean Region. We could geographically group them into four sub-regions, as follows:—

West Asian Littoral	*East African Littoral*	*South Asian Littoral*	*South-East Asian & Australian Littoral*
1. Bahrain	1. Comoros	1. Bangladesh	1. Australia
2. Iran	2. Djibouti	2. India	2. Indonesia
3. Iraq	3. Egypt	3. Maldives	3. Malaysia
4. Kuwait	4. Eritrea	4. Pakistan	4. Myanmar
5. Oman	5. France	5. Seychelles	5. Singapore
6. Qatar	6. Kenya	6. Sri Lanka	6. Thailand
7. Saudi Arabia	7. Madagascar	7. Timor-Leste	
8. UAE	8. Mauritius		
9. Yemen	9. Mozambique		
	10. Somalia		
	11. South Africa		
	12. Sudan		
	13. Tanzania		

It may be seen 'IONS' seeks to provide a regional forum through which the 'Chiefs-of-Navy' of **all** the littoral states of the IOR can periodically meet to constructively engage one another through the creation and promotion of regionally relevant mechanisms, events, and activities. This is also very largely the purpose of the WPNS, in which the navies of the ASEAN States figure equally prominently:- The inaugural activity of the 'IONS' initiative was the "IONS Seminar-2008", which was jointly conducted by the Indian Navy and the 'National Maritime Foundation' (NMF), on 14 and 15 February 2008. The theme of the seminar was ***"Contemporary Trans-National Challenges — International Maritime Connectivity"***. While the seminar witnessed active participation by a galaxy of national and international luminaries, the formal launch of the 'IONS' initiative itself, was effected through two sessions of the 'Conclave-of-Chiefs' — the first held in New Delhi on 15 Feb and the second in Goa, on 16 Feb 08. As had been the intention, it was at this 'Conclave-of-Chiefs', removed from the glare of the media, that the most meaningful progress occurred. Comfortably interacting amongst their peers, the Chiefs-of-Navy ratified the four principal 'Objectives' of the new security-construct, viz:—

(a) *To promote a shared understanding of the maritime issues facing the littoral states of the Indian Ocean and the formulation of a common set of strategies designed to enhance regional maritime security.*

(b) *To strengthen the capability of all littoral nation-states of the Indian Ocean to address present and anticipated challenges to maritime security and stability.*

(c) *To establish and promote a variety of trans-national, maritime. cooperative-mechanisms designed to mitigate maritime security-concerns within the Indian Ocean.*

(d) *To develop interoperability in terms of doctrines, procedures, organisational and logistic systems and operational processes, so as to promote the development of regional naval capacities for speedy, responsive, and effective Humanitarian Assistance and Disaster-Relief (HADR) throughout the region.*

Perhaps of even greater significance, the Chiefs agreed to abide by the draft 'Charter of Business' even while the document was processed for approval in each navy's own governmental hierarchy. With just a year having elapsed since that time, it is a matter of very great satisfaction that the Charter-of-Business has already been brought into its final shape, with the observations and recommendations of all the Chiefs and their relevant national authorities having been incorporated. Of equal import is the fact that the Chiefs, while gathered in conclave, agreed to a set of initial activities. Insofar as the period until 2010 goes, the planned activities — apart from those functional upon port-calls and capability-enhancement measures related to ship-visits — are tabulated below:—

Activity	*Month*	*Remarks*
Capacity-building and capability-enhancement activities, especially (though not limited to port-calls and ship-visits)	Ongoing	
IONS Open Essay Competition 2008	Jan 09	Conducting Authority: Indian Navy
Technical Workshop for Young Officers	Mar 09	Conducting Authority: Sri Lanka Navy
IONS Preparatory Workshop	Jul 09	Proposed Host: Kenyan Navy
IONS Open Essay Competition : 2009	Oct 09	Conducting Authority: South African Navy
Workshop for Young Officers : 2009	Nov 09	Proposed Host: Royal Saudi Naval Forces

Turning to the rotation of the Chairmanship of IONS, it had been agreed, in the course of the inaugural Conclave-of-Chiefs, that the chairmanship should be rotated sequentially through each of the four sub-regions indicated in Table 1. This was so that the somewhat different priorities given even to common challenges, and, of course, such maritime-security challenges as are unique to a given sub-region, could all be given the emphasis and attention that they deserve. The next rotation is to the West-Asian littoral and there are strong expressions of interest from the navies of this sub-region.

Even as we move IONS up to speed, we are aware that there are also other, important sub-regional cooperative constructs within the Indian Ocean Region, some of which do address the changing security environment as well.

A few of these are indicated in Table 3 below. The table has been organised so that countries that are members of more than one cooperative grouping can be readily discerned as lying in the same row. (Observers are indicated by the use of the letter 'O'):—

IONS	*IOR-ARC*	*African Union*	*SADC*	*Arab League*	*GCC*
1. Australia	1. Australia				
2. Bahrain				1. Bahrain	1. Bahrain
3. Bangladesh	2.Bangladesh				
4. Comoros		1. Comoros		2. Comoros	
5. Djibouti		2. Djibouti		3. Djibouti	
6. Egypt	1. *Egypt*	3. Egypt		4. Egypt	
7. Eritrea		4. Eritrea			
8. France	2. *France*				
9. India	3.India				
10. Indonesia	4. Indonesia				
11. Iraq				5. Iraq	
12. Iran	5. Iran				
13. Kenya	6. Kenya	5. Kenya			
14. Kuwait				6. Kuwait	2. Kuwait
15. Madagascar	7. Madagascar	6.Madagascar	1. Madagascar		
16. Malaysia	8. Malaysia				
17. Maldives					
18. Mauritius	9. Mauritius	7. Mauritius	2. Mauritius		
19. Mozambique	10. Mozambique	8. Mozambique	3. Mozambique		
20. Myanmar					
21. Oman	11. Oman			7. Oman	3. Oman
22. Pakistan					
23. Qatar				8. Qatar	4. Qatar
24. Saudi Arabia			9. Saudi Arabia		5. Saudi Arabia
25. Seychelles		9. Seychelles			
26. Singapore	12. Singapore				
27. *Somalia ??*		10. Somalia		10. Somalia	
28. South Africa	13. South Africa	11. South Africa	4. South Africa		
29. Sri Lanka	14. Sri Lanka				
30. Sudan		12. Sudan		11. Sudan	
31. Tanzania	15. Tanzania	13. Tanzania	5. Tanzania		
32. Thailand	16. Thailand	14. Algeria			
33. UAE	17. UAE	15. Angola		12. UAE	6. UAE
34. Yemen	18. Yemen	16. Benin		13. Yemen	
	3. *China*	17. Botswana			
	4. *UK*	18. Burkina			
	5. *Japan*	19. Burundi			
		20. Cameroon		14. Jordan	
		21. Cape Verde		15. Lebanon	
		22. Central African Republic		16. Palestine	
		23. Chad		17. Syria	
		24. Congo			
		25. Congo, DRC	8. Congo (DRC)	18. Algeria	
		26. Cote d'Ivorie	6. Angola		
		27. Equatorial Guinea			
		28. Ethiopia	7. Botswana		
		29. Gabon			
		30. The Gambia			
		31. Ghana			
		32. Guinea			
		33. Guinea-Bissau			
		34. Lesotho	9. Lesotho		
		35. Liberia			

36. Libya		19. Libya
37. Malawi	10. Malawi	
38. Mali		
39. Mauritania		20. Mauritania
		21. Morocco
40. Namibia	11. Namibia	
41. Niger		
42. Nigeria		
43. Rwanda		
44. Sao Tome & Principe		
45. Senegal		
46. Sierra Leone		
47. Swaziland	12. Swaziland	
48. Togo		
49. Tunisia		22. Tunisia
50. Uganda		
51. Zambia	13. Zambia	
52. Zimbabwe	14. Zimbabwe	

On the Pacific side, the several overlapping structures that exist have already been mentioned. Indeed, the ASEAN States are at the core of many of them and may therefore be seen to be the 'hinge' that connects the 'Asian' and the 'Pacific' segments of the Asia-Pacific maritime expanse. It is important to note here that ASEAN maintains inter-organisational contact with several of the constructs within the 'Asia' segment of the 'Asia-Pacific' expanse, such as, the Gulf Cooperation Council and the South Asian Association for Regional Cooperation. Most ASEAN Member Countries also participate actively in the activities of the Asia-Pacific Economic Cooperation (APEC), the Asia-Europe Meeting (ASEM), and the East Asia-Latin America Forum (EALAF). There is a growing recognition that within the maritime domain, initiatives such as the IONS and the WPNS will inevitably be the major components of any pan-Asian security construct. The following table shows the navies that are members and observers of the WPNS construct, with those navies that are common to both, WPNS and IONS being indicated in 'bold' and 'italicised' font:—

Members		**Observers**
1. ***Australia***	10. Papua New Guinea	1. ***Bangladesh***
2. Brunei	11. Philippines	2. Canada
3. Cambodia	12. Russia	3. Chile
4. China	13. ***Singapore***	4. ***India***
5. ***France***	14. South Korea	5. Mexico
6. ***Indonesia***	15. ***Thailand***	6. Peru
7. Japan	16. Tonga	
8. ***Malaysia***	17. USA	
9. New Zealand	18. Vietnam	

A handshake — in the immediate future — between the WPNS and the IONS is inevitable and will synergise the maritime domain throughout the Asia-Pacific. Perhaps we will also see a move towards connectivity with the

Shanghai Cooperation Organisation and perhaps that might eventually lead to the pan-Asian security construct that the Secretary for Defence of the United States of America, Mr Robert Gates, spoke of during the 2008 edition the *Shangri La Dialogue*. This vision, however, lies at a still indeterminate time-to-come. Insofar as the immediate future is concerned, we believe that the IONS and the WPNS movements constitute the keys to addressing the many challenges that face us in the within the Asia-Pacific maritime domain.

By way of conclusion I would like to aver that cooperative maritime strategies within the Asia-Pacific are not limited to the argument of 'guns-versus-butter'. They are, in fact, predicated upon the somewhat revolutionary premise of 'guns ***and*** butter'.

1 **'Capacity-Building'** is most often used in the context of 'material' wherewithal (i.e., the provision of hardware — this could include platforms, infrastructure, equipment or spares), which is provided to entities — usually in developing countries — that have a need to develop a certain 'capacity' to undertake one or more maritime (or naval) role.

2 **'Capability Enhancement'** refers to the realisation of a potential 'aptitude' or 'ability'. In a naval context, it implies that the potential recipient already has the 'capacity' (or some proportion of it) to undertake a naval/maritime role, and our Foreign Cooperation input will now 'enhance' his existing capability to exploit the material wherewithal so as to derive better (hopefully optimal) results. Capability-enhancement is most often by way of intangibles and cognitive processes (examples would include 'training', 'domain-awareness', 'doctrinal-development', etc.). *For instance, a certain navy may well possess operationally viable sea-going Offshore Patrol-Vessels (OPVs). This would be 'capacity'. On the other hand, if the crew aboard the OPV in question did not know how to distinguish between, say, a 'demersal' trawler (one designed to catch fish that live close to the seabed) and a 'pelagic' trawler (one designed to catch fish that swim close to the surface of the sea), it might be unable to establish 'suspicious behaviour' as a function of the depth of water in which it is operating. This is lack of 'capability'.*

3 **ASEAN** = (1) Brunei, (2) Cambodia, (3) Indonesia, (4) Laos, (5) Malaysia, (6) Myanmar, (7) Philippines, (8) Singapore, (9) Thailand, and (10) Vietnam. **ASEAN Dialogue Partners** include (1) Australia, (2) Canada, (3) China, (4) the EU, (5) India, (6) Japan, (7) (8) South Korea, (9) New Zealand, (10) Russia, (11) USA, and the (12) United Nations Development Programme (UNDP).

4 **ASEAN+3** = The ten ASEAN States + China, Japan and South Korea.

5 **APEC** = (1) Australia, (2) Brunei, (3) Canada, (4) Chile, (5) China, (6) Hong Kong, (7) Indonesia, (8) Japan, (9) South Korea, (10) Malaysia, (11) Mexico, (12) New Zealand, (13) Papua New Guinea, (14) Peru, (15) Philippines, (16) Russia, (17) Singapore, (18) Chinese Taipei, (19) Thailand, (20) USA, and (21) Vietnam.

6 ARF = Australia, Brunei, Cambodia, Canada, China, EU, India, Indonesia, Japan, North Korea, South Korea, Laos, Malaysia, Mongolia, Myanmar, New Zealand, Pakistan, Papua New Guinea, Philippines, Russia, Singapore, Thailand, the US, and Vietnam

CHAPTER 22

ASEAN After four Decades: A Tryst with Pragmatic Conviviality and Arc of Understanding with India

Prof. Tridib Chakraborti

The history of the Association of Southeast Asian Nations (ASEAN) may be depicted as a series of important events or milestones, which reflected the sturdy growth of the Association, the development of its agenda, and the decisions that have veritably changed the annals of Southeast Asia. From a regional grouping that initially had to define itself by the fact that it was a regional association and not a military alliance, ASEAN has emerged as a dynamic community of nations in the 21st Century. At the time of its origin, many forecasted that ASEAN would not last long, because many factors were going against it, not least the simmering disputes between and among member countries. But, the fact remains that ASEAN's consensus-building approach to resolve problems facilitated the Association to move forward. Each member learned to recognize its ante for the viability of the Association and the astuteness of ASEAN not being a supranational government that has authority over its individual members. Each member exercises full sovereignty, and that is why ASEAN decisions are reached either unanimously or consensually. ASEAN does not intend to convert itself into a political union under any form of central supra-national authority. Each ASEAN member has always tried to safeguard its national government and identity in accordance with the ideals and aspirations of its people. The ASEAN members are legally bound by the code of conduct embodied in the Treaty of Amity and Cooperation (TAC) where the idea of state sovereignty has remained the cardinal principal. ASEAN sees the diversity in its membership as a source of vigour and stimulation for fostering a strong sense of community and regional solidarity.

During its long journey of more than four decades, ASEAN has experienced a number of critical issues - like the genocidal act of the Pol Pot regime during 1975-78; Vietnam's invasion of Cambodia; transmigration and influx of refugees; drugs, human trafficking and transnational crimes; East Timor crisis; Myanmar's military repression; transnational problems such as the forest fires in Indonesia, low intensity conflicts and terrorism; Muslim separatist movements in Southern Thailand and the Philippines; Thailand's devaluation of the Baht; Cambodia's Coup d'etat in 1997; sacking of Malaysian Deputy Prime Minister, Anwar Ibrahim in the 1990s; the financial crisis of 1997; gender discrimination; Asian Values syndrome; rising Islamic fundamentalism; new forms of terrorism; uneven economic status among ASEAN members; natural calamities like 'Tsunami' and earthquakes; poor human rights records, territorial claims and sub-terrenean tensions among the member states, etc. The ASEAN members, on many occasions, have, unfortunately, failed to resolve some of these divisive issues. Nevertheless, they have pragmatically generated acute, acerbic and critical comments on the governmental policies of the respective countries to resolve the crises, in doing which however, they were confronted with the questions about ASEAN's idea of regionalism and its principles of non-interference and non-confrontation. A majority of the members of ASEAN, except the Philippines, have not endorsed the suggestion of Surin Pitsuan, the then Foreign Minister of Thailand and presently the Secretary General of ASEAN, of the basic premises of ASEAN's central principle of non-intervention and thereby the call for reviewing the implementation of the same. Most of the members also felt that the retention of the principle of non-intervention was essential, since it stresses on "mutual respect for independence, sovereignty, equality, territorial integrity and national identity of all nations".

Undoubtedly their internal problems, with regional and transnational ramifications, appeared to be the most important issue facing the ASEAN members and these issues, time and again have caused serious tensions and divided the countries of Southeast Asia. However, in the context of the outstanding issues like the problem of forest fires and trans-boundary environmental pollution; the scourge of terrorism after 11 September, 2001; South China Sea imbroglio; Cambodian crisis in 1979; the financial crisis of 1997; minimizing the gap between rich and poor ASEAN members; island disputes among the member countries, natural disasters, swelling of infectious diseases etc, the ASEAN members have taken a number of initiatives in their fervent endeavour to resolve them, based solely on dialogue, consultation, cooperation, engagement and mutual interaction, without breaking away from the principle of non-intervention. For the sake of regional cohesion, the members have tried to strike a balance between what is desirable and what is possible, the idyllic and the realistic, desired ends and available means and international involvement and national sovereignty. To the ASEAN members, their very own 'ASEAN Way' is not at all a typical conflict-resolution mechanism, but has rather evolved as a conflict-avoidance instrument, relying on the software arms of regional understanding rather than the hardware elements of formalized, rule-based instrumentalities. During its long years of experience, ASEAN has never been visualized as a mechanism for conflict-settlement and conflict-resolution. It has rather been able to establish itself successfully in conflict-mitigation. The signing of the ASEAN Charter in November 2007, which seeks to establish ASEAN as a legal entity and formally move the region towards an EU-style economic community by 2015, has greatly increased ASEAN's institutional capacity and ability for autonomous action, including the realm of counter-terrorism. Thus, after more than four decades, ASEAN has not only survived, but has developed into an important force internationally, being upheld as an exemplar of regional unity, worthy of emulation.

ASEAN's Success Stories of Regional Cohesion

The ASEAN was established on 8 August 1967 in Bangkok with the five original member countries, namely, Indonesia, Malaysia, Singapore, Thailand and the Philippines. Brunei Darussalam joined the Association on 8 January 1984, Vietnam on 28 July 1995, Laos and Myanmar became members on 23 July 1997 and Cambodia on 30 April 1999. The formation of this regional organization was the product of the lack of peace and stability from which the whole Southeast Asian region was suffering for sometime, together with the ASEAN states' apparent dislike for the interference of the Big Powers in regional affairs, leading to the convergence of political outlook among the non-communist states in the region. The members of this organization came under one umbrella with a collective will to bind themselves together in friendship and cooperation through mutual efforts and sacrifices, in order to secure their peoples' peace, freedom and regional prosperity. After more than 42 years of its performance, based on certain important principles, through trial and error method, ASEAN has emerged as one of the most successful experiments in regional cooperation in the developing world. During these years, there are a number of cases, where ASEAN has performed quite proficiently to demonstrate its ability and strength to tackle many outstanding critical issues, both regional and transnational in nature. Issues like the Cambodian crisis in 1979, forest fires and trans-boundary environmental pollution, the issue of terrorism after 11 September, South China Sea problem, financial crisis in 1997, minimizing the gap between rich and poor of ASEAN members, transnational virulent disease and tsunami calamity, etc. are some of them requiring prime consideration. In all these cases, the ASEAN members have taken a number of initiatives and struggled to resolve them, based entirely on dialogue, consultation, cooperation, engagement and mutual interaction. The paper will highlight some cases where ASEAN has established its strength of unity, based on regional cohesion and mutual understanding.

ASEAN's stand on Vietnam's invasion of Cambodia in 1979

The Cambodian Crisis from May 1975 to December 1989 posed serious problems to the nature of intra-ASEAN state relations. On 7th January 1979, Vietnam invaded Kampuchea with the Soviet Union's military assistance and installed Heng Samrin as the Head of State of Kampuchea by removing Pol Pot.[1] This crisis gradually took an international dimension and got inextricably linked with global power politics. The official ASEAN response was to deplore the Vietnamese invasion and call for the withdrawal of foreign forces from Cambodia, and the dismantling of the Phnom Penh government so that Cambodians could exercise their right of self-determination through elections. To force Vietnam's pull out of Cambodia, ASEAN mobilized the international community and the Security Council to isolate the country diplomatically and economically. As a result, Indonesia and other ASEAN members immediately placed the issue on the agenda of the UN Security Council. The ASEAN members, due to their weakness of combined military strength and lack of enforcement power to use harsh measures on Cambodia, could only prevent the People's Republic of Kampuchea (PRK) from obtaining the Cambodian Seat at the United Nations, and thus, from becoming the legitimate government in Cambodia. Having reached the decision on the basis of conflict-management, the ASEAN countries called on both parties (Cambodia and Vietnam) to employ the 'ASEAN Way' of respecting each other's sovereignty and independence, while refraining from interfering with each other's domestic affairs. The members regarded the retention of the principle since it would be the best way pushing for moderate, constructive policies towards Vietnam as well as consensus instead of hard-line policies, and which ultimately resulted in peace talks and regional negotiations, in spite of their serious differences. On October 23, 1991, the Final Act of the Paris International Conference on Cambodia took place, and the UN Peace Keeping Operations was held under UNTAC in 1993, where the ASEAN followed the "dual-track" diplomacy, based on bilateral political communication with Vietnam on the one hand, and maintaining its commitment to the ASEAN formula, on the other. In fact, in this peace process, ASEAN was credited for the success of eradicating the Soviet threat without the need for use of force, sanctions, threats, which strongly reflected the potency of the principle of non-intervention in resolving the Cambodian Conflict. The achievements of the 'ASEAN Way' in solving and neutralizing the Cambodian imbroglio, which ended the long-term unrest and the Indochina Wars in Southeast Asia, eventually laid the fundamental platform for ASEAN to gain global recognition.

Haze Crisis

The issue of environmental security, as a prime attribute of policy shaping, did not become a chief subject theme of study to the countries of Southeast Asia during the first three decades of the cold war era. Its environmental attentiveness slowly evolved in the 1970s, following the 1972 Stockholm UN Conference on the Environment, following which, it has taken a number of important pledges on environment for the sustainable use and management of natural resources. In fact, in 1992 at the Fifth ASEAN

Ministerial Meeting on Environment, held at Singapore, the ASEAN members pledged "to play an active part in protecting the environment by continuing to cooperate by promoting the principle of sustainable development and integrating it into all aspects of development". Unfortunately, implementation of these environmental declarations has not been an effectual exercise, since many of the individual countries have insisted on putting greater stress on the preservation of their national sovereignty and the recognition of their developing country status. Such an exclusivist consciousness often compromised the environmental concern of the ASEAN members, even in the face of international pressure on them to make concrete contributions to the protection of the earth.[2]

The issue of the preservation of environment was drastically altered in the minds of Southeast Asian countries, following the outbreak of smoke pollution due to forest fires in some parts of Southeast Asian region in 1997 and 1998. These smoke hazards ultimately became a trans-boundary haze problem, due to pollution by smoke, dust, moisture and vapour suspended in air sufficient to spoil visibility, originating from large-scale forest and land fires, that affected other countries in the region. These large-scale fires were often deliberately set by large plantation companies and farmer settlers who come from the more densely populated provinces of Indonesia and were provided homesteads in these provinces, together with the traditional shifting cultivators living in the region for a long time, clearing small sites of planting crops until the soil's nutrients have been exhausted and then moving to other sites by using fire as the most economical way of converting forest land for cultivation. This disaster resulted in several dramatic forest fires and haze episodes since the early 1980s - particularly during the dry seasons of 1982-83, 1987, 1991, 1994 1997, 1998, 2000, 2005, and the most recent one in 2007 - which caused severe damage well beyond the destruction of forest land and ecosystems. In fact, these land and forest fires in Southeast Asia have destroyed more than 3 million hectares of peat lands.

However, the 1997 and 1998 smog crisis posed a stern challenge to every aspect of ASEAN's character and modalities. This unscheduled outburst of haze from forest fire took a heavy toll on travel, environment and human life, besides causing public health disaster in the region with the sharp increase in the number of patients treated for respiratory alignments, lung and heart diseases, reduced fertility and damage to the nervous system, blood cells and kidneys. Such health concerns turned many Southeast Asians decidedly impatient with their leaders. Besides this, serious transport accidents appeared more than co-incidental during this smog period: a Garuda Airbus collided into a mountainside on the approach to Medan in Sumatra, and killed all 256 passengers on board. Also, in the unclear Straits of Malacca, a small Indian cargo vessel hit a large supertanker, killing 20 of the former ship's crew. Further, many traffic accidents were exacerbated by this haze catastrophe. In

Indonesia's easternmost province of Irian Jaya, severe drought had caused staple food crops to fail in the highlands, resulting in an estimated minimum of 500 deaths from mass starvation.[3]

The regional smog events and forest fires impelled the countries of ASEAN to accept measures to overcome the calamity in the form of the "ASEAN Cooperation Plan on Transboundary Pollution," which was agreed to in October 1994, at the ASEAN Ministerial Meeting on the Environment, convened in Kuching, Malaysia. As a follow-up action to this meeting, in June 1995, at Kuala Lumpur, Malaysia hosted the "ASEAN Meeting on Trans-boundary Pollution", where the countries agreed to develop an Asian cooperative plan in order to address the trans-boundary pollution issue, based on several mechanisms like comprehensive measures for prevention, management and control; establishment of an early warning system including identification of focal points for information exchange; building up of national and regional institutional capacity; and establishment of cooperative links with developed countries to assist ASEAN's efforts.[4] An effective result of this meeting was the establishment of a 'Haze Technical Task Force' in 1995. However, these efforts have failed to produce an effective result on the part of the ASEAN countries, since the mechanisms adopted by them moved in a desultory manner. ASEAN was caught between rhetoric and reality, and the haze crisis brought the issue of environmental degradation back to the top of the political agenda. Since the problem affected most of the countries of ASEAN, there was a big question mark about ASEAN's "Principle of Non-Intervention in the Affairs of another Nation."[5]

Against such background of the haze problem over the years, in November 1997, the Senior Officials of the ASEAN countries in a meeting agreed to a regional division of labour, with Singapore taking the lead in monitoring fire hazards, Malaysia concentrating on fire prevention measures, and Indonesia on strengthening fire fighting capability. Following this meeting, the ASEAN Environment Ministers met in Singapore on 22-23 December, 1997 and adopted an ASEAN Regional Haze Action Plan (RHAP) to address problems of haze in the Southeast Asian region. In this meeting, the members of ASEAN had also agreed on their joint effort to combat fires and smoke haze and further avowed that they would continue to look after the environment in their quest for economic development, while simultaneously working closely to set up options for future environmental challenges, especially those arising from the effects of climate change. Revealing these expressions of understanding, this meeting identified three main objectives to develop better management and enforcement so as to prevent fires, to institute cooperative mechanisms to monitor fires, and to build fire-fighting competence.[6] Thus, the signing of RHAP was a turning point in the region's effort to alleviate itself from the damage from periodic trans-boundary haze, and this has laid out the cooperative framework and detailed operational plan to deal with issue in the region.

Following this agreement, on 10 June 2002, all the ten ASEAN member countries in Kuala Lumpur signed the ASEAN Agreement on Trans-boundary Haze Pollution. The agreement entered into force on 25 November 2003. However, while Indonesia took part in the negotiations and signed the agreement, it has not yet ratified the agreement and accepted its obligations as the focal point of the haze crises. At the Ninth ASEAN Ministerial Meeting on Haze (AMMH) held on 11 June 2002 in Kuala Lumpur, the Environment Ministers discussed and finally decided actions to be taken on fire prevention and control in peat-lands. As a result, the ASEAN Peatland Management Initiative (APMI) was developed with various partners and endorsed by the ASEAN Senior Officials on the Environment-Haze Technical Task Force (ASOEN-HTTF) in February 2003.

Finally, on 10 November 2004, the 11th ASEAN Ministerial Meeting on Haze took place in Hanoi, Vietnam. In this meeting, the ASEAN ministers reviewed the enhanced cooperation in addressing land and forest fires as well as trans-boundary haze pollution, and expressed their satisfaction regarding the substantial progress on regional collaborative activities, such as the inventory of fire-fighting resources, the ASEAN Peatland Management Initiative, publication and dissemination of zero-burning and controlled burning practices, early warning information systems, standard operating procedures for monitoring assessment and joint emergency response etc.[7] The major stumbling block, however, lies in implementing these decisions effectively due to ineffective cooperation from Indonesia. Till now, it has not yet ratified the ASEAN Agreement on Trans-boundary Haze Pollution, which naturally reveals a soft weakness of ASEAN, as a political and technical body. What is essential at present is Indonesia's participation in the ASEAN Haze Agreement, and for that an enforcement and liability clause will be incorporated, because those who are responsible for the fires should pay reparations for the victims. This "bite" is desirable to ensure that all the declarations and action plans are made effective enough. One positive development that took place in recent times was that at the Sixth Meeting of the Sub-Regional Ministerial Steering Committee (MSC) on Trans-boundary Haze Pollution, held on 22 October 2008, at Phuket, Thailand, the majority of the members of ASEAN appreciated Indonesia's efforts in effectively implementing its Plan of Action (PoA) in dealing with trans-boundary Haze pollution and congratulated Indonesia for achieving its 50% hotspot reduction target as of mid-October for 2008, compared to 2006. The Meeting also noted that while there has been an increase of hotspot activities in the region, there was no significant corresponding increase in trans-boundary haze. This was attributed to the concerted mitigation actions taken to restrain the fires and improved normal weather conditions. Thus, in spite of the limitations faced by ASEAN members, it is clear that the haze is no longer an individual undertaking of the ASEAN countries, and it receives a coordinated and concerted response from all the members.

South China Sea Crisis

The South China Sea (SCS) remains a major contentious issue among the countries of the Asia-Pacific region. The maritime disputes in the South China Sea have been characterized to be of strategic, diplomatic and economic in nature. The territorial claims in this region (particularly the Paracel and Spratly islands) among the various disputing countries owing to their strategic importance has appeared as the gravest threat in the last part of the 20th century and in the early part of the 21st century. China has been the main claimant over the issue of territorial sovereignty in the South China Sea and also the principal and potential source of threat and uncertainty for the ASEAN countries. The other claimants include the ASEAN countries and Taiwan. The Philippines, Malaysia and Brunei claim specific parts of the South China Sea, while China, Taiwan and Vietnam claim all of its island, islets and reefs; China appears to claim the submerged features as well. These claims and counter-claims over the islands in the South China Sea have culminated in frequent clashes among the disputing countries, of which, the dispute between Vietnam and China in Paracel islands in 1974 and Spratly islands in 1988, and the conflict between China and the Philippines in Mischief Reef in 1995 remain most imperative.[8] Owing to these severe disputes, ASEAN as a regional grouping was forced to undertake initiatives and formulate coherent policy in the face of this crisis, because such frequent disputes threatened the peace and stability of the region as a whole. The collapse of former Soviet Union in 1991 and the phased withdrawal of the US naval and air bases from the Philippines in 1992 created a power vacuum in the region, prompting China to establish its dominion over the Asia-Pacific region with the possibility of Beijing resorting to the use of force in the settlement of disputes in South China Sea.

The conflict management-approaches with reference to South China Sea's Paracel and Spratly islands are different. One reason is that the Paracel conflict is 'de facto' considered to be a bilateral issue between China and Vietnam, whereas the Spratly dispute is considered to be a multilateral one. Furthermore, attempts at negotiations between China and Vietnam have displayed that Vietnam wants to include the Paracel issue on the agenda, but China is not amenable. China considers Paracels to be no issue to negotiate, since it claims full control of the archipelago. The role that ASEAN can play is rather a complex exercise, since four of its member states – Brunei Darussalam, Malaysia, the Philippines and Vietnam – pursue sovereignty claims to all or parts of the Spratly archipelago. This naturally exhibits a situation in which ASEAN cannot play the role of third party mediator between China and these claimants. Nevertheless, the condition in the South China Sea has been brought onto the agenda in the context of the ASEAN – China dialogue, after the ASEAN members in July 1992, signed the ASEAN Declaration on the South China Sea in Manila. In this Manila Declaration, the

ASEAN members did not deal with the problem of sovereign jurisdiction but initiated an effort to disseminate an informal code of conduct based on self-restraint, the non-use of force and the peaceful resolution of disputes. It relied on the norms and principles primarily introduced in the ASEAN-TAC of 1976[9]. Thus, this informal code of conduct for the South China Sea was based on the notions of conflict-management and avoidance rather than conflict-resolution. Despite the overlapping claims, the member states shared an interest in promoting to seek a tranquil solution to the territorial dispute in the South China Sea. In July 1999, at the ASEAN Foreign Ministers Meeting held in Singapore, the Philippines and Malaysia, for the first time put forward a proposal for a 'regional code' with respect to security and economic issues over the Spratly group of islands. However, this draft 'code of conduct' was described mainly as an intra-ASEAN document and ASEAN planned to widen its reach by incorporating China's cooperation and ideas. The ASEAN members sought the extension of these principles through the espousal of a Regional Code of Conduct for the South China Sea, covering all ARF members, through which, they could reduce tensions. China after its initial repudiation has finally signed the Code of Conduct on 4 November 2002.

The Declaration on the Conduct of Parties on South China Sea was a 10-point programme, which was adopted by the governments of the member states of ASEAN and PRC. It re-emphasized the need to peacefully settle the South China Sea dispute, and agreed to "refrain from action of inhabiting on the presently uninhabited islands, reefs, shoals, cays, and other features." In addition, ASEAN and the PRC pledged to resolve territorial issues peacefully and to "respect freedom of navigation in and over flight above the South China Sea."[10] This Declaration was in itself a triumph since it was the first political document concluded between China and ASEAN over the South China Sea issue, bearing a positive significance for enhancing mutual trust between the two sides, and also a progressive step towards the resolution of the crisis, as China for the first time signed a multilateral declaration with ASEAN over the issue, which it had earlier refused to do. However, signing of this agreement has been encumbered by ifs and buts. **First,** the declaration is merely a political statement, not a legally binding document. If one party violates a provision, there is no method for enforcement. **Secondly,** the statement fails to mention any geographic scope, specifically concerning the Spratly or Parcel Island chains. **Finally,** the language of the Declaration on the Conduct of Parties in the South China Sea commits the signatories to cooperative conduct, but history shows that this is unlikely to happen. However, Beijing's accession to the TAC in October 2003 and Tokyo's promise in December that year to ratify the document clearly demonstrates that multilateralism— via ASEAN —is working. Furthermore, at the Eleventh ASEAN-China Summit held on 20 November 2007, at Singapore, the ASEAN member countries further reaffirmed their determination "to the early and full implementation of the Declaration on the Conduct of Parties in the South

China Sea (DOC), towards the eventual adoption of a Regional Code of Conduct in the South China Sea."

Thus, the decades-old South China Sea problem among the disputing countries has been temporarily shelved and presently there is no sign of any tension or clash among the claimants. The drastic alteration of the global order and the prominence of economics as a major determining factor in bilateral relations rather than politics largely reduced the tensions that had existed in the South China Sea. In resolving this crisis, ASEAN's adherence to regional cohesion has played a key role and has generated a favourable and congenial environment in the region. Its initiative of code of conduct undoubtedly shows a desire by the different parties involved to pursue their claims by peaceful means, and openly denounces the use of force in the South China Sea. In that sense, it contributes towards the easing of tensions between the claimant states. By putting off the question of boundaries, it also increases the possibility of reaching agreements on joint oil exploration and development schemes, as well as restoration of peace through collective means, by keeping the principle of maintenance of sovereignty of each country intact in the region. Thus, the South China Sea dispute can be characterized as one that strikes a balance between sovereignty, development and security interests of ASEAN, based on regional cohesion.

Terrorism and Cooperation among ASEAN Members

The internal security troubles in the socio-political structure of Southeast Asia originated mainly due to ethnic/ race conflicts, poverty and under-development, domination of ruling party on the minority community, religion (mainly rise of Islamic fundamentalism), historical bequest, opium and drug related issues, etc. In recent times, the problems in Moluccas Islands, Irian Jaya and Aceh, Southern Philippines, Myanmar, Malaysia (PAS), Southern Thailand (Pattani movement) etc., often create mistrust, dissection and anxiety among neighbouring countries of Southeast Asia, resulting in sharp conflicts of opinions and interests, and thereby placing obstructions towards the realization of a regional security community and a united front against low intensity conflict and terrorism in the region. The terrorist activities of Abu Sayyaf Group (ASG), the Jemaah Islamiah, the Moro Islamic Liberation Front (MILF), the Laskar Jihad, the Front Pembela Islam (Islamic Defenders Front – FPI), the New People's Army (NPA), the Kumpulan Mujaheddin Malaysia (KMM), the Pattani United Liberation organization (PULO), New PULO, the Barisan Revolusi Nationale (BRN), and Majelis Mujahidin Indonesia (MMI) etc, an alliance of about 100 militant and radical groups, have practically disturbed the entire security situation of Southeast Asia.[11] These patterns of terrorism often create regional tensions, and subsequently put barriers towards the realization of regional cohesion.[12] After the 11 September 2001 incident in the United States, the internationalization of the concept of terrorism, low intensity conflicts, insurgency predicament and transnational crimes have become important and dynamic themes of regional politics in Southeast Asia, leading President George Bush describing Southeast Asia as a second front in the 'global war on terror'[13] This was not surprising since the countries like Malaysia, Thailand and the Philippines are already marked significantly in Al- Queda's network and hub of global terrorist activities spanning from East and Southeast Asia to Australia. But the fact remains that the threat of terrorism in this region has been mainly emanating due to domestic constraints rather than being totally related to global matters. The ASEAN members identified the acts of terrorism a menace in the process of their regional cohesion, and felt that the way to deal with international terrorism in the post-September 11 world depended on their ability to forge a coherent message not only for the sake of regional security, but also for the long-term viability of the organization itself.

The ASEAN countries have taken a number of initiatives to counter and resolve this international menace, though a clear difference of opinion on approach to terrorism existed among them. Unlike Singapore, the Philippines, Thailand, Indonesia and Malaysia with predominantly Muslim population expressed their unwillingness to be a part of the US strategy of countering terrorism in this region. At the national level, the Indonesian government termed the issue of terrorism as a political subject and failed to acknowledge this threat as existential in nature. It was also disinclined to connect itself to US views on global terrorism. Malaysia, on the other hand, expressed its serious hesitation regarding linking terrorism with Islam, and considered that terrorism has been essentially transnational in character and is an artifact of Western misdeeds against the broader Muslim community. It also refused to accept the links of Malaysian religious and political organizations to the global Al-Qaeda network. However, Singapore maintains an uncompromising posture on the general issue of terrorism due to its multi-racial state character. It blindly supported the US' way of handling the issue of terrorism, due to its exclusive economic interests. Thailand and the Philippines, on the other hand, are tending to downplay terrorism for the sake of domestic politics. The conflicts in these countries, however, are mostly ethno-nationalist fights resulting largely from an abortive integration of the Muslim population into the mainstream. Thus, there exists a tendency to identify these conflicts as domestic insurgencies with local implications rather than part of global jihad with wider ramifications[14]. In spite of their differences in viewpoint, the ASEAN members at the regional level have taken certain important initiatives to reduce the threat posed by terrorism. On 11 October 2001 in Singapore, at the third ASEAN Ministerial Meeting on Transnational Crime (AMMTC), ministers "strongly condemned all acts of terrorism, in particular, the terrorist attacks of 11 September 2001 on the US," and called all its member states to ratify all relevant international anti-terrorist conventions.

In the seventh ASEAN Summit held on 5 November 2001, in Brunei Darussaalam, the member countries signed the ASEAN Declaration on Joint Action to counter Terrorism. This was ASEAN's initial step to create a unified threat perception of terrorism, in-spite of sharp disagreements among its members. Nevertheless, the declaration was significant as a statement of objective and an acknowledgement that terrorism was a serious long-term issue that had to be faced. To fight terrorism as a truly regional and global endeavour, the ASEAN-related groupings and other regional organizations, such as ARF, APEC, ASEAN+3, ASEAN+1 etc have undertaken a number of schemes, including apparatus of sharing information and astuteness to develop law enforcement and investigation capabilities of the agencies of respective member countries. Besides this, the Joint Communiqué issued in Kuala Lumpur, after the special ASEAN Ministerial Meeting on Terrorism held on 20-21 May 2002, recalled the 2001 ASEAN Declaration on Joint Action to Counter Terrorism adopted at the Seventh ASEAN Summit in Brunei Darussalam, and suggested to advance ASEAN's efforts in the global struggle against terrorism. In this meeting, the ASEAN Ministers also committed "to counter, prevent and suppress all forms of terrorist acts in accordance with the Charter of the UN and other International law, especially taking into account the importance of all relevant UN resolutions" and "to follow-up on this communiqué by entrusting the Senior Officials to execute the Work Programme on Terrorism to implement the ASEAN Plan of Action to Combat Transnational Crime approved on 17th May 2002 in Kuala Lumpur which is deemed to be an integral part of this Communiqué and to review its progress at subsequent meetings of the ASEAN Ministers responsible for transnational crime issues."[15] This meeting once again reaffirmed their regional commitment that "the sovereignty, territorial integrity and domestic laws of each ASEAN member country shall be respected and upheld in undertaking the fight against terrorism".

ASEAN members in their various regional and Summit meetings have taken other initiatives to strengthen the national mechanism of the member-countries to combat terrorism, and agreed carrying out different-counter terrorism training programmes and projects. It has also adopted a variety of institutionalized apparatus, like the ASEAN-EU Meetings, the ASEAN–US Meetings, the ASEAN plus three Meetings, the Inter-Sectional Meeting on Counter terrorism and Transnational crime and so on, where different avowals and joint communiqués were approved to combat terrorism internationally, while respecting the ASEAN principles of territorial sovereignty, integrity and non-interference in domestic affairs of the state. However, these counter-terrorism schemes of ASEAN have not been sufficiently effective due to its loose organizational structure, the non-binding nature of its agreements, and its tradition of non-intervention in the internal affairs of member-states. Nevertheless, on 13 January 2007 at Cebu, the Philippines, the ASEAN

Convention on Counter-Terrorism was drafted and this pragmatically paved the way for a more legally binding approach to cooperation in counter-terrorism. The signing of this agreement would greatly increase ASEAN's institutional capacity and ability for autonomous action, including in the field of counter-terrorism. So far, only Singapore and Thailand have ratified, though no ASEAN member has any crucial reservations about the Convention because they had all agreed to cooperate in combating terrorism.

Besides this, ASEAN, since 2001, has commenced several centres for combating terrorism in the region, including the Jakarta Centre for Law Enforcement Cooperation, the International Law Enforcement Academy in Thailand, and the Southeast Asia Regional Centre for Counter Terrorism in Malaysia, and presently the members of this organization have achieved some success in degrading the operational capabilities of major terrorist groups such as JI and ASG.[16] Even then, ASEAN's counter-terrorism plans have long been hindered by its wobbly organizational configurations, the non-binding nature of its agreements, implications of terrorism as a threat to regional order and its practice of non-intervention in the internal affairs of states. This was further augmented by the fear about adverse domestic reactions following the adoption of a US-led counter-terrorism strategy on a regional basis in Southeast Asia after the 9/11 incident. Therefore, the issue of terrorism has no doubt been treated as a litmus test for ASEAN solidarity, since counter-terrorism cooperation has severely posed major challenges to its principle of non-intervention. Nevertheless, peaceful dialogue and discussion, consultation and consensus are the ASEAN approach, even on the issue of terrorism.

Natural Disasters Management

The episode of earthquake and Tsunami disaster on 26 December 2004, brought not only an unprecedented loss of life and property, but more importantly, removed the geographical and environmental boundaries of the nation-states of South and Southeast Asia. This unparalleled catastrophe forced the alertness among the nation states that disaster management has to be integrated into the conventional development and investment efforts. This destructive natural disaster brought various governments, international organizations, the private sector, humanitarian organizations and community groups on a common promenade and unfalteringly demonstrated their craving for international cooperation, solidarity and partnership. It also exhibited that the nation-states, though segregated by borders, political ideology, race and creed, humanity has the inherent instinct to rise to the occasions, if needed. These disasters have further generated complex emergencies that require urgent and coordinated responses from a broad range of state and non-state actors. Unfortunately, many states of South and Southeast Asia, at the initial level were unable to cope with these complex humanitarian emergencies. and virtually lacked regional capability to respond to this disaster. However, after its initial shock, due to the institutional weakness, the countries of this region induced a level of solidarity that has not been frequently witnessed among the members of ASEAN, since the 1997 Asian financial crisis. This Tsunami disaster, therefore, provided an opportunity to the ASEAN members to come together once again and act decisively to forge the response to the tragedy and to create an impact of regional cohesion and understanding among themselves. Apart from dispatching aid quickly to the areas hit by the tragedy, the ASEAN-led Tsunami Summit, held on 6 January 2005 in Jakarta, was a clear manifestation of ASEAN solidarity leading to initiatives to overcome any further disaster in future include the establishment of the ASEAN Regional Disaster Emergency Response Simulation Exercise (ARDEX-05), which commenced in 2005.[17] The simulation exercise is envisioned to be an annual exercise, bringing together several personnel and mobilizing light-to-medium equipment geared toward providing immediate humanitarian assistance to affected countries in times of natural disaster.

Beyond ASEAN, there are also other ad hoc exercises in disaster management being undertaken within the ARF framework. After the tsunami disaster, the ARF Ministers decided to work together in emergency relief, rehabilitation, and reconstruction, as well as prevention and mitigation efforts in addressing natural disasters.[18] Besides these regional initiatives, humanitarian assistance was provided by external partners to ASEAN, like the United States, European Union, Australia, India and Japan, plus a number of international aid agencies, to overcome this natural catastrophe. Southeast Asian countries held a number of meetings and agreed to enhance cooperation in disaster relief, including prevention and mitigation[19] and specifically, converged on mobilizing additional resources to meet the emergency needs of tsunami victims. They also called upon the international community through the United Nations to convene an international pledging conference for sustainable humanitarian relief efforts and to explore the establishment of "standby arrangements" for other relief efforts. ASEAN also called on donor institutions—the World Bank, Asian Development Bank, and other financial institutions—to provide the necessary funds to support the rehabilitation and reconstruction programme in disaster-stricken areas. More significantly, at the July 2006 ARF Ministerial Meeting, officials from ARF countries discussed the possibility of developing guidelines in improving civilian and military cooperation in humanitarian operations. ASEAN leaders have demonstrated their leadership by bringing together their colleagues from around the world to Jakarta, to take stock of what had happened, and charted out the road ahead in hastening emergency relief operations, coordinating the rehabilitation and reconstruction of the affected areas, and reinforced the need for prevention and mitigation of natural catastrophes. It further exhibited ASEAN at its best in illustrating the effectiveness and drive of the organization, as well as its openness to external powers.

Initiative of ASEAN Integration (IAI) programme

The most critical hurdle of ASEAN is the development gap among member states, which has a powerful impact on the degree of regional engagement. Less-developed ASEAN members, due to their past historical legacies, sometimes feel isolated, owing to their own deficiencies in resources and knowledge while attempting to catch up with the rest of the grouping, particularly in areas of more sophisticated cooperation like free-trade agreements or prevention of infectious diseases. Some members have had very little experience with multilateral cooperation after long years of colonial rule. And some have even employed ASEAN as a shield against external pressure, in order to prolong their brutal regimes. To reduce the gap between developed and developing members of ASEAN, the organization has undertaken the IAI programme as an important initiative and requested all the Full Dialogue Partners to promote this regional cause. For the implementation of the IAI, Vietnam joined other ASEAN members in issuing the Hanoi Declaration on Narrowing Development Gap at the AMM-34 held in Hanoi in 2001. With Vietnam as the chair of the IAI task force, the implementation of IAI has seen some results. IAI currently has 134 projects of which, over 90% have received a total committed aid of US $48 million for developing infrastructure, human resources, information technology, tourism, poverty reduction and an improvement of living standards. In June 2007, Vietnam hosted the Second IAI Development Co-operation Forum to work out a cooperation strategy to implement the IAI in the 2008-2015 periods. Vietnam introduced an important initiative on socio-economic development through the Sub-Mekong Development and Co-operation Programme for poor areas along the East-West Corridor. This initiative has been, no doubt, a clear example of ASEAN's outlook of regional cohesion, base on pragmatic understanding.

Transnational Infectious Diseases

In terms of their transnational character, the avian influenza and infectious diseases etc have emerged as major non-traditional security threats for the countries of Southeast Asia. According to the WHO, new diseases are emerging at an unprecedented rate over the years. The examples include among others: Ebola Hemorrhagic Fever in Africa, the West Nile virus pulmonary syndrome in the United States, and the Nipah Encephalitis in Southeast Asia. Older diseases like cholera and tuberculosis have also re-emerged. These recurring diseases have come back with more virulent strains and are often found to be resistant to currently available first-line antibiotic drugs. Most of these carry virulent pathogens that pose serious challenges to current epidemiological expertise. In Southeast Asia, these infectious diseases have also, posed a brutal danger to human security, especially since the Asia-wide outbreak of the Severe Acute Respiratory Syndrome (SARS) and avian flu.

The SARS experience has clearly exhibited that in this era of globalization, contagious illnesses can quickly damage the security and well being of all members of a country's society and all aspects of its economy.[20] Furthermore, the spreading of infectious diseases such as **HIV-AIDS** caused by human and drug trafficking have also accelerated the devastation of human security in Southeast and East Asia. In 2003, the outbreak of SARS infected more than 8,000 people and killed 500 in this region.[21] This epidemic outburst of SARS, HIV-AIDS and Avian flu naturally caused irreparable damage to the economies of Singapore, Indonesia, Vietnam, Hong Kong, and China, which had the highest toll. This uneven incident has also dented the tourism sector and travel fell steeply as people avoided these and other virus-hit countries, which added to decline in consumer confidence and domestic demand pushed many businesses to the brink of collapse. The overall cost of SARS to Southeast Asia's economies was estimated to have run between US$ 30 and 50 billion—and up to US$ 150 billion worldwide. The speed and impact of the contagion prompted many governments of ASEAN to incorporate the health security as non-traditional security threat in their national agenda. To overcome this crisis, the ASEAN members with their regional efforts have tried to tackle these threats in a concerted way and at the regional level, the key ASEAN initiatives are as follows:

- The ASEAN Expert Group on Communicable Diseases;
- The ASEAN Highly Pathogenic Avian Influenza (HPAI) Task Force;
- The ASEAN + 3 Emerging Infectious Diseases Programme; and
- The Regional Framework for Control and Eradication of HPAI.

Many of these collaborative programmes focus on strengthening the national and regional capacity for disease surveillance and early response and strengthening the capacity to prepare for any pandemic. Within ASEAN, steps to develop a region wide mechanism in rapid disease control have begun with the first exercise held in Cambodia in late March 2007. The exercise, Panstop 2007, was coordinated by the ASEAN Secretariat with the help of the World Health Organization, together with the Japanese government and the Japan International Cooperation System. Besides this, the ASEAN members have implemented other collaborative programmes organized under the framework of the wider forums in the region—APEC and the EAS. Most of the measures outlined in these programmes focus on, among others, strengthening of institutional capacities at national and regional levels to ensure effective and efficient implementation of avian influenza prevention, putting in place disease control programmes and pandemic preparedness and response plans, and enhancing capacity-building in coping with a pandemic influenza. Other measures also include establishing information-sharing protocols among countries and multilateral organizations based on effective, timely and meaningful communication before or during an influenza outbreak.[22] Hence, outside the East Asian regional framework, responses from other dialogue partners of ASEAN and regional preparedness in containing pandemic outbreaks were initiated. A critical step in this direction is in creating mechanisms for effective production and distribution of vaccines and other medicines. Moreover, the United States through the APEC framework, has also initiated the establishment of a Regional Emerging Diseases Intervention (REDI) Center, in partnership with Singapore. Formally launched in 2003 after the SARS outbreak, REDI would assist Asian countries in "tracking, controlling, and researching emerging infections with appropriate resources and expertise."[23] However, despite the keen interest on pandemics in the region, many of these proposed measures from ASEAN, EAS, and APEC still needs more time to be effective in its entirety. The major reasons behind this slackness are — the lack of resources allocated to improving public health systems at the domestic level, poor health infrastructure in many parts of the region, the inadequacies of national and regional capacities to respond to transnational health crises, the lack of contingency planning and coordination among state agencies, reduction in politics of crisis health management, building of credible and effective regional surveillance systems for monitoring infectious diseases, and very little institutionalized regional cooperation in the area of public health policy.

Conclusion

Thus, after more than four decades, ASEAN has not only survived but has developed into an important force internationally, being upheld as a model of regional unity, worthy of emulation. Through its policy of trial and triumph, based on the mindset of regional cohesion, ASEAN has come to play a very constructive and prominent role in developing a sense of regional identity in Southeast Asia and has been largely successful in reducing regional tensions for the maintenance of regional peace and stability. They have adopted clear norms for inter-state relations such as the peaceful settlement of disputes, the rejection of the use or threat of force, and non-interference in another's internal matters. Based on this success story, India in the post-cold war years has developed a non-idealistic linkage with the countries of Southeast Asia. The economic dynamic of this region is at present determined as much by trade, investment and production, coloured with history and cultural leanings. It was only through the formulation of the 'Look East' policy in the early 1990s', that the Southeast Asian region has received its uniform importance in India's policy planning. This in turn has led to a better admiration of the benefits of integrating foreign and economic policies. Such an approach has naturally made the economically vibrant ASEAN countries more attractive towards India, and has led to the new phase of "rediscovery and renaissance" in India's pragmatic outlook towards these countries.

The spiraling of the economic ties with the Southeast Asian countries has quietly led New Delhi into a Second Phase of its 'Look East' policy, marked by creation of arrangements for free trade area and establishing institutional economic linkages between the countries of the region and India.

India, having realized ASEAN's strategic importance in the Asia-Pacific region, has continued its cordiality with the Southeast Asian countries in the 21st century. It also tried to use the ASEAN platform as a catalyst for its further integration with the Asia-Pacific region. Comprehending the potential for gains of the Asian Economic Community (AEC), India has actively searched for cementing its ties with the ASEAN plus three nations by way of involvement in cooperative frameworks both at the sub-regional and bilateral levels. New Delhi's participation in the East Asian Summit might open up a fresh dimension to the efforts at regionalism in Asia, which were hitherto being confined to the countries of Southeast Asia.

References

1. For detailed analysis of this crisis see, Tridib Chakraborti, *India and Kampuchea: A Phase in their relations - 1978-81*, Minerva Associates, Calcutta, 1985.
2. For details, see Tridib Chakraborti, "The Environmental Battlefield in Southeast Asia: The Haze Catastrophe and Regional Responses", in Purusottam Bhattacharya and Sugata Hazra (eds.) *Environment and Human Security*, Lancer's Books, New Delhi, 2003, pp.167-202.
3. Tridib Chakraborti, "Haze Sans Frontiers: The Environmental Calamity, ASEAN Response and India-ASEAN Cooperation on Non-Traditional Security Threats", in V.R. Raghavan (ed.) *India and ASEAN: Non-Traditional Security Threats*, East-West Books (Madras) Pvt .Ltd, Chennai, 2007, pp.112-113.
4. *Annual Report: 1994-95*, ASEAN Standing Committee, ASEAN Secretariat, Jakarta, 1995, p.41.
5. Tridib Chakraborti, n.4, pp.118-119.
6. For details see http://www.haze-online.or.id/help/chronology.php (26 May 2008).
7. For details, see http://www.haze-online.or.id.php, (19 June 2008).
8. For details, see "The Territorial Claims in South China Sea: Probing Persistent Uncertainties", in Arun Kumar Banerji and Purusottam Bhattacharya (eds.), *People's Republic of China at Fifty: Politics, Economy and Foreign Relations*, Lancer's Books, New Delhi, 2001, pp.171-207.
9. *Adopted at the First ASEAN Summit held in Bali in 1976, the TAC constitutes a norm-based code of conduct that enunciates ASEAN's core principles, including the respect for sovereignty and non-interference in the affairs of other states.*
10. David Wiencek, "South China Sea Flashpoint Revisited," *China Brief*, Vol. 2, No. 24, 16 December 2008, http://www.jamestown.org/pubs/view/cwe_002_024_002.htm.

11. For details, see Tridib Chakraborti, "Terrorism and the ASEAN States: A Classification and Prescriptive Analysis," in Omprakash Mishra and Sucheta Ghosh (eds.), *Terrorism and Low Intensity Conflict in the South Asian Region*, Manak Publisher, New Delhi, 2003, pp.316-356.
12. Clive Christie, *A Modern History of Southeast Asia: Decolonization, Nationalism and Separatism*, Tauris Academic Studies, London, 1996, p.192
13. John Gershman, "Is Southeast Asia the Second Front", Foreign Affairs, Vol.79, No.4, July-August 2002, pp 60-74.
14. For details, see Amitav Acharya and Arabinda Acharya, "The Myth of the Second Front: Localizing the 'War on Terror' in Southeast Asia", *The Washington Quarterly*, Vol. 30, No.4, Autumn 2007, pp.80-82.
15. For details, see http://www.aseansec.org/newdata/sammter.htm
16. For details, see http://www.aph.gov.au/library/intguide/FAD/sea.htm
17. ASEAN Agreement on Disaster Management and Emergency Response, Vientiane, 26 July, 2005, *http://www.aseansec.org/17587.htm*
18. See *Chairman's Statement of the Twelfth Meeting of the ASEAN Regional Forum* (ARF), Vientiane, 29 July, 2005.
19. For details, see Statement from the Special ASEAN Leader's Meeting on Aftermath of Earthquake and Tsunami, Jakarta, 6 January, 2005, *http://www.aseansec.org/17067.htm*
20. For more details on SARS and its impacts, see for example, Mely Caballero-Anthony, "SARS in Asia: Crisis, Vulnerabilities, and Regional Responses," *Asian Survey*, Vol. 45, No. 3, 2005, p.475-495; Melissa Curley and Nicholas Thomas, "Human Security and Public Health in Southeast Asia: the SARS Outbreak," *Australian Journal of International Affairs*, Vol. 58, No. 1, 2004,pp. 17-32; and Elizabeth Prescott, "SARS: A Warning," *Survival*, Vol. 45, No. 3, 2003, pp. 162-177
21. For details see, http://www.who.int.com
22. See for example, *APEC Action Plan on the Prevention and Response to Avian and Influenza Pandemics*, 2006/AIPMM/014; and *East Asia Summit Declaration on Avian Influenza Prevention, Control and Response*, at *http://www.www.aseansec.org/18101.htm*
23. See "Regional Emerging Diseases Intervention (REDI) Center," Remarks by Claude Allen Deputy Secretary of Health and Human Resources, 24 May, 2004, *http://singapore.usembassy.gov/utils/eprintpage. html* (accessed 19 October, 2008).

CONTRIBUTORS

1. ***Dr. Karan Singh, Chairman,*** Indian Council for Cultural Relations; and a Member Rajya Sabha. He had been Cabinet Minister and India's Ambassador to the United States.
2. ***Prof. Satish Chandra,*** Former Chairman, University Grants Commission; former Professor of History, Jawaharlal Nehru University. Presently Vice Chairman, Society for Indian Ocean Studies.
3. ***Dr. Kapila Vatsyayan*** is Chairman of Asia Project, India International Centre. She has written extensively on various aspects of Indian culture including countries of Southeast Asia.
4. ***Mrs. Hema Devare,*** wife of Ambassador Sudhir Devare, she lived in Indonesia in the 1990s.
5. ***Prof. Himanshu Prabha Ray,*** Professor of History at the Centre for Historical Studies, Jawaharlal Nehru University; currently Visiting Senior Fellow, Princeton University, U.S.A.
6. ***Prof. Taufik Abdullah*** is former Chairman, Indonesian Institute of Sciences (LIPI). Recipient of the 2006 Association for Asian Studies (AAS) Award for Distinguished Contributions to Asian Studies and numerous international awards and honors.
7. ***Dr. Farish Noor*** is currently Senior Fellow, Rajaratnam School of International Studies, Singapore.
8. ***Dr. H.P. Ray*** is Senior Research Fellow, Asiatic Society, Kolkata.
9. ***Dr. Lakshmi Subramanian,*** former Professor of History in Jamia Millia Islamia, New Delhi is currently in Centre for Studies in Social Sciences, Kolkata.
10. ***Prof. S.J. Stephen*** is at Professor of History, Visva-Bharati, Shantiniketan.
11. ***Prof. Aditya Mukherjee*** is Professor of History and Director, Jawaharlal Nehru Institute of Advanced Studies, Jawaharlal Nehru University, New Delhi.

12. ***Dr. Dilip Chandra*** is former Head, Indonesian Division, All India Radio and currently a Visiting Faculty at the School of Foreign Languages, Ministry of Defence, New Delhi.
13. ***Shri S. Utham Kumar Jamadhagni*** is Senior Lecturer, Defence and Strategic Studies at University of Madras.
14. ***Prof. Baladas Ghoshal*** former Professor, Centre for South and Southeast Asian Studies, Jawaharlal Nehru University, currently Visiting Senior Fellow, Centre for Policy Research, New Delhi.
15. ***Ambassador Sudhir Devare,*** former Secretary, Ministry of External Affaris, Government of India; currently Director General, Indian Council of World Affaris.
16. ***Dr. Amita Batra,*** is Associate Professor, Centre for South and Southeast Asian Studies, Jawaharlal Nehru University, New Delhi.
17. ***Dr. N. Chandra Mohan,*** Professor, Economics and International Business, IILM Institute of Higher Education, New Delhi.
18. ***Prof. Vinayshil Gautam,*** Head, Department of Management Studies, Indian Institute of Technology, Delhi.
19. ***Ambassador Rajiv Sikri,*** retired as Secretary (East), Ministry of External Affaris and is now a Commentator on India's Foreign Policy.
20. ***Prof. P.V. Rao*** is Director, Centre for Indian Ocean Studies, Osmania University, Hyderabad.
21. ***Shri Asad-ul Iqbal Latif*** is a Senior Fellow, Institute of Southeast Asian Studies, Singapore.
22. ***Vice Admiral Pradeep Chauhan*** is with the Indian Navy.
23. ***Prof. Tridip Chakraborti*** is Professor of Southeast Asian Studies, Department of International Relations, Jadavpur University.

INDEX

A

B

D

E

F

G

H

I

N

O

P

T

U

V

W

X

Y

Z